COMPARATIVE LAW

This advanced textbook offers an overview and critical treatment of comparative law, incorporating both traditional and modern approaches to the discipline and an up-to-date survey of the key methodological debates. The fundamental concepts of comparative law are examined through the lens of three main questions: what to compare, why compare, and how to compare.

The study of the objects of comparative analysis (what to compare) begins with a critique of legal positivism to address a plurality of legal concepts. The investigation of the aims of comparative law (why compare) considers the most widespread classifications of legal orders and the diverse approaches to the study of legal change. Finally, the methods of comparative law (how to compare) are analysed, taking into account their different functions. Adopting a contextualised, interdisciplinary approach to the subject with a focus on a range of different legal systems, the author brings in examples from politics and economics to the analysis, highlighting the importance of comparative law for the understanding of modern societies.

Comparative Law: A Critical Introduction will provide a thought-provoking read for advanced-level students and scholars of comparative law.

Alessandro Somma is a full professor of comparative law at Sapienza University of Rome, Italy. He is member of the International Academy of Comparative Law and of the Board of the Italian Association of Comparative Law.

AF849410

COMPARATIVE LAW

A Critical Introduction

Alessandro Somma

Routledge
Taylor & Francis Group
LONDON AND NEW YORK

Designed cover image: Honoré Daumier, Le Défenseur (Counsel for the Defense), c 1862–1865 / AlFA Visuals / Alamy ©

First published 2026
by Routledge
4 Park Square, Milton Park, Abingdon, Oxon OX14 4RN

and by Routledge
605 Third Avenue, New York, NY 10158

Routledge is an imprint of the Taylor & Francis Group, an informa business

© 2026 Alessandro Somma

The right of Alessandro Somma to be identified as author of this work has been asserted in accordance with sections 77 and 78 of the Copyright, Designs and Patents Act 1988.

All rights reserved. No part of this book may be reprinted or reproduced or utilised in any form or by any electronic, mechanical, or other means, now known or hereafter invented, including photocopying and recording, or in any information storage or retrieval system, without permission in writing from the publishers.

Trademark notice: Product or corporate names may be trademarks or registered trademarks, and are used only for identification and explanation without intent to infringe.

British Library Cataloguing-in-Publication Data
A catalogue record for this book is available from the British Library

Library of Congress Cataloging-in-Publication Data
Names: Somma, Alessandro author
Title: Comparative law : a critical introduction / Alessandro Somma.
Description: Abingdon, Oxon [UK] ; New York, NY : Routledge, 2026. |
Includes bibliographical references and index.
Identifiers: LCCN 2025038760 | ISBN 9781032684468 hardback |
ISBN 9781032684444 paperback | ISBN 9781032684499 ebook
Subjects: LCSH: Comparative law | Comparative law—Political aspects |
Comparative law—Economic aspects | Legal positivism | LCGFT: Law materials
Classification: LCC K559 .S6655 2026 | DDC 340/.2—dc23/eng/20250820
LC record available at https://lccn.loc.gov/2025038760

ISBN: 978-1-032-68446-8 (hbk)
ISBN: 978-1-032-68444-4 (pbk)
ISBN: 978-1-032-68449-9 (ebk)

DOI: 10.4324/9781032684499

Typeset in Baskerville
by Apex CoVantage, LLC

To Guido Alpa, in memoriam.

CONTENTS

PART I

What to compare

The law and the legal order

TABLE OF CONTENTS

DOI: 10.4324/9781032684499-1

CHAPTER 1

COMPARATIVE LAW AND CRITIQUE OF LEGAL POSITIVISM

1 A CHALLENGE TO THEORETICAL ORTHODOXY

Comparative law scholars usually present their subject as a reaction to the study of national law. In their perspective, the latter is traditionally seen as carried out in a way that is inappropriate to emphasise alternative points of view than those of their own national order. The comparatists' focus on 'foreign' law leads them to live in a kind of 'transgressive idolatry' in which they relativise what the 'priests of local law' hold to be absolute truths. Rather, they find themselves adopting a plurality of points of view. In this sense, it is often claimed that comparative discourse is 'a rebellious discourse, a counter discourse, a discourse of resistance',[1] and that comparative law represents an instrument of critical knowledge of law which is 'subversive' of the system produced by the 'theoretical orthodoxy'.[2] That orthodoxy, in essence, reduces law to its formal sources of production, and more generally prevents one from 'expanding the agenda of available possibilities'.[3]

For comparative law scholar, legal positivism is a *bête noire* and the main obstacle to critical knowledge of law. The theoretical foundations of legal positivism were defined in the 18th century and are, in many respects, still widely accepted. For its critics, it leads to such a distorted and trivialised image of law, that the claim that this approach can still yield good results belies a mythology.[4]

On closer examination, legal positivism has important merits, especially from a historical point of view. In particular, it was instrumental in overcoming the structures of feudal society, which instituted a static social order based on status differences. In that system, the individual was dissolved within the multiple communities of society: from the family to the religious, from the political to the economic.

The feudal order drew its strength and legitimacy from the fact that it was regarded a natural fact that pre-existed its members, who were unequal from birth and destined to remain unequal throughout their lives. The feudal order, indeed, was secured by a natural law: its addressees could not produce the rules, let alone could they change them. This legitimised the immobility of a society based on the 'axiom of the ontological differentiation of beings' and their 'necessary hierarchical organisation'.[5]

All this was transformed due to changes within natural law theory, which took on the guise of rational law with the Enlightenment. It included principles based on reason as well as nature: in particular, the principle that individuals are free and equal from birth. Crucial to

1 P. Legrand, *Droit comparé*, 5th ed., Paris, 2015, pp. 21 and 24.
2 H. Muir Watt, *La fonction subversive du droit comparé*, in *Revue internationale de droit comparé*, 2000, p. 505.
3 G. Fletcher, *Comparative Law as a Subversive Discipline*, in *American Journal of Comparative Law*, 46, 1998, p. 695.
4 See P. Legrand, *Questions à Rodolfo Sacco*, in *Revue internationale de droit comparé*, 1995, p. 968.
5 P. Costa, *Cittadinanza*, Roma and Bari, 2005, p. 14.

DOI: 10.4324/9781032684499-2

the overthrow of the feudal order, however, was the conceptualisation of natural law as a set of philosophical-moral rules which, as such, could only produce internal ethical constraints. The law, by contrast, was laid down by an earthly legislator; hence, the identification of law with legislation, the only source capable of producing external and therefore legal constraints.[6]

This identification, at the basis of the concept of positive law, was the core of a specific expression of legal positivism: legislative positivism. This was epitomised by the figure of Napoleon Bonaparte, who is regarded as the father of the French Civil Code of 1804. Legal positivism relegated both legal scholars and judges to marginal roles. Scholars had to limit themselves to a mere paraphrase of the text; hence, the School of Exegesis, coined to allude to the secondary role given to legal doctrine until the end of the 19th century (II.1.2). Similarly, judges were expected to apply the words of the legislator to the concrete case, being careful not to modify or distort them. They should simply be 'the mouth that speaks the words of the statute'. They were thus to be the expression of an 'invisible and void' power.[7]

The latter expression derives from Montesquieu's theory of the tripartite separation of powers. However, for Montesquieu, these powers had to be coordinated in order to balance each other.[8] Legislative positivism as it developed in France, instead, interpreted the separation of powers in the light of Rousseauan organicism, which expressed the idea of nation as a collective political body.[9] Hence, the French exaltation of legislative power, which, as the most direct expression of the will of the people, was superior to other powers: in particular to judicial power, considered as a kind of subordinate or delegated power (II.3.5).

In the first half of the 19th century, a distinct form of legal positivism took hold in Germany within the Historical School of Law. It arose as a romantic, and therefore anti-Enlightenment, reaction to the French Revolution and the Napoleonic will to reduce law to legislation. Its main premise was that positive law was the law made by the people, or rather by the 'popular spirit' (*Volksgeist*)[10]: like language and art, law was a cultural achievement. The legislative power was not supposed to produce law, for fear of mortifying the incessant creative impulse of the people, which could not be captured in legislative texts. The task of producing law was to be left to legal scholarship, whose task was to identify the law posed by the people and, above all, to transform it into a coherent and complete system of concepts and rules.

In the second half of the 19th century, Pandectists soon challenged the programme of the Historical School of Law. They used Roman law to bring order to the customary law as the expression of the popular spirit, thus creating a coherent and complete German legal system.[11] The result was a denial of the very premises on which the Historical School of Law was based: by translating the popular spirit into immutable concepts, scholars ended up behaving exactly like the evil for which they claimed to be the remedy. In any case, this is the basis of the scientific positivism promoted by Pandectists, which aims to legitimise a law of a sapiential nature: capable of being intimately harmonious since it is protected from the arbitrariness of political power.[12]

It should be noted that the Pandectist's scientific positivism was only partially overcome in Germany with the codification of private law. This is due to the fact that the German Civil Code of 1896 is largely based on the work of jurists. It also, and above all, depends on the

6 N. Bobbio, *Giusnaturalismo e positivismo giuridico* (1977), Roma and Bari, 2011, p. 90 ff.
7 Montesquieu, *De l'esprit des lois* (1748), Book 11 Chapter. 6.
8 P. Ridola, *Preistoria, origini e vicende del costituzionalismo*, in P. Carrozza, A. Di Giovine and G.F. Ferrari (Eds.), *Diritto costituzionale comparato*, 2nd ed., Roma and Bari, 2014, pp. 749 f.
9 J.J. Rousseau, *Du contrat social ou Principes du droit politique* (1762), Amsterdam, 1762.
10 F.C. von Savigny, *System des heutigen Römischen Rechts*, vol. 1, Berlin, 1840, p. 18 ff.
11 F. Wieacker, *A History of Private Law in Europe* (1967), Oxford, 1995, pp. 341 ff.
12 G.F. Puchta, *Cursus der Institutionen. 1, Einleitung in die Rechtswissenschaft und Geschichte des Rechts bey dem römischen Volk* (1841), vol. 1, Leipzig, 1841.

decision not to introduce definitions of general concepts into the rules of the Code. The aim was to avoid the risk of crystallising the basic categories of law.[13] However, it is clear that the real purpose of such a choice was to give legal scholars considerable leeway. Because the legislature left general concepts undefined, they had the freedom to develop, and indeed create, countless legal rules. In short, legal scholarship was allowed to share with political power a role that would otherwise be incompatible with the ideology of codification.

This is not limited to private law concepts: public law concepts, often quite abstract, were also involved. In this sense, none less than Marx criticised the resulting use and abuse of such concepts, observing that 'each paragraph of the Constitution contains its own antithesis . . . namely, freedom in the general phrase, abrogation of freedom in the marginal note'.[14]

2 LEGAL POSITIVISM AND THE UNIQUENESS OF THE LEGAL RULE

Having set the context of the emerging legal positivism, we can now return to the comparative law discourse on the subversive function of this field. In fact, the intertwining of the two forms of legal positivism – legislative and scientific – sums up what comparative law scholars see as the mentality of national legal scholars, i.e. the main target of their critique.

Indeed, legal positivism is still alive, even if it has lost its lustre in the course of the 19th century, not least because the intimate connection between lawmaking and national state building had waned by the early 20th century. Without such a secure foundation, the 20th century opened with a crescendo of reactions to the theoretical orthodoxy that had dominated the previous century, including scientific positivism as well as legislative positivism.

In Germany, Pandectism, polemically renamed as the jurisprudence of concepts (*Begriffsjurisprudenz*), became the target of the Free Law movement (*Freirechtsbewegung*). Its proponents challenged the idea that 'there is no other kind of law than that recognized by the state', not least because the code has gaps that cannot be filled by recourse to state law alone. The role of 'dogmatics' was also transformed by the Free Law movement. Resorting to 'free law, with the spontaneity of its decisions and the emotional clarity of its content' now seemed inevitable if recourse to 'fictions' was to be avoided.[15]

In France, the critics of legal positivism, who gave birth to the Scientific School, undermined the unchallenged dominance of the Exegesis School. The former, too, was committed to challenging the coincidence of law and legislation and to emphasising the role of 'free scientific research' (II.1.2). However, the result was not the end of legal positivism, but merely a redefinition of its foundations in terms less trivial than those linked to the historical reasons behind its creation. In fact, at the end of the Second World War, these foundations were clearly untenable: the tragedies caused by the conflict had definitively discredited the claims to the absolutisation of the state and its commands (II.1.3).

This led advocates of legislative positivism to rethink the identification of the law with legislation on the assumption, developed by Hart, that obedience to the law does not follow from mere knowledge of its content. Instead, its 'acceptance' by the 'officials of the system' is also relevant. This leads to the recognition that the law contains, in addition to legislation,

13 The Pandectists referred to Javolenus' motto, according to which 'omnis definitio in iure civili periculosa est; rarum est enim, ut non subverti possit' (D. 50, 17, 202).
14 K. Marx, *The Eighteenth Brumaire of Louis Bonaparte* (1857), in K. Marx and F. Engels, *Collected Works*, vol. 11, London, 1979, p. 115.
15 H. Kantorowicz, *The Battle for Legal Science*, in *German Law Journal*, 12, 2005, p. 2011.

precepts that do not derive directly from the legislator, but which are embraced by the legal interpreter.[16]

A stimulus for the innovation of legislative positivism then came from the criticism of Dworkin, who observed that disputes are decided not only on the basis of rules, but also and above all on the basis of policies and principles. Policies refer to 'an improvement in some economic, political, or social feature of the community', while principles refer to 'a requirement of justice or fairness or some other dimension of morality'. Since both policies and principles are not verbalised, it is not possible to reproduce them faithfully from a source. They can only be formulated at the end of an argumentation that inevitably involves the values of the decision-maker. In fact, unlike 'all-or-nothing' rules, principles require 'balancing' and this inevitably involves a degree of discretion.[17]

Because of these criticisms, the adherents of legislative positivism have tried to save their faith by admitting the possibility that positive law contains principles, i.e. that law is the outcome of reflections on the objective law and the subjective judgements of the interpreter.[18] We will return to this point when we will discuss law as an interpretive practice centred on the concrete case, inseparable from its social dimension and therefore irreducible to the representations of legislative positivism, such as the distinction between law as it is and law as it should be (I.1.4).

Other transformations of legislative positivism were imposed in order to counter the repetition of the Second World War and, in particular, to prevent the return of fascism. The affirmation of post-war constitutionalism (I.2.1), soon followed by the attempt to dismantle it (II.3.3), made it necessary to combine the commitment to the defence of the order born out of the defeat of the dictatorship with the non-evaluative approach.[19] This ultimately undermined its practicality: it could only be kept alive by resorting to fictions, useful for preserving theoretical orthodoxy but incapable of concealing the discretion involved in trying to defend the post-war order.

As we already observed, for legislative positivism knowledge of law does not imply obedience to law, since the latter presupposes acceptance of its content. In this sense, the focus is on existing law and not on valid law, i.e. on 'law as it is' and not on 'law as it should be'. And 'it is the task of legal science by virtue of the very concept of science in the modern world . . . to describe the law as it is'[20]: to faithfully reproduce it. However, we know that anyone who reproduces texts necessarily integrates them, and we will see shortly that it is not possible to identify the boundary between the authentic meaning of a text and its integration (I.1.3). Therefore, the claim to be able to faithfully reproduce the law, whether valid or effective, inevitably has the flavour of the ancient claim to be able to be the mouthpiece of the law, or at least to be able to limit oneself to a mere paraphrasing of the normative text.

In other words, whoever purports to describe is on closer inspection part of the prescriptive process. This is as true in the case of the reproduction of valid law as it is in the case where the point of reference is instead the effective law. In the latter case, whoever reproduces the text becomes the amplifier of the rules formulated by its interpreter. This explains the accusation levelled at positivism of promoting a scientistic approach, an aspect to which we shall return on several occasions.

16 H.L.A. Hart, *The Concept of Law* (1961), Oxford, 2012.
17 R. Dworkin, *Taking Rights Seriously* (1977), London, 2013, pp. 38 ff.
18 See P. Chiassoni, *Positivismo giuridico. Una investigazione analitica*, Modena, 2013.
19 See especially, L. Ferrajoli, *Principia iuris. Teoria del diritto e della democrazia*, Roma and Bari, 2007.
20 R. Guastini, *Girovagando nella filosofia giuridica del Novecento*, in *Materiali per una storia della cultura giuridica*, 2018, p. 242 ff.

If we then move away from the reflection carried out at the level of philosophy and general legal theory, we are confronted with a panorama that also indicates a considerable attachment to the traditional understanding of positivism. This is first and foremost the scientific positivism that characterises the customary understanding of many scholars of positive law and, ultimately, a foundation of what is summed up in the term 'Western legal tradition' (II.3.2). But legislative positivism also retains its appeal, as can be seen from the constant reiteration of one of its corollaries: the principle of the uniqueness of the rule.

This principle is more or less explicitly connected to the myth of the completeness and coherence of the legal system, as reconstructed by legal scholarship from the words of the legislator. In fact, if domestic lawyers necessarily register the plurality of available readings of a legal text, they nevertheless end their analysis by inexorably committing themselves to the identification of the only reading that is considered to be correct. In short, they only admit a single legal truth, a single possible interpretation among the many proposed within the scientific community or identified by case law. More precisely, in Sacco's words:

> In our work as territorial lawyers, we honour this principle of unity. Our greatest effort as civil lawyers is to discover the legal model within a given legal system. Given a legal question, we make every reasonable effort to find the answer (in the singular) to the question; we want to find the norm (in the singular) that regulates that given phenomenon. It is true that in order to know this norm we, after reading the code, take a look at the case-law records; it is therefore true that already at this moment of the search for the legal datum we are willing to consider the existence of a statute and the existence of something completely different from legislation. It is true that in practice we Romanist jurists, if in a lying manner we say that we go looking for the law in the statute, in reality we learn about it from books. . . . It is true therefore that from a realistic point of view we learn the legal datum from the book, then we verify it on the code, then we verify it on the case-law; it is true therefore that in a certain way we behave as if at a conscious level we distinguish in our law a statute, a doctrine and a case-law; it is true that empirically we know that there may be cases in which case law does not coincide with doctrine, in which antiquated or unreasonable statute has been superseded by a more suitable interpretation, drawn up by judges or professors. All this is true; but it is also true that, in the web of notions underlying our way of thinking as territorial jurists, we find the idea that the answer to a legal question, within a given system, is only one. There is only one legal truth, which has its source in the statute and is faithfully reconstructed by doctrine and applied by the judges.

It is evident that the statute could be subject to more than one interpretation, but this very circumstance reinforces the principle of the uniqueness of the legal rule. If several interpretations are abstractly possible, it will be said that one of them is correct. The doctrine will set itself the task of identifying it and pointing it out to us. If the doctrine proceeds through fairly vague formulas, case law, closely linked to practice, will enrich the rule with the details that are necessary to complete it. Thus, we return to the axiom of the uniqueness of the legal rule.[21]

In order to better illustrate the distinction between the approach of comparative law scholars to the study of law and the one traditionally adopted by jurists, we shall define the former as the 'external point of view' and the latter as the 'internal point of view'. Before delving into the two concepts, however, we should caution that we are not alluding to a distinction that is now well-established in legal philosophy, i.e. the one that defines as external the point

21 R. Sacco and P. Rossi, *Introduzione al diritto comparato*, 7th ed., in *Trattato di diritto comparato*, dir. R. Sacco, Milano, 2019, p. 56.

of view of the observer who does not feel bound by the content of the rules, and as internal that of the observer who instead uses those rules as the basis of his conduct.[22]

3 AN INTERNAL POINT OF VIEW ON LAW

The legal positivist principle of the uniqueness of the rule – i.e. expressing only one possible meaning – presupposes and reinforces a precise delimitation of the concept of law: it identifies it with the set of rules that, although mediated by legal science, are traceable or attributable to the formal sources of law. This leads to a conception of the analysis of law as a purely technical fact, as a non-evaluative activity with merely applicative purposes. The consequence is a representation of the jurist as an accomplice of political power, whose work is seen as an integral part of the prescriptive moment.[23] This leads to an internal point of view on law, i.e. to seeing the law as a variable independent of the context in which it is produced and applied.[24]

The internal point of view on law produces a very precise image of the legal system, which is seen as capable of providing solutions to all the conflicts generated by the society it seeks to represent in purely formal terms. This view inevitably produces an image of the legal system as a complete and coherent set of rules, without gaps or contradictions in line with the image portrayed by 'legal logicism'.[25] In fact, if one were to admit the existence of such gaps and contradictions, one would end up affirming the need to consider the substantive aspect of the events to which the technical-legal constructions apply. The result would be the valorisation of non-formal sources of law. The famous phrase contained in the French Civil Code, whereby 'a judge who refuses to give judgment on the pretext of legislation being silent, obscure or insufficient may be prosecuted for being guilty of a denial of justice' (Art. 4), is intended to prevent precisely such an outcome.[26]

One needs only consider the interpretive techniques used by lawyers in civil law systems to understand the extent to which the internal view of law is entrenched.

In order to discredit such a view, it would suffice to point out that, in the absence of a specific criterion for selecting the technique to be applied to the concrete case, the determination of that technique is necessarily based on arbitrary or even political evaluations. This would legitimise the conclusion that 'there are as many legal systems as there are methods of interpretation'.[27] However, this is not the focus of the discussion, which aims to shed light on how the various techniques confirm the validity of legal positivism as a reference point for the work of the interpreter. For the most part, these techniques are concerned with how to make the law coincide with legislation, even if this requires the use of fictions. This is the case, for example, with the psychological rule, according to which the interpreter must refer to the intention of the legislator, or with the purposive rule, whereby he must refer to the objectives pursued by the legislator in writing the rule, or again with the historical rule, which is used to justify what could be called the 'conservative legislator hypothesis'.[28]

22 See H.L.A. Hart, *The Concept of Law*, cit., p. 89 ff.
23 Ph. Jestaz and Ch. Jamin, *L'entité doctrinale française*, in *Dalloz*, 1997, Chron., p. 172.
24 V. Pocar, *Guida al diritto contemporaneo*, 4th ed., Roma and Bari, 2012, p. 7 ff.
25 L. Lombardi Vallauri, *La scienza giuridica come politica del diritto*, Firenze, 1974, p. 49 ff.
26 D. Gutmann, *Le juge doit respecter la cohérence du droit. Réflexions sur un imaginaire article 4½ du Code civil*, in G. Fauré and G. Koubi (Eds.), *Le titre préliminaire du code civil*, Paris, 2003, p. 109 ff.
27 L. Lombardi Vallauri, *La scienza giuridica come politica del diritto*, cit., p. 74 quoting Adolf Merkl.
28 See especially G. Tarello, *L'interpretazione della legge*, in A. Cicu, F. Messineo and L. Mengoni (Eds.), *Trattato di diritto civile e commerciale*, Milano, 1980, p. 364 ff.

It is true that these rules are formally imposed on the interpreter, who is forced to adhere to the principles of legal positivism, sometimes by the rules that civil codes devote to resolving legal gaps and contradictions. There are, indeed, only a few cases in which the interpreter is allowed to deviate from these rules, considered as the interpreter's main points of reference. Examples include the Austrian Civil Code of 1811, with its reference to 'principles of natural law' (para. 7), or the Swiss Civil Code of 1907, which, in the absence of statutory provisions and customary law, authorises the interpreter to decide 'in accordance with the rule that it would make as legislator' (Art. 1).

More often, however, even these cautious openings are avoided. This can be seen in particular in the provisions of the Italian Civil Code concerning legal gaps and contradictions. The Italian Civil Code was written during the Fascist period (1942) by a regime that exalted the state as lawgiver and was distrustful of judges, who were suspected of not being aligned with the political power. With regard to gaps, the Italian Civil Code provides that, in the absence of rules applicable to a dispute directly or by analogy, general principles may be applied. However, these general principles must be derived from the legal system of the state (art. 12, preliminary provisions to the Civil Code). The same adherence to the principles of legal positivism is then evident in the rules for resolving contradictions. These rules are intended to give consistency to seemingly contradictory words of the legislator, resorting to criteria such as the hierarchy of sources (art. 1 preliminary provisions), or the succession of laws in time (art. 15 preliminary provisions).

Even if the internal point of view on law is imposed by the legislator, adherence to the maxims of legal positivism remains fundamental to the representation, or rather self-representation, of the jurist. It is necessary for the image that he produces and reproduces of the social functions he is called upon to perform. This obedience, however, increasingly seems to be an attitude aimed at concealing strategies or beliefs anything but positivist, and thus at preserving a certain image of the jurist in society.

In short, legal positivism can be seen as a strategy of the legal professionals, as it relates to their self-legitimation. It is a strategy that focuses on aspects other than those typical of political power. The lawyer must present himself as a resolver of conflicts, distant from the arena of political passions, capable of taking decisions whose value derives from the fact that they are the result of technical evaluations. This is, after all, the characteristic feature of Western law. The legal professional, as the possessor of specialised knowledge, is its inspiring soul and guardian (II.3.2). For this reason, he likes to present himself as the holder of a power that is both rational and traditional. The former is founded on 'a belief in the legality of enacted rules' and thus on the knowledge and reproduction of a complete and coherent legal order. The latter is founded instead on the 'established belief in the sanctity of immemorial traditions'.[29]

It is, above all, private law that provides evidence for what we have said. For this reason, it was precisely in the area that comparative law – with its subversive attitude towards theoretical orthodoxies held to be immutable – first emerged and developed. This can still be seen in the way in which continental private law scholarship searches, almost convulsively, for a connection between its concepts and Roman law, or – to put it better – what is supposed to have been Roman law. The references to Roman law are intended to endow the work of the jurist not only with the chrism of legality, but also with the chrism of the sacredness of principles rooted in time.[30] This also explains the recent attempt to propose a European private

29 M. Weber, *Economy and Society. An Outline of Interpretive Sociology* (1922), vol. 1, Berkeley CA, 1979, p. 215.
30 A.M. Hespanha, *Introduzione alla storia del diritto europeo*, Bologna, 1999, p. 10 ff.

law of a doctrinal nature on a Romanist basis, the result of what could be called a genuine 'Neopandectism' (II.1.1).

All this, while the reduction of the law to legislation is criticised by those who see it as a 'mythology' aimed at making relative and questionable principles seem absolute. However, this reduction is more apparent than real, and if it seems real it is only because it has been supported by 'two hundred years of skilful propaganda'.[31] Moreover, the tragic consequences of a belief in the internal point of view on law have long been evident, and unfortunately often seen in practice, not just in the 20th century: 'if one were to study carefully what has happened in the world since men have kept memory of events, one would readily discover that, in all civilised countries, alongside a despot who commands, one almost always finds a jurist who legalises and systematise the arbitrary and inconsistent wills of the former'.[32]

Our intention here is not to propose a different understanding of the legal phenomenon, perhaps to confer legitimacy on centres of legal production other than those glorified by legal positivism. Rather, it is simply to emphasise its militant character and to expose the ideological charge of the legal positivist faith embraced by national lawyers. At the same time, we want to urge the recognition of the entirely prescriptive underpinnings of legal positivism. This must be countered by a mode of legal analysis that, if not descriptive (which, in any case, would be illusory), is aware of legal positivism's normative value, and denounces it. The call to denounce legal positivism is particularly common among scholars of sociology and legal history, the latter disciplines traditionally associated with comparative law[33]: the maxim that 'history implies comparison' is famous. This maxim is echoed by one that also emphasises the opposite, namely, that 'comparison implies history'.[34]

If legal history and sociology emphasise their essence as knowledge aimed at description and thus at avoiding prescriptions, this is also to accredit their subversive value (I.1.1). This is all the more apparent as the object of study moves culturally and geographically away from the perimeter of Western law. There, it is necessary to consider as 'law' also and above all those sources of normativity that are not considered law from the point of view of the scholar who is unable to abandon his own domestic approach. This, however, does not detract from the fact that one must also avoid the internal point of view of the scholars of the law under examination[35] – i.e. we must avoid taking as binding the representations or self-representations typical of the prescriptive approach cultivated by the latter.

4 FROM POSITIVE LAW TO LEGAL AND SOCIAL NORMS: THE CONTRIBUTION OF HERMENEUTICS

The point of view that the comparative law scholar must adopt is therefore the external one, open to the consideration of legal sources that are often disregarded by those who adopt an internal point of view.

In countries where the law is codified, this requires, first of all, an evaluation of the sources that the theory of the separation of powers does not permit: case law and doctrine.

31 P. Grossi, *Mitologie giuridiche della modernità*, 3rd ed., Milano, 2007, p. 4.
32 A. de Tocqueville, *L'état social et politique de la France avant et depuis 1789* (1836), in *Oeuvres complètes*, vol. 8, Paris, 1865, p. 39 s.
33 M. Brutti and A. Somma (Eds.), *Diritto: storia e comparazione: Nuovi propositi per un binomio antico*, Frankfurt M., 2018 and G.F. Ferrari, *Comparazione e storia*, in *Diritto pubblico comparato ed europeo*, 2021, p. 281 ff.
34 See especially M. Timoteo, *Grammatiche del diritto. In dialogo con Paolo Grossi*, Bologna, 2020, p. 55.
35 See P.G. Monateri, *Methods in Comparative Law*, in P.G. Monateri (Ed.), *Methods of Comparative Law*, Cheltenham and Northampton MA, 2012, p. 9.

Legal positivism sees them as mere repetitions of the legislator's words. Judges and scholars, on the other hand, when they interpret legislation, break the equation that identifies the legislation with the law because they carry out an activity that is not and cannot be merely cognitive. In fact, they start from the black-letter rule and then produce norms that are the result of integrations without clear boundary with the supposedly authentic meaning of the text. Such authentic meaning may exist but remains inscrutable.

In other words, the interpretation of a text is an activity whose characteristics are very different from the interpretation of a natural fact. The former, unlike the latter, necessarily involves an evaluative element, which legal positivism does not deny, but which it relegates to the stage when the text is formulated, i.e. prior to the interpretation delivered by legal professionals. This scheme, however, is a mere fiction since the evaluation and understanding of a text are not distinct phases, both being constitutive of its meaning. In this sense, the 'understanding' of the social sciences cannot be reduced to the 'explaining' of the natural sciences. Explanation is concerned with the objective aspects of knowledge, those without a temporal and spatial dimension, relating to the identification of a given chain of causes and effects. Understanding, on the other hand, means knowing in a subjective sense, that is, in a historical sense, recognising the inextricable link between the observed object and its space-time coordinates.[36] And law cannot be explained, only understood, within the framework of necessarily partial cognitive processes.

This is explained by hermeneutics, which studies the ways in which meaning is attributed to texts, emphasising the role of context and the contribution of the interpreter. It focuses attention on the moment of application since 'one always interprets for the purpose of application', and thus emphasises the relevance of principles as well as rules (I.1.2), and makes it possible to affirm that 'discretion is ineradicable from judicial choices'.[37]

For a long time, hermeneutic scholars were convinced that it was possible to show the multiple combinations of elements directly traceable to the letter of the text and external elements: those that integrate the context in which the text is situated, including the more or less conscious inclinations of the interpreter, or even the general feeling conveyed by the interpreter. This conviction, however, is based on the assumption that it is possible to separate the meaning of the letter of the text from the integrations that contribute to determining its meaning. It is no coincidence that early hermeneutic scholars believed that by interpreting texts in relation to their context, it was possible to derive the 'highest sense'.[38]

However, such a belief appears to be unfounded: hermeneutic scholars now recognise that, if such an operation were possible, it would produce a knowledge that is only seemingly alternative to that sought by legal positivists. It would, in fact, be a knowledge aimed at identifying, if not the single meaning, then the many meanings objectively ascribable to a text, as many as its contexts. Conceived this way, hermeneutics would, in short, boil down to a 'theory of the multiplicity of conceptual schemes'.[39]

On the contrary, hermeneutics must be understood as an intellectual practice that does not merely highlight the 'historicity of the horizons of truth'. Rather, it is an intellectual practice

36 F. Viola and G. Zaccaria, *Diritto e interpretazione. Lineamenti di teoria ermeneutica del diritto*, Roma and Bari, 1999, p. 112, referring to the difference between *Verstehen* and *Erklären* which dates back to Wilhelm Dilthey.

37 G. Zaccaria, *Postdiritto. Nuove frontiere, nuove categorie*, Bologna, 2022, p. 289 ff.

38 F.D.E. Schleiermacher, *General Hermeneutics* (1809–1810), in F.D.E. Schleiermacher, *Hemeneutics and Criticism and other Writings*, Cambridge, 1998, p. 228.

39 P.G. Monateri, *Correct Our Watches By the Public Clocks. L'assenza di fondamento dell'interpretazione del diritto*, in J. Derrida and G. Vattimo (Eds.), *Diritto, giustizia e interpretazione*, Roma and Bari, 1998, p. 200.

constitutive of truth itself: one that produces a 'radically historical truth'.[40] Hence, the well-known assertion of Nietzsche, that 'facts are precisely what there is not, only interpretations',[41] leads to the conclusion that the intellectual process of understanding the normative text is itself productive of the meaning of that text, i.e. of the norm.

At this point, it should be clarified that by invoking historicity as a dimension filtered through the hermeneutic approach, one advances a very different use of history from a Neopandectist legal-historical approach (II.1.1). The latter seeks to identify constants in the succession of conceptual constructions. There, the passage of time is seen as a mere chronological matter, which is reconstructed in retrospect. By contrast, the hermeneutic approaches' references to history reveals a succession of radically different objects, and the temporal dimension is constitutive of their diversity.

But let us return to the external point of view on law, which has been invoked so far in order to extend the notion of the source of law to the various actors who are called upon to deal with the words of the legislator by evaluating not only formal, but also the substantive sources of law. The adoption of an external point of view has an important further consequence: it leads us to take account of all the rules that are capable of steering individual behaviour and relations between individuals. This means that not only legal norms, such as those directly or indirectly linked to the legislator, must be taken into account, but also private norms of behaviour. These include provisions enabled by private autonomy (for example, the definition of manufacturing standards within a business organisation or the codes of conduct adopted by a professional order),[42] but also provisions that emerged in informal communities. These are social norms which express 'a model to which an action relates, or can relate, or must relate'.[43] They possess a de facto coercive value, and incur sanctions in the event of their violation; that is, they serve, as much as legal norms, the imperative distribution of values and resources necessary to satisfy interests and needs.

Of course, social sanctions are not imposed as the result of a trial held to settle a dispute.[44] Social norms, indeed, exist without litigation, unless they can be traced back to the system of legal sources by means of references: as is the case with the 'usages' recognised e.g. by the Italian Civil Code to the extent they are referred to by statutes or regulations (art. 8 preliminary provisions). And yet social sanctions are no less severe, and therefore no less capable of influencing behaviour, than sanctions imposed for non-compliance with legal rules. One might think of the exclusion from the community in which the social rules are recognised, a sanction typically imposed on those who violate these rules. Exclusion determines the isolation of the individual, the severing of his relations with the members of the community, and is all the more effective the more the community is irreplaceable.

To understand the scope of social norms and sanctions, more precisely to highlight their relevance as instruments for controlling and steering individual behaviour and interindividual relations, we can turn to concepts from sociology, which is the science that studies the conditioning of individuals by communities.

In this context, the concept of *homo sociologicus* was defined as opposed to the traditional human reference type in economics: the *homo oeconomicus*. The latter is the individual who is perfectly rational and capable of self-determination, i.e. who knows how to weigh the costs

40 G. Vattimo, *Beyond Interpretation. The Meaning of Hermeneutics for Philosophy*, Stanford CA, 1997, p. 6.
41 F. Nietzsche, *F. Nietzsche, The Will to Power* (1901), New York NY, 1968, p. 267.
42 G. Alpa, *La prassi e i codici di condotta*, in G. Alpa et al., *Le fonti del diritto italiano*, vol. 2, in *Trattato di diritto civile*, dir. R. Sacco, Torino, 1999, p. 119 ff.
43 V. Ferrari, *Diritto e società. Elementi di sociologia del diritto*, Roma and Bari, 2004, p. 42.
44 For example, J. Carbonnier, *Flexible droit: Pour une sociologie du droit sans rigueur* (1992), Paris, LGDJ, 1997, p. 25 ff.

and benefits of his actions on the sole condition that he possesses an adequate level of information about the options he is presented with (IV.2.4). The *homo sociologicus*, on the contrary, is the individual whose conduct is subject to continuous external conditioning, which depends on the role he occupies in particular contexts. This might include expected behavioural patterns that come with membership of a social class, age group, family, and so on. As Dahrendorf explains:

> Social roles are a constraining force on the individual, whether he experiences them as an obstacle to his private wishes or a support that gives him security. The constraining force of role expectations is due to the availability of sanctions, measures by which society can enforce conformity with its prescriptions. The man who does not play his role is punished; the man who plays his role is rewarded, or at least not punished. Social pressure to conform to prescribed role expectations is by no means peculiar to certain modern societies, but a universal feature of all social forms.[45]

Of course, *homo sociologicus* may decide to behave differently from what his role requires, perhaps as a result of an autonomous calculation of the costs and benefits of his alternative behaviour. But non-compliance with behavioural expectations is seen as deviance and is subject to a system of social sanctions: 'If he resists society's demands, he may preserve an abstract and bootless independence, but only at the expense of incurring society's wrath and painful sanctions'.[46]

In short, the law with which the comparatist is concerned is not only that produced by all the actors who, in one way or another, deal with the words of the legislator and who produce the norms composing the legal system. It is also the set of social norms, norms that are not legal from the internal point of view of the law, but that are nevertheless to be included in the list of rules that condition the behaviour of the individual and his place in the multiple communities of which he is a member. And importantly, it is also the rules that are perfectly legal from the external point of view on the law.

Social norms will have less relevance from an internal point of view, the more comparative research concerns Western law. If one moves away from this perspective, then non-legal social norms take on an increasingly important role. Comparative law scholars will find it useful to turn to the teachings of sociology, as we have said, or to those of anthropology, as we shall see shortly (I.2.3). But whether one is considering Western or non-Western law, social norms always help to guide the behaviour of citizens and must therefore be taken into account by those who wish to understand the legal phenomenon by going beyond the internal point of view.

5 THE SUCCESS OF THE JURIST

Legal positivism is criticised here as an obstacle to understanding what law is and what its sources are. This has not just a conceptual or scientific, but also an ideological dimension. Indeed, legal positivism has always been an essential point of reference for the legitimation strategies of Western lawyers. As we have said, and will reiterate at a later point (II.1.5), the Western jurist, lacking a political mandate, cannot but hide his role as a source of law behind the smokescreen of technical or technocratic legitimation. Thanks to the latter, the jurist,

45 R. Dahrendorf, *Homo Sociologicus. On the History, Significance, and Limits of the Category of Social Role*, in R. Dahrendorf, *Essays in the Theory of Society* (1958), Stanford CA, 1968, p. 38.
46 *Ivi*, p. 31.

'a private citizen', sets himself up 'as the legislator of his fellow citizens', endowed with the power to dictate to them 'the rule or rules of conduct that must standardise their social coexistence'.[47] This was sometimes shared by comparative law scholars, who gave birth to the subject as a reaction to the traditional study of law and then succumbed to theoretical orthodoxy they initially wanted to oppose. For example, by the end of the Second World War, when the unease about the combination of law and ideology was particularly palpable and comparatists retreated to the apparent neutrality of legal positivism as a legitimating device.[48]

Of course, technical legitimacy is not enough to explain the 'success of the jurist', which also requires two other factors: the prestige conferred by his alignment with 'the models considered to be most in vogue in the environment in which he has to operate', and the ability to actually solve the problems he has to deal with. The combination of these two factors, together with the technocratic strategy of legitimation, gives rise to the conviction of the 'irreplaceability of the work of the jurist and of legal culture'. This conviction is so deep-rooted that it appears to be unaffected by recurrent criticisms of the role and function of the jurist. More precisely, as Gambaro clarifies:

> The tentative moral of this story, then, is that in Western Europe the technical-legal way of thinking is so ingrained that without the work of legal specialists, not only is it impossible to judge, to help, to advise, but it is even impossible to legislate, at least if one intends to proceed organically and sustainably.[49]

These criticisms have been formulated in relatively recent times, and yet they no longer seem to be current. This is not because we are witnessing the rejection of the jurist's technocratic role, and thus his possible marginalisation as a decontextualised social engineer,[50] who is capable of combining the two variants of legal positivism: accentuating either the ability to reduce law to legislation, or the ability to place the latter within a coherent conceptual framework. The jurist is still a central player, but he is no longer acting out a script of his own making, as was the case in the days when normative texts used a language made up of concepts whose meaning was largely controlled by the jurists themselves.

Things have changed as a result of the vicissitudes in the economic order, or more precisely as a result of the advance of finance and the concomitant retreat of real economy. This evolution has led to the spread of a language dominated by expressions whose meaning is completely beyond the jurist's control. The language of real economy makes the jurist the protagonist insofar as concepts inherited from tradition such as contract, property, or liability are used. While these concepts are obviously still in use, they are now combined with linguistic constructions largely borrowed from economics, such as those used to describe financial instruments.

The role of the jurist as an adherent of legislative or scientific positivism is thus radically modified: the jurist now becomes the mouthpiece of economic laws, or the creator of a conceptual order derived from economic science. In both cases, the jurist fails to seize the opportunity created by the relativising of state law, in the emerging globalised 'legal order', which could have led to a re-founding of the autonomy of the juridical in favour of the jurist.[51]

47 A. Gambaro, *Il successo del giurista*, in *Foro italiano*, 1983, V, c. 86.
48 D. Kennedy, *The Methods and the Politics*, in P. Legrand and R. Munday (Eds.), *Comparative Legal Studies: Traditions and Transitions*, Cambridge, MA, 2003, p. 345 ff.
49 A. Gambaro, *Il successo del giurista*, cit., p. 89 ff.
50 M. Brutti, *La solitudine del presente*, in I. Birocchi and M. Brutti (Eds.), *Storia del diritto e identità disciplinari: tradizioni e prospettive*, Torino, 2016, p. 295 ff.
51 See P. Grossi, *Globalizzazione e pluralismo giuridico*, in *Quaderni fiorentini per la storia del pensiero giuridico moderno*, 2000, p. 551 ff.

In other words, the autonomy of the jurist is abolished, or at least decisively reduced. The possibility of portraying the jurist as a technocrat, legitimated by his specific knowledge, is also downsized. When legal discourse becomes a mere paraphrasing or reproduction of the economic discourse, law loses its *raison d'être*. It becomes post-law, an expression in which the prefix 'post' indicates the negation of 'law': law is now reduced to the mere echo of other social phenomena. The same happens to those who want to use law to regulate social coexistence. The adherents of post-law are the possessors of a knowledge that is no longer capable of interpreting social phenomena, much less of governing them.

The subject is not new. The relationship between law and economics has long been debated, and it has been long argued that law is a mere form while economics the real content of market and even social relations.[52] What is new, however, is the economic reality that leads to the marginalisation of the jurist as a technocrat. If there is no juridical knowledge, as such, the jurist is relegated to the role of simply reproducing economic knowledge through law. This is different from the role of the jurist in the industrial society in which he reconstructed his own centrality by developing, outside the limits of Roman law, which was unsuited to regulating an economic order centred on mass production and consumption, the instruments necessary to regulate phenomena that could not be compressed into individualistic categories.

The new instruments were elaborated on the basis of knowledge produced and reproduced autonomously by jurists, who were able to adapt their constructions to the social dimension indispensable for the development of the economic order.[53] Now, the same jurists have been reduced to the role of guardians of rules about rules: that is, rules about the interpretation or validity of rules. The jurists, however, are without influence on the substance of the relationships that the rules deal with. They can no longer claim 'completely autonomous activity', let alone of claiming a 'kind of proud independence',[54] in a context in which 'the science of law has a purely pragmatic and instrumental value'.

All of this is made worse by a phenomenon that is paradoxical in many respects and that linguists in particular have focused on: while economic language is experiencing a moment of widespread diffusion, fuelled by virtual finance, economic experts do not bother to clarify its meaning for the uninitiated. We can therefore speak of a veritable 'financialisation of language', which coincides, moreover, with the increasing use of English expressions that are a source of further misunderstandings.[55] This gives rise to the 'application of a single language, a single rhetoric with its stylistic features, to all communicative situations'[56]: one of the main characteristics of European law, which 'represents a very peculiar standardisation, charged as it is with factuality and technical dimensions from which it cannot and does not want to separate itself'.[57]

To be clear, the overlap between the language of law and the language of economics and finance is physiological when the former seeks to regulate the latter, as is the case with social phenomena in general. That is to say, when the law deals with information technology, public health, or even climate change, it obviously cannot dispense with the use of the expressions of the sciences that deal with these subjects. In these cases, however, the language of law makes

52 For instance, K. Renner, *The Institutions of Private Law and Their Social Functions* (1929), London, 1949.
53 See A. Somma, *Alle radici del diritto privato europeo. Giustizia sociale, solidarietà e conflitto nell'ordine proprietario*, in *Rivista critica del diritto privato*, 2010, p. 39 ff.
54 G. Capograssi, *Il problema della scienza del diritto*, Milano, 1937, p. 5 f.
55 R. Gualdo, *L'italiano dell'economia*, Roma, 2023, pp. 21 and 34 ff.
56 J.-L. Egger, *Dall'anatocismo allo spread: esperienze di linguaggio finanziario*, in C. Marazzini (Ed.), *L'italiano delle banche e della finanza*, Firenze, 2016, p. 46.
57 P. Grossi, *Il diritto tra norma e applicazione. Il ruolo del giurista nell'attuale società italiana*, in *Quaderni fiorentini per la storia del pensiero giuridico moderno*, 2000, p. 500.

use of the language of the specialised sciences without being subject to it or, in any case, without passively accepting it. The case where the language of law is disciplined by the economic and financial language is different since the former is overridden by the latter. There, economics and finance produce 'truths' that can guide individual behaviour and, above all, legitimise political decisions. All these following solutions that are certainly not new: 'we invent a language based on an imaginary theory', such as economic theories derived from *homo oeconomicus* as the human reference type (I.1.4), and 'we use it to bend reality'.[58]

This way, we obtain further evidence of the continued dominance of paradigms typical of the age of legal positivism: when the economy was desocialised (II.1.9), and law regulated social life by concealing its political dimension. Specialised language has been skilfully used to achieve such a result, at least because it indicates a desire to pursue a 'design to rationalise and disenchant the world' and, in any case, to 'overshadow the complexity and tortuousness of historical factors'.[59]

If this is the case, the subversive function of comparative law should be of interest not only to comparative lawyers concerned with identifying the subject's epistemological status, or at least distinguishing it from that of other fields of legal knowledge. Indeed, the reaction to legal positivism, as a synonym for the reaction to the technocratic approach, is becoming a necessity for legal scholars as such. Once upon a time, they could benefit from legitimation strategies based on outdated paradigms, but which at least contributed to the success of the legal scholar. Now that these strategies are no longer useful, it is necessary to criticise them, or at the very least to stigmatise their obvious anachronism.

To sum up, the success of the jurist is undermined at its roots. He is not in tune with the common sense prevailing in the context in which he operates. Moreover, since he has to deal with rules that can only be understood by recourse to fields of knowledge other than his own, he is less capable of solving the problems he is confronted with. The time has come, therefore, to develop new paradigms capable of enhancing a value-based and non-technocratic dimension of law. The legitimacy of the jurist as a specialist of critical knowledge must be refounded on these values.

SUMMARY

1. Scholars of comparative law ascribe to their subject a subversive function of the theoretical orthodoxy inherited from tradition, in particular that of legal positivism. Legal positivism undoubtedly has the historical merit of having asserted the human nature of rule-making. Nevertheless, the idea that law is made by a legislator, i.e. that it coincides with legislation, is as misleading as the idea that law is produced by jurists and therefore coincides with doctrinal precepts.
2. The more the reasons for its affirmation seemed obsolete, legal positivism came under numerous attacks. First of all, there was the criticism of the school of the Free Law movement against Pandectism, and of the Scientific School against the Exegesis School. Other criticisms focused on the role of principles as unspoken rules for resolving disputes. In response, legal positivism attempted to revise its foundations, which nevertheless persist, albeit in the context of less trivial discussions than

58 J.-P. Fitoussi, *La neolingua dell'economia ovvero come dire a un malato che è in buona salute*, Torino, 2019, p. xii.
59 R. Caponi, *Specialismo e politica nella scienza giuridica*, in *Rivista trimestrale di diritto e procedura civile*, 2022, pp. 354 and 362.

in the past. In particular, these foundations are hidden behind the principle of the uniqueness of the rule, which, on the one hand, admits the plurality of interpretations of the legislator's words but, on the other hand, denies it in the name of a single legal truth.

3. Legal positivism leads to seeing the application of rules as an integral part of the prescriptive moment and therefore as a non-evaluative practice. This determines an internal point of view on law which, on closer inspection, constitutes the core of the legitimation strategies of the Western jurist: technical legitimation, in which the political value of the application of the law must be concealed as incompatible with the recognition of only formal sources of law.
4. Those who wish to describe the phenomenon of law, rather than participate in prescription, must take an external point of view on law. This leads to an appreciation of the substantive sources of law, which must be identified according to the principles of hermeneutics. From this point of view, all those who interpret the law contribute to its creation. Indeed, interpretation is both a cognitive and a creative act and, in this sense, an intellectual practice constitutive of meaning. The external point of view on law then leads one to consider as law all the rules that can guide individual behaviour and interpersonal relations. In other words, it leads us to equate social norms with legal norms, insofar as they affect the imperative distribution of values and resources necessary for the satisfaction of interests and needs.
5. Legal positivism, as a strategy of technical legitimisation of the jurists, has ensured their visibility and social prestige for centuries. However, it is now leading to their slow but inexorable marginalisation. The technique most frequently used today is that developed by economics, reducing the jurist to the mouthpiece of economic laws or, possibly, to the weaver of a conceptual plot determined by economics. This highlights the usefulness of a critical study of law, not only as a practice of comparative law, but also as a redemption strategy for the jurist as such.

CHAPTER 2

AN EXTERNAL POINT OF VIEW ON LAW

1 FROM NORMS TO POWERS: THE POLITICAL DIMENSION OF LAW

Let us return for a moment to consider the role of hermeneutics in the development of the so-called external point of view on law, namely, the approach that undermines the view which reduces law to the rules laid down by formal sources alone. One may disagree with what is summed up in the famous Nietzschean slogan that there are no facts, only interpretations. That is, one may believe, to the contrary, in the possibility of distinguishing between facts and interpretations, and thus reject the idea that the attribution of meaning is an intellectual practice constitutive of truth, and not simply a way of emphasising the historical character of truth (I.1.4). However, it cannot be denied that this idea, which leads to the view that there are no clear boundaries between the cognitive and creative activity of the interpreter, is a convincing description of what jurists usually do when attributing meaning to a normative text.

Indeed, it is easy to see that the lawyer, in assisting a client, is not interested in identifying the authentic meaning of legal rules, or at least not the meaning that is more or less in keeping with the spirit of the law. The lawyer will certainly have to present his interpretation of the rules as respecting the meaning of the law, but in truth he will be interested in the meaning that is most likely to enable his client to obtain, in whole or in part, the desired result. Failure to do so may even expose him to liability for breach of professional ethics, according to which 'a lawyer must always defend his client's interests to the best of his ability and place them above his own interests or those of his colleagues'.[1]

The same can be said of the use of legal rules prior to any dispute. When dealing with other individuals or with public authorities, one will refer to these rules to support his more or less legitimate aspirations and expectations. The latter will constitute the point of reference for the interpretation of these rules, much more than the rules' supposedly authentic meaning, the reconstruction of which pertains to the rhetorical level of argumentation. It is, moreover, the only approach that corresponds to the basis of the jurist's success, i.e. the society's expectations of the jurist (I.1.5).

The same goes for the use of legal texts in the activities of public authorities, especially in their relations with each other, as well as in their relations with citizens. Preference is given to interpretations which, on the basis of specific needs, extend or restrict competences, increase or limit powers and capacities, or affirm or deny rights and obligations. In doing so, the alleged objective meaning of the provisions invoked is disregarded since it may well be incompatible with what is intended to be achieved by the interpretive activity. In all of this, consistency with the mythical conceptual structure of the legal system may be relevant as a rhetorical argument useful in arguing a case, but not as a value to be affirmed *a priori*.

1 Art. 2.7 Model Code of Conduct for European Lawyers.

DOI: 10.4324/9781032684499-3

This suggests that interpretation is an activity that is certainly relevant at a philosophical level, where the aspect of the authentic meaning of a text may come into play, but also and above all as a practice in a broadly political sense – that is, in relation to a precise model of distribution of resources and values in society. This does not turn it into an arbitrary practice, since stressing the political valence of interpretation also means stressing that the final result must 'provide a response, in terms that are comprehensible and rationally acceptable to the surrounding social environment, to the needs that determined those expectations'. This is particularly true in situations where the legislature fails to resolve social conflicts and these are brought before the courts. Underlining what the critics of legal positivism (I.1.2) have pointed out: that 'the starting point of interpretation is not the text . . . but the actual or imagined case and thus the problem or set of problems it poses'.[2]

From this point of view, interpretation has an extra-legal value. It has to deal with the meaning of a text, but must identify, each time, the most convenient among the meanings generally accepted by its addressees as a legitimate source for regulating their behaviour. This is the aspect emphasised by those who speak of hermeneutics as meaning-creation, and in particular of the comparative lawyer as 'involved in a co-constitution of meaning',[3] as they seek to emphasise the main purpose of discursive practices in law, including interpretation. This serves to clarify that they aim to produce and reproduce, through an exercise in rhetoric, or rather formalisms and conceptualisms, values and social arrangements that are useful for favouring some components of society to the detriment of others:

> A powerful exercise in rhetoric, discursive re-presentation privileges, through the chosen narrative structures and tropological choices, certain constituents of the society in which it intervenes, in order to suffocate others. Since the legal discourse situates in the social fabric of the moment the oppressor and the oppressed, it brings out the chronologically determined organisation of power relations within a given society. Through its texts, law thus offers a narrative – moreover an institutionalised narrative – through which a society re-presents itself to itself, provides the image of the society towards which it tends. A legal text, through its normative side, encourages its authors as well as its readers to make certain interpretative choices and adopt certain social perspectives.[4]

This understanding of interpretation emphasises that law in its essence is a way of resolving conflicts over different approaches to the distribution of resources and values. Legal rules crystallise a certain compromise, while the legal system ritualises and, above all, individualises disputes over the application of the rules through the regulation of specific procedures. This does not, however, determine the end of the conflict, which is, moreover, affected by changes in the power relations that inspired the formulation of the rule. This is why the conflict remains, partly outside and partly within the law: it includes the interpretation of rules and procedures in order to alter the terms of compromises reached, or even to overturn them.[5]

The conflictual dimension of law becomes evident when a compromise appears fragile – that is, when the plurality of interests is such as to highlight the partiality of the points of view. And yet the discourse does not change when there is a *de facto* convergence around an interpretative choice, which nevertheless remains the result of a political choice and not, or at least not only, a philosophical one. Even if the consensus around this choice leads one to see it as the result of evaluations alien to the sphere of values, or at least to perceive it as dictated solely by technical reasons.

2 See L. Mengoni, *Diritto e politica nella dottrina giuridica*, in *Iustitia*, 1974, pp. 346 and 350.
3 P. Legrand, *Droit comparé*, 5th ed., Paris, 2015, p. 12.
4 P. Legrand, *Le droit comparé*, Paris, 1999, p. 49 f.
5 A. Somma (Ed.), *Diritti fondamentali e conflitto sociale. Un dialogo tra le discipline*, Roma, 2024.

This view of law, when mediated by emphasising the broadly political character of interpretation, contrasts with the way of conceiving the legal system suggested by normativist theories and the related structuralist approach. After all, for normativist theories the legal system is merely a set of rules to be analysed from the point of view of their validity, coherence, and completeness. These elements exhaust the field of what is meant by law, reduced to a general theory of law, namely, to a science limited to the mere conceptual analysis of law[6] – thus neglecting what is confined to the field of sociology, or even of the philosophy of law, which is therefore belittled: the effectiveness of rules, of their constitutive role for the behaviour of citizens.

This is why normativist theories are concerned with the structure of law and disinterested in its function and in the motives of the interpreter[7]: it would imply a focus on the sources of rules, and thus on the political use of interpretation. This is the background for viewing the legal professional as a mere technician, for qualifying his activity as merely cognitive and acritical.

It is therefore no coincidence that normativist theories fit well with the conception of law advocated by legal positivism, which emphasises the role of the legislative power. In fact, the evaluative moment in the production of rules is given to the legislator and taken away from their addressees. If legal positivism neglects the role of power in the production of law, its emphasis requires a broad notion of power: the ability or 'problematic possibility of bending others to one's own project, regardless of their desire or will'.[8] Indeed, if on the prescriptive level it can be argued that only the legislative power is allowed to produce legal rules, on the descriptive level it should be noted that anyone who has an effective capacity to steer the behaviour of others can do so.

To put it differently, as they use the words of the legislator, all powers end up becoming sources of law albeit in formal compliance with the dogma of legal positivism: identifying an *a priori* meaning of legislative texts rather than promoting choices in a broader political sense. This is why we have stressed that interpreting means exercising power through control over the production of legal discourses, and that the latter are tools to realise and develop systems of inclusion.[9]

Of course, the mechanism just described does not apply only to the case where the source of law is such because it uses the words of the legislator. Particularly in the present era, characterised by the reduction of the role of the state in the production of rules, the words used may be those of the many powers in the political and economic order. We shall return to this point discussing legal pluralism (I.2.3) and globalisation (II.1.9).

The emphasis on the power dimension characterises the democratic and social constitutionalism that was conceived at the end of the Second World War to prevent the return of the regimes that had unleashed that war (I.1.2). It thus stands in stark contrast to the legal positivist tradition. In fact, democratic and social constitutionalism feeds on conflict and, in this sense, legitimises it: it is based on the 'guarantees of even radical diversity', albeit recomposed within an order designed to pursue the 'unity of pluralism'.[10] All of this, however, achieving equal starting points for the parties in conflict, i.e. counter-balancing social weakness with legal strength. This is the meaning of measures aiming at promoting rights for those in a situation of vulnerability and, conversely, at limiting rights for the bearers of social strength, which are therefore forced into a situation of legal weakness.

This is the meaning of the principle of substantive equality, which can be understood as a way of redistributing the weapons of social conflict. It is summed up in the formula that

6 N. Bobbio, *Giusnaturalismo e positivismo giuridico* (1965), Roma and Bari, 2011, p. 42 ff.
7 N. Bobbio, *Dalla struttura alla funzione. Nuovi studi di teoria del diritto* (1977), Roma and Bari, 2007, p. 48 ff.
8 F. Ferrarotti, *Il potere*, Roma, 2004, p. 9.
9 M. Foucault, *L'ordre du discours*, Paris, 1971, p. 10 f.
10 G. Azzariti, *Contro il revisionismo costituzionale*, Roma and Bari, 2016, pp. 34 and 44 f.

public authorities are obliged to remove economic and social obstacles to the full development of the human person and to political, economic, and social participation. This is a formula contained in the Italian Constitution (art. 3), which is the foundation of post-war constitutionalism, or more precisely of the democratic and social constitutionalism that emerged after the defeat of fascism, even if this was reached after the end of the Second World War. Indeed, provisions similar to the one just mentioned, which define the principle of substantive equality in terms of the obligation of public authorities to remove obstacles to its realisation, can be found in the constitutions of Greece (art. 25), Portugal (art. 81), and Spain (art. 9).[11]

We will see that the attempt to downgrade post-war constitutionalism goes hand in hand with the desire to defuse conflict and, in this sense, to depoliticise the social arena. We will also see how all this is aimed at the construction of a neoliberal order through the most disparate instruments: first and foremost, the market for reforms (III.2.1–9).

2 THE CONCEPT OF INSTITUTION AND THE INSTITUTIONAL ANALYSIS

To fully understand the broad political significance of interpretation, it is necessary to move beyond visions of the legal system as a mere set of rules. Normativist theories, in fact, relegate the role and strategies of those who create rules outside the legal sphere, assuming that rules are an ascertainable and immutable fact for interpreters. Institutionalist theories take a different approach: they emphasise the role of institutions as engines of the legal system, as organisations that pre-exist legal rules and condition the production of their meaning.[12] Institutional analysis is thus an essential point of reference for the comparative law scholar, and an indispensable point of view to counter legal positivism as a precondition for making comparisons.

Institutionalism is widespread among scholars of comparative public law, who, in view of the specific nature of their subject, stress the need to adopt 'an institutionalist rather than a normative approach', which pays attention to 'the type of concrete organisation of relations'.[13] Private law scholars also resort to institutional analysis not least because of its relevance for developing an external point of view on law.

Nevertheless, it must be acknowledged that the concept of institution poses problems due to its vagueness. These problems are generally overcome by focusing on more or less stable and permanent organisations. It is pointed out that stable and durable organisations are those that are able to transcend the lives and strategies of their individual members: 'from the simplest, such as the family and the tribe, to the most complex of all, the state'.[14]

This approach is consistent with the earliest reflections on the role of institutions, which were ultimately aimed at challenging a foundation of legislative positivism: the individual had to be let alone in front of the state. This foundation extends back to the French Revolution, and its famous Le Chaplier law, which sought to suppress all intermediate bodies between the citizen and the state.[15] Those who wanted to challenge it shed light on the coexistence between the state

11 A. Somma, *Quando l'Europa tradì sé stessa e come continua a tradirsi nonostante la pandemia*, Roma and Bari, 2021, p. 41 ff.
12 The classic reference is M. Hauriou, *Teoria dell'istituzione e della fondazione* (1931), Milano, 1967 and S. Romano, *L'ordinamento giuridico*, 2nd ed., Milano, 1946.
13 G. Lombardi, *Premesse al corso di diritto pubblico comparato. Problemi di metodo*, Milano, 1986, p. 70.
14 C. Faralli, *Pluralismo e teoria generale del diritto*, in P. Cappellini and G. Cazzetta (Eds.), *Pluralismo giuridico. Itinerari contemporanei*, Milano, 2023, p. 63.
15 G. Cazzetta, *Una consapevole linea di confine. Diritto del lavoro e libertà di contratto*, in *Lavoro e diritto*, 2007, p. 157 f.

and other centres of power and promoted a non-formalist vision of their interaction. In other words, they wanted to look beyond the schemes historically used to dismantle the structures of the *ancien régime* – first and foremost formal equality – to show that they actually concealed a conflict between opposing interests that persisted in the modern state. As Romano clarifies:

> The current state – and this is a typical feature of the state – balances before the law the weak and the strong, the humble and the powerful, whereas it should follow and reflect the instincts of conquest, of heroism, of the struggle between individuals, between different classes and between different races. . . . It is precisely from these contrasts, or rather from a special attitude assumed by them, that the movement that determines a sort of crisis in the modern state receives its greatest force. Within it, and often, as we shall see, against it, a series of organisations and associations multiply and flourish with a luxuriant life and effective power. They set themselves the most disparate special purposes, but they all have a common character: that of grouping individuals according to the criterion of their profession or, better, of their economic interest. . . . With the disappearance and suppression of statuses and guilds, and the reduction of even the municipalities to a minimum, only the individual was placed before the state: the individual, apparently armed with an infinite series of rights emphatically proclaimed and given with no costly generosity, but in fact not always protected in his legitimate interests. While the organisation of the modern state, insofar as it relates to its emergence as the sole sovereign power, no doubt faithfully reflected the new social structure, soon revealed itself to be utterly deficient in regulating, and often in failing to recognise, the groupings of individuals, albeit so necessary in any society that had reached a high degree of development.[16]

In other words, early reflections on legal pluralism mirror the transformations resulting from the transition from bourgeois to industrial society, and its direct consequence: the overcoming of a society which venerated the 'property to the individual and empire to the sovereign'.[17]

This phrase, borrowed from Seneca, was used by the fathers of the French Civil Code to sum up the foundation of civil society: the separation of the political sphere from the economic sphere corresponding to the distinction between public and private law (II.2.4), achieved by means of a pact between the individual and the sovereign. The individual consented to the political sphere being entirely within the hands of the sovereign, freed, as such, from the constraints typical of the *ancien régime*. In return, the sovereign agreed to govern while accepting those conditions that allowed private initiative to develop, in particular by recognising the formal equality of individuals and their economic freedom.

However, the affirmation of equality on a formal level, namely, through the abolition of statuses, did not erase differences which were linked to the transition to industrial society. The industrial society is a class society in which the key division is between the owners of the means of production and the proletariat.[18]

This division was obviously also characteristic of bourgeois society, but it was not the basis of a necessary social immobility. It is true that this society extolled freedom as a fundamental characteristic of the human condition, present from birth and identified with the possession of property rights. However, the appropriation of goods did not require an act of trade, since it could result from mere human activity: 'whatsoever' an individual 'removes out of the state that nature hath provided, and left it in, he hath mixed his labour with, and joined to it something that is his own . . . makes it his property'.[19]

16 S. Romano, *Lo Stato moderno e la sua crisi*, Pisa, 1909, p. 12 ff.
17 *Exposé des motifs de la loi relative à la propriété par le conseiller d'état Portalis*, in *Code civil des français*, vol. 4, Paris, 1804, p. 31.
18 See especially O. Brunner, *Storia sociale dell'Europa nel Medioevo* (1978), new ed., Bologna, 1988, p. 39 ff.
19 J. Locke, *Second Treatise of Government* (1690) (n. 27).

Thus, in bourgeois society, work, even more than property, was the basis of individual freedom and the source of individual emancipation. In fact, labour was a factor of social mobility because it made it possible for everyone to become an owner and, as such, free. However, this was because work was carried out in the context of agricultural and artisanal production and by those who owned the tools of labour and could therefore take its fruits.

The situation is quite different in industrial society, where production is capitalist, and the worker is a wage-earner. Industrial society has to combine the property order with the factory system, that is to say with forms of work organisation characterised by the use of machinery and thus by a strong regimentation and hierarchisation.[20] These modalities alone are incapable of putting workers in the position of owners: workers on the assembly line know no emancipation, and nor do their descendants.

The transition to the industrial society generated considerable conflict, forcing a revision of a fundamental principle of bourgeois society, the imaginary of the individual standing along before the state. Industrial society, in fact, had to rediscover intermediate bodies: on the one hand, in order to counteract social weakness through the collective dimension; on the other hand, in order to discipline and regulate this dimension, that is, to neutralise class conflict and prevent it from overturning the property-based social order. After all, the latter was pursued by part of the nascent workers' movement inspired by the utopian socialism, a socialism of a reformist inspiration which aimed at the construction of a society based on collaboration and brotherhood.[21]

We can now understand why the transition from bourgeois to industrial society is in the background of the early reflections on institutions, as well as the reason that only organisations with a certain stability were considered institutions. However, if we avoid considering organisations that do not have this characteristic as institutions, we end up failing to understand the dynamics of the multiple centres of interest that nevertheless condition social behaviour, above all through precise interpretations of formal legal sources. It is only by assessing such dynamics from an institutional point of view, i.e. by recognising that unstable but nevertheless influential institutions operate within stable and permanent institutions, that we understand the sense of the political use of interpretation (I.2.1).

In other words, in order to contribute effectively to the inclusion of the evaluative moment in the activity of interpreting rules, institutionalist theories must use a particularly broad concept of institution. That is to say, this notion must be capable of encompassing the various legal actors, or at least the most diverse centres of interest that use law in their action.

In short, we should also speak of institutions in relation to unstable organisations when they are capable of directing the behaviour of their members. Of course, we must avoid the risk of blurring the concept to such an extent that it loses its ability to contribute to the knowledge of the legal phenomenon from the privileged point of view of the comparative law scholar. But this should not lead us to neglect the so-called 'semi-autonomous social fields': a term that refers to communities that are capable of producing rules that can influence the behaviour of their members, even though they are 'vulnerable to rules and decisions and other forces emanating from the larger world by which it is surrounded', first and foremost that of state power.[22]

20 For instance, S. Simitis, *The Case of the Employment Relationship*, in W. Steinmetz (Ed.), *Private Law and Social Inequality in the Industrial Age. Comparing Legal Cultures in Britain, France, Germany and the United States*, Oxford and New York NY, 2000, p. 193 f.
21 See especially K. Taylor, *The Political Ideas of Utopian Socialists*, London, 1982.
22 F. Moore, *Law and Social Change: The Semi-Autonomous Social Field as an Appropriate Subject of Study*, in *Law & Society Review*, 7, 1973, p. 719 f.

3 LEGAL PLURALISM AND STATELESS LAW

Institutionalist theories are fundamental to understanding the phenomenon of legal pluralism, a concept that in essence identifies 'the explanatory potential of the legal-political order as an alternative to a monistic account of the order itself'.[23] Legal pluralism helps to define the object of comparison, in particular by making it possible to identify centres of production of rules other than those considered by legal positivist dogma, i.e. different and often conflicting sets of rules all concerning the same case which the law is called upon to regulate.[24] If this were not the case, there would be 'plurality' but not 'pluralism': the former refers to cases where there is a mere juxtaposition of sets of rules, and the latter to cases where there is instead a competition among them.[25]

As we now know, legal positivism was established to support the construction of the modern state. In the modern state, political power is centralised, and with it the power to make binding rules: the monopoly of the legal (I.1.2). This served to undermine the power structures of feudal society, which were all based on the recognition of intermediate bodies and the coordination of their power to produce rules. The modern state presented itself as an institution before which the individual was left alone, and deprived of the support of entities that could otherwise fragment legislative power (I.2.2). This is why principles of legal positivism were developed according to which the interpreters of the words of the legislator, in particular judges and scholars, would simply repeat these words without adding to their authentic meaning. Otherwise, the logic of intermediate bodies would have been exhumed and the division of powers at the basis of the modern state would have been altered (I.1.3).

As is well known, the legislative power of the state has long been in crisis due to the existence of alternative centres of interest both within the state and at the international and supranational level. And in the first case, the erosion is not only due to the system of territorial autonomies: the same effect is produced by immigration, which is the basis of a multiculturalism that is also productive of a multiplication of sources of law,[26] if only from a substantive point of view.

The erosion of the legislative power of the state has problematic implications for a cardinal principle of legal positivism: popular sovereignty. Even from a formal point of view, it can be argued that the myth of legal positivism has not really been downgraded, since it is still possible to trace limitations and cessions of sovereignty back to a decision of the state, which remains the ultimate source of legislative power. And yet, if this is true for the erosion of legislative power by centres of interests authorised or tolerated by the state,[27] the same cannot be said with reference to centres of interests hostile to the state: such as criminal organisations or, in various respects, multinational economic conglomerates.[28]

The legal positivist dogma can only conceal the action of these centres of interest, namely, their capacity to produce rules, which is also exercised by manipulating the words of the legislator. Alternatively, this dogma can recognise this manipulation and try to counteract it by

23 P. Costa, *Il pluralismo politico giuridico: una mappa storico concettuale*, in *Quaderni fiorentini per la storia del pensiero giuridico moderno*, 2021, p. 33.

24 J. Vanderlinden, *Le pluralisme juridique: essai de synthèse*, in J. Gilissen (Ed.), *Le pluralisme juridique*, Bruxelles, 1972, p. 19 ff.

25 M. Delmas-Marty, *Les forces imaginantes du droit*, vol. 2 (*Le pluralisme ordonné*), Paris, 2006, p. 18.

26 B. Pozzo (Ed.), *Multiculturalisms. Different Meanings and Perspectives of Multiculturalism in a Global World*, Berne etc., 2009.

27 A. Somma, *Sovranismi. Stato popolo e conflitto sociale*, Roma, 2018, p. 85 ff.

28 See especially M.R. Ferrarese, *Diritto sconfinato. Inventiva giuridica e spazi nel mondo globale*, Roma and Bari, 2006, p. 76 ff.

declaring as invalid rules considered to be alien to the state's legal system. However, it cannot prevent them from being effective, that is, followed in practice because of the influence exercised by the system of sanctions that affects their violation. A legal positivist would note that mere effectiveness does not make a rule valid, which therefore becomes relevant only from a historical or sociological point of view.[29] But it is precisely this point of view that is indispensable to comparative analysis, which aims to describe how communities function rather than to contribute to establishing how they should function: to 'understand what the law does in society' rather than to 'question what the law is'.[30]

Legal pluralism is an important aspect in the analysis of legal systems where legal positivism has a long tradition, for it highlights the merely programmatic nature of legal monism. The valorisation of pluralism, by contrast, seems indispensable in the study of legal systems in which the legal positivist tradition has not taken root, or at least has played a secondary role compared to that which it plays in systems with codified law. Mattei and Monateri make this point clearer:

> The reality is that wherever there is a sufficiently complex organised society, law cannot but have a plurality of centres of production. The state is but one of these centres. The law produced by the state can be understood as a background of complex, often contradictory precepts, accompanied by complicated and costly enforcement mechanisms. This system constantly competes, and often succumbs, in the face of other information-normative systems. Western scholars tend to miss this reality, known as legal pluralism, when observing the law at home. This phenomenon is certainly more visible in developing countries and is usually seen as a problem by those same ethnocentric observers who fail to notice what is happening daily before their eyes. The real problem, however, is not legal pluralism. The real problem is considering legal pluralism as a problem, rather than the natural configuration of law in any society.[31]

In order to better understand the usefulness of legal pluralism, let us consider African legal systems that have been affected by the dynamics set in motion by colonisation. To describe these dynamics, the image of legal stratification has been evoked, a figure that can be used in the analysis of the law of any society that has undergone frequent and significant legal changes.

Legal stratification refers to the gradual accumulation of normative orders which, from a descriptive point of view, stand side by side, even though, from a prescriptive point of view, they should overlap and partly exclude each other. In fact, it is a characteristic of African legal systems that, in addition to a traditional customary layer, typical of societies with diffused power, a religious layer with an Islamic origin, there is also a colonial layer constituted by the law of the Western occupying countries, and a post-colonial layer also modelled on the law of Western countries (the latter, moreover, being undermined by a return to tradition induced by the growing mistrust of Western models). None of these layers has succeeded in imposing itself on the others, in expressing a set of rules capable of regulating all social relations. The different spheres of these relations have corresponded and continue to correspond, albeit to varying degrees, to different legal layers.[32]

It is no coincidence that legal stratification is discussed mainly in legal anthropology, namely, in the study of the functioning of traditional societies. Nevertheless, methods and

29 See N. Bobbio, *Teoria generale del diritto* (1957–60), Torino, 1993, p. 25.
30 M. Graziadei, *Un compasso allargato. La comparazione giuridica nel mondo attuale e le questioni del metodo*, in *Diritto pubblico comparato ed europeo*, 2024, special issue, p. 29.
31 U. Mattei and P.G. Monateri, *Introduzione breve al diritto comparato*, Padova, 1997, p. 147 f.
32 *Ivi*, p. 148 ff. and R. Sacco, *Antropologia giuridica*, Bologna, 2007, p. 75 ff.

sensibilities of legal anthropology have found important and fruitful applications in the study of modern laws. Indeed, even in modern laws it is possible to reconstruct a dimension that can be defined as 'mythical': for example, a particular the communicative strategy used to 'give society an image of itself that does not correspond to its real structure'.[33]

Among the myths to which legal anthropology has traditionally turned its attention are, most importantly, those fuelled by the dogma of legal positivism, such as the idea that the state is the sole or ultimate source of rules and that there is therefore no room for legal pluralism.[34] Like anthropology, comparative law fights against such a myth and even defines its object of study in terms of a radical critique of legal positivism. In short, both subjects share the desire to deconstruct 'the image that the state as an institution has given of itself'. Both aim at overcoming the normative perspective typically cultivated by political philosophy in order to focus on a conflictual and therefore unstable reality. As made clear by Gardini:

> Anthropological approaches provide an image of how the state constitutes a political, ideological and administrative project whose legitimacy and sovereignty must be constantly reaffirmed through legal and bureaucratic apparatuses, repressive and benevolent instruments, the mobilisation of consensus and the creation of symbolism, the establishment of borders and the continuous confrontation with internal and external actors that shape, limit or reinforce its authority.[35]

Evidently, the same can be said of the history and sociology of law, and it is no coincidence that these fields of knowledge also adopt a legal pluralism perspective.

The sociology of law offers us the first references to legal pluralism, albeit without using the same terminology. We can derive it from a statement of Ehrich, one of the fathers of the discipline who not surprisingly was also an initiator of the Free Law movement (I.1.3). It was he who wrote that 'the centre of gravity of the development of law in our time, as in all times, is not to be found in legislation or jurisprudence, but in society itself'.[36]

Legal history echoes similar statements in the study of pre-modern law, or 'law without a state'.[37] In particular, they recur in research where the law is praised for not being the 'authoritative and binding voice of the holder of sovereignty' because it 'belongs to society and therefore to life'. Under these conditions, legal pluralism becomes a concept used to describe the characteristics of the legal system in contexts where legal absolutism has not taken root:

> It is the ordering of society which, independently from the holders of power, is in search of legal inventions that will guarantee its salvation. And, contrary to what happens under the leaden cloak of the monolithic state (e.g. in mature modernity), where the law is the expression of a central, centralising will (legal monism), we will witness throughout the Middle Ages the triumph of legal pluralism, i.e. the possibility of the coexistence of different legal orders produced by different social groups even if they coexist on a territory subject to the same political authority.[38]

On closer inspection, the possibility of using the category of legal pluralism for the pre-modern period does not appear to be uncontroversial. At that time, social coexistence was also formally regulated on the basis of modalities that encompassed both the territorial and the personal sphere. Instead, legal pluralism should only be discussed in relation to a 'plurality

33 N. Rouland, *Anthropologie juridicque*, Paris, 1988, p. 410 ff.
34 E. Merry, *Legal Pluralism*, in *Law and Society Review*, 22, 1988, p. 869 ff. and J.D. Cesano, *Derecho penal comparado. Una aproximación metodológica*, Córdoba, 2017, p. 60 ff.
35 M. Gardini, *Antropologia dello Stato: un'introduzione*, in *Antropologia*, 2016, 2, p. 9.
36 E. Ehrlich, *Grundlegung der Soziologie des Rechts*, München and Leipzig, 1913, *Vorrede*.
37 R. Seinecke, *Rechtspluralismus in der Rechtsgeschichte*, in *Rechtsgeschichte*, 25, 2017, p. 215 ff.
38 P. Grossi, *L'Europa del diritto*, Roma and Bari, 2007, pp. 6 f. and 15.

of forms of authority and normative codes', including 'those that are informal, subterranean, undeclared, but nevertheless fundamental in giving meaning to social action and guiding the behaviour of social actors'.[39]

Moreover, the use of the category of legal pluralism for the pre-modern period has a militant value, so to speak, in that it does not merely reconstruct an institutional system thrown into crisis by the advent of the modern state: it promotes a kind of return to that system, presenting that period as a more or less explicit point of reference.

Equally militant is the recourse to legal pluralism, not so much to establish the protagonism of more or less informal communities, but to promote new legal subjectivities within the framework of recognition policies. This leads to criticism of the tradition of legal pluralism studies, which is ultimately seen as incapable of really overcoming the statist monism it purports to combat.[40] Those who take such considerations to extremes end up rejecting the term 'legal pluralism', which is seen as the result of legal conceptions based on the centrality of legislation and the state, or at least as incapable of expressing a radical critique of these concepts. Hence, the proposal to use 'multinormativity' in its place, which would imply the desire not to emphasise the reference to the sphere of the 'legal', necessarily doomed to generate the sphere of the 'non-legal', as well as the intention to neglect the sphere of 'illegal norms'.[41]

In short, a debate is raging around the concept of legal pluralism that goes far beyond the stigmatisation of the legal monism of a legal positivist origin. The ultimate aim is to severely limit the state dimension, on the assumption that it can promote a renewed emphasis on society or, similarly, to the 'revival of remote societies'. But this is 'false thinking' because the withdrawal of the state is followed by something quite different: the expansion of the market.[42] This is what we observed when we criticised the lawyer's claim to be a technocrat, convinced that this would enable him to take over the space left vacant by politics. Instead, he is inevitably destined to succumb to the expansion of the economy (I.1.5) and ultimately to become an accomplice in the compression of democratic participation.

4 LEGAL TRADITION AND THE POWER OF THE JURIST

To mark their distance from the legal positivist approach, comparative law scholars who employ the term legal system redefine it an alternative way to the traditional one. In doing so, they make it inappropriate for feeding normativist theories and instead suitable for valorising an external point of view on law. Indeed, comparative law scholars hold that although they use a concept of norm expressive of an internal point of view on law, they intend to concentrate on law from an external point of view: they want to emphasise the space-time context in which the law as a phenomenon manifests itself.[43]

Some comparative law scholars, however, believe that it is difficult to speak of a legal system if one wishes to mark a clear distance from the legal positivist dogma. They then use other terms, which also appear in these pages, where the concept of legal system is used in a

39 F. Dei, *Razionalità e relativismo nell'antropologia giuridica*, in P. Cappellini and G. Cazzetta (Eds.), *Pluralismo giuridico*, cit., p. 82.
40 M.-M. Kleinhans and R.A. Macdonald, *What Is a Critical Legal Pluralism?*, in *Canadian Journal of Law and Society*, 12, 1997, p. 25 ff.
41 Th. Duve, *Was ist Multinormativität? Einführende Bemerkungen*, in *Rechtsgeschichte*, 25, 2017, p. 91.
42 P. Grossi, *L'Europa del diritto*, cit., p. 256 f.
43 For instance, R. David and C. Jauffret-Spinosi, *I grandi sistemi giuridici contemporanei* (2002), 5th ed., Padova, 2004, p. 16 f.

sense that is incompatible with legal positivist orthodoxy: in particular 'legal tradition', 'legal experience', and 'legal culture'.

The use of 'legal tradition' is especially frequent in common law literature, where the term hints to a conception of the law that takes into account, in addition to the typical features of an internal point of view, broadly speaking historical-cultural aspects. These references to the legal tradition, however, do not have particular meanings: they simply echo a legal conception typical of the system of origin of their authors. Historically, in fact, the centralisation of political power in England was not achieved through a revolutionary act, to be followed by a clean break between the era of common law and the era of codified law set by an all-mighty legislator. Not least because the feudal order, as founded and developed by the Normans who conquered England at the beginning of the second millennium, had different characteristics from that of the continent. The English fiefdoms were small in size and the sovereign avoided transferring police powers and tax collection powers to his vassals, as doing otherwise would have excessively weakened his prerogatives. An efficient technocracy was thus formed and developed at the central level, within which it was possible to centralise the administration of justice from the outset and thus accredit the sovereign as the guarantor of peace for the kingdom.[44]

Moreover, in the English legal experience, the convergence between 'unification of law' and 'reformist programmes of absolutism and individualistic and liberal demands' was not realised. It was therefore necessary to base legal certainty on an alternative model, centred on the 'primacy of law as such rather than law as statute'.[45] This is the model presupposed by the declaratory theory of precedent, according to which the courts do not create law but simply discover it. Their decisions 'are the proof of what common law is'.[46]

These are the reasons that common law countries are not well-suited to the statist notion of order, which is traditionally typical of civil law countries. In fact, the former are defined in terms of 'open systems', in which the court of one state can decide by invoking decisions issued by the court of another state: a common practice at the time of *ius commune*, when the courts throughout Europe were 'open to the *interpretatio* of others'.[47] One can then understand why in such a context it is natural and instinctive to see law as a phenomenon that develops predominantly in time, rather than in space – an aspect to which we shall return (II.2.2).

The meaning of references to the legal tradition is clarified by common lawyers in opposition to the concept of 'legal system', which shares the same inspiration of those who use the term 'legal order'. Indeed, those who speak of a system are said to have been educated in a context excessively determined by state sovereignty, and even by the nationalistic exaltation of that dimension. Those, by contrast, who refer to tradition observe law from an external point of view, that is, they take into account all the elements also considered by institutionalist theory. Moreover, and above all, they overcome the reduction of law to a phenomenon linked to the state alone. In this sense, tradition values the interactions between law, society, and politics, to the point of considering law as an expression of a 'culture'.[48] Precisely:

> A legal system, as that term is here used, is an operating set of legal institutions, procedures, and rules. . . . In a world organized into sovereign states and organizations of states, there are

44 A. Gambaro, R. Sacco and M. Graziadei, *Sistemi giuridici comparati*, 5th ed., in *Trattato di diritto comparato*, dir. R. Sacco, Torino, 2024, p. 49 ff.

45 A. Cavanna, *Storia del diritto moderno in Europa*, vol. 1 (*Le fonti e il pensiero giuridico*), Milano, 1982, p. 484.

46 According to the famous expression by Sir William Blackstone: see R. Cross and J.W. Harris, *Precedent in English Law*, 4th ed., Oxford, 1991, p. 27 f.

47 G. Gorla, *Unificazione "legislativa" e unificazione "giurisprudenziale". L'esperienza del diritto comune*, in *Foro italiano*, 1977, V, cc. 98 and 118.

48 J.M. Merryman, *The Civil Law Tradition. An Introduction to the Legal System of Western Europe and Latin America*, Stanford CA, 1969, p. 1 f.

> as many legal systems as there are such states and organizations. . . . Such differences in legal systems are reflections of the fact that for several centuries the world has been divided into individual states, under intellectual conditions that have emphasized the importance of state sovereignty and encouraged a nationalistic emphasis on national characteristics and traditions. In this sense, there is no such thing as the civil law system or the common law system. Rather, many different legal systems exist within each of these two groups or families of legal systems. . . . A legal tradition, as the term implies, is not a set of rules of law about contracts, corporations, and crimes, although such rules will almost always be in some sense a reflection of that tradition. rather, it is a set of deeply rooted, historically conditioned attitudes about the nature of law, about the role of law in the society and the polity, about the proper organization and operation of a legal system, and about the way law is or should be made, applied, studied, perfected, and taught. The legal tradition relates the legal system to the culture of which it is a partial expression. It puts the legal system into cultural perspective.[49]

On closer inspection, however, a study that examines a legal tradition is not immune from flaws, any more than the consideration of the historical dimension of law is. We know, for example, that the analyses produced by the Neopandectists, who take account of the temporal dimension of law in order to identify the traditions that are considered noble and on which to base their constructions (I.1.3), are decidedly flawed. In doing so, they nourish a scientific positivism – perhaps disconnected from legislative positivism, but nevertheless functional to a necessarily internal point of view on law.

Even among comparative law scholars, the legal tradition can be emphasised in broad spatial contexts – in particular those coinciding with the term 'family of systems' (II.2.1). This is, for instance, the case with references to the 'Anglo-American common law tradition' or the 'Romano-Germanic civil law tradition'.[50] These expressions do not, however, refer to arguments centred on the myth of origins (II.3.1),[51] as is the case with Neopandectists: they do not overlook the fact that identities are the result of contaminations rather than a reiteration of models that have remained identical to themselves despite the passage of time. Comparative law scholars speak, in short, of a continental European tradition, aware, however, that they must value it in its constant becoming. As Glenn states:

> Since tradition is best defined as information, however, the (slightest) contact with another tradition implies a variation in the information base of the initial tradition. Its overall identity is no longer what it was, in the sense that the totality of information available to it has expanded. . . . Given any form of contact between traditions, the overall identity of each becomes non-exclusive; each contains elements of the other, which may find support in the various tendencies in the receiving tradition. In today's world there are therefore no pure identities of tradition.[52]

Having said that, references to the legal tradition are not a source of misunderstanding if they are used to identify a more or less defined space that is useful for contextualising the phenomena analysed and thus avoiding distorted uses of history. This is the case, for example, when national legal experiences are discussed, although legal experience as such need not be delimited by state borders.

However, we must avoid overshadowing the distance between the concept of tradition and that of legal order or system as usually understood. This is, if anything, necessary because discussing tradition tends to relativise the connection between the legal phenomenon and its

49 *Ibid.*
50 M.A. Glendon, M.W. Gordon and P.G. Carrozza, *Comparative Legal Traditions*, St. Paul MN, 1999, p. 14.
51 M. Bloch, *Apologia della storia o mestiere dello storico* (1949), Alessandria, 2016, p. 78 ff.
52 H.P. Glenn, *Legal Traditions of the World. Sustainable Diversity in Law*, 5th ed., Oxford, 2014, p. 34.

state dimension. There are indeed 'complex' legal traditions that may have a point of reference in space, but there are also legal traditions that are 'internal' to the complex ones and, above all, 'lateral' traditions that do not have a specific territorial rooting.[53] In particular, the identification of internal and transversal traditions, perhaps in the context of analyses attentive to the theme of legal pluralism, helps to denounce the incompleteness of the legal positivist point of view. We will return to this aspect when discussing the classification of legal systems (II.2.7).

At this point it is necessary to return to the fact that tradition is ultimately information. Indeed, 'that which is brought from the past to the present, in a particular social context, is information'.[54] In other words, references to legal tradition imply the narrative dimension of law. And this leads to further reflections on the role of the jurist as a source of rules, insofar as they are able to control the production of meaning in legal discourse.

Let us turn first to the narrative dimension of tradition. It is a constitutive dimension because tradition, as an essential part of social memory, takes shape through a process of selection and transmission of information about the past. In short, tradition thrives on narratives, which as such are not a kind of faithful distillation of values that have matured over time. Rather, the selection and transmission of information is an arbitrary practice that cannot be reduced to mere uncritical reproduction, any more than the attribution of meaning to the words of the legislator by those who make use of the law.

Reflecting on the narrative dimension of law and its constitutive character for social memory ultimately highlights the power of the narrator and, in particular, the limits of his power in relation to other powers. The narrator, in the field of law as in the field of literature, pursues autonomous strategies capable of imposing themselves on those he necessarily pursues as part of a broader context: his narratives constitute a 'veritable reappropriation' of conventions, a way of legitimising 'different canons, sometimes antagonistic to other reconstructions'.[55]

In other words, thinking of it as narrative, law ends up appearing as an instrument of imperative distribution of values or goods and the power of the jurist ends up being highlighted in its aspects relating to this aim. This is, after all, what traditions aim to do when they become legitimation devices centred on the narration of the past. In the guise of artefactual constructions, they are real 'inventions' designed to establish moments of even fictitious continuity with selected events, for the sole purpose 'to inculcate certain values and norms by repetition'.[56]

5 LEGAL EXPERIENCE

References to legal tradition are widespread in common law systems, where the temporal dimension of law is highlighted more than its spatial one. In continental Europe these references are infrequent, not particularly thought-through and for a long time limited to Roman law and *ius commune* scholars. Comparative law scholars seem to have discovered legal tradition only recently, which leads us to believe that other expressions were used to stress the critical approach of the discipline. We know, for example, that an implicit reference to the notion of legal tradition can be found in the redefinition of the concept of legal system.

53 *Ivi*, p. 364 ff.
54 *Ivi*, p. 13.
55 G. Marini, *Diritto e politica. La costruzione delle tradizioni giuridiche nell'epoca della globalizzazione*, in *Polemos*, 2010, 1, p. 37 f.
56 E. Hobsbawm, *The Invention of Tradition*, Cambridge, 1983, p. 1.

The same applies to concepts not in current use, such as the concept of legal experience, which is relatively widespread in Italian as well as French scholarship.[57] An early use of the term can be found in an initiator of legal realism in the United States, who stated that 'the life of the law has not been logic: it has been experience'. As made clear by Holmes:

> The felt necessities of the times, the prevalent moral and political theories, intuitions of public policy, avowed or unconscious, even the prejudices which judges share with their fellow-men, have had a good deal more to do than the syllogism in determining the rules by which men should be governed. The law embodies the story of a nation's development through many centuries, and it cannot be dealt with as if it contained only the axioms and corollaries of a book of mathematics.[58]

The formula 'legal experience', used to draw attention to the 'human dimensions' and the 'essentially problematic character of the legal phenomenon',[59] began its career during the 1930s, when law was understood in its essence as a product of social interaction: as a 'practical form of the concrete world of men despite its apparent abstractness'. This is not surprising, since these years witness the definitive emergence of intermediate bodies as actors capable of competing with state authority in the political order and with the individual in the economic order. All this was in line with what was advocated by the theorists of legal pluralism, and more precisely by those who understood it as the expression of a pre-modern concept of social life.[60] This is evident in the references to legal experience aimed at challenging the idea that 'only the norm issued and enforced by the state is a legal norm', and at promoting the recovery of 'certain profiles of medieval life, also characterised by the multiplicity of collective disciplines'.[61]

The concept of legal experience is then used and developed by Roman law and legal history scholars always with a focus on the pre-modern dimension of law. Indeed, the concept is linked to the promotion of legal pluralism, and thus used to denounce the ideological character of the reduction of the law to legislation. The ultimate goal is to overcome the legal positivist paradigm because of a distrust towards public powers.

Roman law scholars who use the concept of legal experience stigmatise the approach of those fond of 'closed and delimited systematics' linked to the 'tradition of objective research so dear to positivist scientism'.[62] If that tradition typically derives from an internal viewpoint on the law, legal experience is instead the product of an external view that reinforces the interweaving of three worlds: that of norms and legal scholarship – the only ones to be taken into account by the legal positivist approach – but also and above all that of human behaviour. The latter end up being considered in its essence as a source of legal rules since 'everyone, conscious and unconscious', is 'operator of the legal', contributing to the formation of the legal experience 'with the continuous weaving and reweaving of our relations, even with our omissions, transgressions, violations'.[63] This is all held together by the glue of history,

57 See G. Gurvitch, *L'expérience juridique et la philosophie pluraliste du droit*, Paris, 1935.
58 O.W. Holmes, *The Common Law*, Boston MA, 1881, p. 1.
59 E. Opocher, *Esperienza giuridica*, in *Enciclopedia del diritto*, vol. 15, Milano, 1966, p. 736.
60 P. Costa, *Il diritto come esperienza giuridica. La filosofia di Capograssi nello specchio della storiografia grossiana*, in *Quaderni fiorentini per la storia del pensiero giuridico moderno*, 2023, p. 75 ff.
61 G. Capograssi, *Studi sull'esperienza giuridica* (1932), in Id., *Opere*, vol. 2, Milano, 1959, pp. 213 ff. and 232.
62 R. Orestano, *Introduzione allo studio del diritto romano*, Bologna, 1987, p. 352.
63 R. Orestano, *Della esperienza giuridica vista da un giurista* (1980), in R. Orestano, *Diritto. Incontri e scontri*, Bologna, 1981, p. 505 ff.

which is the essence of legal experience, and the foundation of its irrepressible singularity.[64] As Orestano states:

> The reference to legal experience appeared to me and continues to appear to me as the only one that allows us to look at all this no longer as separate worlds and in a certain sense – to remain in the image – rotating in different orbits, but on the contrary as components of a single and bigger world, within which aspects usually considered separate are instead conceived and seen as interrelated and interacting in a firm relationship, interpenetrated in a whole, all attracted by the same gravitational field: the world of the legal, a world dropped entirely into history, a world that is history, even when it seems to be given to detach itself or detached from it, a world that is history.
>
> The cosmic bodies of such a world consist not of Platonic geometric figures or abstractions, but of historical facts. They are facts brought into being by men, at all times and in all places, consisting of gestures or deeds, actions and behaviour, whether spontaneous or stylised, or the expression of thoughts, conceptual constructions or ideologies: indefinite series of facts, open to the incessant flow of life, with all that is rational and irrational, continuous and discontinuous, rational and contradictory, with all its ideals and egoisms, with all its outbursts of love and dedication that can touch the sublime, and with all its blazing hatreds that can drive one to fanaticisms of the most extreme cruelty and ruthlessness, with all its beauty and ugliness, with all its hopes and tensions, with all its constant struggles, with all its wounds, with all its plagues. In short, life.
>
> Within this new world – obviously only new in the way of considering it, for otherwise it is as old as history – any of the infinite manifestations of the historical concrete, including the most heterogeneous, the most conflicting can finally find a place.[65]

These explanations can certainly be criticised from many angles, not least because of their pre-modern flavour typical of the various theorisations of legal experience. However, it is undoubtedly true, and significant for our purposes, that discussing legal experience means reminding the scholar of the complexity of the set of rules that regulate, or at least influence, individual behaviour and inter-individual relations. In other words, it highlights the incoherence and contradiction of that set, challenging the coherence and completeness that legal positivists instead claim to elevate to an innate characteristic of what they, not by chance, define as the legal 'order'.

The analysis of law as legal experience thus ends up highlighting the confusion between cognitive and creative activity as an inescapable feature of interpretation: both are the prerogative of whoever gives meaning to legal rules, thus becoming their source of production, even if this is not formally recognised (I.2.1). Roman law scholarship critical of legal positivist orthodoxy alludes to the close relationship between experience and interpretation: 'in wanting to know experiences other than our own, contemporary experiences or experiences of the past, we give rise to our own experiences'.[66] And yet the same scheme can describe the way in which law is used by its operators, as well as by the addressees of the rules, engaged in exercising power in the form of control over the production of legal discourse.

From this point of view, experience is always and only in the plural and can manifest itself at least as many times as there are points of view, wills to know or to exercise power. If this were not the case, one would end up assuming the existence of a core of experience which could be claimed to be objective, thus burdening the concept with the same flaws typical of

64 See especially F. Cerrone, *Sull'esperienza giuridica: Capograssi, Orestano, Giuliani*, in *Diritto pubblico*, 2016, in particular pp. 976 f. and 988.

65 R. Orestano, *Della esperienza giuridica vista da un giurista*, cit., p. 506 f.

66 *Ivi*, pp. 516 f. and 528. Also F. De Marini Avonzo, *Rileggere l'introduzione di Orestano*, in *Labeo*, 1988, p. 209 ff.

traditional hermeneutics (I.1.4). The result would be a deficient theory of the historicity of legal orders, neglecting the fact that historicity is rather a constitutive element of orders and their mode of representation.

Roman law and legal history scholars distinguish legal order and legal experience precisely to emphasise the differences between broad spatial or temporal contexts, corresponding to 'a way of living law in history . . . in connection with a certain societal worldview' and 'certain cultural preconditions'. Hence, Grossi's references to medieval or modern legal experience:

> Such a notion necessarily represents something much broader and qualitatively different from any particular positive regime, from this or that political projection; rather corresponds to a cultural area, to a mentality, to a set of customs shaped by fundamental choices of associated living. Hence we will have a distinct legal experience wherever the great questions of the communities that follow one another in history are answered in a specific and autonomous manner within the realm of law; hence the historical legal evolution can be reduced to a sequence of distinct legal experiences, each corresponding to relatively autonomous historical legal moments that the researcher identifies and records.[67]

Comparative law scholars refer to legal experience in more limited contexts, namely, by reference to legal system or legal order. They therefore speak of Anglo-American or continental European legal experience, but also of German, Canadian, or Italian legal experience. However, these narrower understandings of legal experience do not indicate a misuse of categories formulated in other disciplinary contexts, but rather an intention to polemicise with the same approaches criticised by legal history and Roman law scholarship.

However, a clarification is needed. The comparative law scholar who speaks of legal experience does not intend to recover pre-modern visions of society, which is implicitly clarified precisely through the use of the concept also in narrow spatial and temporal contexts.

6 LAW AS CULTURE

The image of 'law as culture' has been invoked to emphasise the unbridgeable distance between the legal positivist approach and that typical of the comparative law scholar. It is particularly apt since the 'law as culture' is the antithesis of a vision of 'law as rule'.[68] However, only in limited cases does the image refer to a new way of understanding what is commonly referred to by the concept of legal order or system.[69] More precisely, it refers to a specific aspect to be taken into account in the study of the legal phenomenon.

This way of understanding legal culture has matured in the field of the sociology of law, where it has begun to be spoken of in terms of the 'components' of the 'legal system as process', albeit in a different sense from that used by theorists of legal tradition. In addition to the 'structural' component, which refers to 'institutions themselves, the forms they take, the processes that they perform', and the 'substantive' component, which refers to the 'output side of the legal system', and therefore, in particular, to the rules, a 'cultural' component has been identified. The latter refers to the 'values and attitudes which bind the system together, and which determine the place of the legal system in the culture of the society as a whole'.[70]

67 P. Grossi, *L'ordine giuridico medievale*, Roma and Bari, 1997, p. 23.
68 For example, M. Van Hoecke and M. Warrington, *Legal Cultures, Legal Paradigms and Legal Doctrine: Towards a New Model for Comparative Law*, in *International and Comparative Law Quarterly*, 47, 1998, p. 498 ff.
69 J. Bell, *French Legal Cultures*, London, 2001.
70 L.M. Friedman, *Legal Culture and Social Development*, in *Law and Society Review*, 4, 1969, p. 33 ff.

However, there is no agreement on the actual meaning of legal culture, in particular its subjective scope.[71] For some, it is relevant only as an internal feature in the sense that it guides the behaviour of the actors in a legal system; i.e. it is only an internal legal culture. For others, it must be taken into account in its capacity to also influence those who are subject to rules; in other words, it is an external legal culture, which relates to the recognition and acceptance of the activity of institutions, influencing aspects such as the rate of litigation and deviance. More precisely, as Friedman puts it:

> We can distinguish between an *external* and an *internal* legal culture. The external legal culture is the legal culture of the general population; the internal legal culture is the legal culture of those members of society who perform specialized legal tasks. Every society has a legal culture, but only societies with legal specialists have an internal legal culture . . . the values, ideologies, and principles of lawyers, judges, and others who work within the magic circle of the legal system.[72]

Additionally, there are different views on the components of legal culture. Some consider aspects that are clearly additional to those considered by the notions of legal system or legal order but tend to favour comparisons focused on commonalities. Others tend to perform the opposite operation and thus list numerous aspects to be taken into account in order to highlight the differences between the various legal cultures, going so far as to argue for the 'irreducibility of cultural differences' and thus for their 'uniqueness'.[73] We will come back to this when discussing the incommensurability of legal traditions (II.1.8).

Nevertheless, the reference to legal culture undoubtedly allows to focus attention on the dynamics that govern the production and reproduction of internal culture by paying attention to elements that are not necessarily taken into account by the concepts of tradition and legal experience. This can be deduced from the numerous and multifaceted questions that need to be asked in order to achieve such a result:

(1) A concept of law. What is law? What is its relationship to other social norms?
(2) A theory of valid legal sources. Who has the power to create law, and under what conditions? What is the hierarchy of the legal sources? How, and by whom, are problems of collision between legal sources solved? What is the respective role of the various legal professions? Are non-legal texts or decisions, such as religious ones, direct sources of law?
(3) A methodology of law, both for the making (at least if there is any deliberate law-making in the legal orders concerned) and for the adjudication of law. This consists in the first place of a theory of interpretation of the law. To what extent do the adjudicators of the law have the freedom and/or the duty to interpret the law? Which methods of interpretation may be used? Do they have any hierarchical relationship? Which is the standard style of writing, e.g. for statutes or for judicial decisions?
(4) A theory of argumentation. Which kinds of argument and of argumentation strategy are acceptable? Are these strictly legal elements, or social, economic, political, ideological, and religious ones as well?

71 D. Nelken, *Legal Culture*, in J.M. Smits (Ed.), *Elgar Encyclopedia of Comparative Law*, 2nd ed., Cheltenham and Northampton MA, 2012, p. 480 ff.
72 L.M. Friedman, *The Legal System: A Social Science Perspective*, New York NY, 1975, pp. 223, 194.
73 Citations in R. Cotterrel, *Comparative Law and Legal Culture*, in M. Reimann and R. Zimmermann (Eds.), *The Oxford Handbook of Comparative Law*, 2nd ed., Oxford, 2018, p. 710 ff.

(5) A theory of legitimation of the law. Why is law binding? What if it conflicts with some other, non-legal, social norms, such as religious norms? What kind of legitimation may give a binding force to the legal rules: a purely formal legitimation or (also) an ideological legitimation (e.g. moral or religious values)? What kind of legitimation gives the whole legal system its binding force? Is it sociological, historical, or axiological legitimation? And, in case of more than one kind of legitimation, in which combination, and under what conditions?

(6) A common basic ideology: common basic values and a common basic worldview. A common view on the role of law in society and on the (active or passive) role of lawyers. A view on which problems are considered to be legal problems, to be solved properly by the legal system, and not just, e.g. moral or economic problems, which remain outside the realm of the law. For Western legal orders this includes, among other things: a rationalist and individualist view on man and society; a positivist view on law: law is generally considered to be valid, independently of its moral content (except in very exceptional cases, such as Nazi law or abuse of rights); an instrumentalist view on law: law is not a spontaneously emerging social ordering, but a technique used by the ruling power to steer society.[74]

The external culture is the main point of reference for comparative public law scholars using the concept of 'constitutional culture'. In Germany, scholars allude to the 'set of attitudes, experiences, value judgements, expectations and thinking . . . and the actions of citizens, groups and even state bodies that refer to the constitution'. In the US the emphasis is on 'that substratum of shared premises that allows a social movement to publicly criticise a particular interpretation of the constitution'.[75]

On closer inspection, the study of legal culture, in addition to enriching the external point of view on law, contributes to refining the techniques used to classify legal systems. In particular, the 'common basic ideology' implies a focus on elements enriched by the study of the legal mentality, which is used by the most innovative taxonomies as a point of contrast with the legal positivist orthodoxy. Indeed, it is precisely the reference to legal culture that allows to go beyond the study of the rules, and ultimately to analyse 'the mental schemes on which their interpretation depends'.[76] We shall return to this point (II.2.3), not least to highlight the links between the study of mentality and the elements that contribute to the identification of legal experience. As we have seen, mentality is also invoked for this purpose, and it is understood as the 'custom' that the law is called upon to regulate, 'expressing the values of a civilisation'.[77]

Last but not least, references to legal culture make it possible to develop a reflection on the relationship between the law and social phenomena other than law. First of all, because they enrich the framework of aspects to be taken into account when attributing meaning to texts: if law constitutes 'an interpretative social practice', one cannot fail to stress that its identity is shaped 'by institutional bodies, but also by non-institutional subjects who contribute to the formation of the practice and its maintenance'.[78]

In short, legal culture allows to relate to the most diverse elements that make up the complex of values implemented by law. It allows to highlight the mechanisms that govern the

74 M. Van Hoecke and M. Warrington, *Legal Cultures*, cit., p. 513 f.

75 A. Di Martino, *Culture costituzionali, storia e comparazione*, in *Rivista italiana delle scienze giuridiche*, 2019, pp. 90 and 95 with reference to the words of Peter Häberle and the thought of Reva Siegel.

76 M. Graziadei, *Il diritto comparato, la storia del diritto e l'olismo nello studio delle culture giuridiche*, in *Rivista critica del diritto privato*, 1999, p. 345 f.

77 P. Grossi, *L'Europa del diritto*, cit., p. 7.

78 B. Pastore, *Semantica della vulnerabilità, soggetto, cultura giuridica*, Torino, 2021, p. 65 f.

formation and dissemination of dominant ideologies in economic matters, and to identify the links with the technical-legal constructions that are tasked with implementing them.[79] Here, too, there are implications for systemological analysis, in particular focusing on the connection between models of capitalism and parts of the Western legal tradition (II.2.9).

SUMMARY

1. The interpretation of law is a philosophically relevant activity, but it also has a strong political impact: by means of a rhetoric focused on the authentic meaning of the normative text, it realises an imperative distribution of values and resources. However, this characteristic is concealed by normativist theories of the legal system, which see it as a set of rules whose validity and overall coherence must be examined. In fact, these theories hide the role of the powers that pre-exist the law and use it to condition the outcome of social conflicts.
2. Precisely these aspects can be brought to light by institutionalist theories of the legal order, through which the effectiveness and function of rules can be analysed, thus revealing the dimension of power. Initially, the concept of institution, developed to shed light on the role of intermediate bodies concealed by legal positivist monism, referred only to stable organisations. Later, the concept was extended to include unstable organisations and, in particular, semi-autonomous social fields.
3. In order to effectively counter the legal positivist orthodoxy, one cannot ignore the valorisation of legal pluralism, whereby the same case is governed by several and sometimes conflicting sets of rules. This approach was developed long ago by anthropology, sociology and legal history and is indispensable for revealing the mythical dimension of law, i.e. legal monism. However, there are numerous cases in which legal pluralism is used to promote rather than to illustrate the crisis of the state dimension, with results very different from those typical of pre-modern societies: the spaces left vacant by politics are reconquered not by society but by the economy.
4. Understood in its traditional sense, the concept of legal order is obviously unsuited to expressing an external point of view on law. For this reason, comparative law scholars redefine it in order to dissociate it from legal positivism and normativist theories. Alternatively, comparative law scholars consider other concepts, such as legal tradition. This concept is used above all in common law, which focuses more on its temporal and therefore historical dimension than on its spatial and therefore territorial dimension. In fact, the latter tends to exalt the state character of law, whereas references to tradition aim to emphasise its interaction with society and politics.
5. In order to underline their rejection of legal positivist orthodoxy, comparative law scholars also draw on the concept of legal experience, coined to criticise the closed and ahistorical systematics widespread among Roman law scholars. The reference to legal experience implies a desire to value not only the world of norms and legal scholarship, but also and above all the world of human behaviour. Hence, the

79 S. Marotta, *Law and Justice in the Society of Economic Inequality*, in *Oñati Socio Legal Series*, 12, 2022, p. 1547 ff.

considerable points of contact with the external point of view on law, starting with the valorisation of the substantive sources of law.

6. Some consider that the concept of legal culture can be used instead of that of legal order. However, this is not what suggests the sociology of law, the discipline which originated the concept. Sociology of law simply considers that the analysis of the legal order must take into account not only the structural and substantive components, i.e. the institutions and rules, but also the cultural component, i.e. those elements that are indispensable for the development of an external point of view on law. In this sense, too, legal culture helps to expose the ideological nature of legal positivist orthodoxy and thus promotes the external point of view on law.

PART II

Why compare

Taxonomy

TABLE OF CONTENTS

DOI: 10.4324/9781032684499-4

3 The comparison between common law and civil law
4 Next: comparative constitutional and administrative law
5 From classifications to rankings: the superiority of common law
6 Next: the New Comparative Economics
7 Continued: law and finance and the theory of legal origin
8 From socialist law to Western law?
9 Latin American law as the periphery of Western law
10 The identity of Latin American law
11 Next: a land of transitions in the clash of models of capitalism
12 The law of the Nordic countries

CHAPTER 3

COMPARING TO UNITE AND COMPARING TO DIVIDE

1 A DISCIPLINE IN SEARCH OF AN IDENTITY

Comparative law is a relatively recent discipline that is still struggling for recognition and integration into university teaching, as well as for its legitimisation within the scientific community. Even current times, characterised by an increasing interdisciplinary perspective and by an international, supranational, and transnational dimension,[1] pose a persistent challenge to the legitimacy of comparative law: it is still perceived as an unnecessary, and at times, an exotic appendage to a conventional legal education. This is not solely due to the persisting primacy of the national dimension, but also to the enduring belief that the internal perspective on law can and must prevail over these novel phenomena.

The reasons for this apparent paradox are easy to understand. The cultural and critical study of law cultivated by comparative law scholars evidently collides with the legitimisation strategies of the jurist (I.1.5), which remain firmly centred on his role as a technical and neutral problem solver (II.3.1). This is the reason for the endurance of legal positivism and for the difficult dialogue with the many scholars still committed to its foundations.

In order to circumvent the difficulties linked to a critical approach, some comparative law scholars offer their understanding of alien law in conformity with the conventional strategies of jurist legitimisation: first of all, those who aspire to contribute to the unification of law within Europe regarding Roman law as a repository of latent principles capable of revealing its deeper unity (I.1.4). These scholars present their work as a technical activity legitimised by its alignment with tradition, thus concealing its political inspiration: the one deriving from the emphasis on the assumed individualist character of Roman law (IV.3.2). All this in order to restore to scholarship the role of source of law and thus to re-propose scientific positivism in a Europeanist key. For this reason, the advocates of such a use of legal comparison have been called Neopandectists.[2]

A closer look reveals that these concessions have not succeeded in securing the visibility and prestige of comparative law: on the contrary, they have produced results that impoverish or disempower comparative law and its cultural project. Indeed, Neopandectism has prevented a methodological renewal in the study of law, thereby thwarting the potential impact on traditional reflection that could have resulted from an awareness of the advantages of the comparative method. In any case, this has not led to the expected result of a greater attention to comparative law, which continues to be used as a valuable instrument for promoting political or cultural operations decided elsewhere (IV.1.3–4). Even the European institutions, considered to be the primary natural interlocutors of the Neopandectists, have

1 A. Vedaschi, *Diritto comparato e interdisciplinarietà: tra innata vocazione e incompiuta realizzazione?*, in *Diritto pubblico comparato ed europeo*, 2021, p. 301 ff.
2 See A. Somma, *Da Roma a Washington*, in P.G. Monateri, T. Giaro and A. Somma (Eds.), *Le radici comuni del diritto europeo. Un cambiamento di prospettiva*, Roma, 2005, p. 218 ff.

DOI: 10.4324/9781032684499-5

disregarded the traditional maxims of civil law. The idea of a unified law based on these maxims thus appears to be a futile academic exercise (II.1.5).

In other words, any discipline trying to legitimise itself by invoking specific objectives is destined to be marginalised. Indeed, if the legitimacy of a given discipline is made to depend on consensus about the aims it claims to pursue, the point of view of its scholars is placed in a subordinate position to the point of view of those entrusted with the task of assessing the merits of those aims.

This is not to suggest that intellectual speculation is an end in itself, eventually assuming the scholar's neutrality and capacity to yield indisputable truths. Nor do we suggest that scientific disciplines can only be regarded as such insofar as they eschew 'ideology'. That would be tantamount to asserting that the study of law can effectively 'expunge culture'[3] – that is, the founding values and worldviews of those who create the rules, as well as those of their addressees (I.2.6). Such perspectives expose the scholar to the risk of being 'instrumentalised by the contingent political interests involved in social conflict', which might be concealed but by no means rendered harmless by the claim to 'guarantee the political neutrality of the application of law'.[4]

It suffices to note that comparative law, for which many aims have been ascribed in order to demonstrate its theoretical and practical usefulness,[5] has ultimately ended up making its legitimacy depend on the strategies of the various disciplines that benefit from its analyses. This approach has not yielded significant results, and in instances where results have been obtained, these have not been definitive or enduring.

Rodolfo Sacco, an initiator of Italian comparative law, emphasised this aspect by addressing the apparent and specious problems of the subject. Contemplating the purpose of sciences in general, he observed that no one would dare to inquire about the purpose of an astronomer's knowledge. Astronomy has undoubtedly had substantial successes, having contributed to the attainment of significant objectives such as the moon landing, and yet its status as a science has never been dependent on those successes. By contrast, comparative lawyers do not dare to assert that their science's legitimacy rests on 'satisfying the need to know'. With Sacco's words:

> First of all, there are those who believe that they are weaving a very special eulogy of comparison by enumerating its purposes in connection with various forms of progress and social prophylaxis, among which are better mutual understanding between peoples, the creation of better public international law, the standardisation and unification of legal norms, and the improvement of national law. There are those who go further, and want to condition the very recognition of the scientific validity of the comparison on its ability to achieve this or that practical aim, specifically to prepare the advent of a better law. Comparative science would be identified with the search for a better model, conducted through the analysis of the foreign model. The speculation of legal models on different legal systems, lacking this purpose, would be pure contemplation, an erudite exercise; it would not be science.[6]

An examination of the objectives pursued by scholars in the field of comparative law shows that certain aims appear to garner more widespread consensus than others. Notably, those objectives pertaining to the promotion of a convergence of national legal systems stand out as they are closely aligned with the critique of both scientific and legislative positivism. Scientific positivism has indeed fostered conceptions of the legal phenomenon as the articulation

3 See V. Denti, *Diritto comparato e scienza del processo*, in R. Sacco (Ed.), *L'apporto della comparazione alla scienza giuridica*, Milano, 1980, p. 211.
4 See L. Mengoni, *Diritto e politica nella dottrina giuridica*, in *Iustitia*, 1974, p. 348.
5 On this, see R. Scarciglia, *Metodi e comparazione giuridica*, 3rd ed., Milano, 2021, p. 43 ff.
6 R. Sacco and P. Rossi, *Introduzione al diritto comparato*, 7th ed., in *Trattato di diritto comparato*, dir. R. Sacco, Torino, 2019, p. 3 ff.

of communities characterised by robust and exclusionary identities, such as those nurtured by the national spirit (*Volksgeist*): a notion that was deliberately accentuated by Nazism.[7] Legislative positivism led to the codification of private law thereby establishing the basis for the legal fragmentation that emerged from the ashes of historical *ius commune*. Moreover, the revival of the ancient unity championed by scholars in the field of comparative law enabled the restoration of the centrality that scientific positivism accords to the legal scholar (I.1.1), whilst liberating him from embarrassing links with old models that history has rejected.

It is important to note, however, that this pattern pertains to private law rather than public law, where nationalist approaches have historically dominated.[8] Undoubtedly, scholars specialising in comparative public law have mostly relinquished the nationalist fervour that once characterised their discipline. Nevertheless, it is important to note certain tendencies that indicate a focus on national and constitutional identity, as well as a more general critical stance towards analyses that emphasise unifying tendencies (I.1.10).

By contrast, the latter remain prevalent among of comparative private law scholars, who have not abandoned their traditional interest in the international unification of law or, more generally, in the convergence of national laws, as well as in taking an active role in this field. To be fair, unification and convergence can also be conceived as works that do not require scholarly input, and yet scholarship never fails to carve out a privileged space. Scholars therefore express their favour for such a use of comparison: a tool considered indispensable to grasp the 'physiological globality of social experience' and nourish the 'coexistence of peoples in the name of shared values and principles'.[9]

In other words, when it seeks to substantiate itself through its purposes, legal comparison presents itself as a comparison that unites. This appears to be the common thread that runs through comparative law from its constitutive phase. However, this does not detract from the fact that a comparison can also be constructed to divide, namely, to exalt identities and thus to disunite, which brings comparative private law closer to the sensibilities of public law scholars. Nor does it detract from the fact that public lawyers can adopt a more cosmopolitan approach with respect to other disciplines: this will be seen after dealing with the comparison that unites (II.1.6).

2 COMPARATIVE LAW AND THE LAW OF CIVILISED HUMANITY

The notion that comparison implies a critical and cultural analysis of law was posited prior to the advent of legal positivism and the widespread adoption of codification as its primary product. We derive it from Montesquieu, considered a precursor in comparative law,[10] who wrote that 'law in general is human reason', and yet added that 'the political and civil laws of each nation ought to be only the particular cases in which human reason is applied'. And more tellingly, Montesquieu emphasised that special attention should be paid to the context in which those laws arose:

> They should be adapted in such a manner to the people for whom they are framed that it should be a great chance if those of one nation suit another. They should be in relation to the

7 Among many, see K. Larenz, *Volksgeist und Recht*, in *Zeitschrift für deutsche Kulturphilosophie*, 1935, p. 40 ff.
8 T. Amico Di Meane, *Sulle spalle dei giganti? La questione metodologica del diritto comparato e il suo racconto*, Napoli, 2022, p. 146.
9 L. Moccia, *Comparazione giuridica come modo di studio e conoscenza del diritto*, in *Rivista trimestrale di diritto e procedura civile*, 2020, p. 18.
10 For instance, A. Mordechai Rabello, *Montesquieu et la codification du droit privé (Le Code Napoléon)*, in *Revue internationale de droit comparé*, 2000, p. 147 ss.

> nature and principle of each government; whether they form it, as may be said of politic laws; or whether they support it, as in the case of civil institutions. They should be in relation to the climate of each country, to the quality of its soil, to its situation and extent, to the principal occupation of the natives, whether husbandmen, huntsmen, or shepherds: they should have relation to the degree of liberty which the constitution will bear; to the religion of the inhabitants, to their inclinations, riches, numbers, commerce, manners, and customs. In fine, they have relations to each other, as also to their origin, to the intent of the legislator, and to the order of things on which they are established; in all of which different lights they ought to be considered.[11]

The spread of legal positivism led to reflections on how to counteract legal particularism in the name of a new unity, which would replace the previous one of the *ius commune*. From the second half of the 19th century onwards, comparisons between national legal systems began to be regarded as a means by which 'to discover numerous similarities between laws, all the more wonderful the more distant in time were the peoples'. These words come from Emerico Amari, who supported the idea of a 'science of comparative legislation' made up of three types of comparison: between customs to identify 'the average man of mankind', between codes to define a 'biology of laws' and between social conditions to achieve a 'social physics'.[12]

A first attempt to match the overcoming of legal positivism with the critical and cultural study of law was made at the International Congress of Comparative Law in 1900 in Paris: an event which is associated with the birth of comparative law as an autonomous science, i.e. with the transition from 'spontaneous' to 'institutionalised' comparison.[13] At the Paris Congress, the identity of comparative law as an 'independent' field of knowledge was finally asserted, particularly in relation to 'two other disciplines with which one might be tempted to confuse it: the comparative history of institutions and sociology'.[14]

We have already mentioned the conflicts that accompanied the definitive transition from bourgeois to industrial society in the period under discussion, mostly arising from the clash between the proprietary order and the factory system (I.2.2). In France, the attempt to appease those conflicts had led to the development of a 'socialist' approach to society. That approach, however, had no intention to overthrow the proprietary order. On the contrary, it aimed to prevent such an outcome through the formulation of 'a social rule capable of imposing itself on the individual'. The aim was to promote the protection of individual rights in a functionalist way, namely, to the extent that their exercise satisfied the duty to contribute to the balance between the various components of the social organism.[15] Or, similarly, to nurture 'solidarism', namely, 'the association of individual actions' to the extent useful to 'maintain the individual in a state of lasting prosperity and security'.[16]

Against the backdrop of these sensitivities, the dismissal of legislative positivism was taking shape. In fact, the image of a legal science as a faithful interpreter of the legislator's words was under attack, so much so that its exponents were called the School of Exegesis.[17] Indeed, that name was chosen to parody their self-representation as authors of mere paraphrases of legislative rules, who fully bought into the myths of the uniqueness of the legal rule and the completeness and coherence of the legal system (I.1.1).

11 Montesquieu, *The Spirit of the Laws* (1748), New York NY, 1949, pp. 6 and 7 (Book I, Chapter 3).
12 E. Amari, *Critica di una scienza delle legislazioni comparate* (1857), vol. 1, Palermo, 1969, pp. 105 ff. and 256 ff.
13 S. Goltzberg, *Le droit comparé*, Paris, 2018, p. 11.
14 R. Saleilles, *Conception et objet de la science du droit comparé*, in Société de législation comparée, *Congrès international de droit comparé*, vol. 1, Paris, 1900, p. 169.
15 L. Duguit, *Les transformation générales du droit privé* (1911), 2nd ed., Paris, 1920, pp. 8 f. and 26 ff.
16 L. Bourgeois, *Solidarité*, 3rd ed., Paris, 1902, p. 61 f.
17 Following J. Bonnecase, *L'Ecole de l'exégèse en droit civil. Les traits distinctifs de sa doctrine et de ses méthodes d'après la profession de foi de ses plus illustres représentants*, Paris, 1924.

Although the role played by scholars was necessarily more significant,[18] for much of the 19th century they stressed their marginal importance in order to show formal deference to legislative positivism. Later, there was a greater awareness of the contribution of the interpreter, who, in fact, played a pivotal role in adjusting the law to cope with the tensions unleashed by the forces of capitalism (I.2.2). The School of Exegesis would thus give way to the Scientific School, which did not contest the primacy of legislation, but at least recognised the need to supplement it with additions derived in particular from 'free scientific research', and above all did so in order to restore the harmony between society and law. That same harmony which had legitimised formal equality as the foundation of bourgeois society, and which the transition to industrial society had put in crisis. Free scientific research was intended to reconstruct the 'immanent law' of which legislation was only an 'imperfect revelation', and which was to be perfected by observing the 'nature of things' and by striving to realise the 'ideal of justice or social utility'.[19]

In short, the Scientific School contested the self-sufficiency of the lawmaker's words, and more generally the claim to isolate the legal datum from the extra-legal datum. Hence, the exhortation to combine the study of positive law with data from the other social sciences, which from the end of the 19th century began to flourish in the teaching programmes of the French law faculties.[20] This also explained the focus on the history and sociology of law, and above all on comparative law, which would not to be limited to the mere comparison of foreign legislation, for otherwise it would have simply reproduced the legal positivist approach. In other words, legal comparison, besides enriching free scientific research, had to track its interdisciplinary approach, and its openness to dialogue between social sciences. It had to be an integral part of the reaction to the centrality of legislation.

We can conclude from this that when comparative law asserted itself as an autonomous science, it was in a sense easy for it to adopt as its *raison d'être* the subversive function *vis-à-vis* theoretical orthodoxy (I.1.1). This, however, does not detract from the fact that the new science had to accredit itself as being aimed at a very precise purpose, which during the Paris Congress of 1900 was derived from the aforementioned distinction between legal comparison, comparative history of institutions and sociology.[21] This was illustrated by Raymond Saleilles, who shared the aims that the Historical School of Jurisprudence indicated for the renewal of the study of law[22]: in particular, to overcome the centrality of legislation in order to stabilise capitalist modernisation (II.1.1.).

The comparative history of institutions relates to the study of the 'legal and social institutions of each people considered in their own reality', possibly undertaken to ascertain whether useful indications can be derived from it to 'explain the institutions of peoples whose social status is more or less assimilable'. From this point of view, the use of the 'comparative method' is an expedient useful to the historian of law to 'fill in the gaps presented to him by the institutions of a country through what he can learn about the institutions of similar peoples'. Sociology, instead, is responsible for the study of the 'laws that govern the constitution, development and, in general terms, the organic life of societies'. Its approach is in many respects common to that developed by historicism, but purged of the emphasis on the national dimension which is considered an obstacle to the valorisation of the 'international interpenetration

18 Ph. Jestaz and Ch. Jamin, *La doctrine*, Paris, 2004, p. 72 ff.
19 F. Gény, *Méthode d'interprétation et sources en droit privé positif. Essai critique* (1919, 1st ed. 1899), 2nd ed., vol. 2, Paris, 1954, p. 223.
20 J.-L. Halpérin, *Histoire du droit privé français depuis 1804*, Paris, 2001, p. 171 ff.
21 T. Amico Di Meane, *Sulle spalle dei giganti?*, cit., p. 138 ff.
22 A. Aragoneses, *Un jurista del modernismo. Raymond Saleilles y los orígenes del derecho comparado*, Madrid, 2009.

of customs and traditions', and thus to the recognition of the 'natural laws relating to the creation and development of law'.[23]

Comparative law at the beginning of the 20th century aimed at something different and indeed at something more: at prescribing rather than describing. Unlike the comparative history of institutions, it was not limited to the mere contemplation, or to 'findings of fact that do not imply any element of creation or legal construction to be deduced'. Nor was it content, like sociology, to derive 'natural laws of social development' that once identified must simply be 'respected'. Rather comparative law aimed to 'create' and 'construct': while its starting point was the data provided by comparative institutional history and sociology, it used that data as a basis for activating a deductive process to find out the 'ideal that seems to impose itself on the legal initiative of mankind considered at a given moment in its history'.[24]

In other words, comparative law pursued a very specific 'practical purpose'. It was dedicated to the 'critical study of each foreign law considered from an economic and social point of view', in order to then 'identify points of contact likely to correspond to a motion of evolution common to several countries' and then 'orient the policy of law of the various countries in a perceptibly similar social situation'. In doing so, comparative lawyers abandoned the mere description of the phenomenon of law in order to become prescriptive. They aimed to show the 'ideal lines of legal progress', thus elaborating models of legal policy to inform the development of legal systems, and thereby contributing to crafting 'the common law of civilised humanity'. A law 'that is for the states as a whole what it was, in countries where there were different customs or different local laws, such as ancient France or Germany before its civil code, the progressive and scholarly construction of a unitary law formed above and beyond legal differences'.[25]

On closer inspection, not everyone shared such a universalising approach, albeit mitigated by the exclusive reference to private law and by the belief that the common traits of only those laws that shared the same level of 'legal civilisation' should be exalted.[26] However, most scholars established a link between legal comparison and the identification of the common traits of national laws, thus highlighting what later became a constant in the comparison of laws: its conception as a search for the features that unite, rather than those that divide.

Previously, others, moving from an evolutionist philosophy of history, had placed comparative law at the service of a 'theory of progress'; i.e. they had referred to it as a 'legal doctrine of universal civilisation'.[27] It was now added that comparative law ended up fulfilling the same role attributed to canon law or Roman law at a time when legislative positivism had not yet fuelled the myth of codification. At the same time, it was suggested that this would not reproduce the abstract schemes typical of rational natural law, as this was countered by the calls to emphasise the diversities rooted in traditions or in specific historical developments.[28]

3 COMPARATIVE LAW AND WORLD WARS

Although devoted to overcoming the nationalist and the legal positivist paradigm,[29] the Paris Congress of 1900 could not depict comparative law as a science truly devoted to universalism,

23 R. Saleilles, *Conception et objet de la science du droit comparé*, cit., p. 169 ff.
24 *Ivi*, p. 173 f.
25 *Ivi*, pp. 174 ff. and 181.
26 See D.S. Clark, *Nothing New in 2000? Comparative Law in 1900 and Today*, in *Tulane Law Review*, 75, 2001, p. 875 ff.
27 E. Amari, *Critica di una scienza delle legislazioni comparate*, cit., p. 156.
28 For instance, I. Tambaro, Art. *Legislazione*, in *Digesto italiano*, vol. 14, Torino, 1902–1905, p. 424 f.
29 R. Sacco, *One Hundred Years of Comparative Law*, in *Tulane Law Review*, 75, 2001, p. 1166 f.

not even in its guise as the private law of civilised nations. This was not least because the congress focused on French law as a point of reference for the convergence of national laws. All of this accompanied by 'a marked Eurocentrism that was anything but immune to colonialist and imperialist pathologies', such as those that hinted at a sort of 'legal evangelisation' of non-European peoples.[30]

In many respects, the First World War did not significantly change the comparative law agenda, which had to deal with a landscape characterised both with increased legal fragmentation and greater convergence in the efforts to overcome that fragmentation. The war ended with the collapse of the German, Austro-Hungarian, Ottoman, and Russian Empires and thus with an increase in the number of states, but also with a new awareness of the possibilities for a rapprochement of their private law systems. Indeed, the conflict had definitively 'overthrown individualism', just as the French Revolution had 'overthrown feudalism', showing that the construction of an order capable of reconciling 'the opposing interests of capital and labour' could no longer be postponed.[31]

This was the background to the establishment of the International Institute for the Unification of Private Law (UNIDROIT) in 1926, which was an initiative undertaken by the newly formed League of Nations. The latter was an international organisation that arose at the conclusion of the First World War 'for the purpose of promoting international cooperation' and 'realising the peace and security of states' (Preamble to the Covenants of the League of Nations). Under its auspices, UNIDROIT was entrusted with the task of 'studying ways of harmonising private law among states or groups of states and gradually preparing the adoption by the various states of uniform private law legislation' (Art. 2 Statute). These harmonising efforts occurred against the backdrop of the rise of fascism across the Continent, which evidently had considerable implications for the comparative law agenda. Even so, the desire to promote convergence between national private law systems was not in question. Fascism sought, after all, to eliminate political freedoms, but only to reform economic freedoms in order to overcome the '*impasse* reached by liberal capitalism'.[32]

It is therefore not surprising that UNIDROIT was founded in Rome, where its headquarters are still located, and where it was christened by Mussolini, who used the occasion as a moment of international projection of the fascist regime.[33] It was not by chance that the first president of UNIDROIT, Vittorio Scialoja, and the first secretary general, Pietro De Francisci, both scholars of Roman law, were Italian: the former was convinced that the legal unity of the 'civilised nations' could be achieved by emphasising Roman law,[34] the latter that the fascist revolution represented 'a return to Roman grandeur'.[35] Beyond the rhetoric dear to fascism, this still equates the unification of law limited to private law and above all, based on the principles recognised by so-called advanced countries from a evolutionist point of view.

This approach was indicted at the conclusion of the Second World War, if only to reject the ideology of the regimes that had provoked it. More generally, it was argued that the comparison of laws did not have to correspond primarily to a national interest and that, although it was initially intended to bring about the unification of laws endowed with a certain degree

30 T. Amico Di Meane, *Sulle spalle dei giganti?*, cit., p. 148 ff.
31 N. Stolfi, *La rivoluzione francese e la guerra mondiale*, in *Rivista di diritto pubblico*, 1922, I, p. 387 ff.
32 K. Polanyi, *The Great Transformation. The Political and Economic Origins of Out Time* (1944), Boston MA, 2001, p. 194.
33 See A. Somma, *I giuristi e l'asse culturale Roma-Berlino. Economia e politica nel diritto fascista e nazionalsocialista*, Frankfurt M., 2005, p. 311 ff.
34 V. Scialoja, *Discorso per l'inaugurazione di Unidroit*, in *Zeitschrift für ausländisches und internationales Privatrecht*, 1928, p. 478.
35 P. De Francisci, *Ai giuristi italiani (Discorso inaugurale del I Congresso giuridico italiano)*, in *Lo Stato*, 1932, p. 674.

of homogeneity, the ultimate aim to be pursued was the construction of a 'common law of the mankind'. Sarfatti captures the mood in the post-war years very clearly:

> Whereas formerly the comparing of laws of different countries with one's own laws was done primarily for national ends, for example, as an aid to legislators in the task of law making or as an aid in the appraisal of practical solutions to problems reached by the application of principles common to several legal systems, this particular function becomes today one of secondary importance. That which is worthy of particular consideration today is the aspect of comparative law which has for its object a continuous *rapprochement* among the various legal systems being compared and which seeks to discover in their apparent diversity a common substratum of institutions and concepts so that there finally may be discovered a sufficient body of principles universal enough that their development may point to a day of ultimate unification of law. . . . To achieve this goal we should give attention to the gradual elimination of existing differences among legal systems in force among peoples of equal culture, particularly where the economic conditions producing the legal problems are similar. We should likewise make an effort to reduce the number of divergent legal systems where such divergence no longer has a reason for existence in the political, moral or social character of the nations in question. Thus we should move on to an ultimate unification of law in the form of a consciously desired common law of all mankind.[36]

In short, the emphasis on comparative law as a unifying science seemed an inevitable consequence of the times humanity was living through and of the suspicion with which, in the aftermath of the world conflict, one was inclined to view comparisons aimed at highlighting differences. All of this was accompanied by a rebirth of natural law, exalted in its essence as a barrier against the drifts of legal positivism, that is, as a 'supra-legal law' to be invoked to strike at 'legal injustice'.[37]

It was in this climate that the International Association of Legal Studies (IALS) was founded under the auspices of the United Nations Educational, Scientific and Cultural Organisation (UNESCO). According to the intentions of its promoters, its task was to spread the study of comparative law, to which they attributed objectives very similar to those later evoked to stress the social prophylactic functions of that subject. As René David, a father of French comparative law, observed:

> One of UNESCO's tasks, according to the statute that has just been agreed, is to promote studies in comparative law and international law. This is an essential task of UNESCO: peoples will not truly understand each other if they do not learn to know each other; knowledge of the institutions they have given themselves and the conceptions they have of law and justice, the way these conceptions are realised, are necessary to this knowledge that will generate understanding. Politicians in the various countries are frequently recruited from among jurists: they will be better prepared to deal with the difficulties that arise in international relations if they have learned, in their professional training, through the study of international law and comparative law, to be familiar with the diversity of legal principles and viewpoints accepted in the various countries.[38]

On closer inspection, the era we are talking about was not, however, immune from the revival of evolutionist visions of law, which even conditioned the list of sources of international law included in the Statute of the International Court of Justice, which in fact includes the

36 M. Sarfatti, *Comparative Law and the Unification of Law*, in *Tulane Law Review*, 26, 1952, p. 317.
37 G. Radbruch, *Gesetzliches Unrecht und übergesetzliches Recht*, in *Süddeutsche Juristen-Zeitung*, 1946, p. 105 ff.
38 R. David, *Observations sur le rôle possible de l'Unesco en matière de droit comparé*, Paris, January 21st, 1947, Unesco/Cons.Jur./1/1947. Also A. Tunc, *La contribution possible des études juridiques comparatives è une meilleure compréhension entre nations*, in *Revue internationale de droit comparé*, 1964, p. 47 ff.

'general principles of law recognized by civilized nations' (art. 38). The formula had been borrowed from the Statute of the Permanent Court of International Justice that had arisen within the League of Nations (art. 38). The evolutionist inspiration of those rules was also evident from the specification that in its composition the court must be a 'representation of the main forms of civilization and of the principal legal systems of the world' (art. 9). Having said that, the climate seemed to have changed, at least in part: the international unification of law, a theme that was particularly emphasised at the Paris Congress of 1900, was not mentioned as one of the main aims of comparative law. Rather, the mutual understanding between peoples in different national systems took precedence over the prospects of convergence of those systems.

Furthermore, the concept of 'civilised nations' was not charged with particular meanings. It was used to stigmatise the crimes of which the fascist regimes were guilty and not to revive patterns inherited from the past. It was now admitted that there are several 'civilisations', all of which shared 'a common horror at certain acts of barbaric behaviour, for example, the destruction of big cities, the killing of women and children, the poisoning of defenceless soldiers, the expelling of whole populations from their homeland, the using of force or compulsory labour as a means of political coercion or as a punishment for holding or expressing political view'.[39] By the way, international law was born and developed from an ambiguous relationship between its universal character and the underlining of the distinction between civilised and non-civilised communities, which was used as a justification for European colonialism and imperialism.[40]

Having said this, the end of the Second World War coincided with the development of an international framework that was decidedly more complex than that of the immediately preceding historical period. Among the Western countries, the United States had emerged as the hegemonic power capable of undermining the primacy of Europe. Above all, alongside the Western countries, other entities destined to complicate the international arena were emerging, namely, the socialist countries and the so-called Third World countries.[41]

Although now more difficult to achieve, the international unification of law continued to represent a founding purpose of comparative law as a science, which was constantly reaffirmed over time: so much so that for many it remains the main purpose of the subject.[42] And even when such a purpose is not made explicit, comparison is for the most part practised in a unifying key, namely, to highlight the commonalities between the objects being compared. We shall see that it is only recently that a marked attention to the protection of identities has emerged (II.1.7–10).

4 THE CLIENTS OF COMPARATIVE LAW

Before focusing on comparison that divides, it is useful to identify the expectations of those who can be considered as 'clients' of comparative law[43]: national legislators and legal professionals. When doing so, however, we will not follow the usual distinction between the study of

39 E. Sauer, *Universal Principles in International Law*, in *Transactions of the Grotius Society*, 42, 1956, p. 188.
40 M. Koskenniemi, *The Gentle Civilizer of Nations: The Rise and Fall of International Law 1870–1960*, New York NY, 2012, p. 127 ff.
41 M.J. Bonell, *Comparazione giuridica e unificazione del diritto*, in G. Alpa et al., *Diritto privato comparato. Istituti e problemi*, 4th ed., Roma and Bari, 2012, p. 4 ff.
42 In particular, K. Zweigert and H. Kötz, *An Introduction to Comparative Law* (1996), 3rd ed., Oxford, 1998, p. 28 f.
43 J. Basedow, *Comparative Law and Its Clients*, in *American Journal of Comparative Law*, 62, 2014, p. 821 ff.

foreign law and comparative law.[44] Describing foreign law in fact presupposes the translation of concepts that lack that correspondence which is typical of the hard sciences; in other words, it requires their homologation, and this evidently implies a comparative exercise, as best illustrated by the scholars of legal translation.[45]

But let us return to the clients of comparative law, and also of foreign law, whose approach can be regarded as the same from at least two points of view. First of all, they do not demand the unification of law, or in any case comparisons aimed at producing a law designed for the whole of mankind or to replace national laws with shared foundations. Also, the clients of comparative law are not interested in what we have summarised in terms of its subversive character (I.1.1): not because they expect a faithful reproduction of legal positivist dogmas, but because their attention is focused on formal legal sources and their application.[46]

In other words, the clients of legal comparison do not intend to develop an external point of view on law, and more fundamentally have no interest in the connections between law and other social phenomena like politics or the economy. This is not surprising, since national legislators and legal professionals are called upon to solve concrete problems and not to speculate on the way to reach this objective. Indeed, this is the specific interest of comparative law scholars, and the main point of reference for defining the epistemological status of comparative law.

If this is the case, the comparative law to which its clients turn is not very different from that practised before it was recognised as an autonomous science. At that point, comparative law scholarship simply compared the formal sources of law without any critical bite. Today, as at that time, comparative law scholars are called upon to perform a servant's role.[47] They must, in particular, provide information on foreign law, e.g. those of interest to the courts under private international law.[48] Not to mention laws that are useful for economic operators who, through their legal advisers, wish to know the rules governing the operation of foreign or international markets.

It was precisely to meet these practical needs that the first national associations of comparative law were formed. The oldest, the French *Société de législation comparée* (Society of Comparative Legislation), was founded in 1869 and its name is surely telling. While its founders intended to promote a critical and cultural study of law, in line with Montesquieu's theory of law (II.1.1),[49] the association's main activity consisted in providing translations of foreign legislative texts, as well as periodical publications to inform the public about new foreign legislation.[50]

If the French example was not faithfully followed in Germany, it was only because of the spread of scientific positivism. Even so, German lawyers were not immune to the mindless reproduction of legislative texts. While the *Internationale Vereinigung für vergleichende Rechtswissenschaft und Volkswirtschaftslehre* (International Association for Comparative Legal Science and Political Economy), founded in Berlin in 1894, was meant to adopt a critical approach, it produced a large amount of information on the formal sources of law.

44 For instance, K. Zweigert and H. Kötz, *An Introduction to Comparative Law* (1996), cit., p. 6.

45 In particular, V. Jacometti and B. Pozzo, *Traduttologia e linguaggio giuridico*, Padova, 2018.

46 *Ivi*, p. 839 ff.

47 É. Lambert, *La fonction du droit comparé*, vol. 1, Paris, 1903, p. 8 ff.

48 For instance, Art 14 Statute 218 of 1995 in Italy provides that, to ascertain foreign law, the judge may interrogate experts of specialised institutions.

49 É. Laboulaye, *Études sur l'esprit des lois de Montesquieu*, in *Revue de droit international et de législation comparé*, 1869, p. 161 ff.

50 See P. Allorant and W. Badier, *La Société de législation comparée: boîte à idées du parlementarisme libéral de l'empire libéral à la République opportuniste*, in *Clio@Themis*, 13, 2017, p. 1 ff.

Similar was the fate of the *Gesellschaft für vergleichende Rechts- und Staatswissenschaft* (Society for Comparative Science of Law and State), an association founded in Germany during the same period.[51]

In the common law world, the problems of understanding legislative language was not a concern, and comparative law scholars were instead enlisted for more practical matters. Hence, in 1895, the London-based Society of Comparative Legislation was established, which focused its attention on the United States and the British Empire, whose imperial possessions extended to countries such as Canada, India, and Australia. Studies on the laws of colonised populations and dominions, useful to political and economic powers in their expansionist plans, were particularly in demand. Moreover, the very reference in the association's name to legislation, rather than law and jurisprudence, points to alignment with the demands of the clients of comparative law.[52] While this was happening, in England the study of common concepts of positive law had become established under the name of comparative jurisprudence. This discipline promoted comparisons between 'mature' national laws in order to identify 'a system of universal principles of positive law'.[53]

As we have anticipated, the practical aims of the comparative approach taken by the first scientific societies were not only appreciated by legal professionals. Even the legislators of the time made use of comparative research when drafting the most important statutes. So much so as to conclude that 'comparative law was invented in Europe in order to be integrated into legislative activity'.[54] To realise this, one need only consult the preparatory works of the German Civil Code of 1896, which abound, article by article, with references to the Austrian Civil Code of 1811, the French Civil Code of 1804, the Italian Civil Code of 1865, the Dutch Civil Code of 1838, and the Swiss Code of Obligations of 1881.[55] This tendency is widespread in that period, a point noted at the Paris Congress of 1900, where it was emphasised that 'the preparatory work on the codes at the end of the century gave ample space to investigations into foreign legislation'.[56]

On closer inspection, the link between legislation and comparison is longstanding, although the assessment of this association is more mixed. In some cases, it bore witness to a certain openness on the part of national legislators, namely, their desire to show that state sovereignty was 'neither closed nor absolute'.[57] In other cases, the link between legislation and comparison appears more superficial, or at least ill-conceived, e.g. because of comparison being reduced to confront national law and Roman law.

Over time, the use of comparison by national legislators has grown and become more sophisticated, at least because it fulfils what is achieved in hard sciences by experimentation (III.1.1): social sciences are not sciences operating 'by trial and error'.[58] National legislators must therefore aspire to produce good quality rules because their subsequent improvement is a slow, complex, and costly process. That is why comparison has become a substitute for experiments, and its use a unifying tool.

51 In particular E. Wadle, *Einhundert Jahre Rechtsvergleichende Gesellschaften in Deutschland*, Baden-Baden, 1994, p. 23 ff.
52 G.F. Ferrari, *Il diritto comparato nella giuspubblicistica britannica dall'inizio dell'Ottocento alla prima guerra mondiale*, in *Diritto pubblico comparato ed europeo*, 2017, p. 37 ff.
53 F. Pollock, *The History of Comparative Jurisprudence*, in *Journal of the Society of Comparative Legislation*, 5, 1903, p. 74.
54 H.P. Glenn, *Vers un droit comparé intégré?*, in *Revue internationale de droit comparé*, 1999, p. 843.
55 *Motive zu dem Entwurfe eines Bürgerlichen Gesetzbuches für das Deutsche Reich*, 5 vol., Berlin and Leipzig, 1888.
56 É. Lambert, in Société de législation comparée, *Congrès international de droit comparé*, cit., p. 45.
57 J.D. Cesano, *Consideraciones sobre algunas de las funciones del derecho comparado*, in *Cuaderno de derecho comparado*, 2018, p. 15.
58 I. Tambaro, Art. *Legislazione*, cit., p. 425.

Having said this, we must not lose sight of the fact that the use of comparison does not alter the ultimate function of legislation, which is to formalise a compromise between several options for regulating a given matter. It is therefore misleading to state that the best solution to a given problem can be identified through comparison: 'better regulation' transforms the law into 'a consumer good, a product that is offered in the market of rules and chosen by those who will see that rule applied'. Moreover, the concept of better regulation conceals its submitting to 'economic logic',[59] and more precisely denotes a neoliberal way of interpreting the economic order (II.2.9).

The use of comparative law by the national legislator may result from an autonomous decision, or be prompted by legal science. It represents an effective expedient to promote law reform, which demonstrates the political value of comparisons. Indeed, there is a tradition of using comparative law for instrumental purposes in several disciplines such as civil and criminal procedure, criminal law, and labour law[60] (IV.1.3).

The use of comparative research is becoming an established practice. Sometimes, such a practice appears to be undemocratic. One only has to think of legislative outsourcing, the practice whereby private entities and in particular large law firms are entrusted with the task of drafting legislation.[61]

The sovereign debt crisis is an emblematic example. At that time, Freshfields, an international law firm, drafted legislative provisions to stabilise the German banking system. This only became public knowledge because the then German Minister for the Economy wanted to prepare an alternative project by having it drawn up by another international law firm, namely, Linklaters. The alternative proposal was written on the firm's letterhead, which is why its background was revealed, sparking a lively debate also in the media.[62]

Even if one disregards such cases, the recourse to comparison by national legislators is a practice the real impact of which must be carefully assessed. Indeed, this recourse may be the expression of a communicative strategy intended for public discourse, that does not reveal the real reasoning behind the choices made by the legislator. This, at least, can be deduced from two salient examples, namely: the codification of criminal procedural law in Italy, and the codification of civil law in China. They are emblematic because of their different contexts and, above all, of the breadth of the intervention.

The first example relates to the drafting of the Code of Criminal Procedure 1988, currently in force, which replaced inquisitorial with adversarial trials. The inquisitorial model had been a central feature of the Italian criminal process of the previous Code of Civil Procedure of 1930 and therefore was tainted by association with the fascist period. The adversarial model is typical of common law countries and can possibly be traced back to the Magna Carta. It is based on the distinction between the roles of the prosecutor and the judge and on the formation of evidence in the trial through the confrontation between prosecution and defence. In the inquisitorial model, derived from the canon law trial, the roles of the prosecutor and the judge overlap, and evidence is introduced into the trial by the prosecution. However, whether the Code of Criminal Procedure has actually achieved the transition from one model to the other remains disputable. In fact, it is not entirely accurate to say that the trial was previously informed by the inquisitorial model, and in the same way it cannot be said

59 T.E. Frosini, *Legislazione e comparazione*, in *Diritto pubblico comparato ed europeo*, 2015, p. 73 ff.

60 See A. Somma and V. Zeno-Zencovich (Eds.), *Comparazione e diritto positivo. Un dialogo tra saperi giuridici*, Roma, 2020.

61 S. Haberl, *I legislatori occulti. Outsourcing legislativo ed espertocrazia nell'ordinamento tedesco*, in *Politica del diritto*, 2018, p. 431 ff.

62 J. Krüper, *Lawfirm – legibus solutus? Legitimität und Rationalität des inneren Gesetzgebungsverfahrens und das Outsourcing von Gesetzentwürfen*, in *Juristen-Zeitung*, 2010, p. 655 ff.

that the current trial fully complies with the requirements of the adversarial model.[63] Thus, the use of comparative law by the national legislator, even when it is called upon to carry out reforms that are intended to bring about convergence with foreign law, may well conceal a purely rhetorical function. In other words, it is intended to introduce into the public discourse concepts that do not correspond to what is actually practised by the legislator.

The same is true, albeit for different reasons, of the codification of civil law in China, for which the legislative body of the Chinese National People's Congress set up a commission in the late 1990s to study the feasibility and issue guidelines on its possible content. The commission first focused on some preliminary questions, analysing the main Western codification models and assessing their compatibility with the Chinese legal experience. To this end, a questionnaire was prepared and distributed to a number of European academics, consisting of a first part with general questions on codification and a second part with questions on more specific aspects. Among other things, the questionnaire asked whether the various sources of obligations should be regulated in a uniform way, where rules on the rights of the person should be included, and whether procedural rules should be incorporated in the code.[64] The text was completed in 2020 accompanied by declarations stating that the legislator intended to base the codification on Roman law.[65] Nevertheless, we should be cautious in our assessments since the value attached to the codification of civil law in a Western system is certainly not the same as in other contexts, especially when it is not the result of an endogenous development, but rather a requirement for membership of the World Trade Organization.[66]

5 COMPARATIVE LAW AND SCHOLARLY UNIFICATION OF LAW

Although national legislators are among the main clients of comparative law, it cannot be said that they use it to promote the unification of law, which is instead the constitutive purpose of the discipline (II.1.2). National legislators undoubtedly resort to comparative law in order to extol the similarities between their own law and the law they claim to be inspired by. Nevertheless, unification is essentially irrelevant to their agenda, at least where it is not the expression of hegemonic projects.

More precisely, it was only in the era in which legal positivist schemes prevailed, that national legislators could be considered the protagonists in the international unification of law. Things have changed since then, not least because of the emergence of supranational bodies such as the European Union, to which nation states have ceded some of their sovereignty and, with it, prerogatives to unify their laws.[67]

What has not changed is the interest and support of scholars for the international unification of law, which has always been considered a natural fact, and which aligns with a widespread feeling even among non-lawyers. This sentiment is illustrated by the irony of Voltaire who marvelled at the fact that travellers in his time changed laws as often as they changed

63 R. Orlandi, *The Italian Path to Reform: Italy's Adversarial Model of Criminal Procedure*, in *Italian Law Journal*, 5, 2019, p. 565 ff.

64 A. Somma, *La codificazione civile nel terzo millennio: riflessioni storico e politico normative*, in *Materiali per una storia della cultura giuridica*, 2004, p. 329 ff.

65 A. Saccoccio and S. Porcelli (Eds.), *Codice civile cinese e sistema giuridico romanistico*, Modena, 2021.

66 L. Siyi, *Looking Back and Thinking Forward: The Current Round of Civil Law Codification in China*, in *The International Lawyer*, 52, 2019, p. 450.

67 M.J. Bonell, *Comparazione giuridica e unificazione del diritto*, cit., p. 10 ff.

horses, or by the famous exclamation of the scientist Blaise Pascal in the mid-17th century: 'a strange justice that is bounded by a river!'[68]

The ways in which this sentiment is expressed may change, but the sentiment itself is a fixed point. Some view the unification of law as the inevitable consequence of the increasing standardisation of social relations wrought by processes of globalisation (II.1.9). Others focus instead on what is considered an innate vocation of the sciences in general: the vocation to universality, which in the case of legal science takes on the characteristics of rediscovering an ancient common root.[69]

A well-known expression of the unificatory zeal is an initiative launched in the 1960s that has become something of an icon for comparative studies: the Cornell Seminars on Contract Formation, which sought to reconstruct the common core of contract under the direction of Rudolf Schlesinger.[70] The initiative was born out of an observation reflected in the provision of the Statute of the International Court of Justice mentioning the general principles recognised by civilised nations among the sources of international law (II.1.3): the observation that 'legal scholars and practitioners throughout the world have become increasingly convinced that the legal systems of most nations, or perhaps of all, have certain elements in common'. All this notwithstanding diversity in 'cultural traditions'. As Schlesinger remarked:

> Somewhat similar terms, such as 'common core', 'common denominators', and 'the common law of mankind', have become current in scholarly discussions. These various forms of words may not be synonymous, but all of them express a basic underlying assumption that the differences between legal systems, described in countless comparative studies and daily observed in practice, relate largely to details; that behind and beyond these details there are shared and connecting elements; that these elements can be identified; and that it should be possible, without resorting to mere generalities, to formulate these elements in normative terms.[71]

We will return to the Cornell Seminars to focus on the methodology they used: the so-called factual approach (IV.2.3). For now, it's enough to note that these seminars were the result of a technocratic approach, aimed to observe the phenomenon of law without reference to its context, and to identifying the reasons for the convergence of national laws.[72] However, that approach cannot and should not be presented as neutral, if only from the point of view of the way rules are produced: it expresses an approach similar to that of scientific positivism since it aims to accredit legal science as the source of the production of rules.

Something similar can be said of the efforts that positive law scholars devote to the construction of European private law and, unsurprisingly, accompanied with a deep dissatisfaction for the way in which it is conceived and imposed from above.[73] Their criticism relates to the fact that European private law consists of sectoral regulatory acts, which they consider too fragmentary and chaotic to be reduced to the categories to which they are accustomed as scholars of a national legal system. Hence, the production of a considerable number of scholarly contributions that limit themselves to commenting on European directives and regulations, and often paraphrasing them, in accordance with the classic canons of legislative positivism. Or, alternatively, the attempts to reconstruct improbable systematics capable of

68 See A.F. Schnitzer, *Vergleichende Rechtslehre*, Basel, 1945, p. 49 ff.
69 A. Tripiccione, *La comparazione giuridica*, Padova, 1961, p. 90 and V. Varano and V. Barsotti, *La tradizione giuridica occidentale*, 7th ed., Torino, 2021, p. 12 ff.
70 R.B. Schlesinger (Ed.), *Formation of Contracts: A Study of the Common Core of Legal Systems*, New York NY, 1968.
71 R.B. Schlesinger, *The Common Core of Legal Systems*, in K.H. Nadelmann, A.T. von Mehren and J.H. Nazard (Eds.), *XXth Century Comparative and Conflicts of Law. Legal Essays in Honor of Hessel E. Yntema*, Leiden, 1961, p. 65 f.
72 G. Frankenberg, *Comparative Law as Critique*, Cheltenham and Northampton MA, 2016, p. 59 ff.
73 See the contributions in L. Moccia (Eds.), *I giuristi e l'Europa*, Roma and Bari, 1997.

giving coherence to the words of the European legislator, whose shortcomings and dangerous deviations from an undefined tradition are then denounced (I.1.5).

This is also why, decades ago, initiatives were launched to build a European private law from below. However, those initiatives did not have in mind innovative ways of building a democratic consensus around choices concerning the regulation of social coexistence. On the contrary, the intention was to concentrate the power to indicate the forms and content of unification in the hands of legal scholars and meanwhile to create a European legal science.[74]

Of course, scholars had to rely on pre-existing materials, in particular the civil codes and their re-reading in the light of case law, to construct a supranational connective tissue capable of holding national laws and national case law. After all, this is what scholarship has always done when it has claimed or defended its power to produce law: it has concealed it by qualifying its work as aimed at providing a system, and not at creating rules. In so doing, it has rediscovered its ancient vocation to be the driving force behind the identification and development of what constitutes the core of common European law, in the wake of a tradition that began in the Middle Ages and was abruptly and foolishly interrupted by the codifications produced since the modern age.[75]

On closer inspection, however, those codifications had only partly cracked the unity of legal science. They all appeared and still appear to be related to the French and German civil codes, and French and German were the dogmatic categories used by the various national scholarships to interpret the words of their legislators and judges. Subsequently, a contribution to the dialogue between European legal scholars came from the system of fundamental rights drawn up by post–World War II constitutionalism (I.2.1), variously used to re-read the codifications in the light of a changed social reality. It is by this route that the formal unity of the 'subject of law' built up by the modern state, which had suppressed status differences but produced class differences, was broken (I.2.2).

On the basis of these forms of spontaneous convergence of national private laws in the 1980s a group of European scholars coordinated by the Danish professor Ole Lando initiated the drafting of the Principles of European Contract Law (PECL). This projected involved contributions from lawyers from the 12 member states of the then European Economic Community. It did so while taking care to maintain a critical distance with respect to the European and national institutions of origin in order to preserve scholarly autonomy and independence in the production of a work with a strong political and economic impact.[76]

The Principles of European Contract Law were finalised at the beginning of the new millennium and presented as immediately available instruments for cross-border trade to which private parties could refer as a modern *lex mercatoria*. As a distillation of common solutions, they then offered themselves as a model for the case law and legislative development of national contract law, and of course as a basis for future initiatives at the European level.[77]

The latter use was emphasised on the occasion of the European Union's 6th Framework Programme for Research and Technological Development (2002–2006), when the Commission promoted and financed the establishment of an international network of European private law scholars and entrusted it with the task of providing a 'Draft common frame of reference' for European contract law. The intention was to bring together the best solutions adopted at national level and the *acquis communautaire*, thus immediately providing useful principles,

74 A. Somma, *Introduzione critica al diritto europeo dei contratti*, Milano, 2007, p. 17 ff.

75 As stigmatised by Neopandectists: for instance, R. Zimmermann, *Roman Law and European Legal Unity*, in A. Hartkamp et al. (Eds.), *Towards a European Civil Code*, Nijmegen, 1994, p. 65 ff.

76 O. Lando, *European Contract Law*, in *American Journal of Comparative Law*, 31, 1983, p. 655.

77 The Commission on European Contract Law, *Principles of European Contract Law*, Parts I and II, The Hague, 2000; Part III, The Hague etc., 2003.

definitions, and rules to improve the coherence and quality of European law, as well as forming the basis for a possible future 'optional instrument'. That was intended to be an unspecified 'modern body of rules particularly adapted to cross-border contracts in the internal market'.[78]

The network of scholars recruited by the European Commission did not have the same independence that characterised the Lando Commission. In fact, the drafting of the Common Frame of Reference was done in accordance with the maxim that 'the principle of freedom of contract needs to be emphasised as crucial', so much so that 'should rules be mandatory, this should be clarified and justified'. In addition, a committee of economic stakeholders was set up (Cfr-net), mainly consisting of companies' representatives and legal professionals whose views were virtually binding for the network of scholars. The latter were required to attend seminars on topics identified by the stakeholders, where the line to be followed was determined. As the First Annual Progress Report clarified:

> Before workshops, the research drafts are posted on the dedicated website. Those CFR-net members who have registered an interest in the specific topic are invited to examine the drafts and comment. After workshops, CFR-net experts are invited to summarise their contribution to the discussion in writing. The Commission prepares a report which reflects the comments raised by CFR-net members in the workshop, their written contributions and the reactions of researchers. The reports specifically identify policy issues, in particular those relevant to the consumer contract law acquis, as well as horizontal questions. The researchers have 6 months to react to the CFR-net comments summarized in the Commission report, by taking them on board in their revised drafts, or, in case of disagreement, by explaining the reasons.[79]

The Common Frame of Reference was completed in the late 2010s and covered a much broader scope than originally envisaged: it comprises 'definitions, principles and model rules of European private law'.[80] In the meantime, it has been used as the basis for a further project commissioned by the European Commission, which aimed at increasing its practical usability. The project, called Feasibility Study, however, had no particular use: it merely inspired the drafting of a Proposal for a Regulation on a 'Common European Sales Law',[81] which was later withdrawn.

This illustrates in an exemplary manner, and contrary to the claims of Neopandectists, the role actually played by academics in the construction of European private law as an 'open building site'.[82] Even if they fostered the development of a European legal science, they did not manage to restore it to the splendours of the era of historical *ius commune*, when it could indeed be considered a source of law. On the contrary, comparative law scholarship has been degraded to a mere translator in technical terms of agendas which are developed in other contexts, in particular by economic stakeholders, which use that scholarship to become themselves the sources of European private law. This is what is left of the success of the jurist (I.1.5).

The fate of the Principles of International Commercial Contracts[83] is different, but only in part. Those principles were elaborated within the framework of UNIDROIT by scholars

78 Communication from the Commission to the European Parliament and the Council – A more coherent European contract law – An action plan, 12 February 2003, 2003/68 fin., para. 90.

79 First Annual Progress Report on European Contract Law and the Acquis Review, COM (2005) 456 fin., p. 3.

80 See Ch. von Bar et al. (Eds.), *Principles, Definitions and Model Rules of European Private Law. Draft Common Frame of Reference*, Munich, 2009.

81 Proposal of 11 October 2011, Com/2011/635 fin.

82 G. Alpa, *Lineamenti di diritto contrattuale*, in G. Alpa et al., *Diritto privato comparato. Istituti e problemi*, cit., p. 341.

83 The latest edition of *Unidroit principles of international commercial contracts* is from 2016 (the first one is from 1992): see M.J. Bonell, *The Law Governing International Commercial Contracts and the Actual Role of the Unidroit Principles*, in *Uniform Law Review*, 23, 2018, p. 15 ff.

whose status appears to be similar to that of those who drafted the Common Frame of Reference. They were selected by an international organisation and their work was therefore ultimately scrutinised by the states of which the organisation is composed. In other words, the Principles were packaged at the instigation of those who, at least formally, did not represent specific interests but, rather, aimed to mediate between opposing interests: this is why they included provisions the purpose of which is to impose 'ethical conduct between the parties' and a 'duty to cooperate'. Perhaps this is the reason that their use is relatively limited, and for the most part not attributable to an initiative of the contracting parties: it depends on an initiative taken during arbitration proceedings or on the occasion of a dispute decided by the courts, where they have 'a supplementary function' only. This, however, does not detract from the fact that the Principles have been used as a source of inspiration for the drafting of national rules,[84] and that in so doing they have ensured a certain influence for legal science as the driving force behind the unification of law. The unifying value of comparative law is therefore confirmed.

6 THE JUDICIAL USE OF COMPARATIVE LAW

A different way of constructing European private law, which has long been discussed among comparative law scholars, is to rely on the creativity of national judges rather than on the contribution of legal scholarship. Judges are called upon to embark on pan-European hermeneutic paths, where the supreme courts of the member states attribute mutual persuasive authority to foreign precedents,[85] thereby fostering the emergence of common approaches. This is buttressed nowadays by numerous formalised or informal networks through which dialogue is stimulated between national courts in Europe and elsewhere, including constitutional courts, and between these and supranational or international courts.[86]

It should be noted that this requires the judicial use of foreign law, and therefore of comparative law, outside the cases in which this is imposed by private international law.[87] In other words, it is a complementary and optional use, a rhetorical expedient to be resorted to in the context of arguments aimed at promoting the approximation of national laws. It is not, therefore, the use to which we referred when discussing legal professions as clients of comparative law (II.1.4).

This proposal, like that of proceeding by scholarship, is also supported by references to the historical *ius commune* tradition, when courts resorted to foreign law to resolve disputes submitted to them.[88] In common law jurisdictions, this practice is still widespread, as it is the corollary of a legal culture centred on the temporal, rather than spatial, dimension. In civil law countries, on the contrary, the courts' references to foreign law have been prevented by the process of centralisation of the production of law that culminated in codification (I.2.4). In any case, there has been no shortage of initiatives to rebuild a dialogue between national courts – initiatives that are the more insistent the more the crisis of the myths embodied in

84 R. Peleggi, *Diritti nazionali e comparazione attraverso le lenti del diritto uniforme dei contratti*, in M. Graziadei and A. Somma (Eds.), *Esperienze giuridiche in dialogo. il ruolo della comparazione*, Roma, 2024, p. 47 ff.

85 Already L. Ruffini Gandolfi, *Per l'uniforme interpretazione ed applicazione di un futuro codice europeo dei contratti*, in *Rivista di diritto civile*, 2000, p. 727.

86 D.S. Law and M. Tushnet, *The Politics of Judicial Dialogue*, in M. Tushnet and D. Kochenov (Eds.), *Research Handbook on the Politics of Constitutional Law*, London, 2023, p. 286 ff.

87 P. Ridola, *La giurisprudenza costituzionale e la comparazione*, in G. Alpa (Ed.), *Il giudice e l'uso delle sentenze straniere. Modalità e tecniche della comparazione giuridica*, Milano, 2005, p. 17.

88 See G. Gorla, *Il ricorso alla legge di un luogo vicino nell'ambito del diritto comune europeo*, in *Foro italiano*, 1977, V, c. 91 ff.

codification is felt – and thus to proceed with an integration of the law, perhaps by way of references to legal interpretation.

In the Italian legal experience, for example, the law requires that in those cases in which a dispute cannot be decided through application of a specific rule, the judge shall refer to those concerning similar cases or analogous matters, and then to the general principles of the state legal order (art. 12 preliminary provisions to the Civil Code). In the intention of the legislator, this last reference was intended to prohibit judges from resorting to foreign law and thus undermining the identity of the national law. However, such a prohibition was relativised from the outset: it would not have covered references to the national scientific tradition, and through it to Roman law and the *ius commune*. It was then suggested that the reference to foreign law was permissible if required by the historical interpretation of a provision borrowed from a foreign legal system. Since the Italian Civil Code had a French fabric written in a language borrowed from German scholarship, this opened up quite a few prospects for the judicial use of foreign law. Subsequently, it was proposed to legitimise this use through references to analogy, which, unlike general principles, does not mention the requirement of statehood.[89]

In Swiss law, the same outcome could well be based on what is laid down, in much more explicit terms, in the Civil Code (*Zivilgesetzbuch*). In that Code, in the event of a gap that cannot otherwise be filled, the judge is allowed to formulate the rule 'that he would adopt as legislator' (art. 1) (I.1.3). And since legislators are now accustomed to looking at solutions devised abroad, courts are also entitled, if not obliged, to do so.

We may at this point also recall the reference in the Austrian Civil Code (*Allgemeines bürgerliches Gesetzbuch*) to the principles of natural law as a source of last resort to fill any gaps (para. 7) (I.1.3). Some consider that through this reference the UNIDROIT Principles of International Commercial Contracts and the Principles of European Contract Law elaborated by the Lando Commission may be considered sources of law (II.1.4).[90]

These and other possible grounds for the optional judicial use of comparison do not only concern cases where it explicitly promotes forms of international unification of law.[91] There are also cases in which that use simply contributes to legitimising the adoption of innovative solutions, perhaps in contrast to what is deemed to be the letter of the law or a prevailing scholarly interpretation.[92] Even in these cases one ends up using comparative law to unify laws, at least in the context of legal orders belonging to the same cultural tradition, which is thus incentivised to change along shared lines. It is however self-evident that the persuasive force of the reference to a foreign law is all the more impactful the more this expresses the same basic values of the receiving legal order. This emerges particularly from the decisions of the constitutional courts of Western countries, which are increasingly committed to the recognition of new rights, and increasingly careful to support their decisions through legal arguments centred on the comparison with systems belonging to the same cultural traditions.[93]

A well-known Italian decision exemplifies how references to foreign models can be used to develop national law in a way that appears to contradict the letter of the relevant statute. This is the decision of the Constitutional Court that undermined the principle of the absolute inexcusability of ignorance of the criminal law (art. 5 of the Penal Code), denying in particular

89 P.G. Monateri and A. Somma, *Alien in Rome. L'uso del diritto comparato come interpretazione analogica ex art. 12 preleggi*, in *Foro italiano*, 1999, V, c. 47 ff.

90 For instance, W. Posch, *Judikative Rechtsangleichung: ein Weg zur Europäisierung des Privatrechts?*, in *Zeitschrift für Europäisches Privatrecht*, 1998, p. 521 ff.

91 A. Gambaro et al., *L'uso giurisprudenziale della comparazione giuridica*, Milano, 2004 and B. Markesinis and J. Fedtke, *Judicial Recourse to Foreign Law: A New Source of Inspiration?*, London and New York NY, 2006.

92 More recently E. Adamo, *Diritto civile e argomentazione comparativa*, Napoli, 2018.

93 L. Pegoraro and A. Rinella, *Introduzione al diritto pubblico comparato*, Padova, 2002, p. 267 ff.

that this principle finds application in cases of unavoidable error of law. The Constitutional Court relaxed the letter of the statute when there is an 'objective impossibility of knowledge of the precept' and the law is not within the 'specific knowledge of the individual'. This orientation is based on arguments accompanied by historical information and reference to numerous European and non-European criminal codes. As the Constitutional Court declared:

> From the point of view of history and comparative law, it must be emphasised that the principle of the irrelevance of ignorance of the law has never been positively affirmed in its absoluteness. On the contrary, it can be said that the history of the principle coincides with the history of its exceptions: from Roman-Classical law, under which it was permissible for women and minors under the age of twenty-five to be ignorant of the law, through the glossators and canon law, to the current comparative law regulations (West-German, Austrian, Swiss, Greek, Polish, Yugoslav, Japanese criminal codes, etc.), there are so many exceptions to the absoluteness of the principle under discussion, that the Italian code can be said to have remained isolated in this matter, not even followed by the Portuguese penal code.

There is more. The Constitutional Court also points out that further measures, such as the provision of mitigation of punishment for cases of avoidable ignorance of the criminal law, could be devised by the legislature, as supported by a solution found in the German penal codification.[94]

As evidence of the judicial use of comparative law to support solutions opposed by the scholarship, we may recall a German decision on liability for non-pecuniary damage. The German Civil Code establishes that such damage can be compensated only in cases established by law (par. 253), which does not explicitly mention the case of damage to the general right of personality (*allgemeines Persönlichkeitsrecht*). This latter, indeed, is a doctrine constructed by case law in the mid-'50s by resorting to the constitutional provisions declaring human dignity inviolable (art. 1) and establishing the right to the free development of personality (art. 2).[95]

Scholarship agreed with that legislative choice, noting that it was intended to protect the freedom of the press, which would be undermined by overly extensive forms of personal protection. The German Federal Supreme Court recognised the need to balance the two positions and in particular to give priority to the latter only in cases of significant harm. Thus, the fundamental rights system remains in balance, whereas it would not be so if the possibility to compensate non-pecuniary damages for infringement of the general right of personality were excluded in absolute terms. According to the Court, the conclusion that this is a balanced solution is confirmed by Swiss law, whose Code of Obligations (*Obligationenrecht*) contains the following provision: 'any person whose personality rights are unlawfully infringed is entitled to a sum of money by way of satisfaction provided this is justified by the seriousness of the infringement and no other amends have been made' (art. 49). Indeed, this solution has not resulted in 'an inadmissible attack on the constitutionally protected freedom of the press, or even an inadmissible threat to this freedom'.[96]

It is certainly true that there are not many cases in which national courts explicitly make references to foreign law when they are not required to do so. And yet there are far more cases in which such a reference remains under the radar, i.e. where it operates implicitly.[97] This is generally true, but all the more so in civil law systems, in which the openness of the courts to

94 Constitutional court, 24 March 1988, n. 364.
95 BGH, 25 May 1954, I ZR 211/53.
96 BGH, 5 March 1963, VI ZR 259/60.
97 G. Alpa, *Comparazione e diritto straniero nella giurisprudenza della Corte di Giustizia dell'Unione europea*, in *Contratto e impresa*, 2016, p. 879 ff.

comparative law is greater than what might emerge from a superficial reading of their decisions, and used as a point of reference for imitation.

7 POSTMODERN COMPARATIVE LAW

Comparative law, although used primarily to legitimise convergence of national laws, if not their international unification, may well achieve its opposite. That is, it can serve to help distinguish a national law from others and thus justify its continuing otherness. In these circumstances, one can speak of an identity-based comparative law. That is, when viewed from the perspective of its unificatory function, comparative law may serve to destroy or at least to prevent the unity of law.[98]

The choice of the relevant foreign law for comparison with domestic law is obviously central for whether it is used constructively or destructively. If the foreign law is embedded in a context similar to that of domestic law, namely, if it is the expression of similar political and economic as well as social and cultural values, then arguments suggesting the appropriateness of convergence will be particularly effective. If, on the contrary, the foreign law does not present these characteristics, namely, if it appears to be the law of a context with different values, it is clear that the comparison can only serve to support divergence.

A paradigmatic example of the latter case is a decision of the Court of Monza, in Italy, concerning so-called surrogacy or gestational surrogacy contracts. These refer to a situation where a woman uses her own egg (traditional surrogacy), or another woman's egg (gestational surrogacy), which is fertilised by the intending father's sperm. In jurisdictions where this form of assisted procreation is permitted by law, either altruistically or for payment, the pregnant woman does not acquire the legal status of parent, which is granted instead to those on whose behalf she carries the pregnancy to term, to whom the child must be surrendered immediately after birth.

The subject is notoriously controversial and the disputes particularly heated between those who favour freedom of choice and those who, invoking ethical and moral reasons but also the social implications of the practice, aim to ban it.[99] All of this has repercussions on the validity of the surrogacy or gestational agreement, which are particularly relevant in cases where the pregnant woman does not wish to perform it, i.e. hand over the child to the intended parents.

In Italy, gestation for others is now explicitly prohibited by the Statute on Medically Assisted Procreation (Law 40 of 19 February 2004), based on the conviction that surrogacy 'intolerably offends the dignity of women and deeply undermines human relations'.[100] The statute punishes with imprisonment from three months to two years and a fine of between six hundred thousand and one million euro 'anyone who, in any form, carries out, organises or publicises surrogacy' (art. 12).[101] The decision of the Court of Monza was rendered before the introduction of this prohibition at the request of a couple who had asked for the specific performance of a surrogacy agreement. The claim was supported by references to the US legal experience, in which the matter was and still is regulated by state laws, ranging from the prohibition of surrogacy to its recognition, possibly even for payment. In particular, reference

98 A. Somma, *L'uso giurisprudenziale della comparazione nel diritto interno e comunitario*, Milano, 2001, p. 170 ff.
99 In this regard, A. Di Martino, *Pensiero femminista e tecnologie riproduttive. Autodeterminazione, salute, dignità*, Milano, 2020.
100 Corte costituzionale, 22 November 2017, n. 272.
101 Law 169 of 4 November 2024 clarified that the conduct constitutes a universal crime: it is punishable even if the acts are committed abroad.

was made to a decision of the Superior Court of New Jersey, which in the late 1980s ordered the specific performance of a surrogacy agreement, and which has aroused some interest in the Italian scholarship.[102]

The New Jersey Court had affirmed the validity of the surrogacy agreement because it had found it to be functional to the right to procreation, as well as to realise the 'best interests of the child'. In the Court's view, this required a decision in favour of the intended parents: partly because the surrogate mother's mental health appeared to be unstable and partly because of the family situation, which included reference to their wealth.

This decision was overturned in some respects by the New Jersey Supreme Court, which invalidated the surrogacy agreement and thus reaffirmed the surrogate mother's parental authority. However, it referred the final decision to another court, reaffirming that such decision had to be made in accordance with the best interests of the child. That latter court then granted the intended parents' custody of the child and held that this solution fulfilled the child's best interests, confirming that such interest should also be considered in light of the material life conditions that the intending parents could provide.[103]

It is precisely these arguments that are discussed by the Court of Monza, which explicitly distances itself from the solution adopted by the Superior Court of New Jersey 'on which the plaintiffs' defence strongly insists'. This is because the Italian legal system does not recognise any 'fundamental, constitutionally guaranteed right of the biological father to procreation by any reproductive means', just as it does not take into consideration the child's 'interest in becoming part of the family that can ensure him the greatest well-being'. More precisely, as the court declared:

> The combined provisions of Articles 2 and 30 of the Constitution have been interpreted by the Constitutional Court . . . in the sense that they take as their primary value the promotion of the personality of the developing human being and his upbringing in the most suitable place for that purpose: to be found first of all in the family of origin and, only in the event of the latter's incapacity, in a substitute family. . . .
>
> On the other hand, given that Article 2 of the Constitution, in guaranteeing human rights in general, necessarily refers back to the subsequent norms in which those rights are particularly taken into account, so that, if the violation of one of those rights is excluded, the violation of Article 2 of the Constitution is also excluded. . . . The Charter does not recognise an actual right to procreation as a particular aspect of the more general right of personality . . . since it cannot be inferred from any provision that the desire or even the interest in offspring (in itself, of course, far from being illegitimate) has been elevated to the dignity of a subjective right or, in any case, that the authors of the Constitution had considered a concept of paternity or maternity merely negotiated, that is to say, detached from any biological basis, relegated to the exhaustive governance of private autonomy and liable to erase natural ones from the legal world.
>
> After all, the very institution of special adoption, often called into question in this matter, by analogical comparisons, even though it ultimately satisfies the would-be adoptive parents' desire for fertility, presupposes the existence of the adoptable child and, therefore, the child's primary need for protection (and, therefore, not only and not primarily the wish of the infertile couple), who finds it impossible to remedy, within the biological family – the privileged model, as we have seen in the constitutional design, of the integral development of the personality in the evolutionary phase – to an ascertained state of complete deprivation of moral and material assistance, and is rigidly garrisoned by a penetrating preventive

102 *In re Baby M*, 537 A.2d 1227, 109 N.J. 396 (N.J. 1988). See Superior Court of New Jersey, 31 march 1987, in *Foro italiano*, 1988, IV, c. 97 ff. with case-note by G. Ponzanelli.

103 For instance, J.V. Feinerman, *A Comparative Look at Surrogacy*, in *Georgetown Law Journal*, 76, 1988, p. 1837 ff.

> and subsequent control of the public authority (intended, moreover, to verify, essentially, not so much the prospect of economic well-being, as the affective and educational capacity of the community of insertion).[104]

We can, at this point, generalise the scheme that is used in the judicial use of comparison in a destructive key and compare it with the scheme that is used in its constructive use. Both cases concern laws that, in ethnocentric terminology, are considered to be proper to civilised humanity. In the case of constructive use, however, the desire to promote unification has exaggerated the similarities and neglected the differences. These differences could have been identified by a more careful examination of the context in which the technical-juridical solution operates. Instead, the context has been emphasised in the case of the destructive use of legal comparison to underline the differences destined to emerge when the technical-legal solution is anchored to the concrete events which constitute its background. That is what we have indicated as legal tradition (I.2.4) or legal experience (I.2.5) or even legal culture (I.2.6).

As we have said, comparative law has traditionally pursued goals that highlight identities rather than differences, presenting the latter as merely apparent. In other words, it has been a comparison that unites, rather than a comparison that divides, and too often devoted to realising the conditions of human progress conceived as a unidirectional motion towards an inescapable goal. However, following Glenn, this is a misrepresentation of the etymological meaning of 'comparison', which implies putting on an equal footing, not with a view to making objects homogeneous, but to allow the 'peaceful coexistence of what is considered equal'. All this regardless of the differences between the objects being compared, which on the contrary must be preserved.[105] Per Legrand:

> Comparison must re-inscribe (i.e. deconstruct) the singularity in which each law is always already inscribed in order to allow one's own and the foreigner to cohabit in the hospitality of comparison without their difference being hidden, i.e. in recognition of and respect for a specificity through which anyone who can claim to participate in an understanding in the strongest sense of the term must pass: recognised difference is the condition of any authentic encounter.[106]

If all this has been overlooked, when not openly opposed, it is because comparative law has traditionally placed itself at the service of modernity. And this has on the one hand produced identity tensions, such as those traceable to the process of nation-state building, but on the other hand also and above all triggered a forced standardisation of human relations: what in Weberian terminology has rendered life 'more stereotyped'.[107]

In other words, modernity has fought against tradition and the pluralism of identities. It has assigned to comparison the task of pandering to ethnocentrism and social Darwinism, which are called upon to strengthen and propagate the new course. In this sense, Friedrich Nietzsche argued that modernity was the 'age of comparison', in which to devote oneself to the comparison of different worldviews, something previously prevented by spatio-temporal ties, i.e. when 'every culture still enjoyed only a localized domination'. It was precisely the culture of comparison that would finally allow 'a selecting out among the forms and customs of higher morality whose objective can only be the elimination of the lower moralities'.[108]

104 Trib. Monza, 27 October 1989.
105 H.P. Glenn, *The National Legal Tradition*, in *Electronic Journal of Comparative Law*, 11, 2007, p. 15.
106 P. Legrand, *Le droit comparé*, 5th ed., Paris, 2015, p. 94.
107 M. Weber, *Economy and Society* (1922), Los Angeles CA and London, 1978, p. 729.
108 F. Nietzsche, *Human, All too Human* (1878), Cambridge, 1986, p. 24.

Exactly this project is contested by postmodernity, a complex and variegated set of cultural options held together by the purpose of opposing the unifying tendencies of modernity, of combating its aspiration to the 'programming of the social whole'.[109] It is also a denunciation of the failure of those tendencies which, at best, were capable of creating a new hierarchy of power, characterised by strong mobility at the top and invincible and debilitating immobility at the bottom.[110]

From the critique of modern comparison as a unifying practice, the proposal has arisen to develop a postmodern comparative law[111]: a composite approach exactly like postmodernism as such,[112] which shares its militant character. Indeed, postmodern comparison claims to highlight diversity against attempts to stifle it through the exaltation of commonalities, and focuses attention on the 'coordinates of time and place' and even on 'transience': to promote 'the cultural identity of peoples as well as of individuals', thereby elevating pluralism to 'legal value'. All this is meant to enable the peaceful coexistence of differences. As Jayme states:

> Among the founding values of postmodernity is the recognition of the multiplicity of lifestyles and people's refusal to universalise individual points of view. To make this statement more precise, it can be said that it accepts the idea of non-assimilability. . . . In the perspective outlined, we are not simply referring to narrow autonomies: it is a question of approaching the unfamiliar, of adapting the contradictory. Comparing according to the canons of postmodernity thus means testing the approach of different systems towards those aims.[113]

It should be noted that the development of global law does not make such intentions anachronistic, because its propositions are interpreted locally: law is not 'atopic' because as a 'linguistic act' it can never produce 'universal meaning'. In this sense, 'comparison does not have a unifying, but a multiplying effect', which leads it to naturally oppose 'the axiomatisation of similarity and the imperialism of the equal'.[114]

If this is the case, postmodern comparison induces a relationship with history that is the opposite of that of those who use references to the past as a rhetorical device aimed at concealing breaks in the evolution of legal experience, as is the case in the construction of European private law according to the maxims of Neopandectism (II.1.1). Postmodern comparative law avoids considering excessively broad temporal extensions since this would end up erasing or severely limiting the impact of the elements on which diversity is based. It disdains the 'historically consolidated datum' in order to 'focus on the contemporary, whose fate appears uncertain'.[115]

8 THE INCOMMENSURABILITY OF LEGAL TRADITIONS

The pursuit of the protection of identities makes comparative law a militant science. Yet it is difficult to reconcile this view with the idea that, indeed as a science, comparative law must aim to describe the characteristics of the objects it observes, highlighting both the original

109 J.-F. Lyotard, *The Postmodern Condition: A Report on Knowledge* (1979), Minneapolis MN, 1984, p. 12.
110 Z. Bauman, *The Individualized Society*, London, 2001, p. 38.
111 Citations in A. Peters and H. Schwenke, *Comparative Law beyond Post-Modernism*, in *International and Comparative Law Quarterly*, 49, 2000, p. 803 ff.
112 M. Siems, *Comparative Law*, 2nd ed., Cambridge, 2018, p. 115 ff.
113 E. Jayme, *Osservazioni per una teoria postmoderna della comparazione*, in *Rivista di diritto civile*, 1997, I, p. 813 ff. As well as Id., *Internationales Privatrecht und postmoderne Kultur*, in *Zeitschrift für Rechtsvergleichung*, 1997, p. 230 ff.
114 P. Legrand, *Le droit comparé*, cit., pp. 88 and 102 f.
115 E. Jayme, *Osservazioni per una teoria postmoderna della comparazione*, cit., p. 814.

traits but also, where appropriate, the aspects on which they converge. Of course, when a legal system is studied emphasising its spatiotemporal coordinates, then points of divergence, rather than convergence, emerge almost naturally (III.1.1). And yet, when it claims to describe rather than prescribe, comparative law cannot anticipate the outcome of its analysis, assuming it as the predetermined end goal of the comparison. That is to say, those who define comparison as a science aimed at detecting analogies and differences cannot reduce themselves to fabricating descriptions in which differences are *a priori* assumed to the detriment of patterns of convergence.

The intention here is not to give the impression that comparative law must, and above all can, provide objective measurements of similarities and differences, thus assuming a scientistic point of view. Such a point of view gives social sciences the same characteristics as natural sciences, disguising their explanations as objective and neutral rather than necessarily partial (I.1.4). Instead, it must be stressed that its alignment with a specific purpose – serving an identity-oriented or conversely homogenising discourse – cannot in itself determine the merits of a comparison. This is what we have observed with regard to the international unification of law, a constitutive aim of comparison as an autonomous science, which is still considered by many to be its main *raison d'être* (II.1.2). And we cannot but reiterate this at a time when the ideal of reconstructing comparative law as a field of knowledge based on exaltation of differences is becoming commonplace wisdom. In this way, new aims end up promoting old and now outdated approaches.

In other words, it cannot be said that the comparative law scholar, even when he emphasises the context of the analysed technical-legal constructions, can ignore convergence. Likewise, one cannot conclude that comparison and unification of law are irreconcilable. However, this is precisely what is argued by those who claim that 'respect for otherness is not the result of a comparison of laws: it is its prerequisite'. Per Legrand:

> It is at the beginning of his research that the comparative law scholar must become aware of the fact that there is something that can be called and perceived as his own law, his own legal culture, his own culture, and that there is something else that is not, that differs from it. The consciousness of this otherness will then be brought to the fore in all theories and, in so doing, in all practices of comparison. It then becomes clear that comparison will not have a unifying effect, but a multiplying one. Moreover, the promoter of the unification of law is the exact opposite of the comparative lawyer (to claim to devote oneself to comparative legal studies and the internationalisation of law is to embroil oneself in a contradiction from which the most fertile imagination will not be able to manufacture credibility).[116]

It is no coincidence that these assertions come from a scholar who extols law in its essence as a discursive practice, whose meaning is constituted through interpretation, as clarified by proponents of an inescapable nihilistic vocation of hermeneutics (I.1.4). From such a point of view, comparative law takes on the contours of a comparison between unique and contingent discourses about law, focused on what gives those discourses their otherness and 'ambiguity', neglecting those aspects from which to derive 'analogies and parallels'. Hence, the definition of comparative analysis as 'differential' analysis, developed from the observation that 'law knows only diversity', and that legal systems, considered as 'traditions', are 'incommensurable'.[117]

116 P. Legrand, *Le droit comparé*, cit., p. 102 f.
117 P. Legrand, *L'analyse différentielle des jurisculture*s, in *Revue internationale de droit comparé*, 1999, p. 1053 ff. As well as P. Legrand (Ed.), *Comparer les droits, résolument*, Paris, 2009.

On closer inspection, differential analysis, as opposed to the 'integrative' analysis of those who task comparison with 'identifying points of convergence, similarity, analogy, interaction and mutual influence between legal systems and cultures',[118] boasts a long tradition. Even at the Paris Congress of Comparative Law of 1900, there was a desire to emphasise the 'distinctive features' of the 'legislations or customs of different peoples' as a point of reference for the formation of families of 'original legal systems'.[119] This showed, however, the possibility of reconciling, on the one hand, a focus on the identity of legal experiences and, on the other, their comparison. This possibility is instead denied by those who consider that incommensurability means 'the absence of common measures between two laws',[120] i.e. the inability to identify a *tertium comparationis* for them (IV.1.1).

And therein lies the problem: the identity of a law emerges from emphasising its otherness from other laws, but this necessarily presupposes comparison in the first place. Hence, the theorists of differential analysis fall into a contradiction. On the one hand, they distinguish between incommensurability and incomparability, affirming the former and denying the latter[121] and, on the other hand, they end up deriving incomparability from incommensurability when they do not deem it possible to find points of reference for comparison.

As we have said, this conclusion appears unacceptable first of all because it subordinates the legitimacy of comparison to its pursuit of a well-defined purpose, be it the exaltation of commonalities or the underlining of differences. One can certainly question the practicability of comparisons between objects that have developed in contexts too distant from each other, but not also conclude that the emphasis on the context always implies unbridgeable distances.

In short, the contrast between 'claims of cultural uniqueness' and the will to discover 'universal features of human social and conceptual life' has a long history,[122] as long as the history of comparative law as an autonomous science itself: as we have seen, the aspiration to the unification of law in an evolutionary key is constitutive of the birth of the discipline (II.1.2). However, this does not justify the confusion which stems from the uniqueness claim, which does not concern the scientific legitimacy of the comparison, but rather its appropriateness or practicability from a moral or possibly political point of view.

As an example, take the analysis of exceptionally dramatic historical events such as the Holocaust. The incomparability of the Holocaust is the subject of lively discussions. These are not, however, conducted on the basis of scientific concerns. Its incomparability does not concern the alleged impossibility of comparing that event with other crimes against humanity, but rather the moral and political implications of using such a comparison as way of revisiting German national history from an absolutory perspective.[123]

A similar confusion characterises those who claimed the incomparability of socialist law with bourgeois law, apodictically regarded as evidence of the superiority of the former over the latter.[124] Here, too, we were not dealing with evaluations concerned with the scientific dimension of the comparison, but instead with the affirmation of the supposed primacy of

118 F. Tap, *L'apport du droit comparé à la scientificité du discours constitutionnaliste*, in *Revue internationale de droit comparé*, 2018, p. 9.
119 A. Esmein, *Le droit comparé et l'enseignement du droit*, in *Bulletin mensuel de la Société de législation comparée*, 1900, p. 379.
120 P. Legrand, *Le droit comparé*, cit., p. 75.
121 *Ibid.*
122 L. Rosen, *Comparative Law and Anthropology*, in M. Bussani and U. Mattei (Eds.), *Cambridge Companion to Comparative Law*, Cambridge etc., 2012, p. 73 f.
123 For instance, E.R. Piper (Ed.), *Historikerstreit. Die Dokumentation der Kontroverse um die Einzigartigkeit der nationalsozialistischen Judenvernichtung*, München and Zürich, 1987.
124 In this regard, J. Hazard, *Socialism, Legislation and Delegalisation*, in T. Daintith (Ed.), *Law as an Instrument of Economic Policy – Comparative and Critical Approaches*, Berlin and New York NY, 1988, p. 268.

planned economy over market economy, and more generally of models promoted by the Soviet Union over those sponsored by the United States.

9 GLOBALISATION AND COMPARATIVE LAW

Globalisation is a phenomenon whose Western roots have been highlighted by the social science, which have shed light on its consisting in the worldwide diffusion of what represents the essence of the West: a political order centred on democracy and an economic order based on capitalism (II.3.1). The latter, however, is the main trigger for globalisation: it is the expansion of markets, and contextually the standardisation of consumption, that inspires the circulation of cultural models and lifestyles, traditions and ways of thinking, best summarised in the expression 'McDonaldization'.[125] All this fuelled by imperialist and colonialist dynamics considered typical of 'western rationality', even if concealed under the smokescreen of rhetorical discourses concerning the exportation of a political order based on democratic participation.[126]

That said, globalisation also concerns the spread of the Western political order, an aspect whose complexity depends on disagreements on the role of the state.

For some, the state has lost much of its relevance, and indeed is the main loser of globalisation. This can be deduced from the features deemed typical of global law, which is a law without legislation, expressing itself mostly through international treaties, decisions of courts and arbitration bodies, and practices and private norms of a contractual nature. It is also a law without territory, conceived for a space that cannot be contained within defined boundaries, in which sources of various origins coexist. It is therefore a law without society, conceived for communities identified on the basis of the interests shared by their members, for the most part specific and mediated by the role they assume in the economic order.[127] Finally, it is a law produced in a way that is distinct from the traditional democratic law making, as it is strongly technocratic in nature. It is, in particular, largely produced by undefined 'epistemic communities', that is, 'networks of professionals with expertise in a specific field'.[128]

On closer analysis, this description of global law is vitiated by the fact that it is produced in opposition to the traditional way of understanding law, that is to say, to legal positivist paradigms that in many respects are no longer current. The discourse of global law highlights how those paradigms are still substantially widespread, although formally repudiated. In fact, it is not a description at all, since it appears more an attempt to contribute to the formation of global law rather than to faithfully describe its characteristics: it is a description with performative value.[129]

In reality, even in times of globalisation, the state does not have a marginal role. First of all because, otherwise, globalisation would represent a 'union of humanity' and would therefore eventually become an unrealistic dreamlike scenario. Instead, the global dimension needs the local dimension to emerge and therefore both are 'mutually constitutive rather

125 G. Ritzer, *The McDonaldization of Society*, 3rd ed., London, 2000.

126 H. Muir Watt, *Globalization and Comparative Law*, in M. Reimann and R. Zimmermann (Eds.), *The Oxford Handbook of Comparative Law*, 2nd ed., Oxford, 2019, p. 599 ff.

127 M.R. Ferrarese, *Prima lezione di diritto globale*, Roma and Bari, 2012, pp. 54 ff. and 145 ff.

128 P.M. Haas, *Introduction: Epistemic Communities and International Policy Coordination*, in *International Organization*, 46, 1992, p. 3.

129 A. Di Martino, *Circolazione delle soluzioni giuridiche e delle idee costituzionali. Questioni di metodo comparativo e prassi tra culture costituzionali e spazi globali*, in *Dpce online*, 2021, p. 778.

than oppositional'.[130] Moreover, globalisation requires an institutional architecture whose construction and development necessarily imply the activity of public authorities. It is probably no coincidence that the last few decades have been characterised by a multiplication of state entities.[131]

However, this does not detract from the fact that it is a different state from the one to which post-war constitutionalism refers, i.e. the constitutionalism designed to prevent democracy from being swallowed up by capitalism (I.2.1). The state in line with the expectations of globalisation is ultimately the state shaped by neoliberal orthodoxy (II.2.9), which aims to make the functioning of capitalism historically possible. And from that perspective, the state strives to compress democracy (II.2.7), i.e. to achieve a 'weak and domesticated legislature' reduced to dealing with issues of no external relevance, in order not to hinder the formation of 'an increasingly powerful and private executive'. Precisely, as Sassen puts it:

> There is a novel type of segmentation inside the state apparatus, with a growing and increasingly privatized executive branch of government aligned with specific global actors, notwithstanding nationalist speeches, and a hollowing out of the legislature whose effectiveness is at risk of becoming confined to fewer and more domestic matters. A weak and domesticated legislature weakens the political capacity of citizens to demand accountability from an increasingly powerful and private executive, since the legislature gives citizens stronger standing in these matters than the executive.[132]

Similarly, it can be argued that globalisation implies the universalisation of modernity and in particular of the nation state, combined with the use of penetrating surveillance practices. Perhaps nation states as a whole constitute an essential articulation of a 'transnational state': the former being called upon to realise at the local level the conditions for making capitalism historically possible, and in this sense to pander to the instances of the global level represented by the latter.[133] All this confirms that the spatial dimension of law, inextricably linked to the mechanisms set in motion by modernity, cannot be considered a legacy of the past: we are not confronted with a 'deterritorialisation of the world', but with a 'new territorialisation'.[134]

This reading is in line with analyses of globalisation that place the beginning of the phenomenon in the 1970s, when the first international initiatives to reverse the trend whereby democracy had become an obstacle to the development of capitalism began to take shape. Think, for example, of the Trilateral Commission and its report 'on the governability of democracies'.[135] Clearly, the same reading cannot be invoked by those who link the birth of globalisation to the birth of the capitalist world order in the 16th century.[136] But the more historical reading, however, is affirmed if one only thinks back to the 19th century, when the market became the main instrument of resource allocation, over and above the hitherto prevailing forms of allocation: the redistributive transaction and the socially obligatory gift-giving.[137] This situation posed such a threat to the survival of society that it necessitated the

130 M. Graziadei, *What Does Globalisation Mean for the Comparative Study of Law?*, in *Journal of Comparative Law*, 16, 2021, pp. 528 and 536.
131 Already M. Shapiro, *The Globalization of Law*, in *Indiana Journal of Global Legal Studies*, 1, 1993, p. 37 ff.
132 S. Sassen, *Neither Global nor National: Novel Assemblages of Territory, Authority and Rights*, in *Ethics & Global Politics*, 1, 2008, p. 72.
133 W.I. Robinson, *Theories of Globalization*, in G. Ritzer (Ed.), *The Blackwell Companion to Globalization*, Malden MA and Oxford, 2007, pp. 131 and 138.
134 C. Poncibò, *Geografia del diritto: un'introduzione*, Torino, 2021, p. 54.
135 M. Crozier, S.P. Huntington and J. Watanuki, *The Crisis of Democracy: On the Governability of Democracies*, New York NY, 1975.
136 J. Osterhammel and N.P. Petersson, *Geschichte der Globalisierung. Dimensionen Prozesse Epochen*, München, 2003.
137 K. Polanyi, *Primitive, Archaic, and Modern Economies: Essays of Karl Polanyi*, Boston MA, 1968, p. 8.

intervention of the state, which was called upon to stem the expansion of the markets by reasserting its national dimension. This was done in the United States through the New Deal and thereby by democratic means, while in Europe the same aims were pursued by fascism, and thereby sacrificing the political order to the needs of the economic order. In other words, by suppressing political freedoms in order to reform economic freedoms (II.1.3).

This is not to deny the peculiarities of our age compared to previous ones. And yet it is undeniable that the present era is also characterised by the expansion of markets, which is at the root of the impoverishment of society and, therefore, of the claim to the state to restore forms of defence against the intrusiveness of the market. It is as well undeniable that demands for return of the nation state have inspired the affirmation of violent and exclusionary identities, which does not necessarily imply the sacrifice of political freedoms, but at least a tendency towards their limitation. At the same time that state action in support of globalisation processes is not questioned, identity conflicts are fuelled in order to overshadow redistributive conflicts. In this regard, some of the countries that joined the European Union on the occasion of eastward enlargement offer particularly fitting examples (III.2.5).

Having summarily reconstructed the scenarios that have fuelled and are in turn the product of globalisation, we can deal with the specific point of view of comparative law and its practitioners.

The impression is that globalisation has brought about results that helped to raise awareness of the meaning of the subversive function of comparative law (I.1.1). It has led to a more critical approach to certain statements of principle concerning the inadequacy of traditional paradigms.[138] All this with obvious benefits from the point of view of the dialogue between comparative law and the other disciplines engaged in casting an external gaze on the law, whose scholars point out that the unifying approach constitutes an objective obstacle.[139]

The first aspect on which globalisation has prompted reflection relates to the constitutive purpose of comparative law: the use of comparisons as a stimulus to the unification of law or at least the relativisation of differences between national laws. We have seen that globalisation does not only go hand in hand with homogenising impulses, or rather that these impulses are present and yet have to face an apparent paradox: they can only be imposed through action at the local level. The tension between the latter and the global level leads to question the traditional focus of comparative law on the unification of law. At the very least, the tension brings out the manifold implications of a cultural agenda centred entirely on convergence, and highlights the contextual opportunity to nurture identity discourses. Not as the default purpose of comparisons, as claimed by postmodern comparative law (II.1.7), but at least as an approach that must be acknowledged as being neglected for too long.

Globalisation then offers comparative law scholars interesting ideas for developing their critique of the theoretical orthodoxy that underlies the traditional discourse on law. First and foremost, global law calls into question the reduction of law to legislation and thus the underlining of its state dimension.[140] If global law is a law without legislation, without territory and without society, then legal pluralism must be taken into serious consideration. Legal pluralism in fact describes not their mere juxtaposition, but the confusion and possibly conflict between sets of rules. All this can be applied not only to the analysis of the succession of legal systems

138 R. Scarciglia, *Diritto globale e metodologia comparativa: verso un approccio verticale?*, in *Diritto pubblico comparato ed europeo*, 2015, p. 1011 ff.
139 K. Lerch, *Das Verschwinden der Unterschiede. Vom Nutzen und Nachteil der vergleichenden Methode für die Rechtsgeschichte*, in *Rechtsgeschichte*, 3, 2003, p. 38 ff.
140 H. Muir Watt, *Globalization and Comparative Law*, cit., p. 600 ff.

over time, but also to the circulation of legal systems produced by the circulation of persons in particular due to migration (I.2.3).

The same applies to the critique of evolutionism, which we know is at least covertly present in many legal analyses, including those of comparative lawyer. This critique, too, may benefit from the characteristics of global law, as indeed has been the case in the field of anthropology[141]: in particular, that which specialises on multiple modernities, to which we will return (II.3.7).

10 NEXT: FROM GLOBAL CONSTITUTIONALISM TO CONSTITUTIONALISMS

We have provided numerous examples of scholars who are aware of the subversive value of their knowledge and in various ways who are committed to promoting a cultural and critical study of law, and producing within this framework comparisons aimed at enhancing the identity dimension. We have also stated that those who practise postmodern comparative law, while criticisable to the extent that they make comparisons with a predetermined outcome in mind (II.1.7), show a remarkable awareness of the subversive nature of comparative law.

Another sign that comparative law scholars are aware of the impact of globalisation on their discipline is the clarification that globalisation should be spoken of in the plural, i.e. that 'there are a number of globalizations going on'. And these globalisations are not to do with the 'spread of western technology, open markets and human rights' as is the case with the Western model, but rather with values aligned with at least two other models that also claim hegemony: the Islamic model and the Chinese model. Then, there is the chthonic tradition (II.2.6), which does not claim hegemony and yet seems in many ways the best equipped to make itself universal. Per Glenn:

> The world is too complicated, however, to be caught in a single dichotomy of a growing 'us' and many, smaller, 'thems'. It is rather the case that each tradition, or at least each of the major ones, has within it the potential to globalize, to be used for purposes of domination in a way which suppresses, by manifold means, variant opinion. There now appear to be three main candidates in a race to globalize: the west, islam, and east Asia. No one is able to foresee the result of such a race, and some argue that other traditions, notably the chthonic one, hold the key to human and ecological survival. So it is unlikely we are heading for a single, cosmopolitan, world culture since *a* cosmopolitan culture implies that somebody's culture is cosmopolitan, while those of other are not.[142]

It must be said at this point that such an awareness appears to be more widespread among comparative public law scholars and less so among those who resort to comparisons in private law.[143] This may come as no surprise since it is above all in public law that one finds measures with 'high political content' or 'high ethical content', whereas private law is primarily concerned with the economic order[144]: a domain which is less devoted to promoting diversity. And yet this only partly explains the different sensitivity to identity. Even the economic order may

141 R. Robertson and K.E. White, *What Is Globalization?*, in G. Ritzer (Ed.), *The Blackwell Companion to Globalization*, cit., p. 56.

142 H.P. Glenn, *Legal Traditions of the World*, 5th ed., Oxford, 2014, p. 51 f.

143 R. Michaels and N. Jansen, *Private Law beyond the State. Europeanization, Globalization, Privatization*, in *American Journal of Comparative Law*, 54, 2006, p. 843 ff.

144 T.E. Frosini, *Rappresentanza e legislazione nell'età della globalizzazione*, in *Annuario di diritto comparato e di studi legislativi*, 2017, p. 199 f.

well be regulated with attention to identities, and if this is not the case, the reason certainly does not lie in some sort of natural tendency. We are indeed faced with choices of values, and those concerning the expansion of markets have an undoubted neoliberal inspiration. We know that this inspiration is problematic for the balance between capitalism and democracy (II.2.8). It is, in fact, precisely the necessity to balance capitalism and democracy that inspired democratic and social constitutionalism, which from the market promotes the anchoring of the economic order to the state dimension in order to defend society (II.1.9).

Reflecting on constitutionalism offers interesting insights into the current debate between those comparative public law scholars who emphasise unifying tendencies, and those scholars who are sensitive to identity claims.

The debate on 'global or post-national constitutionalism or constitutionalism beyond the state' is exemplary. That debate frames constitutionalism as a way to make up for the growing inadequacy of the national level in the effort to 'keep politics in check' and in particular to promote 'human rights, democracy and the rule of law'.[145] This is an extremely wide-ranging and rich debate, which has documented the successes of the formula 'global constitutionalism', but also numerous controversial aspects. Criticism focuses on three main aspects.

The first criticism has to do with the ethnocentric connotation of global constitutionalism, which is moreover evident if one considers its distinctive features. The critique is not so much concerned with its Western foundations, but with its specifically liberal declination.[146] Indeed, global constitutionalism does not include the features of democratic and social constitutionalism, with the result that the affirmation of democracy does not take into account the need to preserve it from capitalism and therefore ends up being a mere statement of principle. The conception of democracy referred to is, moreover, one centred on 'public voting', which therefore does not take into account the real 'opportunity for citizens to participate in political discussions and to influence public choice'. All of this overlooks the fact that democracy is not an exclusively Western practice, and in particular that history offers examples of how it has been practised in other continents as well, and how this has occurred in accordance with 'long traditions of public discussion'.[147]

The second aspect on which critics of global constitutionalism have focused is its apolitical dimension: its being the result of dynamics developed within communities lacking the characteristics of people communities. That is, global constitutionalism is not the expression of communities built around shared values and as such capable of expressing constituent powers, but rather technocratic communities that arose more to neutralise social conflict than to nurture it as the foundation of democratic participation. Furthermore, the lack of a common ideal and value base prevents the development of the forms of solidarity that are indispensable to legitimising a redistribution of resources alternative to the one realised through the market. In other words, it prevents the development of democratic and social constitutionalism, making only its neoliberal declination possible.[148]

As we know, technocracy is a typical feature of global law as a whole (II.1.9), which is certainly not diminished by the fact that here we are dealing with rules placed at the top of the sources of law system. Indeed, this character is reinforced by the emphasis on the dialogue between the courts as a catalyst for global constitutionalism (II.1.6), celebrated as a source of

145 A. Wiener et al., *Global Constitutionalism: Human Rights, Democracy and the Rule of Law*, in *Global Constitutionalism*, 1, 2012, p. 1 ff.
146 L. Pegoraro, *Blows against the Empire. Contro la iper-Costituzione coloniale dei diritti fondamentali, per la ricerca di un nucleo interculturale condiviso*, in *Annuario di diritto comparato e di studi legislativi*, 2020, p. 450 f.
147 A. Sen, *The Argumentative Indian. Writings on Indian History, Culture and Identity*, New York NY, 2005, p. 13.
148 Already F. von Hayek, *The Economic Conditions of Interstate Federalism*, in *New Commonwealth Quarterly*, 5, 1939, p. 131 ff.

'superior rationality' produced in a forum that is 'impartial by definition' and 'alien to political dialectics'.[149]

This brings us to the third aspect highlighted by critics of global constitutionalism, namely, its ineffectiveness. It may well be that 20th century constitutionalism contained within national borders has betrayed the universalist inspiration of its origins, and yet it must be admitted that it has ensured respect for fundamental rights. The same cannot, however, be said of 'rights without a sovereign'. They are 'ethereal' or alternatively effective only insofar as their implementation is ultimately ensured by entities directly or indirectly connected to a state. More precisely, as Azzariti argues:

> Cosmopolitan rights appear, in effect, without history, almost despot-less. Rights without a sovereign. Rights without historical subjects of reference (bearers) who, through their claims, assert their demands. Even today, states impose the supranational domination of rights, asserting their traditional prerogatives: within their own borders on the basis of the principle of imperium, in international relations by adopting the acts or putting in place the facts necessary for their assumption in the various concrete legal systems. . . . In fact, it cannot be denied that those rights, historically realised in specific political and cultural contexts, and valid for qualifying the legal system in relation to a territorially closed and homogeneous space, at the moment they are projected into the great spaces lose their deepest ties with the concreteness of politics and with the political subjects within the state that had worked to make them prevail. This ultimately renders cosmopolitan rights weak, makes them ethereal.[150]

On closer inspection, critics of global constitutionalism have not limited themselves to highlighting these and other controversial aspects of the concept. They have also elaborated alternative categories, capable on the one hand of capturing the specificities of non-Western models, and on the other of not unduly diluting the notion of constitutionalism, still relating to practices of power limitation and legitimisation. Among these categories, we will briefly consider Andean constitutionalism, referring to legal experiences belonging to the Western legal tradition, and two constitutionalisms traceable to non-Western systems: Islamic and Chinese (II.3.1).

Islamic constitutionalism is an alternative to Western constitutionalism because it disregards the requirement of statehood and thus territoriality: the community of reference is a religious one regardless of the physical location of its members. Nevertheless, the *sharia*, the set of precepts of divine derivation and as such considered a source of law, contains provisions concerning the limitation of power, establishes constraints concerning the promotion of community welfare, and protects positions comparable to fundamental rights. Chinese constitutionalism displays features that can be traced back to developments in recent decades, when the country reformed its economic order in a capitalist direction (II.2.9), incorporating some elements not far removed from the Western concept of fundamental rights protection and rule of law. These features coexist with aspects, such as the collective dimension of rights and the role of the party in the institutional architecture of the state, which make Chinese constitutionalism an alternative to Western constitutionalism but not also to constitutionalism as such.[151]

Andean constitutionalism, whose foundations were formalised in the Ecuadorian constitution of 2008 and in the Bolivian constitution of 2009, is expressive of Latin American identity. It is founded on a mixture of Western and chthonic elements (II.3.8), which is expressed through the full recognition of legal pluralism and the qualification of the state

149 P. Bianchi, *Miti e leggende del costituzionalismo globale*, in *Ambiente Diritto*, 2023, 4, p. 15.
150 G. Azzariti, *Il costituzionalismo moderno può sopravvivere?*, Roma and Bari, 2013, p. 63 f.
151 A. Di Martino, *Circolazione delle soluzioni giuridiche e delle idee costituzionali*, cit., p. 833 ff.

as plurinational. This model of constitutionalism is then complemented by what has been defined in terms of the caring state as opposed to the welfare state: while the latter constitutes a compromise between economic freedoms and social justice and promotes sustainable development, the former pursues social justice as the overriding objective and aims at an integral protection of nature. In short, the caring state is an evolution of the welfare state into forms capable of nurturing a renewed harmony between man and the environment.[152] If Latin American law is considered the most entitled to claim global hegemony, as we have just recalled, it is precisely because it emphasises this fundamental characteristic.

Other constitutionalisms can, of course, be identified, and indeed we have already moved in this direction when we discussed democratic and social constitutionalism. It emerged in the European context after World War II (I.2.1), and then came under threat with the rise of neoliberalism in such a way as to herald a different model of constitutionalism (II.2.9). What we have reported so far, however, is sufficient to document the current aspirations towards a use of comparison aimed at investigating identities rather than reasons for convergence. This proves that the constitutive approach to comparative law, exacerbated by the processes of globalisation, has finally entered a crisis or at least needs a period of decisive mitigation.

SUMMARY

1. Perhaps because it is still struggling for its full recognition, comparative law likes to legitimise itself by pointing to goals valued by other disciplines, first and foremost the international unification of law. In doing so it condemns itself to subalternity and ultimately to irrelevance, as can be seen considering the contributions of comparative lawyers to Neopandectists. It is then preferable to claim as the sole purpose of the subject the increase of knowledge useful for the cultural and critical study of law, i.e. the recovery of its political dimension.
2. Comparative law as an autonomous science arose as reaction to a focus on legislation and as a differentiation from comparative history of institutions and from sociology. It arose with two precise aims: to enhance the collective dimension of law in order to prevent the overthrow of the proprietary order, and to promote the international unification of law. This happened on the basis of paradigms that are in many respects ethnocentric and evolutionist, not always expressive of an effective reaction to the focus on legislation, such as those relating to the identification of the common law of civilised humanity.
3. At the end of World War I, the international unification of law remained the primary aim pursued by comparative law, albeit within the framework of nationalist paradigms aimed at sustaining the proprietary order: first and foremost, those promoted by fascism to crush political freedoms in order to reform economic freedoms. The end of World War II marked the transition towards a comparison aimed at promoting the formation of a common law of mankind. Evolutionism remains an inspiration, as can be seen from the reference to the general principles of law recognised by civilised nations referred to in the Statute of the International Court of Justice.

152 S. Bagni, *Le forme di Stato in America latina*, in Ead. and S. Baldin (Eds.), *Latinoamérica. Viaggio nel costituzionalismo comparato dalla Patagonia al Río Grande*, Torino, 2021, p. 52 ff.

4. The clients of comparative law, national legislators and legal practitioners, pursue a different agenda from that of scholars. Although they favour comparison that unites, they are not particularly interested in the international unification of law, nor do they promote a cultural and critical study of law: they pursue practical aims and are therefore focused on formal sources of production and their application. The use of comparative law by national legislators is well-established and long-standing. It may be stimulated by scholars interested in promoting reforms or it may result from an endogenous impulse, possibly followed by analyses contracted out to public or private entities. In the latter case, it can result in legislative outsourcing, which is problematic because it produces an erosion of democracy.

5. Among comparative law scholars, the interest in the international unification of law has never waned. It has, however, produced research which is indifferent to the cultural dimension of law, as can be seen by considering the Cornell Seminars and the efforts undertaken to build a European private law. To pursue the latter goal, the formation of a supranational legal science has been promoted, which, however, has achieved disappointing results: it has taken on the limited task of translating into technical terms the agenda developed by market operators. The contribution of the scholars who, within the framework of UNIDROIT, have drafted the Principles on the law of international commercial contracts is somewhat different. And yet this confirms the necessity of reserving for comparative law the task of nurturing the critical study of law, rather than pandering to the aims indicated by other fields of legal knowledge.

6. The international unification of law can be pursued by promoting the formation of common judicial approaches, and in this sense by fostering the judicial use of comparative law. This is a complementary and optional use, to be combined perhaps with the choice of recognising reciprocal persuasive effect to the decisions of the highest courts of the systems involved in unification. In common law countries this corresponds to a long-standing practice, whereas in civil law countries one can only invoke sibylline references contained in the statutory provisions on the interpretation of the law.

7. The judicial use of comparative law may promote the adoption of innovative solutions opposed by the legislature or scholarship. The same use may, however, promote resistance to innovation in the context of an identity-based use of comparative law, aimed at exalting the differences between legal systems. This is what may be called the destructive use of comparison, as opposed to the constructive use typical of unifying comparisons. The exaltation of differences is assumed as the end goal of postmodern comparative law, which is committed to opposing the projects of international unification of law.

8. The identification of differences cannot constitute an indisputable aim of comparison, just as the unification of national laws cannot. This aim is argued by comparative law scholars for whom the discipline only requires a differential analysis: the latter, as a critical and cultural study of laws, can only lead to an awareness of otherness and thus to the finding of the incommensurability of laws. If, however, laws are devoid of common measures, then incommensurability becomes incomparability, which may at most be relevant as a moral or political statement, but not as a scientific one.

9. Globalisation is portrayed as the process through which the democratic political order and the capitalist economic order find planetary diffusion, all accompanied by a decisive downsizing of the state. On closer inspection, however, the state constitutes a fundamental actor in globalisation since this implies the spread of neoliberalism: the latter requires the attribution to the public authorities of the task of presiding over the market and compressing democratic participation. This reproduces 19th-century patterns, when the expansion of the markets posed such a threat to the survival of societies that they sought protection from the state: sometimes granted while respecting the democratic system, as in the US New Deal, and sometimes in complicity with its collapse, as was the case with fascism. That being said, globalisation and its implications are forcing comparative law to reassess its constitutive unifying vocation, to develop reflections on legal pluralism and to stigmatise the evolutionist dimension that has characterised comparative law for too long.

10. Globalisation intends to promote the planetary diffusion of Western models, thereby neglecting the presence of other models that could also be accepted beyond the areas where they have been elaborated and experimented upon: the Islamic and Chinese models, and to some extent the chthonic tradition. In short, globalisation should be spoken of in the plural, which is recognised in particular by comparative law scholars with a public law sensibility. The latter discuss global constitutionalism, but also constitutionalisms: in particular Andean, Islamic, and Chinese constitutionalisms, which differ from the Western but still relate to the limitation and legitimisation of power. All this while global constitutionalism is stigmatised as an ethnocentric, technocratic, and fundamentally ineffective construct, if not as a catalyst for neoliberal arrangements.

CHAPTER 4

SYSTEMS AND FAMILIES OF SYSTEMS

1 COMPARATIVE LAW AND THE MAPPING OF POLITICAL BODIES

In many respects, comparative law as an autonomous science originated as taxonomy,[1] in other words as an attempt to identify groupings of national legal systems on the basis of their main characteristics, usually referred to as 'families'. Legal scholars have devoted themselves with great assiduity to the endeavour of grouping legal systems by family.[2] Even before the 20th century, references to families or similar concepts were common, but they did not appear to be particularly well thought-out and rooted in a robust macro-comparison. Indeed, until the 19th century, interest in micro-comparison was more prevalent,[3] as we know from the research conducted within the first comparative law scientific societies (II.1.4).

From such a point of view, the Paris Congress of 1900 reversed the trend, perhaps because of the tension between those who wanted to devote themselves to universal law, and those who wanted to consider only the law common to systems with the same level of civilisation (II.1.2). The second option required the identification of those systems, i.e. to the construction of homogeneous groupings or families of systems, and their classification. As we will see (II.2.4), this also explains how that construction was carried out from a Western point of view, which is inevitable for those who are used to describing the world by reference to evolutionist and ethnocentric categories.

This does not imply, however, that this is the only reason for the inherent partiality of systems classifications. Particularly within the West – but also in relation to possibly competing regions – the identification of families, and before that of a system representative of that family, is the result of cultural choices supported by comparative analyses. If one views law essentially as an instrument of power (I.2.1), it follows that comparative law is expressive of a governance project,[4] and legal taxonomy is a field of knowledge concerned with the creation of a 'geography of laws'[5] or 'geography of political bodies'. Per Monateri:

> The theory of law systems attempts to divide the world into a relatively small number of models of the legal-political organisation of human societies. The problem is grouping social organisations according to some principle that makes it possible to represent the global reality of the planet in relation to the laws that govern it. Of course, the very moment a map of local

1 G. Resta, *Le tassonomie e la comprensione del comparatista*, in *Diritto pubblico comparato ed europeo*, 2017, p. 1197 ff. and V. Zeno-Zencovich, *Comparative Legal Systems. A Short Introduction*, 2nd ed., Roma, 2019, p. 1.

2 For an overview, M. Siems, *Comparative Law*, 2nd ed., Cambridge, 2018, p. 88 ff.

3 For instance, W. Hug, *The History of Comparative Law*, in *Harvard Law Review*, 45, 1932, p. 1027 ff.

4 Da. Kennedy, *The Methods and the Politics*, in P. Legrand and R. Munday (Eds.), *Comparative Legal Studies: Traditions and Transitions*, Cambridge, 2003, p. 345 ff.

5 C. Poncibò, *Diritto comparato e geografia*, in *Rivista critica del diritto privato*, 2014, p. 187 ff.

DOI: 10.4324/9781032684499-6

> legal orders is produced, this in turn presents itself as an ordering of sense of the world. Indeed, from this point of view, it is quite clear that this presents itself as an ordering of orders, insofar as it gives a particular local law a general sense that, by localising it, identifies it in relation to a sense giving context.[6]

Hence, as tools for organising reality,[7] the classifications of systems, or rather their mapping, are, on closer inspection, functional to producing ranking of systems. Both result from the transformation of 'legal models' into 'ideological entities corresponding to large political entities'.[8] In this sense, taxonomy constitutes a form of geopolitics, which is used to produce a 'world hierarchy of the great families', as well as an 'internal hierarchy within each of them, between the representative type and the represented type'.[9]

Scholarship attentive to the geopolitical dimension of comparative law has traced this way of conceiving taxonomy back to the classification proposed by Adhémar Esmein, who was one of the leading figures at the Paris Congress of Comparative Law in 1900. There, Esmein considered it useful to classify systems on the basis of their 'original' character, evidenced by emphasising their 'historical formation', as well as some undefined aspects, namely, 'their general structure and distinctive features'. The result reflected the balance between the powers of the time and the division of the world into their respective areas of influence, corresponding to the following 'families or groups': Latin, Germanic, Anglo-Saxon, Slavic, and Islamic,[10] representing, respectively, the sphere of power of the French Third Republic, Victorian England, the German Reich, Tsarist Russia, and the Ottoman Empire.

About 20 years later, during a period characterised by the collapse of the Russian, Ottoman, Austro-Hungarian and German empires, Esmein's classification came to be viewed as 'obsolete'. In the volume dedicated to the 50th anniversary of the *Société de législation comparée* (II.1.4), the French scholar Henri Lévy-Ulmann identified families of systems by emphasising in addition to the 'ethnic' dimension, the sources of law and the ways in which law evolves. The result, largely conceived as a description of private law aspects, was the identification of three families or 'great systems': continental countries with written and codified law, English-speaking countries with 'jurisprudential custom', and Islamic countries with a religious character, which were characterised by an 'almost absolute immobility'.[11] In this way, the distinction between French and German law was recomposed in favour of a category, continental law, which was obviously intended to enhance the hegemonic role of France: the role of the codes in the system of sources is the distinguishing feature of continental law, and the French Civil Code is the code *par excellence*.

It should be noted that classifications aimed at unifying the European continent's legal systems were also successfully deployed to explain legal systems that, compared to the French, were considered peripheral. In Italy, for example, Michele Sarfatti used such classifications, although at the same time specifying that a distinction had to be made between purely Latin codes and Germanic codes, the former modelled on the French example. However, this was not, Sarfatti added, the point of reference for continental identity, which was based instead on the Justinian Codex as adapted by the School of Bologna to 'western political society'. The Codex, to be

6 P.G. Monateri, *Geopolitica del diritto. Genesi, governo e dissoluzione dei corpi politici*, Roma and Bari, 2013, p. 11.
7 G. Pascuzzi, *Conoscere comparando: tra tassonomie ed errori cognitivi*, in *Diritto pubblico comparato ed europeo*, 2017, p. 1184.
8 L.-J. Constantinesco, *Traité de droit comparé*, vol. 3, Paris, 1983, p. 475.
9 P.G. Monateri, *Geopolitica del diritto*, cit., p. 12.
10 A. Esmein, *Le droit comparé et l'enseignement du droit*, in *Bulletin mensuel de la Société de législation comparée*, 1900, p. 379.
11 H. Lévy-Ulmann, *Observations générales sur les communications relatives au droit privé dans les pays étrangers*, in Société de législation comparée, *Les transformations du droit dans les principaux pays depuis cinquante ans*, vol. 1, Paris, 1922, p. 85 ff.

considered a 'body of Italian Roman law',[12] thus ended up restoring centrality to a national law that otherwise assumed a residual position with respect to the French paradigm.

The category of continental law, on the other hand, could not accommodate the identity claims of Latin American law scholars, who showed understandable irritation with taxonomies that condemned them to the role of periphery to a distant centre. A way out was found by taking advantage of the fact that, before the Second World War, many Latin American countries experimented with democratic governments. Only in a few cases this was successful, and generally only for a short time. However, there was a widespread desire to distance themselves from what was happening in the West at the time, particularly with regard to the rise of fascism in southern Europe, but also socialism in the East.

Hence, the proposal of groupings that exalted the democratic vocation of certain Latin American legal experiences, which was highlighted by taking the historical origin of the codifications of civil law as a point of reference. Admittedly, democracy was spoken of here in a limited sense, to hint to the fact that in the New World inequalities based on class, race or nationality had not been fostered.[13] This was enough to mark the difference with what had happened in Europe in the 19th century. In this perspective, the Argentine Enrique Martínez Paz distinguished between a 'barbaric customary law' typical of England, a 'barbaric Roman' law such as the French and German, a 'barbaric Roman canonical law' to which the Spanish and Portuguese legal experiences could be traced, and a 'democratic Roman canonical law'. The latter included 'democratic liberal' regimes, such as the Brazilian, 'democratic social' experiences, such as the Swiss, and 'democratic social' orders, such as the Soviet.[14]

Particular geopolitical awareness was shown by the classifications proposed at the conclusion of the Second World War, designed to position the hegemonic national legal systems within the world division dictated by the new balance of powers: the United States had definitively emerged as the reference point among common law legal systems, and had placed itself at the head of the Western bloc in its opposition to the Soviet bloc.[15]

The most representative classification of the new balances is the one proposed by the French scholar René David. He sought to identify the distinguishing features of the various laws by first considering elements of a legal rather than an extra-legal nature, albeit identified from an external point of view. In addition to their 'historical origin', factors such as the 'professional culture' of lawyers, their 'working techniques', their 'vocabulary' and their 'concepts' were considered. Moreover, the differences that existed with respect to such 'technical' characteristics should not obscure the similarities on the 'ideological' level: that concerning 'conceptions of justice', 'religious or philosophical beliefs' and 'political, economic or social structures'. From such a point of view, it was necessary to relativise the distinction between countries with codified law and English-speaking countries, both of which were to be considered part of the 'western world founded on the moral principles of Christianity, on the political and social principles of liberal democracy, and on a capitalist economic structure'. Only in this context could a distinction be made between codified and non-codified laws, the former being traced back to the Romano-Germanic family, within which German and French law are merged, with the latter being placed in a dominant position.[16]

12 M. Sarfatti, *Introduzione allo studio del diritto comparato*, Torino, 1933, p. 51 ff.

13 D.F. Esborraz, *La individualización del Subsistema jurídico latinoamericano como desarrollo interno propio del Sistema jurídico romanista. II La contribución de la Ciencia Jurídica argentina en la primera mitad del siglo XX*, in *Roma e America*, 2007, p. 82 nt. 214.

14 E. Martínez Paz, *Introduccíon al estudio del derecho civil comparado*, Córdoba, 1934, p. 154 ff.

15 See U. Mattei, *The Cold War and Comparative Law. A Reflection on the Politics of Intellectual Discipline*, in *American Journal of Comparative Law*, 65, 2017, p. 567 ff.

16 R. David, *Traité élémentaire de droit civil comparé*, Paris, 1950, p. 215 ff.

The Western world was obviously contrasted by the Soviet world, founded on the socialist creed and on alternative beliefs to those of the West in all the areas mentioned earlier (II.3.7). Alongside the families that had arisen around the protagonists of the incipient Cold War, one could then recognise three other systems of law in an absolutely subordinate position: the Muslim, the Hindu, and the Chinese. In a publication a few years later, David traced these to the category of 'philosophical or religious systems', including, in addition to Muslim law and Hindu law, Far Eastern, Chinese, and Japanese law, as well as the law of Africa and Madagascar.[17]

The merging of French and Germanic law, i.e. the identification of the Roman-Germanic system as a family dominated by the former law, was not universally endorsed. During the same period a group of comparative law scholars from different backgrounds – the Frenchman Pierre Arminjon, the Russian Boris Nolde and the German Martin Wolff – all offered a more complex picture. They distinguished seven different families of systems that had arisen around as many 'centres of legal irradiation', whose characters were assessed 'independently of external factors': French, Germanic, Scandinavian, English, Russian, Islamic, and Hindu.[18] In this way, the opposition between capitalist and socialist systems was blurred, Germanic law regained its identity in relation to French law, and the country of origin of the common law regained ground in relation to the US.

2 NEXT: BETWEEN GEOPOLITICS AND LEGAL GEOGRAPHY

It has been said that comparative law, when it devotes itself to the mapping of political bodies, can be considered a form of geopolitics. This assertion needs some clarification, at the very least because of the bad press that geopolitics has enjoyed and to some extent still enjoys, long held to be expressive of imperialist and militarist tendencies on the one hand, and determinist and evolutionist tendencies on the other.

One of the discipline's founders identified the struggle of states for the conquest of a 'living space' as the driving force of international politics, considered as a dynamic fuelled by a sort of biology of political bodies.[19] And it was precisely this conception of geopolitics that found favour with the Nazi regime, within which it fuelled 'the power ambitions of the German Reich'. This was unfortunate for geopolitics, which was understandably considered incompatible with the goal of building an international order founded on democracy and aimed at promoting peace. At the same time, the world that emerged from the defeat of Nazism was not founded on a 'geographical division of the globe', as the polarisation produced by the Cold War was first and foremost the result of an 'ideological division'[20] and, more precisely, the result of a clash between ideologies relating to the political and economic order.

The end of the Cold War did not immediately affect the fate of geopolitics, marginalised by renewed determinist and evolutionist tendencies fuelled by the outcome of the clash between socialism and capitalism. Indeed, there was a widespread conviction that the victory of the Western bloc would have led not only to the death of ideologies and thus to the 'end of history', but also to the pacification of the planet and thus to the 'end of geography'.[21] The defeat of socialism would, in short, have marked the point of arrival in the evolution of

17 R. David and J.E.C. Brierley, *Major Legal Systems in the World Today* (1966), London, 1968, p. 18 ff.

18 P. Arminjon, B. Nolde and M. Wolff, *Traité de droit comparé*, vol. 1, Paris, 1950, p. 47 ff.

19 F. Ratzel, *Der Lebensraum. Eine biogeographische Studie*, in K. Bücher (Ed.), *Festgabe für Albert Schäffle zur siebenzigsten Wiederkehr seines Geburtstages*, Tübingen, p. 103 f.

20 For instance, G. De Ruvo, *Governare il caos. La geopolitica come pensiero dell'ordine*, in G. De Ruvo (Ed.), *Storia e filosofia della geopolitica*, Roma, 2024, p. 23 ff.

21 K. Dodds, *Geopolitics: A Very Short Introduction*, Oxford, 2019, p. 3.

humanity: the definitive affirmation of an order centred on political and economic freedoms, that is, on the combination of democracy and capitalism. At the end of the Cold War, the combination of democracy and capitalism was conceived not so much as an identifying trait of the Western experience, but as the natural foundation of society on a planetary level.[22]

As we know, this view has turned out to be deeply flawed. Not so much, and not only, because democracy has not really crossed the borders of the West, but also and above all because it is precisely in the West that it appears anything but rooted. Indeed, there are many indications that the balance between capitalism and democracy is precarious and destined to shift in favour of the former, for instance, in times of economic and financial crisis: when, to save the market from autophagy and preserve it from social conflict, authoritarian regimes first and then totalitarian regimes are established (II.1.3). In other words, capitalism can function without democracy, namely, in a context in which the combination of democracy and capitalism, i.e. the basis of the Western experience and the reason for its planetary success, is not realised.

Hence, the renewed interest in geopolitics, which for some years now has been widely used as a key to interpreting current events by scholars to whom we owe the renewal of the discipline. This renewal was based on the abandonment of imperialist and militarist tendencies, just like those of a determinist and evolutionist nature which explained its long marginalisation. Nevertheless, states persevere in understanding geopolitics in terms of power politics, related to military, economy, and technological prowess. Geopolitics can therefore constitute a useful framework for analysing the different modalities in which hegemonic projects are supported and nurtured.

These modalities undoubtedly include mappings of legal orders, which identify centres and peripheries of the world.

To better understand this point, we can usefully turn to geography of law or legal geography, which is a recently established discipline. Legal geography makes use of comparison and by so doing seeks to fulfil a 'subversive' function.[23] Indeed, legal geographers want to 'interrogate the legal from a critical geographic perspective' and thus unveil the ways in which 'assumptions about space . . . work to stabilize the validity of seemingly obvious propositions, identities and the very meaning of law'. As Delaney et al. put it:

> This convergence of legal and geographical perspectives on the social has at least three significant consequences. First, by reading the legal in terms of the spatial and the spatial in terms of the legal, our understandings of both 'space' and 'law' may be changed. Old stabilities begin to reveal gaps and tensions. New questions and research topics emerge. . . . Second, taking legal themes such as the connection between law as discourse or representational system and law as power seriously opens up a variety of questions about how – by what actual practices, in relation to what social or political projects – social space is produced, maintained or transformed. . . . Third, and more significant, by reading the social (the political, historical, and cultural) in terms of the spatio-legal – that is, in terms of new questions and understandings generated by the convergence – we may develop new insights into the constitution of social life more generally and into the terms, conditions and consequences of social change. . . . The legal and the spatial are, in significant ways, aspects of each other and as such, they are fundamental and irreducible aspects of a more holistically conceived social-material reality. This irreducible interpretation is more indicative of what might better be seen as a fusion or even, in some cases, an identity.[24]

22 F. Fukuyama, *The End of History and the Last Man*, New York NY, 1992.

23 A. Kedar, *Expanding Legal Geographies. A Call for a Critical Comparative Approach*, in I. Braverman, N. Blomley, D. Delaney and A. Kedar (Eds.), *The Expanding Spaces of Law. A Timely Legal Geography*, Stanford CA, 2014, p. 95.

24 D. Delaney, R.T. Ford and N. Blomley, *Where Is Law?*, in Iid. (Eds.), *The Legal Geographies Reader*, Oxford, 2001, pp. xv and xvii f.

The geography of law has first of all shown how the spatial dimension of law, and thus the basis of the geopolitical use of comparative law, constitutes an offshoot of modernity and ultimately a corollary of the pact between the individual and the sovereign: the pact whereby the former is entitled to property and the latter to empire (I.2.2). In fact, both refer to the spatial dimension, thus marking a difference from the typical institutions of pre-modern times, when the temporal dimension prevailed. And when, moreover, authority was not expressed through the identification of a territory over which it exercised its influence, but rather through 'bundles of rights of varying intensity'.[25]

We owe to the geography of law the development of a way of understanding space that is an alternative to its old representation as a mere container and to the conception according to which it is relevant only insofar as it conditions social phenomena. The latter is the dominant conception among comparative lawyers committed to explaining the differences between systems by starting from the 'natural environment' and thus from the 'geographical situation of a country'.[26] Geography of law, instead, has developed the thinking of geographers who have contested the image of space as a 'passive locus of social relations', arguing for its centrality as an element through which hegemony is exercised. All this, highlighting how it is 'a product' resulting from 'the same global process of commodities, money and capital'.[27]

The production of space takes place by recourse to numerous techniques, including, of course, law, which is therefore not shaped by space. On the contrary, it contributes to shaping space even beyond the boundaries of the political body that produces it.[28] This does not mean that spatiality does not condition social phenomena,[29] but rather it is no longer 'simply a passive reflection of social and cultural trends, but an active participant'. To put it succinctly: 'geography is constitutive as well as representative'.[30]

The shaping of space through law does not only concern the construction of the political order, concerning both the way political bodies exist and the relations between them. It also concerns the economic order, to support which the political bodies produce the rules and create the institutions functional to redistributing wealth in accordance with the ideologies that guide their actions.

Here, too, there is a lateness in recognising the dynamics relating to the production of space, which economics has often regarded as a 'stable context or site for historical action'. This neglects a dynamic that has been central to the construction and development of capitalism. Per Harvey:

> To begin with, the suspicion lurks and many a theory of imperialism asserts that the survival of capitalism into the 20th century has been assured only through the transformation of space-relations and the rise of distinctive geographical structures (such as core and periphery, First and Third worlds). The 'innovation waves' that others . . . see as so fundamental to the absorption of surpluses of capital and labor power over time have often had everything to do with the transformation of space – railroads and steamships, the automotive industry, aerospace and telecommunications. The multinational corporation, with its capacity to move capital and technology rapidly from place to place, to tap different resources, labor markets, consumer markets and profit opportunities, while organizing its own territorial division of labor, derives much of its power from its capacity to command space and use geographical differentials in a way that the family firm could not.[31]

25 C. Poncibò, *Geografia del diritto: un'introduzione*, Torino, 2021, p. 2 ff.
26 B. Grossfeld, *Geography and the Law*, in *Michigan Law Review*, 82, 1984, p. 1511.
27 H. Lefebvre, *The Production of Space* (1974), Oxford, 1991, pp. 11 and 26.
28 I. Castellucci, *Geodiritto. Il diritto come dimensione della geopolitica e del conflitto*, in *Gnosis*, 2020, 2, p. 27.
29 E.W. Soja, *Seeking Spatial Justice*, Minneapolis MN, 2010, p. 18.
30 B. Warf and S. Arias, *The Reinsertion of Space into the Social Sciences and Humanities*, in Iid. (Eds.), *The Spatial Turn. Interdisciplinary Study*, London and New York NY, 2009, p. 10.
31 D. Harvey, *Spaces of Capital. Towards a Critical Geography*, Edinburgh and New York NY, 2001, p. 325.

Thus, if space is central to the development of the economic order, and this is constituted by practices in which law plays a fundamental role, the geopolitical significance of its use is further confirmed. We will examine and deepen this aspect by discussing the current clash between civil and common law systems within the Western legal tradition (II.3.2).

3 THE STYLE OF SYSTEMS AND THE LEGAL MENTALITY

So far, we have considered the geopolitical significance of the mappings of political bodies proposed from the emergence of comparative law as an autonomous science until the end of the Second World War and the outbreak of the Cold War. Subsequent taxonomies continue to reflect Cold War arrangements, and yet seem to be conditioned by a resurgent competition between national laws within legal families. In particular, one can point to the competition between the French and German systems within the family of civil law.

At the beginning of the 1970s, two German authors, Konrad Zweigert and Hein Kötz, published an introduction to comparative law that was destined to become the reference work for comparative law scholars. From a geopolitical point of view, their classificatory scheme followed those that sought to restore the visibility of German law, which had been obscured by the emphasis on the opposition between the socialist bloc and the West, as well as by the attempt to portray the latter as characterised by the distinction between common law countries and countries of the Romano-Germanic family. Zweigert and Kötz, in fact, took up the classification proposed by Arminjon, Nolde and Wolff, and distinguished four Western families: one Roman, one Germanic, one Anglo-American and one Scandinavian. These were contrasted by a socialist family and three 'remaining' families: Far Eastern law, including Chinese and Japanese law, Islamic law, and Hindu law.[32]

Particularly interesting and influential is the criterion used to create the classification, which was preceded by an emphasis on the principles of subject matter relativity and temporal relativity. According to this analysis, each proposed grouping must be related to a specific branch of the legal system – for example, private law, as in the case of Zweigert and Kötz – and take into account the historical context, since a change in it can lead to very different classification results. Having said this, the proposed taxonomy aims to group national legal systems according to a concept that is widespread in linguistics and the visual arts, but also in the social sciences: the concept of style, which is not new to comparative reflection.[33]

The 'style of a system' is determined by factors of a legal nature, even if they are derived from an external point of view on law, and thus, at least implicitly, by extra-legal events. The latter, however, are not emphasised, as the disregard of legal criteria of classification is deemed to produce unreliable results: as the ones resulting from David's taxonomy (II.2.1), which was indeed criticised by Zweigert and Kötz.[34]

The first factor influencing the style of the system is the 'historical development' of the legal orders. The distinction between the common law and civil law models is based on this, the emphasis on which would motivate the limited usefulness of Western law as a category: 'the independent historical development of the common law makes it necessary to classify it separately, and the same is true of Islamic and Hindu Law'. Above all, the valorisation

32 K. Zweigert and H. Kötz, *An Introduction to Comparative Law* (1969–71), 1st ed., vol. 1, Oxford, 1977, p. 67. See now Iid., *An Introduction to Comparative Law* (1996), 3rd ed., Oxford, 1998, p. 72 f.

33 Citations in G. Samuel, *An Introduction to Comparative Law Theory and Method*, Oxford e Portland OR, 2014, p. 51 f.

34 K. Zweigert and H. Kötz, *An Introduction to Comparative Law* (1969–71), cit., p. 61 ff.

of historical facts tends to emphasise the difference between the Roman family and the Germanic family. Indeed, it would be inappropriate to compare the legal systems in which Pandectism has been widely used with those in which it has not, just as it would be inappropriate to compare the legal systems affected by the circulation of the French Civil Code with those in which codification has instead used other reference models.[35]

To these distinctions could be added those relating to the way in which the centralisation of political power came about. These dynamics took shape in the Middle Ages in the case of common law, while they and are rooted in a revolutionary act at the dawn of modernity in civil law (I.2.4). The historical evolution of the dynamics relating to the centralisation of political power can help explain the roots of the different models of capitalism that have taken hold in the two component families of the Western legal tradition (II.3.5).

The style of the system is then conditioned by the 'legal mentality', a concept that others have defined as 'the collective mental programme' or the 'cognitive structure' through which to understand 'how a community thinks about the law'.[36] Zweigert and Kötz do not provide a definition, preferring to resort to an exemplification. Indeed, they note that the legal mindset refers to, for example, the tendency towards abstraction and deductive reasoning typical of civil law and rooted in its scholarly origins, or the opposite tendency towards the empirical approach and inductive reasoning typical of common law systems:

> If we may generalise, the European is given to making plans, to regulating things in advance, and therefore, in terms of law, to drawing up rules and systematising them. He approaches life with fixed ideas, and operates deductively. The Englishman improvises, never making a decision until he has to. As Maitland said, he is an empiricist. Only experience counts for him; theorising has little appeal; and so he is not given to abstract rules of law. Convinced, perhaps from living by the sea, that life will controvert the best-laid plans, the Englishman is content with case-law as opposed to enactments.[37]

Legal mentality affects also the 'tendency towards anti-formalism' typical of civil law, exemplified by the circumstance whereby 'agreement creates contractual obligations, no matter how it is expressed', and the opposite formalist inclination of common law, well represented 'in developed Anglo-American law, in the Statute of Frauds'. Then, the centrality that the law has assumed in the West as an instrument for regulating social conflicts is linked to profound differences in legal mentality, as is the opposite tendency towards their harmonious resolution by means of alternative instruments to the law, which is instead typical of the Far East.[38] Finally, it is worth noting the contrast between the individualism fostered by Roman law and the communitarianism typical of Germanic law, to which we shall return (IV.3.2).

As is clear, and as systems style theorists point out, the analysis of legal mentality in particular requires the use of tools such as those provided by the sociology of law, and thus nourishes an external viewpoint on law. It implies the valorisation of extra-legal data or, alternatively, the consideration of law according to schemes that cannot be reduced to Western ones.[39] This is reflected in the references to the legal mentality used by legal historians to criticise the legal absolutism of modernity and to celebrate instead the concept of law typical of the Middle Ages (I.2.6).

35 *Ivi*, p. 63 f.
36 P. Legrand, *European Legal Systems Are Not Converging*, in *International and Comparative Law Quarterly*, 45, 1996, p. 60.
37 K. Zweigert and H. Kötz, *An Introduction to Comparative Law* (1969–71), cit., p. 64.
38 *Ivi*, p. 64 f.
39 See A. Gambaro, *The Trento Thesis*, in *Global Jurist Frontiers*, 4, 2004, p. 1 ff.

Having said this, the study of mentality has a particularly prestigious tradition, being linked to the New History: a current that arose in the first half of the last century to criticise the reduction of history to major events and figures, i.e. to shift the focus from the elites and the institutions they dominated, to the 'mass of society'.[40] At the same time as it called for an interdisciplinary or at least multidisciplinary study, i.e. including the perspectives of social sciences such as politics, economics, and anthropology, New History promoted the study of mentality as the study of 'the particular way of thinking and feeling of a people, of a certain group of people'. It called for this in order to develop a 'history of cultural systems, systems of beliefs, of values, of intellectual baggage within which mentalities were formed, lived and evolved'.[41]

But let us return to the style of the system and note that it is not only the legal mentality that invites an external viewpoint on the law. The same applies to 'ideology', a component of the style emphasising the role of 'political or economic doctrines or religious belief' as having 'a distinctive effect' on law: a role particularly manifest in socialist systems and religious legal systems, respectively.[42] It should be noted, however, that Zweigert and Kötz do not intend here to discuss the ideologies that govern the production of Western law, which could emerge if only an external viewpoint on law were adopted: something that the two German comparative law scholars avoid doing. That is to say, it is fair to assume that they did not really want to abandon the internal point of view on law, which thus remains their prevailing perspective, as well as the main weakness of the proposed classification.

The internal point of view also plays a leading role in the assessment of the last two factors of the system's style: the identification of characteristic 'legal institutions', as well as of the 'choice of sources of law' and the relevant 'methods of interpreting and handling them'. The first factor contributes, for instance, to the identification of the peculiarities of the Germanic family – typically the doctrine of the 'legal act' (*Rechtsgeschäft*) – within the civil law family. The second factor, which includes the characteristics of 'the court machinery and rules of procedure', justifies the traditional way of distinguishing between the Romano-Germanic and the Anglo-American family, focused on the 'supposed opposition between statutory and case-law systems'.[43]

Be that as it may, the analysis of the style of the system makes it possible to develop a critical approach to the study of law, an approach that is not emphasised, and possibly even thwarted, in the studies on the comparative method by Zweigert and Kötz (III.1.3). This applies in particular to the analysis of legal mentality, which makes it possible to shed light on the aspects referred to by the concept of ideology, which has been valorised in the study of legal culture (I.2.6).

The geopolitical significance of the taxonomies proposed after the conclusion of the Second World War was influenced by an internal competition within the civil law family, in particular between French and German law. This is the ultimate meaning of the different classifications proposed by David and by Zweigert and Kötz between the 1950s and the 1970s. The taxonomies that were subsequently elaborated essentially reflect this arrangement, exalting alternatively French or German law. They depart from it, however, when they base their mapping on more innovative criteria, in particular those aimed at relativising state law as a point of reference for classification: we shall see this when dealing with classifications by forms of social control (II.2.6), or by legal traditions or cultural families (II.2.7).

40 P. Ariès, *Storia delle mentalità* (1979), in J. Le Goff (Ed.), *La nuova storia*, Milano, 1983, p. 146.
41 J. Le Goff, *Le mentalità: una storia ambigua*, in Id. and P. Nora (Eds.), *Fare storia* (1974), Torino, 1981, pp. 246 and 254.
42 K. Zweigert and H. Kötz, *An Introduction to Comparative Law* (1969–71), cit., p. 66.
43 *Ivi*, p. 65 f.

This does not detract from the fact that new clashes between systems or families of systems have taken place and are still taking place, faithfully reproduced in the proposed taxonomies which thus retain their geopolitical significance. Those clashes relate above all to a competition between common law and civil law, conducted against the background of the models of capitalism (II.3.4). All this, while laws other than Western law are neglected, or possibly taken into account in order to draw them within the spheres of influence of the two souls of Western law (II.3.1), and thus to enlist them in the clash between models of capitalism.

4 THE TAXONOMIES OF COMPARATIVE PUBLIC LAWYERS: CRITICISM OF THE CRITERIA OF PRIVATE LAWYERS

The principle of relativity warns against the partiality of classifications of legal systems, the outcome of which depends in particular on the spatial-temporal dimension and the sector of the legal system under consideration

The impact of relativity by subject matter can be appreciated especially with reference to the distinction between public and private law. Notoriously, the distinction has an ideological character, or at any rate is historically linked to the intention to emphasise proprietary individualism as the foundation of the economic order, and to use it as a barrier to the spread of holistic paradigms.[44] All this is in accordance with patterns which, on the one hand, allowed the affirmation of bourgeois society and, on the other, were undermined by the transition to industrial society. In the latter, the need to deal with market failures and repress social conflict led to the invasion of the economic sphere by the holistic mechanisms typical of the political sphere (I.2.2).[45] Nevertheless, the training of academic lawyers, including comparative lawyers, is still strongly influenced by the distinction between public and private law, particularly in terms of the topics typically chosen as a point of reference for study and reflection.

In the light of this, it can be said that the taxonomies referred to so far are the obvious fruit of a private law sensibility: while they give more or less weight to other identifying features of the legal systems considered, they end up exalting those relating to the system of legal sources. Everywhere the fundamental distinction is in fact between common law and civil law systems, which presupposes the valorisation of the circumstance that codified law characterises the latter, whereas in the former courts are formal sources of law. This difference, even if its actual scope needs to be reconsidered, is undoubtedly relevant for both public and private law scholars, and yet traditionally is emphasised by the latter: the code *par excellence* is the civil code, in particular the French code.

For comparative public law, the question of classifications has become relevant at a later stage. For a long time, scholars concentrated on deep-rooted differences between the law of different states perceived as insurmountable: commonalities indispensable for the development of taxonomies became impractical.[46] When it became relevant, the question revealed a different sensibility from that typical of scholars of comparative private law. The criticism of classifications derived from a private law perspective is clear-cut, because it serves the

44 For instance, G. Bognetti, *Introduzione al diritto costituzionale comparato*, Torino, 1994, p. 159 ff.

45 More in A. Somma, *Alle radici del diritto privato europeo. Giustizia sociale, solidarietà e conflitto nell'ordine proprietario*, in *Rivista critica del diritto privato*, 2010, p. 39 ff.

46 B. Sordi, *Le strade della comparazione tra pubblico e privato: uno sguardo alle origini*, in *Quaderni fiorentini per la storia del pensiero giuridico moderno*, 2022, p. 18.

purpose of creating inadmissible hierarchies between the two fields of legal knowledge. Per Pizzorusso:

> It should be noted that the idea of limiting the classification to private law seems totally unacceptable. Not only does it negate the usefulness and importance of the results obtained – which should strictly speaking be considered inapplicable to all other branches of law, which now constitute a large majority – but also reflects the antiquated legal conception according to which private law is the real law, while public law and especially constitutional law are something akin to political science or sociology.[47]

Those who favour taxonomies derived from the private law perspective not only imply its superiority to the public law perspective, but also end up fuelling the image of the jurist as technocrat, even if it is largely in crisis (I.1.5). Thus, overlooking the fact that when discussing private law doctrines, it cannot be irrelevant 'whether they are employed, for example, in the context of a democratic regime or an authoritarian regime'.[48]

Others point out that only by overcoming the private law perspective it is possible to grasp the emergence of a 'Western European legal tradition', particularly recognisable by focusing on events of interest to public law scholars: in particular, the development of a liberal constitutionalism, derived from the 'political doctrine according to which (continental) sovereignty is born limited by (Anglo-American) rights'.[49]

Others have emphasised that, over the decades, a 'western concept of legality' has emerged centred on values such as 'political representation' and 'economic freedoms', and that this has further undermined the 'explanatory potential' of the distinction between common law and civil law. All this consolidated by a 'wave of democratisation' that has 'homogenised, at least formally, most legal systems on the demo-liberal model'.[50]

On closer inspection, comparative lawyers with a private law sensibility do not overlook the commonalities between common law and civil law, which are celebrated in the context of reflections on the Western legal tradition (II.3.2). That said, the criticism of the taxonomies of the private lawyers is correct if it aims to show how private lawyers ignore the commonalities emerging from the history of constitutionalism. However, this is not true for analyses devoted to 'liberal democracies', which present 'transversal similarities' that 'overcome and obscure other more radical differences'.[51] Indeed, the debate on constitutionalism as a concept can be criticised for its traditional Western derivation, which, on the one hand, overlooks the differences within the regions where it was conceived, and, on the other hand, fails to take into account points of contact with other regions of the world (II.1.10).

Having said that, there are good reasons to believe that the different ways of regulating the economic order, which are typically attributed to common law and civil law systems, can also be a useful point of view for the scholars of comparative public law. This is particularly the case with regard to aspects such as the way in which the state carries out its tasks of regulating economic life, both when this is a matter of mediated direction, and therefore intended to reproduce the dynamics of the competitive market, and in cases of direct direction, including planning activity.[52]

47 See A. Pizzorusso, *Sistemi giuridici comparati*, 2nd ed., Milano, 1998, p. 173.
48 *Ibid.*
49 M. Barberis, *Europa del diritto*, Bologna, 2008, p. 116.
50 A. Reposo, *Macrofamiglie, sistemi e sottosistemi di produzione del diritto*, in G. Morbidelli et al., *Diritto pubblico comparato*, 4th ed., Torino, 2012, p. 168 f.
51 L. Pegoraro and A. Rinella, *Diritto costituzionale comparato. Aspetti metodologici*, Padova, 2013, 119 f.
52 In this regard, P. Ridola, *Preistoria, origini e vicende del costituzionalismo*, in P. Carrozza, A. Di Giovine and G.F. Ferrari (Eds.), *Diritto costituzionale comparato*, 2nd ed., Roma and Bari, 2014, p. 768 ff.

We will return to this point, in order to verify the possibility of elaborating a taxonomy centred on models of capitalism (II.2.9). For the time being, it is sufficient to point out the considerable relevance in this field of fundamental rights, which is typically studied and stressed by scholars of comparative public law. It is precisely the analysis of the link between models of capitalism and the system of fundamental rights that reveals the regressive tendencies that mainly affect common law systems. It also allows us to explore the transformation that civil law systems are undergoing as a result of the spread of concepts characteristic of the US experience. This transformation is one in which systems that were once attentive to the socialisation of the economy are now inclined to clearly support 'the flexible man's demands for freedom'.[53]

5 NEXT: THE PROPOSED TRADITIONAL CRITERIA

As we know, public comparative law scholars refer to the taxonomies used by private comparative law scholars, whose commitment is acknowledged to be 'absolutely predominant'.[54] That said, the former show a greater awareness than the latter that 'comparison cannot be reduced to sterile lists of historically, politically, economically and socially heterogeneous legal orders'.[55] Public lawyers more than private lawyers then recognise the 'ineluctable variability and incompleteness of the cataloguing' and even more fundamentally that 'the main characteristic and prevailing trend in comparative law is the hybridisation of models',[56] to which we shall return when discussing the limits of taxonomy (II.2.6).

Along with the classifications borrowed from private law scholars, public law scholars add other taxonomies that have long been consolidated and widely used in textbooks on the main topics of public and constitutional law. These include taxonomies relating to the form of state, the form of government, constitutional models, electoral and party systems, constitutional justice, the judiciary, fundamental rights and freedoms, relations between centre and periphery, administrative models, and so on.[57]

Also these classifications can have a strong geopolitical connotation, and a certain ethnocentrism in the choice of parameters for mapping. This is, moreover, inevitable, given that they have largely been chosen to classify Western legal systems and are therefore focused on aspects centred on those systems. All of this reinforced by an evolutionist approach that characterises the taxonomies of public law scholars, also aimed at documenting how Western models are the point of arrival of a development that will sooner or later spread worldwide.

The latter approach is particularly evident in the classification by form of state, which is a Western concept *par excellence*: it identifies the form of political organisation that has arisen in the European region since the 17th century,[58] even if most claim to use it with

53 P. Ridola, *Diritto comparato e diritto costituzionale europeo*, Torino, 2010, pp. 143 and 180.
54 L. Mezzetti, *Tradizioni giuridiche e fonti del diritto*, Torino, 2020, p. 1 ff.
55 G.F. Ferrari, *Civil Law e Common Law*, in P. Carrozza, A. Di Giovine and G.F. Ferrari (Eds.), *Diritto costituzionale comparato*, cit., p. 798.
56 C. Bassu, *Le famiglie giuridiche e le fonti del diritto*, in T.E. Frosini (Ed.), *Diritto pubblico comparato. Le democrazie stabilizzate*, Bologna, 2019, p. 57 ff.
57 For instance, P. Carrozza, A. Di Giovine and G.F. Ferrari (Eds.), *Diritto costituzionale comparato*, cit., p. 804 ff. As well as M. Tushnet, *Advanced Introduction to Comparative Constitutional Law*, 2nd ed., Cheltenham e Nothampton MA, 2018, p. 49 ff. and M.-C. Ponthoreau, *Droit(s) constitutionnel(s) comparé(s)*, 2nd ed., Paris, 2021, p. 482 ff.
58 A. Di Giovine, *Stato e forme di Stato*, in A. Di Giovine et al. (Eds.), *Lezioni di diritto costituzionale comparato*, Milano, 2017, p. 39.

a broader meaning: a meaning that also includes 'the set of rules . . . typical of antiquity and the Middle Ages . . . with reference to which terms such as *polis*, *res publica* and the like are used'.[59]

Indeed, the chronological sequence of the various forms of state shows how, over the centuries, there has been a 'general growth over time of the protection of subjective situations' and, conversely, 'a progressive shift of power from the sovereign to the citizens and their representatives'. The first form is the absolute state, in which 'the power of the prince . . . is depersonalised and concentrated in the hands of the sovereign', who interprets the general interest and aims to realise it through the formation of an embryonic administrative apparatus. This is followed by the police state or enlightened absolutism, which aims to 'pursue the welfare of the population' and implements the first interventions in the economic and social field to this end. It is then the turn of the liberal state, a one-class society and minimal state 'with the aim of guaranteeing the activities of the bourgeoisie', therefore founded on the separation of powers and on the principles of formal equality and legality. The evolution is completed with the multi-class democratic state founded on universal suffrage, whose action is characterised by 'strong interventionism in the economic and social field' in line with the recognition of substantive equality.[60]

One reason that such an evolutionist classification is criticised is because of its misleading unilinear trajectory: the Short 20th Century did not only see the transition from the liberal state to the democratic state, but also and above all the authoritarian state at the basis of the fascist regimes, and the socialist state that arose to prepare the transition that never took place to communism. A further reason to criticise the classification will be considered when dealing with the balance between capitalism and democracy to which neoliberalism refers: it is indifferent to the fate of democracy and admits its compression if necessary to remedy market failures (II.2.9). Here too, as with the authoritarian state and the socialist state, there is an expansion of the prerogatives of those in power and a regression of the prerogatives of those subject to them.

Also problematic is the tendency to reduce the classification of state forms to a contrast between those that 'allow pluralism' and those that 'deny it', mirroring the Kelsenian contrast between 'democracy and autocracy'.[61] In this way, freedom is indeed exalted to the detriment of the promotion of equality, with the risk of reducing democratic and social constitutionalism to an ephemeral affair, if not a mere accident, to be neglected in favour of classifications that elevate the liberal state to a point of arrival in the evolution of forms of government.

As mentioned, evolutionist tendencies are widespread and characterise other classifications of public law scholars, such as the one concerning fundamental rights and freedoms. These are tendencies that also exist in other disciplines, as we can derive from the famous and long-standing view of rights as developing in an incremental process, where social rights mark the final destination of a track that began with the recognition of civil and political rights.[62] Similarly, comparative lawyers adopt the 'generations of rights' discourse: from freedom rights relating to civil or so-called negative freedoms, to political rights concerning participation in political life, to social rights aimed at promoting freedom from want, up to the new generations of rights including privacy, the environment, access to the web, and so on. Even if the most updated among them adopt terms that are hardly compatible with evolutionism: they

59 A. Pizzorusso, *Sistemi giuridici comparati*, cit., p. 181.
60 L. Cuocolo, *Le forme di Stato*, in T.E. Frosini (Ed.), *Diritto pubblico comparato*, cit., p. 95 ff.
61 G. De Vergottini, *Diritto costituzionale comparato*, 11th ed., Milano, 2022, pp. 147 and 167.
62 Following T.H. Marshall, *Citizenship and Social Class*, Cambridge, 1950.

observe that the development of rights in the global context highlights 'at the judicial level . . . the absence of instruments' of protection and 'at the political level . . . their scarce influence'.[63]

But let us return to the classification by forms of state in order to consider attempts to remedy the shortcomings we have mentioned, and in particular its ethnocentric connotation. It should be noted that this cannot be overcome by resorting to an overly broad concept of the state, as this would end up including too many experiences and, in the end, produce classifications of little scientific value. Hence, the proposal to include situations where there is 'a recognised centre of power, a complex organisation, both military and bureaucratic, and an effective fiscal system'. As Pegoraro and Rinella state:

> The generic term 'state' then means . . . an enduring juridical-political community of supra-local extension, with a minimum population density and some degree of complexity of social organisation, which coordinates human coexistence internally through law and justice and externally provides military and diplomatic protection.[64]

In this way it is also possible to include in the comparative lawyers' classifications 'historical forms of state outside the West' that 'present the substantial Westphalian characteristics of the European-style state' such as those we find in some pre-Columbian Latin American or Chinese societies since 1600 BC.[65] This finally removes from the West the exclusivity of a form of social organisation which, on closer inspection, can be found in other parts of the planet, possibly in earlier periods than follow the Westphalian paradigm. Equally useful and opportune are analyses of forms of state capable of going beyond the mere appearance of labels imposed by the West on social organisations that have developed outside its borders, perhaps as a result of the so-called exportation of democracy. In order to do this, it is necessary to equip oneself with the tools made available by the study of legal pluralism, with which to enhance substantive elements beyond the internal point of view on law (I.2.3), as well as those relating to the study of legal mutation, which are useful for critically analysing the spread of legal models and its dynamics (II.1.2).

6 THE LIMITS OF TAXONOMY

We know that comparative law scholars understand the concept of legal system in a different sense from that of followers of legal positivism: they redefine it in terms in line with an external viewpoint on law (I.2.4). In this sense, we can conclude that the classification into families of systems does not constitute a practice that re-proposes paradigms that are now discredited.

Nevertheless, it cannot be said that classifications by families portray legal systems in a way which brings their identities to the fore. Those portraits are necessarily the product of an integrative comparison, which aims to highlight commonalities: a classification that, in order to highlight the identity of systems, would find a particularly large number of families would not be useful.[66] The reason that grouping by families is so widespread among comparative lawyers, even if that eventually produces trivializations, is largely because it is considered an irreplaceable didactic tool.[67] It is, moreover, an indispensable point of reference for micro-

63 A. Algostino, *Diritti*, in A. Di Giovine et al. (Eds.), *Lezioni di diritto costituzionale comparato*, cit., pp. 113 ff. and 123.

64 L. Pegoraro and A. Rinella, *Sistemi costituzionali*, 2nd ed., Torino, 2024, p. 39 quoting Bernd Marquardt.

65 *Ivi*, p. 38 ff.

66 See M. Rheinstein, *Einführung in die Rechtsvergleichung*, 2nd ed., München, 1987, p. 82.

67 In particular, E. Agostini, *Droit comparé*, Paris, 1988, p. 25 and H. Kötz, *Abschied von der Rechtskreislehre?*, in *Zeitschrift für Europäisches Privatrecht*, 1998, p. 493 ff.

comparison: without reference to families of systems, the comparison of individual legal doctrines would be an extremely complex and possibly impracticable exercise.[68] Comparative lawyers thus also recognise that, as a founding aspect of all sciences, 'knowledge implies ordering the manifestations of reality by comparing and grouping them'.[69]

The legislator can also profit from the classification. On its basis, it can identify the legal systems that share the same basic characteristics, and thus those that can be open to 'reciprocal influences'.[70] Similar systems, in other words, are those to which one may turn to look for models to import or from which one could draw inspiration. As we shall see better, however, such a point of view indicates a formalist view of legal change, ultimately disregarding the foundations of comparative research (III.1.3).

As we know, the mapping proposed by Zweigert and Kötz was particularly successful (II.2.3). It has been used and re-proposed by quite a few scholars despite the fact that it was not updated at the end of the Cold War. The collapse of the Soviet bloc was simply followed by the deletion of the part of their textbook devoted to the relevant family of systems, which made it possible to 'save sixty pages'.[71] David's classification proposal (II.2.1), updated to consider the post-Soviet Russian legal system, only cautiously placed side by side with the Romano-Germanic family, is also particularly popular. In that system, as we will show in more detail (II.3.7), socialist conceptions of law would persist, at the very least at the level of mentality, and strong influences of the common law model would also manifest themselves, particularly in the banking and financial sectors.[72]

On closer inspection, David's classification is still celebrated but also questioned, above all in order to stigmatise the heterogeneous character of the Romano-Germanic family, and ultimately its inability to represent the identity of legal systems other than those linked to the French one. In a certain sense, this is the approach adopted by the most widely read textbooks in Italy, where there is a lamentable lack of consideration for the peculiarities of German law and the law of the Scandinavian countries, to which we will turn shortly (II.3.10). In addition, there are also accusations of ethnocentrism because of the lack of treatment of Latin American law[73]: we will go also into this aspect in more detail later (II.3.6).

Both David's and Zweigert and Kötz's classifications because they exemplify a private law perspective, are criticised by comparative lawyers and by those interested in shedding light on the foundations of continental European or, more generally, Western law. Yet these classifications are not rejected by textbooks, which, on the contrary, take them into consideration on the basis of what Zweigert had mentioned in an essay a few years earlier.[74] A notable example is the taxonomy of Swede Ake Malmström, who at the end of the 1960s identified four main groups of systems: a Western group, a non-communist Asian group, an African group, and a socialist group. The Western group, however, was not described in predominantly unifying terms, as in David, but according to criteria similar to those proposed by Zweigert and Kötz:

68 M. Siems, *Comparative Law*, cit., p. 48 and G. Samuel, *An Introduction to Comparative Law Theory and Method*, cit., p. 50.
69 G. Cuniberti, *Grands systèmes de droit contemporains. Introduction au droit comparé*, 4th ed., Paris, 2019, p. 22.
70 M. Fromont, *Grands systèmes de droit étrangers*, 3rd ed., Paris, 1998, p. 5.
71 K. Zweigert and H. Kötz, *Einführung in die Rechtsvergleichung*, 3rd ed., Tübingen, 1996, p. v. See also Iid., *An Introduction to Comparative Law* (1996), 3rd ed., Oxford, 1998, p. v.
72 R. David and C. Jauffret Spinosi, *Les grands systèmes de droit contemporains*, 11th ed., Paris, 2002, pp. 19 f. and 125 ff.
73 A. Gambaro, R. Sacco and M. Graziadei, *Sistemi giuridici comparati*, 5th ed., in *Trattato di diritto comparato*, dir. R. Sacco, Torino, 2024, p. 15.
74 K. Zweigert, *Zur Lehre von den Rechtskreisen*, in K.H. Nadelmann, A.T. von. Mehren and J.N. Hazard (Eds.), *Twentieth Century Comparative and Conflicts Law. Legal Essays in Honor of Hessel Yntema*, Leiden, 1961, p. 24 ff.

it comprised a continental European family, a Latin American family, a Scandinavian family, and a common law family.[75]

On the whole, however, among public comparative lawyers a distrust of the classifications in use among private lawyers seems to prevail. These may also be discussed in general terms, and yet the focus is on taxonomies tailored to the specific aspect considered by comparative public law (II.2.5). By considering and combining the results obtained in these areas, it will be possible to elaborate 'multi-layered classifications', or alternatively to identify 'systems' and 'subsystems', all the while avoiding the simplifications that could conceal the specific features of the experiences classified.[76]

It should be noted that such an approach is also successful among private comparative lawyers, who indeed consider it a point of reference for developments in the discipline. Its future could include analyses 'oriented towards themes and problems underlying every legal experience'. As Moccia states:

> The scenario of a possible new epistemological statute of the comparative study of law opens up to view here. As a study no longer tied to the territorial dimension of the boundaries of the legal world map, within which to place this or that system . . . according to a dichotomous logic of oppositional distinction (aut aut), that is, of classification of individual systems or groups of systems identified as belonging to this or that legal family. . . . But instead addressed to the spatial dimension of forms of rationality expressing ways of thinking about law in relation to fundamental questions of (every) legal experience.[77]

But let us return to the accusation of ethnocentrism levelled at David's classification. On closer inspection, this critique can be addressed to many other classifications by families of systems, and probably at classifications *tout court*. The latter, indeed, often seem the typical product of a discipline unable to renew itself, as well as the product of a markedly Western and continental European approach, 'dominated by abstraction and the spirit of the system'.[78]

Some call, therefore, for the abandonment of taxonomies, which, they say, are instruments irremediably affected by methodological flaws (II.2.12). Others see this solution as too drastic and prefer the elaboration of new classifications designed to highlight the identity of certain systems traditionally placed in a subordinate position, such as Latin American ones. This is what has been done by Martínez Paz's classification (II.2.1), and the sense of a more recent taxonomy identifying a South American law, a continental European law and a customary law, the latter including the English and African experiences (II.3.8).[79]

If the classifications express for the most part an ethnocentric approach, it is often due to the fact that, although comparisons have an encyclopaedic vocation, non-Western laws are often little known and difficult to know by Western scholars, not least because of language barriers (II.3.1). This, at any rate, does not exclude other explanations, such as a Western inclination to classify the other, sooner or later destined to produce rankings aimed at demonstrating its inferiority. This evidently stems from the consideration of Western development as development as such, considered a universal measure from the point of view of evolution, even if it is based on the specific characteristics of a well-defined, and ultimately limited, part of the planet.

75 A. Malmström, *The System of Legal Systems*, in *Scandinavian Studies in Law*, 1969, p. 127 ff.
76 Cfr. A. Pizzorusso, *Sistemi giuridici comparati*, cit., p. 175 f. and L. Pegoraro and A. Rinella, *Introduzione al diritto pubblico comparato*, cit., p. 54 ff.
77 L. Moccia, *Comparazione giuridica come modo di studio e conoscenza del diritto*, in *Rivista trimestrale di diritto e procedura civile*, 2020, p. 22.
78 G. Cuniberti, *Grands systèmes de droit contemporains*, cit., p. 26.
79 M.G. Losano, *I grandi sistemi giuridici*, Roma and Bari, 2000, pp. 175 ff. and 257 ff.

If we then consider the expression 'family of systems' we see that it not only has an inherently ethnocentric connotation, but is also directly designed to evoke and reproduce an internal order within the same grouping. In fact, the concept of the family refers to a hierarchical and organicist conception of community, which recalls the existence of intangible relations of subordination justified by their functional dependence. Indeed, the concept has been used by linguistics since the 19th century as a means of classifying data obtained through the comparison of languages, at that time conceived as an attempt to reconstruct the protolanguage common to Indo-European languages (IV.1.1). In other words, and once again, to establish and naturalise relations between a centre and a periphery.

The same applies to the expression most frequently used by German jurisprudents: *Rechtskreis*, literally 'legal circle'. It was derived from the concept, elaborated in the field of ethnography, of *Kulturkreis*, i.e. 'cultural circle', and is therefore intended to indicate a greater focus on the extra-legal dimension.[80] The scholarship that coined the latter concept, however, shows embarrassing links with Nazism. And even if we want to disregard this aspect, which in truth is hardly negligible, we cannot ignore the fact that the cultural circle is used in an exclusionary sense, i.e. to delimit one culture from the others and prevent its contamination. This, among other things, can be seen in the use of the concept in the well-known and controversial study of the so-called 'clash of civilisations'.[81]

Nor can we overlook that *Rechtskreis* alludes to a centre from which a culture, or a law, radiates, and a periphery that has more or less voluntarily received it, in the context of an inevitably hierarchical relationship.

7 BEYOND FAMILIES OF SYSTEMS: FORMS OF SOCIAL CONTROL

Even if references to systems and families of systems do not imply an internal point of view on law, groupings based on those concepts can hardly avoid references to the state.[82] This constitutes further evidence of more or less explicit and conscious ethnocentric character of classifications by families of systems: in this context the state is conceived as a 'rational' political body, as such 'ideally expressed in universal terms' and incapable to 'tolerate the possibility of other systems within itself'.[83]

An initial attempt to go beyond this approach came from the Romanian comparative lawyer Léontine-Jean Constantinesco, who turned his gaze beyond 'modern' societies in order to identify classification criteria that would be usefully applicable to 'traditional' and 'primitive' societies. He described traditional societies as societies 'belonging to ancient cultures that still exist today', while primitive societies were defined as contemporary societies that 'ignore writing and history'. In order to obtain classifications that are suitable for traditional and primitive societies, it is necessary to start from the values at the basis of societies as such, which must be analysed taking into account their pre-existence with respect to the possible development of legal systems called upon to recognise and protect them. And eventually called upon to conceal these basic values, as shown by the fact that in traditional

80 In particular U. Kischel, *Rechtsvergleichung*, München, 2015, p. 221.
81 S.P. Huntington, *The Clash of Civilizations and the Remaking of World Order*, New York NY, 1996.
82 See M. Carducci, *Ragione politica della comparazione e costituzionalizzazione delle tassonomie*, in *Diritto pubblico comparato ed europeo*, 2017, p. 1113 ff.
83 H.P. Glenn, *Legal Traditions of the World*, 5th ed., Oxford, 2014, p. 54 f.

and primitive societies the 'fundamental choices' and 'aims' are more recognisable than in modern societies.[84]

In short, the classification of legal systems must emphasise the fact that they belong to the same 'civilisation', identifying the same 'lifestyle', the same 'teleological ethical context' and the same 'material environment'. And it must bring out the link between the type of civilisation and the law reconstructed in its 'determining elements'. This allows to go beyond statehood and nationality, which Constantinesco sees as the result of a historical era abruptly interrupted by the horrors of the Second World War. However, it does not allow to overcome a hierarchical view of the relationships within each grouping, which is evident in the use of the terms 'legal circle' and 'cultural circle'.[85]

A different attempt to create classifications not tainted by ethnocentric approaches, explicitly presented in these terms, can be attributed to Jacques Vanderlinden, a Belgian comparatist, who not by chance was also a scholar of legal anthropology. Starting from a notion of legal system freed from the requirement of statehood, Vanderlinden proposed to group laws on the basis of the 'dominant source', namely, the prevailing 'mode of formulation of law', and to focus only at a later stage on events such as 'ideology or technique'. In this way, one can distinguish four systems: a 'customary system' generated by the behaviour of members of society, a 'doctrinal system' centred on the rules produced by the scholars, a 'jurisprudential system' based on the precepts of judges, a 'legislative system' based on the commands formulated at the top, and a 'revelatory system' linked to a deity.[86]

Vanderlinden's taxonomy puts the nature of statehood into perspective insofar as it allows for polythetic classifications (II.2.10), i.e. the possibility of placing the various national orders within several groupings. They are therefore ideal models rather than boxes into which these legal orders fit exclusively and definitively. All these revealing features that are otherwise overlooked by prescriptive accounts, those which consider only the formal sources of law and conceal legal pluralism.

Ugo Mattei and Pier Giuseppe Monateri's proposed classification also aims to emphasise legal pluralism and to relativise the state in a similar way. They group legal experiences on the basis of the instruments used to organise coexistence: to exercise 'social control', as anthropologists would say, or to promote 'social incentive', in the words of economists. In each national legal system, it will be possible to identify a hegemonic instrument, the use of which will determine the residual character of the other instruments, without however condemning them to irrelevance. It should be noted that, from a Western point of view, only one of the instruments would have a normative character. However, in order to underline their preference for an understanding of law that emphasises the subversive function of comparison, the two scholars stress that the instruments of social control identified 'are all endowed with the requisite of legality in the taxonomical sense'.[87]

The first instrument of social control considered is law, secularised and clearly distinct from politics, which as such identifies the Western legal tradition (II.3). This instrument is typical of the 'professional hegemony family', i.e. continental European and Anglo-American law, regardless of the distinction between common law and civil law. This distinction is relativised, but also invoked to discuss a kind of superiority of the Anglo-American model. The latter is 'leading' insofar as it has affirmed the subordination of political power to the law since the time of Edward Coke (II.3.2). Common to both poles of Western law, however, is the

84 L.-J. Constantinesco, *Traité de droit comparé*, vol. 3, Paris, 1983, p. 435 ff.
85 *Ivi*, p. 456 ff.
86 J. Vanderlinden, *Comparer les droits*, Diegem, 1995, p. 334 ff.
87 U. Mattei and P.G. Monateri, *Introduzione breve al diritto comparato*, Padova, 1997, p. 61.

distinction between law and religion, and even between law and morality, dating back at least to the early Middle Ages.[88]

Let us now consider the former socialist countries of Eastern Europe, Africa, and Latin America, classified on the basis of elements which, as Mattei and Monateri warn, show a strongly evolving picture. These countries are traced back to the 'political hegemony family', as politics does not appear differentiated from law as an instrument of social control. As Mattei and Monateri state:

> Our second family, which marks another cardinal point, contains all the systems in which the political and legal moments are not separated, in the sense that the two circuits have not carved out autonomous spheres of competence. The Western observer might say that there is no legalisation of the political moment, but rather a politicisation of the legal moment. . . . In these systems, institutional solutions tend to be centralised according to a model of direct regulation determined by a political will that does not tolerate competition from other decentralised models of institutional choice. The countries belonging to this family appear bent on achieving a political objective, seen as a good in itself, to the attainment of which law is functionalised (e.g. food self-sufficiency, market economy, communism).[89]

The situation is different in Muslim, Hindu, and Far Eastern countries such as China and Japan, which make up the 'traditional hegemony family'. Here, religious or philosophical tradition, rather than law or politics, is used to regulate social coexistence. In Mattei and Monateri's words:

> In these systems, alongside the technical juridical social organisation (the law of the professional jurists, in other words) there is a very important sphere of legal relations that are governed by rules of a different nature. Strictly religious rules in Muslim systems and traditional rules with a philosophical origin in Far Eastern systems. The jurists' law itself (the westernised one) ends up being impregnated and largely conditioned by the presence and social force of this alternative circuit.[90]

The taxonomy centred on systems of social control or incentive makes it possible to place a national system in one group, while at the same time highlighting the presence of characteristics typical of another group. This leads to the admission of polythetic classifications, just as in the case of the classification that emphasises the mode of legal production.

8 NEXT: LEGAL TRADITIONS AND CULTURAL FAMILIES

Although Mattei and Monateri intend to present their taxonomy as immune to an ethnocentric bias, as do comparative public lawyers using this taxonomy,[91] it cannot be denied that it is conditioned by that bias. The identification of the Western legal tradition as being founded on the divorce between law on the one hand and religion and politics on the other is indeed the pivot around which the strategies of self-representation and reproduction of that tradition revolve. Organising the classification of legal experiences on the basis of those concepts, then, means observing non-Western laws through Western lenses, thus producing inevitably

88 *Ivi*, p. 66 ff.
89 *Ivi*, p. 71.
90 *Ivi*, p. 70 ff. Also U. Mattei, *Three Patterns of Law. Taxonomy and Change in the World's Legal Systems*, in *American Journal of Comparative Law*, 45, 1997, p. 5 ff.
91 G.F. Ferrari, *Civil Law e Common Law*, cit., p. 779 f.

partial analyses. We will return to this point when discussing the Western legal tradition and its cultural foundations (II.3.2).

It should also be noted that Mattei and Monateri, who also state that 'all legal systems must be considered equally important, regardless of the hegemonic model within them', end up fostering an evolutionist approach when they stigmatise systems in which the 'political layer' is 'particularly conspicuous'. The law of those systems is in fact regarded as 'developmental and transitional law', which is why they seem to 'have inherent in them a kind of transitional nature'.[92] This presupposes that they are destined sooner or later to become professional hegemony systems, and in this sense to follow a line of progress along Western lines.

Finally, if one regards legal discourse as a technique to enhance values (I.2.1), the distinction between law, politics, and tradition loses its meaning. It becomes a distinction centred on the rhetorical strategies of power legitimisation rather than on the aims pursued through those strategies. And a taxonomy which avoids reflection on the connection to power legitimation ends up inexorably feeding an internal point of view on law.

In short, even if a classification appears remarkable insofar as it avoids references to the legal system or order, showing the intention to reject approaches which are incompatible with the subversive aspiration of comparative law (I.1.1), it is not safe from criticism. Nor is it safe from the temptation to create a geopolitics that elevates Western law and, conversely, denigrates non-Western laws or those that lack the characteristics considered typical of the former.

An attempt to elaborate a taxonomy that is not reproductive of ethnocentric schemes, and thus resistant to geopolitical tendencies such as those just denounced, derives from classifications that focus on legal tradition. This is a concept that, as we know, is disassociated from the state dimension, and which aims to observe the law by emphasising its interaction with society and politics (I.2.4). Additionally, those who base their taxonomy on legal tradition also want to take into account the criticism of taxonomies as such.

A number of scholars use legal tradition as a point of taxonomical reference even if they often end up devising groupings that are sometimes the same as those to which the families of systems refer. Head, for instance, considers that there are three 'great traditions', namely, the common law, the civil law, and the Chinese tradition, and some 'minor' ones, i.e. the socialist, Islamic, Jewish, and indigenous traditions.[93] Mousourakis, by contrast, identifies traditions from their intertwining with external legal culture (I.2.6), which leads to the identification of African, Asian, Islamic, and Western traditions.[94]

The preference of comparative public lawyers for taxonomies centred on the legal tradition should also be emphasised. They also take into consideration the 'classificatory categories proper to comparative public law' – for example, when they refer to the 'fundamental ideology', which implies a reference to the form of state understood in its essence as 'a set of principles, values, fundamental goods, and rights that a single constitutional system assumes as the load-bearing axis around which its own continuity and perpetuation over time is expressed'.[95]

Particularly successful is the taxonomy proposed by the Canadian scholar Patrick Glenn, whose reflections on the concept of legal tradition we have already illustrated. This concept is explicitly used to draft maps and not hierarchies, as well as to dissociate the former from references to statehood. For Glenn, there may be a territorial rootedness of complex traditions, but

92 U. Mattei and P.G. Monateri, *Introduzione breve al diritto comparato*, cit., pp. 62 and 71 ff.
93 J.W. Head, *Great Legal Traditions. Civil Law, Common Law, and Chinese Law in Historical and Operational Perspective*, Durham NC, 2011, p. 18 ff.
94 G. Mousourakis, *Comparative Law and Legal Traditions. Historical and Contemporary Perspectives*, Cham, 2019, p. 153 ff.
95 L. Mezzetti, *Tradizioni giuridiche e fonti del diritto*, cit., p. 34.

these may include internal traditions, and they may also be crossed by transversal traditions (I.2.4). This is done in order to produce polythetic classifications (II.2.10), demonstrating a desire to draw on legal tradition in order to move beyond classificatory criteria centred on the exclusivity of framing.

Glenn distinguishes seven legal traditions: chthonic, Talmudic, civil law, Islamic, common law, Hindu, and Confucian. Almost all of them indicate groupings taken into account by other classifications. The identification of the Jewish tradition as an autonomous experience, as well as the separate treatment devoted to the chthonic tradition, is a novelty compared to traditional taxonomies, though not necessarily to those centred on legal tradition. The chthonic tradition is the primordial legal tradition, which 'simply emerged, as experience grew, and orality and memory did their work'. Despite the variety of 'chthonic people', one can indeed identify common features in their legal traditions. In addition to informality in enunciating law and implementing it, common features include the inseparable link between law and the community's belief system, and the holistic striving for harmony in internal relations and with the order of nature.[96] This is not much different from a pre-modern, and more precisely medieval, Western law model, the era in which 'political power seems to renounce its ordering task in the legal dimension' and 'the sphere of the legal and the factual tend to merge'.[97]

In short, chthonic law is 'mixed in with other important messages', all aimed at emphasising its otherness from Western law, with its claim to be dissociated from politics and tradition. If Western law, as the law of modernity, is highly individualised and founded on the concept of subjective right, chthonic law conceives of the individual only as 'submerged in the past and the wider community', which is why 'an individual power – or *potestas* – to obtain the object of the individual will' is not conceivable. Neither is a concept of individual rights or interests conceivable; on the contrary, tradition 'stands four-square against it, on all fronts'.[98]

It must be said at this point that the traditions identified by Glenn, which 'appear presently as the major ones in the world', do not claim to exhaust the spectrum of traditions of the world. The proposed model is, moreover, the result of choices because the 'recognition of any legal tradition thus involves choice' and is inevitably affected by the limits imposed by available knowledge: 'it may be . . . that there are other legal traditions – of thought, of expression, or of sources – which are still more profound and which await investigation, and recognition, as being of primary importance'.[99]

These clarifications help to introduce the cultural aims of Glenn's taxonomy, which are declaredly opposed to those of classifications that more or less explicitly aim to establish hierarchies between families of systems and, within them, between systems.

By discussing the chthonic tradition, the Canadian comparative lawyer has first and foremost contributed to the promotion of legal pluralism, understood as the rediscovery of legal stratifications beyond the context of societies affected by rapid legal change, which is the usual context in which it is studied (I.2.3). In fact, Glenn emphasises that the chthonic tradition operates in all societies, even in those brought under the category of the so-called developed countries. Moreover, he intends to go beyond the evolutionist point of view and thus promote pluralism as such. His intention is 'reconciling legal traditions', or at least promoting the development of mutual relations in a climate of 'sustainable legal diversity'.[100]

96 H.P. Glenn, *Legal Traditions of the World*, cit., p. 62 ff.
97 P. Grossi, *L'ordine giuridico medievale*, Roma and Bari, 1997, p. 57.
98 H.P. Glenn, *Legal Traditions of the World*, cit., p. 72 ff.
99 *Ivi*, p. 361 f.
100 *Ivi*, pp. 365 ff.

The current historical phase, however, seems to lead in the exact opposite direction, and this can be deduced by considering the most recent studies of comparative economics. These can, moreover, draw on much of the comparative law literature that, as we have seen, more or less explicitly reproduces ethnocentric schemes.

Before we deal with this it is necessary to refer to the concept of 'cultural family', which in many ways overlaps with that of legal tradition. This concept derives from sociology and anthropology, where it highlights fundamental oppositions, such as that between rationalism and irrationalism, or between individualism and collectivism. Hence, the identification of four cultural families: one 'western' individualist and rationalist and three 'non-Western', namely, African, Asian, and Islamic, perceived as collectivist and irrational. The latter are, however, considered as such because they do not recognise a distinction between law on the one hand and morality and religion on the other.[101] That leads therefore to the classification being seen a projection or self-representation of Western law rather a genuine attempt to identify the characteristics of non-Western laws.

We will have the opportunity to explore this aspect in more detail (II.3.2). For now, it is enough to stress how pervasive the geopolitical significance of classifications is: a tendency that is almost impossible to resist. This constitutes further confirmation that comparative law discourse, insofar as it aims to understand and not also to explain, unlike the discourse of the natural sciences (I.1.4), is ultimately the victim of an irrepressible partiality.

9 MODELS OF CAPITALISM: RHINE AND NEO-AMERICAN

For a long time, comparative economics was focused on comparing radically alternative models, analysing in particular the differences between capitalism and socialism: the first being centred on private property and free competition, and the latter associated with public ownership of the means of production and economic planning. The collapse of the Soviet bloc and the end of the Cold War, perceived by many as the irreversible victory of capitalism and in this sense the end of history (II.2.2), prompted a comparison of its different historical realisations,[102] including those resulting from a mixture of Western economic models and alternative Western cultural traditions.[103]

While comparative economics had previously aimed to demonstrate the superiority of capitalism over socialism, especially with regard to imperfect forms of the former capable of leading to a transition to the latter, it now wanted to identify which model of capitalism could provide the best performance. The ideological clash was over and reflection focused on technocratic aspects: those concerning the optimal level of state intervention in the economy, or the ideal system of industrial relations, or the best performing type of welfare. Hence, the intertwining of the study of models of capitalism and the classification of legal systems, which were recognised at this point as having the capacity to shape the economic order. This intertwining has been emphasised since the 1960s by the New Institutional Economics, and more recently by the New Comparative Economics.

We will shortly deal with the research carried out within the framework of these currents of thought (II.3.3), and more fundamentally, with the method used to produce the

101 For instance. M. Van Hoecke and M. Warrington, *Legal Cultures, Legal Paradigms and Legal Doctrine: Towards a New Model for Comparative Law*, in *International and Comparative Law Quarterly*, 47, 1998, p. 502 ff.

102 For instance, P.J. Boettke et al., *The New Comparative Political Economy*, in *Review of Austrian Economics*, 18, 2005, p. 281 ff.

103 See J.B. Rosser jr. and M.V. Rosser, *Comparative Economics in a Transforming World Economy*, 3rd ed., Cambridge Ma, 2018.

measurements from which the best model of capitalism is identified (III.1.4). It is first necessary to describe the models of capitalism identified by comparative economics, and to highlight the systems of legal and social norms that constitute their backbone.

The era in which the comparison between capitalisms develops follows the overthrow of the Keynesian compromise that formed the basis of the so-called Glorious Thirties[104]: the period between the end of the Second World War and the mid-'70s in which public intervention in the economy, aimed at full employment and the redistribution of wealth, was pursued. This overthrow allowed the emergence of neoliberalism, whose theoretical elaboration had actually been worked as early as the late 1930s. Neoliberalism, from the outset, was conceived as a creed according to which the state must intervene in the economy not to socialise it, namely, to promote emancipation against the functioning of the market, but to impose the functioning of the market on society: to transform its economic laws into laws of the state and in this sense use competition as an instrument of political steering of individual behaviour. The idea was also to reduce social inclusion to inclusion in the market, by which the sole criterion for the redistribution of wealth becomes the market mechanism.[105]

In other words, the variety of models of capitalism emerges in the form of the clash between Keynesianism and neoliberalism. This clash concerns larger issues than those considered by comparative law taxonomies,[106] and yet it allows the nexus between economic and legal models to emerge in the context of the transformations characterising the Western legal tradition (II.4.4 ff.).

The first taxonomy to which we should refer is that proposed by Michel Albert, a French economist with a Catholic background, who in a research paper published in the early 1990s contrasted 'neo-American capitalism' with 'Rhine capitalism'.

The former asserted itself in the United Kingdom and the United States through Margaret Thatcher and Ronald Reagan, who initiated the reaction to the Keynesian compromise that had long characterised the economic policies of both countries. The Keynesian compromise was to be combated with a renewed faith in the market's ability to regulate itself, which supposes a conflictual vision of social relations and their reduction to economic relations. That vision also affects the conception of the company to which the sole aim of maximise shareholder profits is attributed, with labour relations reduced to mere market relations, thus tending towards worker flexibility and precarity.[107]

It is also typical of neo-American capitalism to consider social security as an incentive to inactivity and thus unproductivity. In this vision, poverty and unemployment are the typical condition of individuals who 'lack the drive and determination to adapt to the requirements of the labour market'. This is why neo-American capitalism contemplates a reduced tax burden as a redistributive instrument, while entrusting social security to the market and promoting the privatisation of goods such as health or education. The aversion to redistributive measures also inspires wage policies, which fastens to the principle that there must be a clear differentiation. This has, among other things, the function of stimulating self-sacrifice in labour activity: 'individuals are to be paid individually, according to output'.[108]

104 See J. Fourastié, *Les Trente glorieuses ou la révolution invisible de 1946 à 1975*, Paris, 1979.
105 A. Somma, *Diritto e capitalismo. Leggi dello Stato e leggi del mercato nella costruzione della soggettività neoliberale*, in M.G. Bernardini and O. Giolo (Eds.), *Teorie critiche del diritto*, Pisa, 2017, p. 295 ff.
106 In addition to the books mentioned in the following pages, see R. Dore, *Stock Market Capitalism Welfare Capitalism. Japan and Germany versus the Anglo-Saxons*, Oxford, 2000; G. Esping-Andersen, *The Three Worlds of Welfare Capitalism*, Princeton NJ, 1990; D. Coates, *Models of Capitalism. Growth and Stagnation in the Modern Era*, Cambridge and Malden MA, 2000 and M. Regini, *Modelli di capitalismo. Le risposte europee alla sfida della globalizzazione*, Roma and Bari, 2000.
107 M. Albert, *Capitalism against Capitalism*, London, 1993, p. 20 ff.
108 *Ivi*, p. 7 and 8.

Finally, it is typical of neo-American capitalism, centred as it is on the figure of the shareholder, to elevate the stock market as the main channel for financing companies, thus stimulating a relentless financialisation of the economy.[109]

Opposite to neo-American capitalism is the so-called Rhine capitalism, realised in Germany, which is in some respects similar to that typical of other Northern European countries and Japan. This variety of capitalism encompasses a vision of firms as complex communities in need of harmony, just like the state community as a whole, and therefore governed through a vast network of neo-corporative structures. A vision somewhat connected to the circumstance that banks, and not the stock exchange, are the main channel of corporate financing. As Albert states:

> The map of the different realms of power and authority within the modern capitalist company is still being drawn, and on it depends the nature of the capitalist enterprise itself. Are companies to be bought and sold by their owners (the shareholders) like any other commodity or merchandise? That is the Anglo-American view; but according to others the company is in fact a community, a complex organism in which the prerogatives of the shareholders must be balanced with those of management – who in turn are more or less co-opted by the banks and (implicitly, at least) by employees. This power-sharing model – held together with the glue of consensus – is characteristic of the German and Japanese approach to company organisation. . . .
>
> As important company shareholders, banks enjoy a privileged status and their views are listened to, on at least two accounts: first, through direct ownership of a portion of the capital; and, secondly, through voting rights exercised on behalf of shareholders who bank with them. . . . Conversely, the banks' largest single shareholders tend to be these same industrial groups. . . . This interpenetration of banking and business interests forms the warp and weft of an industrial-financial fabric which is both stable and highly resistant to outside factors.[110]

This kind of entrepreneurial communitarianism reverberates in the organisation of work, which is centred on stable and lasting contractual relations, and which above all is not bent to the desire to maximise shareholder profit. Typical of Rhine capitalism is then the cooperative resolution of conflicts between employers and workers, and a management of the firm that includes the participation of the latter: the shareholders are not the lords of the enterprise; rather, the fate of the company is decided by involving all its components, and in part the social community in which the firm operates.[111] Finally, the particular extension of the state and social security provided by Rhine capitalism also fulfils the function of inducing cooperation, as well as social harmony in general. It is, in fact, characterised by high pension and health expenditure, financed by an equally high tax burden, as well as a limited privatisation of goods that serve to satisfy social rights.[112]

More broadly, neo-American and Rhine capitalism can then be differentiated by taking into account their relationship with democracy.

Neo-American capitalism is inspired by neoliberalism, i.e. a theory and practice aimed at imposing the functioning of the market. Prominent in neoliberal thought is the suggestion that economic power must be scattered, as its concentration represents an obstacle to competition and more precisely to competition's role as an instrument for steering the conduct of citizens: if individuals are let alone in the market, they are inevitably doomed to react automatically to

109 *Ivi*, p. 62 ff.
110 *Ivi*, pp. 12 and 107 f.
111 A. Somma, *Giustizia o pacificazione sociale? La codeterminazione nello scontro tra modelli di capitalismo*, in *Politica del diritto*, 2015, p. 549 ff.
112 M. Albert, *Capitalism against capitalism*, cit., pp. 114 ff. and 150 ff.

its stimuli.[113] The economic power to be scattered is not only that of the enterprises, but also that of the workers, who are thus hindered in the exercise of their collective rights. By joining forces, indeed, workers can impose a price for their performance that differs from that resulting from the free encounter of labour supply and demand. More generally, neoliberalism entrusts the state with the task of acting as a 'market police',[114] which thus shows indifference towards the fate of democracy. If its compression and even extinction is necessary to support competition, as was the case with fascism (II.1.3), then this is accepted.

The balance between capitalism and democracy envisaged by Rhine capitalism is different. This is because the Keynesian compromise, when promoting full and good employment, produces an increase of labour power. Moreover, Rhine capitalism is inscribed within an architecture that is in every way similar to that of democratic and social constitutionalism (I.2.1), not least because of their common attention to social rights and welfare in its essence as an indirect wage. Moreover, while this model of capitalism also aims to contain conflict, it does not achieve such an objective by deleting workers' economic power. On the contrary, it recognises the need to consolidate it in order to make it a countervailing power capable of confronting capital, according to a sensibility which is also shared with democratic and social constitutionalism.[115]

The distinction between neo-American capitalism and Rhine capitalism presents analogies with the distinction, formulated in the same period, between 'liberal market economies' and 'coordinated market economies'. Here, too, attention is focused on the conflictual or cooperative character of the relations between companies and workers, thus again contrasting the solutions adopted in the United States with those typical of the German context. Coordinated market economies, in fact, are such insofar as state authorities have nurtured the construction of neo-corporative structures for solving problems between workers and companies, and perhaps for the definition and implementation of social policies in general. In liberal market economies, on the other hand, firms rely on the market mechanism to animate their internal and external relations, which therefore end up becoming predominantly unstable and conflictual.[116]

The differences in the type of industrial relations and social policies sponsored by coordinated market economies and liberal economies are in line with the traits highlighted in the comparison between Rhine capitalism and neo-American capitalism. In the former, wage levels are as a rule set by agreements between capital and labour concluded at the central level, and are complemented by generally extensive welfare measures: a solution also useful to produce cooperation at the level of the firm and social peace in general. On the contrary, in liberal market economies, industrial relations are regarded as comparable to any other market relations. Therefore, social policies are kept at a minimum level since that allows to 'reinforce the fluid labour markets'. It is also worth mentioning that there is a different approach to labour relations: stable and long-term in coordinated market economies, precarious and short-term in liberal market economies.[117]

113 F. Böhm, *Die Bedeutung der Wirtschaftsordnung für die politische Verfassung*, in *Süddeutsche Juristen-Zeitung*, 1946, p. 141 ff.
114 A. Rüstow (1938), in S. Audier, *Le Colloque Walter Lippmann*, Lermont, 2012, p. 469 f.
115 Citations in A. Somma, *Polverizzare il potere economico. Il neoliberalismo e la neutralizzazione del conflitto sociale, le cause della sua crisi e i tentativi di superarla*, in A. Somma (Ed.), *Diritti fondamentali e conflitto sociale*, Roma, 2024, p. 424 ff.
116 P.A. Hall and D. Soskice, *An Introduction to Varieties of Capitalism*, in Iid. (Eds.), *Varieties of Capitalism*, Oxford and New York NY, 2001, p. 6 ff.
117 *Ivi*, p. 51.

10 NEXT: THE CONVERGENCE OF MODELS OF CAPITALISM AND THEIR SPATIAL DIMENSION

The mappings of capitalist models discussed, like others proposed in the same period, depict a situation that in many ways no longer seems relevant, not least because the end of socialism was accompanied by a convergence of these models and their institutional architectures.

Among scholars, this evolution was somewhat foreseen and imagined as a process destined to produce a new model of capitalism, within which elements typical of the old models would be in balance. However, in reality, neo-American capitalism and liberal market economies, rather than of Rhine capitalism and co-ordinated market economies, triumphed. This had been anticipated by Albert, who had identified a number of areas in which, aided by stimuli from European law, Rhine economies were 'increasingly falling under the spell of American politics, culture and media', while neo-American capitalism was about to become the reference point for 'a whole new ideology of capitalism'.[118] S much so that Albert again, more recently, stigmatised what he referred to as the 'Americanisation' of the foundations of the capitalist order.[119]

As we have seen, Rhine capitalism was characterised by a close relationship between companies and banks, the latter being the main financiers of the former, on the basis of a system of cross-holdings designed to strengthen the position of a vast number of stakeholders. And it is precisely in this sphere that the greatest changes can be seen, all of which can be traced back to the process of financialisation of the economy: the capital market is now the main channel for financing companies, and thus the main institution around which to redraw the map of capitalism.[120] This explains the emphasis on shareholders and their expectation of immediate profits, as opposed to the medium and long-term expectations of the other corporate stakeholders.

To sum up, as Albert anticipated, in continental European economies too companies have been submitted to the 'logic of finance':

> The logic of finance itself . . . is . . . to seek out markets offering the least resistance, the fewest rules, and the greatest opportunities for initiative and innovation – but also presenting the highest risks (whether of dishonest dealings or of outright crashes). On both accounts, then, financial globalization is the principal means by which the ultra-liberal model is disseminated throughout the world. Its power is such that even the best-organized economies – the Rhine economies – are unable to fight back effectively. Added to its media appeal and historic successes, the neo-American model has thus managed to infiltrate its Rhine counterpart by means of a Trojan horse filled with financiers and brokers.[121]

Equally unbalanced is the convergence of models of capitalism in terms of liberalisation and privatisation in fields that in continental Europe were protected from competition. The same is true for state and social security, which even in Germany, the homeland of Rhine capitalism, have been strongly downsized. This has led to a marked reduction in the state's capacity to realise human rights of primary importance, with health and education in the lead, as well as to promote worker protection. The latter is increasingly accepted only to the

118 M. Albert, *Capitalism against Capitalism*, cit., pp. 7 f., 169 and 253.
119 See M. Albert, *Capitalismo contro capitalismo dieci anni dopo*, in *Il Mulino*, 2001, p. 390.
120 Already P.G. Cerny, *International Finance and the Erosion of Capitalist Diversity*, in C. Crouch and W. Streeck (Eds.), *Political Economy of Modern Capitalism*, London etc., 1997, p. 173 ff.
121 M. Albert, *Capitalism against Capitalism*, cit., p. 189 f.

extent necessary and sufficient to produce pacification and social cooperation, while the goal of emancipation has been abandoned.[122]

In other words, the key difference between neo-American and Rhine capitalism concerned how they conceiving the redistribution of wealth: in the former the task was entrusted mainly to the market, while in the latter it was conceived as a matter for political institutions. Today, the current 'convergence' between the two varieties of capitalism is rather a generalisation of the approach cultivated by neo-American capitalism, namely, a tendency to reduce sociality to that allowed by the market, or social integration to market integration.

Emblematic from such a point of view is the replacement of universal welfare with the so-called activating welfare state, mirroring the dismissing of full employment policies and the spread of those concerning mere employability. Full employment policies were obtained through the active commitment of public authorities to create and preserve job opportunities, while mere employability policies concern the ability of workers to stay on the market. All this is accompanied by instruments such as the guaranteed minimum income, paid on condition that the unemployed person makes himself available to work, which is the characteristic manifestation of the aforementioned activist welfare state.[123]

11 NEXT: THE NEW STATE CAPITALISM

It was precisely the neoliberal creed that was at the root of the global financial crisis of 2007, which not by chance erupted in the homeland of neo-American capitalism. The crisis produced a precipitous return to extensive forms of state direction of the economy and Keynesian-style anti-cyclical policies, following a trend that began under the presidency of George W. Bush and was continued, and intensified, under the presidency of Barack Obama. The latter's favour for forms of health care, not comparable to European ones and yet very different from those envisaged by neoliberal orthodoxy, should also be mentioned.[124]

These post-2007 changes have led some to believe that the convergence between models of capitalism was more balanced than what could be said so far, or even that it had led to the diffusion of a new model of capitalism, defined in terms of a 'new state capitalism'. Its distinctive feature is a focus on pragmatic intervention which depends on context[125] rather than on an ideological commitment to intervention per se. Precisely this measured approach makes the potential of new state capitalism, which, on the one hand, favours interventions by public authorities and, on the other, avoids undermining free market.[126]

New state capitalism has long been described as the characteristic approach of the BRICS: Brazil, Russia, India, China, and South Africa.[127] After the 2007 crisis, because of the manner in which it was tackled, some thought it could also include the United States, or that the latter was gearing up to incorporate aspects of this model of capitalism.

122 M. Heinrich, *Agenda 2010 und Hartz IV. Vom rot-grünen Neoliberalismus zum Protest*, in *Prokla*, 2004, p. 477 ff.
123 A. Somma, *Abolire il lavoro povero. Per la piena e buona occupazione*, Roma and Bari, 2024, p. 110 ff.
124 So-called Obamacare: see B.R. Furrow, *Regulating Patient Safety: The Patient Protection and Affordable Care Act*, in *University of Pennsylvania Law Review*, 159, 2011, p. 1727 ff.
125 A. Musacchio, S.G. Lazzarini and R.V. Aguilera, *New Varieties of State Capitalism: Strategic and Governance Implications*, in *Academy of Management Perspectives*, 29, 2015, p. 120 ff.
126 C.A. McNally, *How Emerging Forms of Capitalism Are Changing the Global Economic Order*, in *AsiaPacific Issues*, 107, 2013, p. 3.
127 See L. Scaffardi, *Pensare l'im-possibile: Brics, tra miraggio e realtà*, in Ead. (Ed.), *Brics: Paesi emergenti nel prisma del diritto comparato*, Torino, 2012, p. 147 ff.

In fact, this was clearly not in line with the denunciation of market interventionism typical of neoliberal ideology. This can be seen in particular from the Troubled assets relief programme supported by the then Treasury Secretary Henry Paulson. The programme envisaged that in exchange for the purchase of assets from credit institutions, the state would obtain preferential shares, i.e. that it would become an entrepreneur itself[128]: a solution adopted also within the Automotive industry financing programme.[129]

On closer inspection, however, the measures listed, and later measures adopted by President Joe Biden, did not mark a departure from neoliberalism. The latter does not set itself against public intervention, which is in fact acknowledged as indispensable to the functioning of capitalism: neoliberalism entrusts the state with the task of preventing or correcting market failures. And this was exactly the sense of those interventions which led some to believe that a movement of neo-American capitalism towards Rhine capitalism was taking place. Those interventions, moreover, were intended to support and certainly not oppose the functioning of the competitive mechanism.

All this, while Rhine capitalism has gone the opposite way, as we have seen considering Germany as its homeland. Rhine capitalism has now lost many of its peculiarities, not least as a result of the action exerted by the European Union, which is the interpreter and guarantor of neoliberal orthodoxy on this side of the Atlantic. This was no more evident than during the sovereign debt crisis (III.2.7), as well as during the crisis that followed COVID-19 pandemic (III.2.8). We can already observe that in this latter case, too, states reacted with measures that have been wrongly considered inconsistent with neoliberalism.

12 BEYOND TAXONOMIES: FROM ANALOGY TO GENEALOGY

The spread of neo-American capitalism is accompanied by the circulation of the common law model (III.1.4–6), but not to such an extent as to bring about a reclassification of the systems classically traced to the civil law tradition. In other words, what we have discussed regarding the clash of models of capitalism relates to transformations that cannot be grasped through the taxonomies in use among comparative law scholars.

However, this is not the only reason that many promote the overcoming of taxonomies as such.

In the comparative literature on the sense and usefulness of taxonomies, and in particular of families of systems, it is emphasised that the principle of relativity prevents taxonomy from 'imprisoning the pulsating and changing reality of a legal system in a fixed scheme'.[130] Similarly, it is pointed out that classifications correspond to 'ideal types'; i.e. they have no actual correspondence in reality.[131] Others observe that classifying necessarily implies resorting to simplifications, and that therefore taxonomies 'in the long run may prevent one from dealing with the complexity of problems', which is why their function is 'temporary'.[132] Nonetheless, there are increasing reflections on the possibility of radically rethinking

128 *Emergency Economic Stabilization Act* del 2008.

129 For instance, S.M. Davidoff, *Uncomfortable Embrace. Federal Corporate Ownership in the Midst of the Financial Crisis*, in *Minnesota Law Review*, 95, 2011, p. 1733 ff.

130 M. Serio, *Osservazioni brevi su forme, mezzi e classificazioni della comparazione giuridica*, in P. Cerami and M. Serio (Eds.), *Scritti di comparazione e storia giuridica*, Torino, 2011, p. 21.

131 M. Pargendler, *The Rise and Decline of Legal Families*, in *American Journal of Comparative Law*, 60, 2012, p. 1043.

132 G. Pascuzzi, *Conoscere comparando: tra tassonomie ed errori cognitivi*, in *Diritto pubblico comparato ed europeo*, 2017, p. 1196.

classifications, in such a way as to make them sensitive to subtle and ongoing process such as the convergence of models of capitalism.

A first way to achieve this consists in over-emphasising the principle of relativity (II.2.2), i.e. in identifying groupings that are only valid for the specific aspect the comparative lawyer is dealing with, as realised within a specific literary genre: that of atlases.[133]

Alternatively, traditional classifications can be maintained, while revising their structure.[134] This may be achieved by adapting them to comparative exercises 'in a weak form', which aims to avoid monothetic taxonomies such as those characterised by mutual exclusivity and joint exhaustiveness.[135] Indeed, as we have seen considering taxonomies not relying on the statehood and nationality of law (II.2.5), polythetic classifications are possible.

Polythetic taxonomies involve legal phenomena capable of simultaneously falling into more than one category, or possibly finding no place in any category at all. This is what happens with classifications to which 'fuzzy logic', developed in mathematics to allow the formation of 'fuzzy sets', is applied. In Baldin's words:

> Traditional set theory assumes that one can clearly distinguish who belongs and who does not belong to a set, taking the notion of belonging according to the true-false condition as a paradigm. In contrast, fuzzy sets theory, put forward in 1965 by the mathematician Zadeh, imagines classes with vague contours and admits that objects belong to the classes only to a certain extent, diluting the dichotomous result that, in the pursuit of precision, can lose sight of meaning. Fuzzy sets break with Aristotelian principles because they conceive of uncertain collocation – extending the paradigm of membership through the notion of the degree of membership – whereas traditional set theory instead establishes an exact threshold at which an object may or may not belong to a class.[136]

When applied to the convergence of models of capitalism, it would follow that civil law systems would end up being included among common law systems. The solution would make it possible to avoid certain rigidities of the traditional taxonomies, and yet the mere softening of the criteria used to compose families of systems does not in itself lead to a greater attention to the transformations taking place.

More interesting thus is the proposal to represent families of systems by taking into account 'reciprocal intersections', aiming at the identification of 'a common impact zone' and thereby emphasising that they do not constitute 'static and isolated entities'.[137] This proposal should be read in conjunction with that of those who wish to emphasise the category of mixed systems, namely, those with characteristics typical of different groupings, as it naturally tends to take into account the dynamics underlying the variable combination of these characteristics.

The category of mixed systems has traditionally been used to identify mixtures of common law and civil law elements, in particular with reference to Quebec, South Africa, and Louisiana. At a later stage, the category was extended to include any type of mixture, first and foremost those in which religious law or customary law appear, in the context of researches

133 See F. Galgano (Ed.), *Atlante di diritto privato comparato*, 5th ed., Bologna, 2011 and G.F. Ferrari (Ed.), *Atlante di diritto pubblico comparato*, Torino, 2010.

134 E. Mostacci, *Schemi di classificazione e comparazione giuridica: un regno immenso e anonimo*, in *Diritto pubblico comparato ed europeo*, 2017, p. 1173 ff.

135 L. Pegoraro and A. Rinella, *Sistemi costituzionali comparati*, Torino, 2017, p. 27 and S. Bagni, *Oltre i modelli e i sistemi di giustizia costituzionale e convenzionale: alcune riflessioni di metodo*, in *Diritto pubblico comparato ed europeo*, 2017, p. 1070.

136 S. Baldin, *Riflessioni sull'uso consapevole della logica fuzzy nelle classificazioni fra epistemologia del diritto comparato e interdisciplinarietà*, in *Revista General de Derecho Público Comparado*, 2012, p. 11 ff.

137 R. Scarciglia, *Metodi e comparazione giuridica*, 3rd ed., Milano, 2021, p. 91 ff.

focused on legal pluralism (I.2.3) and those open to substantive sources of law (I.1.4).[138] Under these criteria, however, it is easy to say that all systems are ultimately mixed. And even if one were to consider this conclusion too extreme, one should still recognise that the category is necessarily broad and heterogeneous,[139] and that as such it is not able to mirror the transformations we are dealing with.

That said, the idea has been applied to the European Union, viewed as a mixed system supporting the convergence of models of capitalism (II.2.10), i.e. a catalyst for transformations of national laws in line with neo-American capitalism. This emerges from the proposal to combine the concept of mixed system with the idea of competition between legal systems: European law should be left to the free choice of private individuals, called upon to select the rules deemed most suitable to their interests.[140] The neoliberal inspiration of this solution is the same of the idea of competition between legal systems, which not by chance has been theorised and practised in the United States and has become a typical feature of globalisation.[141] It is precisely for this reason that it is criticised in the European context,[142] as we will see in more detail here (III.1.7).

In short, it seems that classification as such, even when revisited and modified in order to emphasise the dynamic aspect of the phenomena studied, is incapable of achieving that result. It is based on an observation of commonalities without any consideration for the contaminations underlying legal change (II.4.1), as well as the reasons for those contaminations.[143] In other words, classification provides a monolithic representation of the legal experience. It also reflects a desire to catalogue the world, but only to satisfy a very 19th-century and Western need for order, rather than a real desire to know the other.[144]

This justifies the proposal to abandon analogical comparison in favour of genealogical comparison, namely, to focus on the dynamics of the circulation of legal models. The result will be a sort of mapping of the transformations undergone by legal systems as a result of these dynamics. For instance, in our case, the mapping that starts from the identification of the US experience as the system embodying the neoliberal model and of common law as the vehicle of its diffusion, and then reconstructs the features of that circulation, including the related conflicts in Europe and in particular in civil law experiences.

More precisely, the mapping can take the form of the family tree, or alternatively the wave pattern. The former appears to be more suited to an evolutionist approach to legal change, and therefore needs to be complemented by the latter in order to support diffusionist views (III.1.2). As Örücü clarifies:

> In linguistics, the 'tree model' of language development reflects an evolutionary approach and is the one generally used to explain ramification and divergence. The 'wave theory', on the other hand, showing that changes can spread like waves over a wide area, can also handle the equally important forces of convergence, as 'diffusion'. . . . This combined approach indicates a way forward for an understanding of how legal systems function, change and develop.[145]

138 In particular J. Du Plessis, *Comparative Law and the Study of Mixed Legal Systems*, in M. Reimann and R. Zimmermann (Eds.), *The Oxford Handbook of Comparative Law*, 2nd ed., Oxford and New York NY, 2019, p. 474 ff.

139 U. Kischel, *Rechtsvergleichung*, cit., p. 224.

140 J.M. Smits, *Mixed Jurisdictions: Lessons for European Harmonisation?*, in *Electronic Journal of Comparative Law*, 3, 2008, p. 151 ff.

141 H. Muir Watt, *Globalization and Comparative Law*, in M. Reimann and R. Zimmermann (Eds.), *The Oxford Handbook of Comparative Law*, cit., p. 617.

142 Citations in A. Somma, *Mercificare il diritto. La via liberista alla tutela della differenza*, in A. Zoppini (Ed.), *La concorrenza tra ordinamenti giuridici*, Roma and Bari, 2004, p. 58 ff.

143 G. Samuel, *An Introduction to Comparative Law Theory and Method*, cit., p. 57 f.

144 T. Amico di Meane, *Metodologia e diritto comparato alla ricerca della creatività. Verso un approccio flessibile*, in *Annuario di diritto comparato e di studi legislativi*, 2019, pp. 168 and 174.

145 E. Örücü, *A General View of Legal Families and of Mixing Systems*, in Id. and D. Nelken (Eds.), *Comparative Law. A Handbook*, Oxford and Portland OR, 2007, p. 171 ff.

It should be noted that even this approach is not exempt from criticism. Consider that the genealogical method is the one used to invent traditions; for example, to describe the spread of Roman law doctrines as the bottom-up foundation of European private law, artfully used to support a market regulation in line with the principles of neoliberalism (II.1.1). And yet one cannot fail to take note of the fact that 'today's legal world is a world of contaminations rather than a world divided into legal families'.[146] Indeed, 'legal families have disintegrated in exactly the same way as natural ones, with second or third marriages, same-sex marriages, cohabitation agreements, in vitro fertilisation, surrogate motherhood, plurality of stepfathers, mothers, brothers, sisters, and so on'.[147]

This very aspect is highlighted by those who use the legal tradition as a reference point for taxonomy. In particular by those who use legal tradition cautiously, and who stress that it indicates ideal types whose characteristics must be observed in their interactions with others: 'there are no pure traditions' because 'hybridity is the rule'.[148]

A similar approach is promoted by social sciences other than law, in particular history, where the genealogical perspective seems the most appropriate to conceptualise what are now widely accepted points. This follows from the lessons of the New History (II.2.3), according to which the scholar's attention must not be captured by the search for origins, understood as the roots of the experiences studied, but rather by the reconstruction of identity as the ongoing, and never complete, result of interactions. This is, among other things, because 'the idol of origins' leads to 'confusing ancestry with explanation' and prevents us from seeing how the latter requires analysing the 'social conditions of the moment'. In short, it leads us to give in to the temptation to provide 'the explanation of the very recent in terms of the remotest past'.[149]

SUMMARY

1. Legal comparison as an autonomous science originates as taxonomy, i.e. as the classification of national laws into families of systems. This activity inevitably leads to the drawing up of rankings aimed at identifying the hegemonic family and, within this, the hegemonic national law. Comparative law produces geographies of political bodies and can therefore be likened to geopolitics. This explains the classifications that during the 20th century reflected the balance of powers, for instance, by emphasising the emergence of US law to replace English law as the centre of the common law family, or by reproducing the dialectic between French and German law in the civil law family.
2. Through taxonomy, law takes on geopolitical significance. Geopolitics as a science was born to support the conquest by states of their living space, which is why it was compromised and long marginalised. It is, however, a useful science to decipher the behaviour of political bodies, and in particular the role of law as an instrument at the service of their hegemonic aspirations. Especially when geopolitics is combined with the geography of law, which sheds light on the dynamics through which law constitutes space, challenging both the traditional representation of space as a

146 P.G. Monateri, *The Weak Law: Contaminations and Legal Cultures*, in *Transnational Law & Contemporary Problems*, 13, 2003, p. 591.
147 V. Zeno-Zencovich, *Comparative Legal Systems*, cit., p. 98 f.
148 Th. Duve, *Legal Traditions. A Dialogue Between Comparative Law and Comparative Legal History*, in *Comparative Legal History*, 6, 2018, p. 32.
149 M. Bloch, *The Historian's Craft* (1949), Manchester, 1954, pp. 32 and 29.

mere container and the notion that it is relevant only insofar as it conditions social phenomena. This appears useful to understand the dynamics of the political order, but also of the economic order safeguarded by political bodies.

3. Among the proposed classifications, the one that refers to the style of the system is still widespread. This refers to a broad complex of data: historical evolution, legal mentality, political-economic doctrines, religious beliefs, particular legal institutions, sources of law, and peculiarities of judicial organisation and procedure. Those who use the style of the system to create classifications stress the relativity of classifications in terms of subject matter and time: very different results can be obtained depending on the areas of the legal system and the periods considered.

4. Classifications into families of systems are traditionally drawn up by private comparative lawyers. For this reason, they attach considerable weight to differences in the system of legal sources and emphasise the distinction between common law and civil law: a practice which is rightly stigmatised by public comparative lawyers. Anyway, the distinction between the two poles of the Western legal tradition proves to be central, even if one focuses on the different way in which the economic order is regulated in the two families: an aspect relevant to both private and public law.

5. Comparative public lawyers use the taxonomies of comparative private lawyers, but complement them with groupings related to their own specific interests. These taxonomies too can also be geopolitical in nature and suffer from evolutionist biases. This is particularly the case with those based on state forms, which ultimately aim to accredit the liberal state as a global reference model, thereby also debasing the constructions promoted by democratic and social constitutionalism. This can be countered by adopting a non-ethnocentric notion of the state, and yet this does not detract from critically assess Western concepts used to describe non-Western legal experiences.

6. Classification by families of systems is a useful teaching tool and a reference point for micro-comparison. However, it is the result of an integrative comparison which, by its very nature, tends to disregard the identities of the classified systems, which are often derived from evolutionist and ethnocentric tendencies. These tendencies are typical of a Western approach to law, which is interested in creating classifications in order to then establish rankings, as can be seen from the expressions used in the taxonomies: family of systems and *Rechtskreis*.

7. Classifications by families of systems can also be criticised because they rarely disregard the statehood and nationality of the laws considered, thus concealing legal pluralism. Hence, the suggestion of grouping according to criteria able to emphasise traditional and primitive societies or using polythetic classifications that concentrate on the dominant mode of law-making. It is also worth mentioning the taxonomy that focuses on the instruments of social control and incentive, which may well coexist within the same national system. This taxonomy identifies three families: professional hegemony, political hegemony, and traditional religious or philosophical hegemony.

8. The taxonomy centred on instruments of social control and incentive is driven by ethnocentric motives insofar as it amplifies the self-representation of Western law as law separated from politics and religion. The classification according to legal traditions, instead, is protected from these biases, which is also significant because these traditions can coexist within the same state entity: this is particularly the case with the chthonic tradition, i.e. the primordial tradition, which is present to varying degrees in all societies. However, the reference to legal traditions may well conceal ethnocentric biases, such as those that emerge from taxonomies centred on the concept of the cultural family.

9. The link between legal rules and the economic order has long been emphasised so that it is possible to classify legal orders according to the model of capitalism to which they are linked. Hence, the interest in identifying these models, to which comparative economics has been devoted since the collapse of the socialist bloc in order to identify the most efficient one. In particular, a neo-American capitalism has been identified, as opposed to a Rhine capitalism, the former in line with neoliberal orthodoxy and realised in the United States and the United Kingdom, and the latter developed as the basis of the Keynesianism, especially in Germany. The two models can also be distinguished in terms of their relationship with democracy: Rhine capitalism promotes it by supporting full employment, while neo-American capitalism is prepared to sacrifice it if the ultimate goal of ensuring the functioning of the market requires it.

10. Many have conjectured a convergence of capitalist models towards a new model that incorporates elements of the old. This convergence is indeed taking place, but in the form of the predominance of neo-American capitalism over Rhine capitalism. This can be deduced from the fact that in Germany the financialisation of the economy is advancing, massive privatisation and liberalisation plans are being implemented, welfare is being cut back and the labour relationship is being reduced to a simple market relationship. Evidence of the success of the neo-American capitalism can also be seen in the spread of policies aimed at employability rather than full employment.

11. For some time now, a new model of capitalism is being discussed: the new state capitalism, which differs from the old one in that it lacks the old ideological charge and comprises levels of interventionism differentiated according to the concrete needs of the moment. One speaks of this, firstly, with reference to the emerging economies of the so-called BRICS countries and, secondly, with reference to the way in which the United States responded to the 2007 crisis. At least in the latter case, however, it is doubtful that neoliberalism has really been abandoned. Indeed, the latter does not disdain the intervention of public powers, indispensable to the historical functioning of capitalism, with the level of intervention being functional from time to time to pursue such an objective.

12. Traditional classifications are criticised for their inability to capture the dynamic aspect of transformations in the legal sphere. Some remedy this shortcoming by overemphasising the principle of relativity, i.e. by composing groupings that are valid for only one specific aspect. Others resort to polythetic classifications that do not meet the requirements of mutual exclusivity and joint exhaustiveness. Still others emphasise the mutual overlaps between families of systems or value the category of mixed systems. The dissatisfaction with those expedients has led to a more radical solution: the overcoming of the analogical approach in favour of a genealogical one, able to focus on the dynamics that govern the circulation of models. This approach is in line with the view of historians who are committed to reconstructing identities as the fruit of interactions and who, in this perspective, marginalise the search for roots.

CHAPTER 5

THE WESTERN LEGAL TRADITION

1 WESTERN LAW AND LEGAL ORIENTALISM

Analysing the ways in which legal systems are classified, we observed how the practice of creating classifications constitutes an expression of a Western approach to the study of the law, expressive of ethnocentric tendencies. From such a point of view, the classification of non-Western laws appears to be aimed at enhancing those features that are presented as peculiar characteristics of Western law. These classifications then can only show an approximate knowledge of the essence of non-Western laws, which can only in part be motivated by difficulties in mastering the amount of data necessary to produce taxonomies with a scientific foundation. Indeed, there is a widespread belief that non-Western laws are not the proper material for scholarly analysis. All this must be considered in the light of the geopolitical significance of classifications to which we have repeatedly drawn attention, which concerns not only relations between Western laws but also between them and other laws (II.2.2).

It is precisely that geopolitical significance that forms the background to the more traditional classifications. It will suffice to recall Adhémar Esmein's early-20th-century taxonomy, which identifies the spheres of influence of the great powers of the time and therefore includes a Slavic group linked to the Russian Empire and an Islamic group to the Ottoman Empire. Similarly, René David's taxonomy drew on cold war politics: in his classification, the West is opposed in particular to the countries of the socialist bloc (II.2.2). The end of this bloc has led to an over-emphasis on the differences between the West, on the one hand, and China, Islamic countries, and Russia on the other, best illustrated by the contrast between democracies and autocracies (II.2.5).

We have also referred to classifications in which non-Western law is presented with the primary aim of bringing out features that are supposed to be constitutive of Western law. Paradigmatic is the taxonomy based on forms of social control, which establishes a sort of hierarchy whereby professional hegemonic orders are considered superior to those with political or traditional hegemony. In so doing, it bases the superiority of Western law on its separation from politics and religion, and conversely the inferiority of non-Western law which has not yet experienced that separation (II.2.7). The same scheme is reproduced in the classifications by cultural families, which are centred on the representation of Western law in its essence as a complex of rules administered by holders of specific expertise. This shows that it is not only the traditional taxonomies – those based on the state dimension of classified laws – that must be critically analysed, but also the more innovative ones. They disregard the dimension of statehood and yet do not innovate with respect to traditional ethnocentric motives.

It should be noted, however, that what we have just highlighted is certainly not the fault of legal scholars alone. The latter follow a practice defined as 'orientalism', through which 'European culture' has 'acquired greater strength and a sense of identity by opposing itself to the East, and making of it a sort of complementary and, so to speak, subterranean self'.

DOI: 10.4324/9781032684499-7

Orientalism does not only identify a 'geographical reality', but above all develops 'configurations of power' whereby 'the relationship between East and West is a question of . . . complex forms of hegemony'. More precisely, as Said clarifies:

> Orientalism can be discussed and analysed as the corporate institution for dealing with the Orient – dealing with it by making statements about it, authorizing views of it, describing it, by teaching it settling it, ruling over it: in short, Orientalism as a Western style for dominating restructuring, and having authority over the Orient.[1]

Hence, and by analogy, the idea that one can also speak of 'legal orientalism', which has developed particularly in the context of post-colonial studies to bringing out the colonialist character of certain representations of non-Western laws.[2] Legal orientalism is indeed a practice that focuses on the role of law in the Western production of the East, indicating 'a set of interlocking narratives about what is and is not law' and an 'epistemological practice' useful for instituting forms of 'colonialism without colonizers'.[3]

Let us now turn to consider the taxonomies that are criticised for their lack of knowledge of non-Western laws. They, too, are the product of ethnocentric biases and ultimately the expression of the hegemonic projects: they are geopolitical devices.

This is particularly evident in reconstructions that dilute the complexity of non-Western law, especially Chinese law, where its socialist component is concealed. Such an outcome is achieved, for instance, by favouring 'purely geographical criteria', perhaps combined with an overestimation of the Confucian tradition,[4] an aspect to which we shall return (II.3.7). Alternatively, one can emphasise the evolutions of Chinese law that bring it closer to Western law, in particular the penetration of market economy and rule of law, which are presented as 'compatible not only with capitalism and democracy, but also with socialism of the Chinese type'.[5] The two strategies are apparently contradictory in that the former emphasises the traditional components of the Chinese legal experience, while the latter seeks to emphasise innovation. In both cases, however, the result is the erasure of the identity of the Chinese legal experience.

That being said, it is difficult to differentiate between cultural shortcomings and geopolitical motives in the classification of non-Western laws, at least those not considered as 'residual laws'. This is the case with Zweigert and Kötz's taxonomy, which uses the expression 'remaining law' to refer to Far Eastern law, including Chinese and Japanese law, Islamic law, and Hindu law (II.2.3). On closer inspection, the latest edition of their handbook has not re-introduced the phrase 'remaining laws'; more importantly, it has raised doubts about the opportunity of lumping Chinese and Japanese laws together, and noted the danger of overestimating the Confucian tradition: China, after all, 'is still a socialist country', while Japan is not.[6] On the whole, however, the depiction of non-Western law retains an implicit tone of superiority for Western law and intends to promote it in geopolitical terms.

In other respects, the description of non-Western law is affected by a certain 'passion for faraway places and civilisations'. The result are caricatured descriptions, interested only in 'outward appearances, local colour and the picturesque'.[7] Exoticism, a phenomenon linked to orientalism, which particularly affected art and literature from the 18th century onwards and

1 E.W. Said, *Orientalism* (1978), New York NY, 1979, p. 3.
2 J. Husa, *A New Introduction to Comparative Law*, Oxford and Portland OR, 2015, p. 138.
3 T. Ruskola, *Legal Orientalism. China, the United States and Modern Law*, Cambridge MA and London, 2013, pp. 10 and 198 ff.
4 Noted by G. Sabatino, *Contraddizione e conflitto nella teoria del diritto cinese. Osservazioni diacroniche*, in A. Somma (Ed.), *Diritti fondamentali e conflitto sociale. Un dialogo tra le discipline*, Roma, 2024, p. 365 ff.
5 M. Siems, *Comparative Law*, 2nd ed., Cambridge, 2018, p. 95.
6 K. Zweigert and H. Kötz, *An Introduction to Comparative Law* (1996), 3rd ed., Oxford, 1998, p. 287.
7 A.G. Garneri, *L'esotismo*, in M. Aime and D. Papotti (Eds.), *Piccolo lessico della diversità*, Trieste, 2018, p. 83.

then declined in the 19th century, seems to have survived among comparative law scholars. One could speak of legal exoticism in the same way as one speaks of legal orientalism.

What we have referred to does not exhaust the panorama of comparative law literature, which includes classifications in which non-Western laws are presented in a way that avoids orientalism and legal exoticism, as well as geopolitical drifts. Admittedly, these classifications, too, come up against an unavoidable fact, namely, the difficulties associated with the need to take into account a considerable amount of data, the understanding of which requires unusual skills. And yet the use of suitable methods of investigation may well contribute to obtaining an acceptable result.

It is hardly surprising that the reference to legal traditions, in particular, constitutes a cornerstone of the classifications we are discussing. This is because the range of groupings identified is much more articulated than that which results from recourse to families of systems. In the latter case, the tendency to differentiate concerns at most Western law, whereas non-Western laws are inevitably destined to be represented in terms which are totally unsuited to bringing out their identity.[8] This is not a peculiarity limited to Patrick Glenn's taxonomy, to which we have already given ample attention (II.2.8); the same is true for other authors who, not by chance, stress the need to abandon 'the Eurocentric perspective' in order to finally give space to 'experiences traceable to cultural contexts that do not coincide reductively with those of Europe or of European origin'.[9]

We will return to this when discussing the efforts to emancipate Latin American law from the traditional models according to which it is seen as a degraded periphery of the Western centre (II.3.8). The theme will then emerge again when considering those scholars who seek to prevent classifications of from becoming rankings (II.3.4).

2 A COMMON HISTORICAL ORIGIN AND VOCATION

We have already discussed the Western legal tradition when considering the taxonomy by instruments of social control and incentive: typically, Western is the use of law as an instrument for directing individual and collective behaviour, dissociated from politics as well as religion and philosophy (II.2.7). Also classifications by families of systems, however, use the same concept by including, for example, the determination of 'how much law matters to its inhabitants' among the criteria for classifying a country's law. This is done to distinguish between states 'with a long legal tradition' and states 'with no real legal tradition or where law is subordinated to religion or ideology'.[10] Similarly, among the commonalities between civil law and common law systems is the fact that both affirm the 'autonomy of law', namely, its being 'relatively distinct from morals, politics and religion'.[11]

The authors of the classification by instruments of social control and incentives trace the divorce between politics and law back to the time and work of Edward Coke, an English jurist and politician of the late 16th and early 17th centuries. This was the period in which the construction of an economic order based on market freedoms began and, from this point of view,

8 With exceptions: in particular A. Gambaro, R. Sacco and M. Graziadei, *Sistemi giuridici comparati*, 5th ed., in *Trattato di diritto comparato*, dir. R. Sacco, Torino, 2024, p. 345 ff.

9 L. Mezzetti, *Tradizioni giuridiche e fonti del diritto*, Torino, 2020, p. 33.

10 R. Legeais, *Grands systèmes de droit contemporains*, Paris, 2004, p. 85 ff.

11 G. Mousourakis, *Comparative Law and Legal Traditions. Historical and Contemporary Perspectives*, Cham, 2019, p. 154.

the divorce in question was functional to limit the royal prerogatives in this matter, particularly those relating to the Crown's power to grant monopolies.[12]

During his years as chief justice of the Court of Common Pleas, Coke inspired two fundamental decisions on what we would now call the relationship between the judiciary, the executive, and the legislature. The first circumscribed the royal prerogatives, establishing in particular that the courts could ascertain and determine their extension, taking into account what was established by the rules of common law and those laid down by Parliament: 'the King cannot change any part of the common law, nor create any offence, by his proclamation, which was not an offence before, without parliament'.[13] The second decision was based on the power of the courts to review acts of Parliament, which could be declared invalid if they violated 'law and reason', were 'repugnant', or were 'impossible to be performed'.[14]

In this way, the superiority of common law over civil law would be evidenced: it was the first to develop a form of social control authentically based on law. The same did not happen in the civil law countries, which, it is claimed, would have avoided European totalitarianisms if only they had been more rigorous in achieving a complete 'legalisation of the political criterion'.[15]

If the historical reconstruction of the divorce between law and politics places the English experience at the centre of the common law tradition and thus of the Western legal tradition, the current structure of the common law is instead described with characters artfully chosen to ascribe a hegemonic position to the US-American system. It is in the latter that, starting with an old decision of the Supreme Court,[16] the power of the courts to review legislative acts has been established, which, moreover, was considered implicit in the constitutional design by its inspirers. In the words of Hamilton:

> A constitution is, in fact, and must be regarded by the judges, as a fundamental law. It therefore belongs to them to ascertain its meaning, as well as the meaning of any particular act proceeding from the legislative body. If there should happen to be an irreconcilable variance between the two, that which has the superior obligation and validity ought, of course, to be preferred; or, in other words, the Constitution ought to be preferred to the statute, the intention of the people to the intention of their agents. Nor does this conclusion by any means suppose a superiority of the judicial to the legislative power. It only supposes that the power of the people is superior to both; and that where the will of the legislature, declared in its statutes, stands in opposition to that of the people, declared in the Constitution, the judges ought to be governed by the latter rather than the former. They ought to regulate their decisions by the fundamental laws, rather than by those which are not fundamental.[17]

This power to review legislative acts, originally conceived in a common law country, has since spread to other Western countries through the provision in their constitutions of a system of constitutional review entrusted to special judges of the law. These judicial bodies operate according to legal and not political criteria and they have transformed Parliament from a 'vehicle for the manifestation of the nation's supreme general will' into a power 'bound by norms, principles and values'. It was therefore only by adopting the schemes developed in the currently hegemonic common law countries that civil law countries implemented the principle of the superiority of law over politics, thus certifying the divorce between the former and the latter.[18]

12 F. Nania, *Le origini della 'freedom of trade' in Inghilterra e la lotta contro i regi monopoli*, in *Diritto pubblico comparato ed europeo*, 2018, p. 939 ff.
13 *Case of Proclamations*, 1610.
14 *Dr. Bonham's Case*, 1610.
15 U. Mattei and P.G. Monateri, *Introduzione breve al diritto comparato*, Padova, 1997, p. 67.
16 *Marbury v. Madison*, 1803.
17 *Federalist Paper* No. 78 (A. Hamilton, *The Judiciary Department*).
18 A. Gambaro, R. Sacco and M. Graziadei, *Sistemi giuridici comparati*, cit., p. 38.

Let us now consider the divorce between law and religion, reconstructed in the wake of the events that have affected Western law since the Gregorian Reformation, that is, the initiatives taken by the Church in the 11th century to emancipate itself from secular powers.

The US-American scholar Harold Berman has in this regard spoken of a veritable papal revolution, which had overall repercussions on the typically Western way of conceiving values and institutions in European national systems, including the English.[19] In fact, what characterised the papacy of Gregory VII, was not only the affirmation of absolute power of ecclesiastical institutions over matters of their direct interest, such as the appointment of their leaders or the choice for the celibacy of priests. The reforms also affected canon law, which should be codified by resorting to techniques borrowed from Roman law, the study of which was rediscovered and promoted in particular through the foundation of the University of Bologna: the oldest university in the world, founded in the city that belonged to Matilda of Canossa, vassal of the pope.

In Berman's reconstruction, the papal revolution was the constitutive act of the Western legal tradition, insofar as it laid the foundations for the development of a society characterised by specific methods of allocating rights and duties, settling disputes and implementing a specific form of social control or incentive typical of legal systems based on professional hegemony (II.2.7). This created a principle that has not been disturbed by other dramatic events that have marked Western history: from the Protestant Reformation to the October Revolution, via the American and French Revolutions. They all created new legal systems, but they did not deviate from the model that had been followed since the Gregorian Reformation.[20]

More precisely, all the events from which legal scholars derive their legitimacy (I.1.3 and I.1.5) are characteristic of the Western legal tradition, as a tradition initiated by the papal revolution: the clear separation of the legal institutions from other institutions, the administration of the law being entrusted to professionals with specific training, who are called upon to give coherence to the rules produced by the legal institutions, thus allowing the law to develop as an organic system. In Berman's words:

> The principal characteristics of the Western legal tradition may be summarized, in a preliminary way, as follows:
>
> (1) A relatively sharp distinction is made between legal institutions (including legal processes such as legislation and adjudication as well as the legal rules and concepts that are generated in those processes) and other types of institutions. Although law remains strongly influenced by religion, politics, morality, and custom, it is nevertheless distinguishable from them analytically. Custom, for example, in the sense of habitual patterns of behavior, is distinguished from customary law, in the sense of customary norms of behavior that are considered to be legally binding. Similarly, politics and morals may determine law, but they are not thought to be law – as they are in some other cultures. In the West, though of course not only in the West, law is considered to have a character of its own, a certain relative autonomy.
> (2) Connected with the sharpness of this distinction is the fact that the administration of legal institutions, in the Western legal tradition, is entrusted to a special corps of people, who engage in legal activities on a professional basis as a more or less full-time occupation.
> (3) The legal professionals, whether typically called lawyers, as in England and America, or jurists, as in most other Western countries, are specially trained in a discrete body of higher learning identified as legal learning, with its own professional literature and its own professional schools or other places of training.

19 H.J. Berman, *Law and Revolution. The Formation of the Western Legal Tradition*, Cambridge MA, 1983.
20 H.J. Berman, *Law and Revolution II. The Impact of the Protestant Reformations on the Western Legal Tradition*, Cambridge MA, 2006.

(4) The body of legal learning in which the legal specialists are trained stands in a complex, dialectical relationship to the legal institutions, since on the one hand the learning describes those institutions but on the other hand the legal institutions, which would otherwise be disparate and unorganized, become conceptualized and systematized, and thus transformed, by what is said about them in learned treatises and articles and in the classroom. In other words, the law includes not only legal institutions, legal commands, legal decisions, and the like, but also what legal scholars (including, on occasion, lawmakers, judges, and other officials talking or writing like legal scholars) say about those legal institutions, commands, and decisions. The law contains within itself a legal science, a meta-law, by which it can be both analysed and evaluated . . .

(5) In the Western legal tradition law is conceived to be a coherent whole, an integrated system, a 'body', and this body is conceived to be developing in time, over generations and centuries.[21]

Berman's reconstruction, although on the one hand it implies the superiority of Western law over other laws, on the other hand does not seem to place a specific legal experience in a hegemonic position within the tradition inaugurated by the papal revolution. Indeed, if one identifies Roman law as a joint reference point for common law and civil law experiences, it is difficult to argue for the superiority of the former over the latter.

And yet this is precisely what happens when attention is focused on the values considered to be fundamental to the Western legal tradition, which are seen as the main common ground, far more solid than the technical legal one, between common law and civil law experiences. It is at this level that a more obvious hierarchy between Western legal systems is re-established, again with the aim of placing common law systems in a privileged position.

The dimension of values has long been analysed by the literature which proposes to classify laws according to their ideological imprint rather than their technical characteristics. From this point of view, the law that supports Christianity, liberal democracy, and the capitalist economy is Western (II.2.1). However, the last two elements in particular can be interpreted in more than one way. There is, after all, more than one model of capitalism, corresponding to more than one way of conceiving the relationship between the economic order and the political order, and hence more than one way of understanding democracy (II.2.9). Traditionally, Western law has been reduced to a 'system of subjective rights', called upon to promote the 'will of the individual', in a context that devalues economic and social rights, to which 'it would be misleading to attribute a connotation identical to that of human rights'.[22] And this is tantamount to considering as Western the common law understanding of democracy and capitalism, and to imagining a line of development for civil law countries which, in an evolutionist key, can only be considered ameliorative insofar as they renounce wide margins of political interference in the economic sphere.

This is the background for understanding the current clash between common law and civil law, to which we will turn shortly (II.3.4). We first have to report on other, apparently less turbulent phases of the confrontation between the poles of the Western legal tradition.

3 THE COMPARISON BETWEEN COMMON LAW AND CIVIL LAW

When comparative law, elevated to the status of a science, took its first steps, the points of reference for analysing the law were those functional to nourishing legal positivist discourses.

21 *Ivi*, p. 7 ff.
22 P. Stein and J. Shand, *Legal Values in Western Society*, Edinburgh, 1974, pp. 91 and 158.

Of course, at the beginning of the 20th century, the centrality of the legislation was under attack, inconsistent with the growing awareness of substantive sources of law, especially judicial decisions. And yet the traditional approach (I.1.2), according to which 'modern civil states are founded on the clear separation of the judiciary from the legislature', persisted among continental European national law scholars. No conclusions were drawn from the observation that 'the judiciary is drawn, consciously or otherwise, to blunt the force of the statute, to circumvent it, to abrogate it by indirect and simulated means'.[23]

It was in this climate that the comparison between common law and civil law developed, widely regarded for a long time as 'comparative law *par excellence*'.[24] On closer inspection, it did not characterise comparative research from the outset, at least because the first classifications focused on other contrasts which were considered fundamental, such as those concerning the attitude towards Roman law.[25] That being said, when the comparison between the two poles of the Western legal tradition became essential, it served disparate purposes, for which it was sometimes necessary to emphasise the aspects of convergence between the two models, and sometimes to distinguish them in order to bring out their irreducible difference.

At the beginning of the last century, scholars recalled the period when codified law systems included case law among the formal sources of law, as it was the case for the decisions of the Roman praetors. Looking at subsequent developments, it was noted that codification had failed to monopolise the sources of law: the centrality of legislation had given way to the recognition for the courts of a power incompatible with legal positivist orthodoxy. This was considered a consequence for the 'impotence of legislative assemblies to legislate', which was a phenomenon also known in England, where, however, the courts were able to solve the problems posed by 'laws incompatible with modern life' in the exercise of 'even broader powers than the Roman praetor'.[26] Nevertheless, the comparison between civil law and common law was made by emphasising that the two models were based on radically different arrangement of the system of legal sources. The code was preeminent in the first case and the decisions of the courts in the second.

In short, what prevented one from looking away from the system of sources of law in establishing the difference between common law and civil law was the different force formally attributed to case law. In common law they constituted binding precedents for the future, as established by the rule of *stare decisis* since the English judicial reforms of the 19th century. In civil law, case law could at best aspire to persuasive authority, to indicate and support a possible line of interpretation which could, however, be disregarded and superseded at any time. On this basis, private comparative lawyers in particular have long developed their classifications and constructed the main dichotomy within the Western legal tradition (II.2.1).

The distinction between common law and civil law derived from the differences in the system of sources is, however, unreliable. This is due first of all to the developments that have characterised both systems with regard to case law. In common law systems, *stare decisis* has been expressly loosened, if not in its vertical scope, concerning the obligation of lower courts to follow the precedents of higher courts, in its horizontal scope, concerning the obligation of courts to follow their own precedents. The latter obligation, which does not exist at the level of lower courts as they are considered to have no creative function, has long not applied to

23 E. Piola Caselli, Art. *Giurisprudenza*, in *Digesto italiano*, vol. 12, Torino, 1900–1904, p. 845.
24 G. Gorla, Art. *Diritto comparato*, in *Enciclopedia del diritto*, vol. 12, Milano, 1964, p. 934.
25 M. Pargendler, *The Rise and Decline of Legal Families*, in *American Journal of Comparative Law*, 60, 2012, p. 1047 ff.
26 E. Piola Caselli, Art. *Giurisprudenza*, cit., p. 846.

US-American and English higher courts, while at the intermediate level there are many exceptions and derogations, especially in the US.[27]

In addition, written law plays a prominent role in common law systems: it is indispensable to fulfil the growing tasks assigned to public authorities in managing, even if only indirectly, the economy and society. So much so that the United States even resorted to codification to harmonise commercial matters throughout the country, regulated in the *Uniform Commercial Code* launched at the beginning of the 1950s as a model of doctrinal production for state legislatures. One could also add the role that written law has played in the United Kingdom in the development of the social security system as well as in the development of private law compatible with the process of legal unification in the European area, which is a role that is unlikely to be called into question as a result of leaving the European Union.

In civil law systems, by contrast, there is a growing need to blur the seemingly unbridgeable gap between persuasive authority and the binding nature of a case law, at the very least because of the increasing tendency of many supreme courts to follow their own rulings. Moreover, a growing inertia of the legislature in codified law systems has determined an inclination to resort to litigation in order to obtain the production of rules. This phenomenon, known as regulation through litigation, can be seen in the most burning issues of the day and for the most diverse purposes: e.g. in the attempts to establish, through litigation, the compensability of damage caused by climate change or to limit the right to abortion.[28]

Moreover, the highest courts of civil law countries are increasingly attributing persuasive value to each other (II.1.6), thereby setting in motion mechanisms typical of common law systems as open systems (I.2.4).

However, if with reference to the system of sources one can verify a convergence 'in the facts' of common law and civil law systems,[29] the same cannot be said of other aspects that identify what we have called the style of a system. This relates, in particular, to legal mentality and the conceptual categories used by lawyers (II.2.2). Considering these and other aspects, the rhetoric of convergence must necessarily give way to a rhetoric of divergence. Or alternatively, it must appear as a rhetoric because the over-emphasis of similarities or differences between systems is a fact that is essentially rooted in cultural sensitivities and the point of view of the observer.

It is necessary to bear these considerations in mind in order to assess the debates on the construction of European unity, in the context of which comparisons between common law and civil law systems have obviously been made in order to document the possibility of rapprochement as well as its political practicability. All this was accompanied by a call for a general 'revision of English legal history', designed precisely to accompany the process of European integration, which needed to find points of contact between legal cultures once reconstructed as radically alternative.[30]

Many scholars have embarked on this path, in particular by revisiting the events of the second half of the 19th century which, if they did not initiate the convergence of the two poles of the Western legal tradition, at least created the climate in which it could take place. In fact, it was at this time that some important reforms in the United Kingdom brought about the merger of the jurisdiction of the common law and equity courts and the abolition of the system of forms of action. This led to the development of substantive law according to canons

27 Ad es. U. Mattei and E. Ariano, *Il modello di common law*, 5th ed., Torino, 2018, p. 177 ff.

28 L. Serafinelli, *La privatizzazione del conflitto politico. Aborto, armi da fuoco e cambiamento climatico nell'esperienza statunitense*, in A. Somma (Ed.), *Diritti fondamentali e conflitto sociale*, cit., p. 391 ff.

29 G. Alpa, *L'arte di giudicare*, Roma and Bari, 1996, p. 17.

30 H.J. Berman, *Law and Revolution. The Formation of the Western Legal Tradition*, cit., p. 18.

that were less distant from those typical of civil law countries, and which were also made more accessible by the spread of a scientific approach to the study of law in the common law.[31]

Consider, then, what has been observed in the construction of a European private law, an area in which the friction between the two poles of the Western legal tradition seems particularly acute. However, common lawyers, through the lord chief justice of the Court of England and Wales, felt that even the idea of a code, if limited to contractual matters, was no longer taboo. This is demonstrated by the willingness of the Westminster Parliament to proceed in this direction since the 1960s,[32] a 'sensational' turning point that was compared to 'the fall of the Berlin Wall which is a symbol of the end of the political opposition of national blocs'.[33] For their part, civil lawyers have accepted not to resort to contractual good faith as a vehicle of 'values authoritatively superimposed on the regulation planned by the parties'.[34]

These facts, however, are not unanimously invoked to document the convergence between common law and civil law. A different kind of rhetoric seeks to identify and emphasise the irreconcilable differences between the two systems. These differences may concern values, which however are related to historical phases closer to us, as documented in relation with the clash between models of capitalism (II.2.9). The same differences can involve conceptual categories as well as legal mentality typical of the common law and civil law systems. In the light of these latter differences, some argue that it would be impossible even to think of achieving the unification of private law in Europe, which could be qualified as a veritable act of 'imperialism'.[35]

4 NEXT: COMPARATIVE CONSTITUTIONAL AND ADMINISTRATIVE LAW

The relationship between common law and civil law is not only a topic for private comparative law scholars: public comparative lawyers, too, deal with it. They either support the idea that the two poles of the Western legal tradition are on the way to substantive convergence or, on the contrary, that unbridgeable distances are destined to remain so.

Even in comparative public law such reflections concern the aspect that is privileged in comparative private law, namely, the analysis of the system of sources. Those who nurture the image of a rapprochement between common law and civil law recall the prominent role that social legislation has assumed in the United Kingdom since the Industrial Revolution, or the massive recourse to federal legislation that in the United States has long undermined judicial state law.[36] Others, more attached to traditional representations, instead highlight the 'crucial difference' between binding precedent and the hierarchy of sources as elements of 'system stabilisation'.[37]

31 See the contributions in M. Reimann (Ed.), *The Reception of Continental Ideas in the Common Law World 1820–1920*, Berlin, 1993 and in J. Gordley, H. Jiang and A.T. von Mehren, *An Introduction to the Comparative Study of Private Law. Readings, Cases, Materials*, 2nd ed., Cambridge, 2021, p. 3 ff.

32 Lord Woolf, *Introductory Remarks*, in Accademia dei giusprivatisti europei, *Code européen des contrats*, vol. 1, Milano, 2004, p. xxxiii.

33 G. Gandolfi, *Prefazione*, in H. McGregor, *A Contract Code: Drawn Up on Behalf of the English Law Commission*, Milano, 1993, p. v.

34 C. Castronovo, *Prefazione all'edizione italiana*, in Commissione per il diritto europeo dei contratti, *Principi di diritto europeo dei contratti*, Parte I e II, Milano, 2001, p. xl.

35 For instance, P. Legrand, *Antivonbar*, in *Journal of Comparative Law*, 1, 2006, p. 13 ff.

36 G.F. Ferrari, *Civil law e common law*, in P. Carrozza, A. Di Giovine and G.F. Ferrari (Eds.), *Diritto costituzionale comparato*, 2nd ed., Roma and Bari, 2014, p. 792 f.

37 C. Bassu, *Le famiglie giuridiche e le fonti del diritto*, in T.E. Frosini (Ed.), *Diritto pubblico comparato. Le democrazie stabilizzate*, Bologna, 2019, p. 73.

At the centre of the reflections are then the consequences of the United Kingdom's exit from the European Union, namely, the conclusion of a path that has been a point of reference for documenting the convergence of common law and civil law, not least because of the encouragement to use legislation as a source of law. According to some, the exit should not have a particular impact, at the very least because it is not capable of reversing trends that are now established in matters where the influence of the supranational level has been most marked.[38] Others point to the United Kingdom's membership of the Council of Europe, which, moreover, inspired the adoption of the Human Rights Act of 1998, i.e. the measure by which the European Convention on Human Rights was incorporated into that legal system.[39] And indeed, although it has been suggested that it should be replaced by a British Bill of Rights precisely to emphasise the political significance of Brexit, this measure remains a cornerstone of the British constitutional architecture.

We know, however, that comparative lawyers with a publicist background, even if they take the system of sources as a point of reference for their taxonomies, focus their analysis on other aspects (II.2.4). As a rule, those aspects are not relevant for the affiliation of a leal system to one of the two poles of the Western legal tradition[40]: taxonomies relating to forms of state or government, or even to electoral systems, tend to be transversal.

This does not detract from the fact that there are cases where the distinction between common law and civil law has a certain relevance and testifies to a convergence between the two families of systems. This is the case, for instance, with regard to the independence of the judiciary with particular reference to the figure of the lord chancellor, who in the United Kingdom traditionally held prerogatives incompatible with the principle of the tripartition of powers. He was indeed a member of the government and at the same time the head of the judiciary and the speaker of the House of Lords, thus being linked to the executive, judicial, and legislative powers. A reform some years ago radically altered such an arrangement, in particular by establishing the Supreme Court as the authority of last resort in place of the Appellate Committee of the House of Lords finally separated from the legislative power, and also by removing the lord chancellor from the top position of the judiciary.[41]

In public law, among the events in which the distinction between common law and civil law is relevant, the system of recruiting judges and the way they interpret their role militates in favour of maintaining a clear separation.[42] In civil law systems, judges are considered to be bureaucrats selected on the basis of their technical expertise, which is evidently justified by the legitimisation strategies of legal scholars in line with the dogmas of legal positivism (II.1.5). In common law systems a political-representative selection prevails, which is justified by the recognition of the not merely technical role of judges.[43] This is why with their decisions they exercise 'a constitutional political role as well',[44] and importantly highlight any disagreements within the court. In civil law countries, on the contrary, decisions are taken in the name of an abstract entity, and there is great suspicion or even rejection of any point that is not of a

38 For instance, L. Serafinelli, *To Change or Not to Change? Le conseguenze della Brexit sul diritto dei consumatori nel Regno Unito*, in *Contratto e impresa Europa*, 2021, p. 37 ff.
39 R. Legeais, *Grands systèmes de droit contemporains*, cit., p. 48.
40 For instance, G. Lombardi, *Premesse al corso di diritto pubblico comparato. Problemi di metodo*, Milano, 1986, p. 49 ff.
41 *Constitutional Reform Act* del 2005.
42 R.A. Macdonald and H. Kong, *Judicial Independence as a Constitutional Virtue*, in M. Rosenfeld and A. Sajo (Eds.), *The Oxford Handbook of Comparative Law*, Oxford, 2013, p. 850 ff.
43 For instance, L. Pegoraro and A. Rinella, *Sistemi costituzionali*, 2nd ed., Torino, 2024, p. 403 ff.
44 A. Pizzorusso, *Sistemi giuridici comparati*, 2nd ed., Milano, 1998, p. 220.

purely technical nature. This is best illustrated by the desire to isolate judges from the public debate surrounding the events they have to deal with.[45]

A classic theme in the comparison of common law and civil law involving public law matters is that of the role of administrative law within Western legal experiences.

This branch of the legal system originated in France following the French Revolution, which as we know was the event to which we owe the centralisation of political power in the hands of the sovereign (I.2.2). We due to this event a prima facie contrast between the French system and the English system. Only in the former the relationship between citizens and the public administration was governed by a special body of rules and disputes were settled by special bodies, whereas in the latter it was fundamentally governed by private law and ordinary judicial authority. In English literature, this contrast continued over time, so much so that until the second half of the 19th century an irremediable contrast was discussed between *droit administratif* and the rule of law. The former conceived to grant special protection to 'servants of the state', the latter to nurture a system in which 'individual freedom is thereby more thoroughly protected . . . against oppression by the government'.[46]

The contrast between an English tradition in which 'the statesman is the one who aspires to make his decision by rendering justice', and a French tradition in which 'the statesman is the one who wishes to decide with authority rather than to render judgement',[47] is in many respects caricatural. Firstly, because it does not fit the US-American experience,[48] and secondly because it disappeared long before the era to which we have just referred. Even in the United Kingdom, as a result of the dynamics triggered by the Industrial Revolution, the development of public authorities and of a discipline aimed at supporting their action in forms similar to those known in civil law countries occurred as a result of the dynamics triggered by the French Revolution.[49] After all, no complex social body can renounce organising itself through an administrative apparatus.[50]

This obviously does not detract from the fact that there are also considerable differences that characterise the administrative law of common law countries with respect to civil law countries. These are, however, in constant flux and above all the outcome of a circulation of solutions that initially showed an expansive capacity of the continental European categories but later on highlighted the success of Anglo-Saxon notions.

We find evidence of this tendency considering that three models of administrative law have been identified: in addition to the French and English models, there is also the German one.[51]

As we have said, the French model of administrative law is the one that inaugurates the autonomy of the subject as a discipline of a centralised and hierarchical administration, complemented by a special jurisdiction. In Germany, the development of administrative law has been slower, as has the process of state-building, which is moreover federal in nature and within which administrative justice is not a specific jurisdiction. In the United Kingdom, administrative law, born as a response to the industrial revolution, led to the development

45 Citations in A. Somma, *When Law Goes Pop. La rappresentazione massmediatica del diritto*, in *Politica del diritto*, 2005, p. 481 ff.
46 A.V. Dicey, *Introduction to the Study of the Law of the Constitution* (1915), Indianapolis IN, 1982, p. 213 ff.
47 M. D'Alberti, *Diritto amministrativo comparato. Mutamenti dei sistemi nazionali e contesto globale*, Bologna, 2019, p. 18 ff.
48 H.P. Nehl, *Administrative Law*, in J.-M. Smits (Ed.), *Elgar Encyclopedia of Comparative Law*, 2nd ed., Cheltenham and Northampton MA, 2012, p. 21.
49 G. Della Cananea, *Il nucleo comune dei diritti amministrativi in Europa. Un'introduzione*, Napoli, 2019, p. 17 ff.
50 G.F. Ferrari, *Civil law e common law*, in P. Carrozza, A. Di Giovine and G.F. Ferrari (Eds.), *Diritto costituzionale comparato*, 2nd ed., Roma and Bari, 2014, p. 663.
51 R. Scarciglia, *Diritto amministrativo comparato*, Torino, 2020, pp. 17 and 113 ff.

of an apparatus with growing prerogatives and responsibilities, which was matched by the development of an administrative justice.[52]

However, the United Kingdom is also the system in which, since the 1980s, a form of management of public administration based on criteria borrowed from the business world has been experimented. This form of management, called New Public Management, is oriented towards efficiency and interaction between public and private subjects, and centred on labour relations without the traditional characteristics of public employment.[53] All this has aroused growing interest in civil law countries, ultimately reflecting the spread of Anglo-Saxon economic models as models aimed at promoting liberalisation and privatisation in line with neoliberal ideology (III.2.2).

5 FROM CLASSIFICATIONS TO RANKINGS: THE SUPERIORITY OF COMMON LAW

As we know, the idea of the Western legal tradition is based on aspects that go beyond the technical features: it also refers to the ideological level, and in particular the common reference to political democracy and the economic principles of capitalism (II.2.2). This dimension, too, just like the technical one, inspires discourses emphasising commonalities, as well as discourses underlining differences.

In the past, the reference to capitalism as the foundation of the Western legal tradition has been used to balance a sort of sense of inferiority of common law system with respect to civil law system. It was indeed observed that the former could be considered more 'undeveloped' than the latter from a technical legal point of view, but also that the situation was reversed if 'economic development' was considered instead. As Merryman clarifies:

> It bears repeating that the civil law tradition is older, more widely distributed, and more influential than the common law tradition. In these senses, at least, it is more important. It should be added that many people believe the civil law to be culturally superior to the common law, which seems to them to be relatively crude and unorganized. . . . Hence a lawyer from a relatively undeveloped nation in Central America may be convinced that his legal system is measurably superior to that of the United States. . . . He will recognize our more advanced economic development, and he may envy our standard of living. But he will find compensatory comfort in thinking of our legal system as undeveloped and of common lawyers as relatively uncultured people.[54]

The sense of inferiority of the common law system could derive from what Max Weber had said about the inadequacy of capitalism as a catalyst for 'that form of rationalization of the law which has been peculiar to the continental West ever since the rise of Romanist studies in the medieval universities'.[55] However, this approach has been superseded by those who have sought to establish a link between the capitalist model typical of the USA and the related model of democracy, from which the superiority of the legal system underlying both models is inferred.

52 G. Napolitano, *Introduzione al diritto amministrativo comparato*, Bologna, 2020, p. 39 ff.
53 For instance, F. Bignami, *Comparative Administrative Law*, in M. Bussani and U. Mattei (Eds.), *The Cambridge Companion to Comparative Law*, Cambridge etc., 2012, p. 147 f.
54 J.H. Merryman, *The Civil Law Tradition. An Introduction to the Legal Systems of Europe and Latin America*, Stanford CA, 1969, p. 3.
55 M. Weber, *Economy and Society* (1922), Los Angeles CA and London, 1978, p. 892.

This conclusion was reached after the US legal system replaced the English one as the representative experience of the common law tradition, which occurred when the former assumed the role of world hegemonic power after the Second World War. In this climate, the characteristics of the model of democracy considered typical of common law systems are reconstructed starting from the observation that, in the United States, the separation of powers was realised in such a way as to allow their reciprocal balancing, thus emphasising the well-known model described by Montesquieu. This is in contrast to the solution adopted in continental Europe, following the French experience based on the centrality of legislation, which has characterised the history of French institutions and has led to a re-reading of Montesquieu in the light of Rousseau's theories. The latter held that legislative power, insofar as it was closer to popular sovereignty, was superior to the other powers, which were considered somewhat delegated (I.1.1). This is why in civil law systems, unlike common law systems, the idea that powers are placed on the same level and are called upon to limit each other is rejected or at least questioned. And this is why the civil law systems, unlike common law ones, soften the opposition between legislative power and executive power, both considered as articulations of a mechanism designed to allow the will of the people to express itself.[56]

All this leads to a characteristic feature of common law systems concerning the distribution of legislative power between parliament and the courts. The former mainly issues 'rules of organization' for 'governing the apparatus of government', whereas the 'rules of just conduct which form the basis of the spontaneous order of society at large' are usually produced by the courts and hence are conceived as emerging bottom-up from society. More precisely, as Hayek states:

> While in political theory the making of law has traditionally been represented as the chief function of legislative bodies, their origin and main concern had little to do with *the law* in the narrow sense in which we have considered it in the last chapter. This is especially true of the Mother of Parliaments: the English legislature arose in a country where longer than elsewhere the rules of just conduct, the common law, were supposed to exist independently of political authority. As late as the 17th century, it could still be questioned whether parliament could make law inconsistent with the common law. The chief concern of what we call legislatures has always been the control and regulation of government.[57]

If the production of law by the courts fuels a spontaneous order, it is because they operate by virtue of a 'fragmented knowledge', and not also of a 'planning mind', as is the case if the source of rule production is a legislator.[58] Hence, there is a radical difference from what happens in civil law countries, where the rules of conduct are famously contained in codes; i.e. they derive from an act of parliament. And it is precisely this feature that would make them less suitable for providing satisfactory protection of subjective economic rights: they are subordinate to the will of the public authorities and therefore of relative value. This is why the identifying features of common law systems include their efficiency, to a far greater extent than can be said for civil law systems.[59]

On closer inspection, the conclusion clashes with that of a copious literature inclined to see in the civil code the instrument through which the bourgeoisie affirms its own system of

56 For instance, P. Costa, *Cittadinanza*, Roma and Bari, 2005, p. 41 ff.
57 F.A. von Hayek, *Law, Legislation and Liberty*, vol. 1, Chicago IL, 1973, p. 124.
58 R. Caponi, *Processo civile e conflitto sociale*, in A. Somma (Ed.), *Diritti fondamentali e conflitto sociale*, Roma, 2024, p. 112 ff.
59 See R.A. Posner, *Some Uses and Abuses of Economics in Law*, in *University of Chicago Law Review*, 46, 1979, p. 281 ff.

values,[60] and thus a complex of rules that is certainly not defective from the point of view of its capacity to nurture efficiency. This is equivalent to saying that the identification of common law as an efficient system is the result of considerable simplifications and distortions of historical data. Is against the backdrop of these simplifications that one has to discuss the differences between the common-law and civil-law systems from the point of view of the different varieties of capitalism (II.2.7).

6 NEXT: THE NEW COMPARATIVE ECONOMICS

The theories used to deepen the contrast between neo-American capitalism and Rhine capitalism, and thus to amplify the differences between the two poles of the Western legal tradition, are those borrowed from New Institutional Economics. This focuses its attention on the costs incurred by market actors due to the 'rules of the game in a society', which can thus be assessed from the point of view of their overall impact on the 'performance of economies over time'.[61] Advocates of New Institutional Economics have long been convinced that the costs related to the rules of the game are directly proportional to the degree of interference by public authorities in private activity. Hence, the conclusion that state intervention will lead to market failure, and the claim that the flourishing of markets is a feature of limited state intervention.[62]

This scheme is evidently based on the old premise that the promotion of economic freedoms necessarily leads to achieving the best possible distribution of wealth. In the past, this premise has not led to any conclusions about the relationship between the qualities of an economic order and the law on which it is based. On the contrary, as we know, the celebration of the superiority of neo-American capitalism or liberal market economies coexisted with the assertion of the technical-juridical inferiority of common law systems to civil law systems. The perspective has now changed, leading to the conclusion that the quality of a model of capitalism depends on its reliance on Anglo-American rather than continental European rules of the game (II.3.5).

This conclusion was mainly supported by the scholars who at the beginning of the new millennium created the New Comparative Economics, an approach whose methods and aims were presented in a study on the requirements set by national laws for starting a business. The study, funded by the World Bank, comes to conclusions that are in line with what public choice theorists have been saying since the 1960s[63]: interventionist national laws serve only political professionals, state bureaucrats, and the businesses they support, while discrete national laws benefit markets and fuel economic growth. More precisely, in the words of Djankov et al.:

> An analysis of the regulation of entry in 85 countries shows that, even aside from the costs associated with corruption and bureaucratic delay, business entry is extremely expensive, especially in the countries outside the top quartile of the income distribution. We find that heavier regulation of entry is generally associated with greater corruption and a larger unofficial economy, but not with better quality of private or public goods. We also find that the countries with less limited, less democratic, and more interventionist governments regulate entry more heavily, even controlling for the level of economic development.

60 The obvious reference is A.-J. Arnaud, *Essai d'analyse structurale du Code civil français. La règle du jeu dans la paix bourgeoise*, Paris, 1973.
61 D.C. North, *Institutions, Institutional Change and Economic Performance*, Cambridge, 1990, p. 3.
62 R. Coase, *The Problem of Social Cost*, in *Journal of Law and Economics*, 3, 1960, p. 1 ff.
63 J.M. Buchanan and J. Tullock, *The Calculus of Consent. Logical Foundations of Constitutional Democracy*, Ann Arbor MI, 1962.

> This evidence is difficult to reconcile with public interest theories of regulation but supports the public choice approach, especially the tollbooth theory that emphasizes rent extraction by politicians. . . . Entry is regulated more heavily by less democratic governments, and such regulation does not yield visible social benefits. The principal beneficiaries appear to be the politicians and bureaucrats themselves.[64]

Hence, the conclusion that the common law tradition, insofar as it typically establishes 'limited governments', is to be preferred to the civil law tradition with its 'proclivity to intervene in economic life'.[65]

For the proponents of the New Comparative Economics, the superiority of common law countries over civil law countries is assumed across numerous dimensions and supported by a theory. The latter has been propounded in a study that seeks to identify the optimal relationship between state order or dictatorship and private disorder, both of which can undermine the market if not properly balanced. The study claims to take into account the specific context in which the economic models are set, and thus not to draw universally valid conclusions. However, thanks to the scientistic method used (III.1.4), this is precisely what happens, unsurprisingly to the benefit of the common law.

The authors of the study argue that an excess of order, like an excess of disorder, leads to violations of property rights. In the first case, as a result of abuses by public authorities; in the second, as a result of illegitimate actions by competing market actors. This justifies the intervention of the state, which is called upon to minimise the social costs of private disorder and dictatorship through an optimal level of interference: that relating to the so-called 'institutional possibility frontier', coinciding with 'the efficient institutional choice for a given society or a sector within a society'.[66]

7 CONTINUED: LAW AND FINANCE AND THE THEORY OF LEGAL ORIGIN

On the basis of this outline, the common law and civil law traditions are reconstructed in their historical development, albeit with great simplifications and ideological distortions, and compared in particular with regard to the legal rules for the protection of property rights. The context in which the rules are applied is then assessed, and then the effectiveness of the rules, or what economists call the capacity to produce good economic performance. All this happened at the same time as comparative law scholars were seriously questioning classifications by family of systems in general and the distinction between common law and civil law in particular which, in turn, demonstrates the substantive and methodological distance that separates their subject from economics.[67]

From the very beginning, as the proponents of the New Comparative Economics note, the common law tradition was able to ensure a favourable legal environment for the functioning of the market. Indeed, in England, the Crown at a very early juncture succeeded in centralising political power and thus in exercising control over its belongings. As a result, the Crown was able to guarantee property rights through a system of firm rules produced by the courts and efficiently administered by independent judges. The civil law tradition, represented by French law, is described in opposite terms. For a long time, the political power there

64 S. Djankov et al., *The Regulation of Entry*, in *Quarterly Journal of Economics*, 117, 2002, p. 1 ss.
65 *Ibid.*
66 S. Djankov et al., *The New Comparative Economics*, in *Journal of Comparative Economics*, 31, 2003, p. 595 ff.
67 M. Pargendler, *The Rise and Decline of Legal Families*, cit., p. 1043 ff.

was subject to centrifugal forces that determined an institutional possibility frontier incompatible with the efficient functioning of the market: in order to counteract these forces, a codified private law was required, administered by judges who were hardly independent from politics. And this situation has remained essentially unchanged, despite changes over time that might well have inspired solutions similar to those of the common law.[68]

This explains, in a simplistic and ideological manner as we have said, the poor performance of the French legal system and of those that have taken it as a model. And the same goes for the almost anthropological inferiority of the civil law tradition as a whole, and conversely the better results obtained by the systems that have instead imitated the law of English origin.

The fact that Romanist legal systems are less efficient than those based on English law had already been suggested in a research study that is considered to be a kind of manifesto of the Law and Finance movement, a movement that re-proposes the themes traditionally dealt with by the Law and Development movement, with an emphasis on aspects related to financial markets.[69]

That research is dedicated to the protection of the rights and prerogatives of the investor, i.e. of the main actor in a system of financing entrepreneurial activities centred on the capital market, which is typical of neo-American capitalism and liberal market economies (II.2.9). The research led its authors to formulate conclusions centred on the 'legal origin' of national legal systems, i.e. on the consequences deriving from the imitation of the law of the European colonising powers: an imitation that was initially obligatory, but in time also attributable to autonomous choices.[70]

The age of colonialism began in the 16th century as a result of the expansionist policies of European countries. Among the main protagonists of this historical phase, which formally ended only in the second half of the last century, England contributed to the spread of the common law system, particularly in North America, India, and Australia. The other European colonisers, France, Germany, the Netherlands, Portugal, and Spain, belonged to the civil law tradition, which reached Latin America and numerous African countries by this route. The conclusion drawn from the legal origin of the national systems analysed is that the imitation of English law led to the development of a high level of investor protection, which was lower in cases where the reference models were civil law. This, once again, was due to the characteristics of the latter system: it favours excessive interference by public authorities in defining the rights of shareholders, stakeholders, and creditors in general.

That the legal origin of a national legal system can influence its economic performance has not only been argued with reference to commercial and company law. The same has been said with regard to other branches of law, and in particular concerning the regulation of employment contracts, industrial relations, and the social security system. In this context, common law countries entrust the solution of market failures to private bargaining, in line with what happens in neo-American capitalism. In contrast, in civil law systems the emphasis is placed on characteristics typical of Rhine capitalism, which entrusts the supervision of the economic order to public authorities and makes considerable use of social security (II.2.9). In this way, systems whose legal origin is English achieve better levels of employment and

68 S. Djankov et al., *The New Comparative Economics*, cit., p. 604 ff.
69 In particular L. Pes, *Teorie dello sviluppo giuridico. Dal movimento di "law and development" all'esperienza neoliberale*, Trento, 2012.
70 R. La Porta et al., *Law and Finance*, in *Journal of Political Economy*, 106, 1998, p. 1113 ff.

wages, whereas Romanistic systems are noted for resulting in illegality and unemployment, especially youth and female unemployment.[71]

For the theorists of legal origin, taking civil law as a model can only be admissible in extreme cases; for example, when the law is called upon to cope with epochal transformations, such as those that accompanied the Great Depression of 1929 or the tragedy of the Second World War. In these cases, it is indeed appropriate for countries to adopt 'civil law solutions', but outside these very limited circumstances 'the common law approach to social control of economic life performs better than the civil law approach'. Concluding, La Porta et al. state:

> First, legal rules and regulations differ systematically across countries, and these differences can be measured and quantified. Second, these differences in legal rules and regulations are accounted for to a significant extent by legal origins. Third, the basic historical divergence in the styles of legal traditions – the policy implementing focus of civil law versus the market-supporting focus of common law – explains well why legal rules differ. Fourth, the measured differences in legal rules matter for economic and social outcomes.[72]

The ideological inspiration of the theory of legal origin is obvious and does not require any particular reflection to denounce or to demonstrate it. Nor is it necessary to spend much time commenting on the fact that the superiority of the common law is largely based on assessments relating to the quality of the regulation of the financial markets, whose limits have, over time, been exposed. Indeed, the 2007 crisis provided clear evidence of how harmful hostility towards public intervention in the economy is for the community.[73] Additionally, it prompted a reconsideration of the assumptions on which that hostility was based, not least in the light of the at least initial transformed role assumed by public authorities in the USA (II.2.11).[74]

We might add, too, that the impact of legal origin on the economic performance of an organisation is far more limited than other elements. Prominent among these are economic policy choices, which in turn are influenced by highly influential events, such as wars. Consider, in particular, that civil law countries, unlike common law countries, were devastated by the Second World War and that this forced choices with implications on the functioning of the economic order.[75]

It is, moreover, instructive to mention some of the assumptions of the theory of legal origin in order to critically evaluate the classification criteria it makes use of. While in some cases this operation is relatively uncontroversial, in others it is decidedly problematic and debateable. It is exemplary in this regard that Chinese law is supposed to have a German legal origin, since China has imitated certain German legislative models.[76] Moreover, the identification of the legal origin constitutes a decidedly arbitrary move if it concerns mixed systems (II.2.12). Some of those latter systems, what's more, include jurisdictions that regulate sectors of the market according to civil law models and nevertheless possess a flourishing economy.[77]

The truth is that, although the proponents of the New Comparative Economics claim to value social norms alongside legal ones, they end up focusing their attention on the latter. The techniques used for comparison, which claim to provide objective and unobjectionable

71 J.C. Botero et al., *The Regulation of Labor*, in *Quarterly Journal of Economics*, 119, 2004, p. 1339 ff.

72 R. La Porta et al., *The Economic Consequences of Legal Origins*, in *Journal of Economic Literature*, 46, 2008, p. 326 f.

73 On this, A. Gambaro, *Common Law e Civil Law: evoluzione e metodi di confronto*, in G. Alpa et al., *Due iceberg a confronto. Le derive di common law e civil law*, Milano, 2009, p. 28.

74 L.-M. Fairfax, *The Legal Origins Theory in Crisis*, in *Brigham Young University Law Review*, 2009, p. 1571 ff.

75 M.J. Roe, *Legal Origins, Politics and Modern Stock Markets*, in *Harvard Law Review*, 120, 2006, p. 462 ff.

76 See M. Siems, *Legal Origins. Reconciling Law & Finance and Comparative Law*, in *McGill Law Journal*, 52, 2007, p. 65 f.

77 For instance, K. Kim, *Mixed Systems in Legal Origins Analysis*, in *Southern California Law Review*, 83, 2010, p. 693 ff.

measurements, such as those produced by numerical or quantitative comparison, are equally problematic. We will consider this aspect in more detail in discussing comparative law methodology (IV.2.5), also in order to relate it to another shortcoming of the theory of legal origins: its neglect of the fact that the imitation of legal models never ends in their faithful reproduction and therefore does not in itself constitute sufficient evidence of belonging to a family of systems (III.1.3).

8 FROM SOCIALIST LAW TO WESTERN LAW?

In all the major classifications, the socialist countries linked to the Soviet Union formed an autonomous group. Common to those countries was the adherence to the historical and dialectical materialism sponsored by Marxism-Leninism, according to which the foundation of the social order is economic in nature and thus conditioned by the relations inherent in production. In this perspective, the evolution of law reflects the changing power relations underlying those relations, and hence the social order as an economic order. This explains the transition from feudalism to capitalism, and from the latter to socialism, which, however, is not yet the last stage of the evolutionary path. For Marxism-Leninism, this ends with the advent of communist society, which is a classless society and thus an order without contrasts, in which law loses its function.[78]

This explains the peculiar character of socialist countries. They conceived of law as being inseparable from politics, or alternatively, thinking of the ideal society, they decreed its imminent end.[79] However, this outcome never materialised and the particularity of socialist law was reduced to its being subservient to an economic order centred on the planned economy and a political order founded on the supremacy of the single party.[80] As David and Brierley clarify:

> In 1917 Russia seceded from the Western world and began to build a new type of society. The society to be created is a communist one under the aegis of fraternity, where there will be no more State and no more Law. These will have been made superfluous by a new feeling of social solidarity developed through the disappearance of the capitalist world's antagonisms: the need for coercion will have disappeared, and social relations, to be ruled primarily by communist morality, will only be subject to simple rules of economic organization and necessity. Up to the present, this ideal of a communist society has not been achieved in the U.S.S.R., where in our time only a socialist state has been created, characterized economically by the collectivization of the means of production, and politically by the omnipotence of the Communist Party.[81]

Both west and east of the Iron Curtain, and in line with the geopolitical relevance of taxonomy analyses (II.2.2), the contrast between socialist law and Western law was the main theme of the comparative analyses conducted during the Cold War years.[82] These analyses focused on the characteristics of the economic order, which was a particular theme of the private law literature, or on those of the political order, more closely examined by authors with

78 For instance, N. Reich, *Marxistische Rechtstheorie*, Tübingen, 1973 and K.A. Mollnau et al. (Eds.), *Marxistisch-leninistische Staats- und Rechtstheorie. Lehrbuch*, 3rd ed. (Ost-), Berlin, 1980, part. p. 13 ff.

79 See R. Guastini (Ed.), *Marxismo e teorie del diritto*, Bologna, 1980 and H. Collins, *Marxism and Law*, Oxford and New York NY, 1982.

80 In particular K. Zweigert and H. Kötz, *An Introduction to Comparative Law* (1969–71), vol. 1, Oxford, 1977, p. 293 ff. and P. Biscaretti di Ruffia, *Introduzione al diritto costituzionale comparato*, 5th ed., Milano, 1984, p. 70 ff.

81 R. David and J.E.C. Brierley, *Major Legal Systems in the World Today* (1966), London, 1968, p. 119.

82 Citations in Z. Kühn, *Comparative Law in Central and Eastern Europe*, in M. Reimann and R. Zimmermann (Eds.), *The Oxford Handbook of Comparative Law*, 2nd ed., Oxford and New York NY, 2019, p. 184 ff.

a public law sensibility.[83] The contrast also involved other features which were not explicitly ideological, such as those by scholars who defined Soviet law as the product of a 'revolutionary' act, as an 'improvisation', and contrasted it with Western law which was 'the result of a slow and progressive development'.[84]

While identifying the peculiarities of the law of the socialist countries, comparative law scholars did not fail to point out that, before being absorbed by the Soviet bloc, many of them were part of the Western legal tradition. This particularly concerned countries such as Czechoslovakia, Croatia, Poland, Slovenia, and Hungary, whose law was heavily indebted to Austrian, French, or German law. The same could also be said of the Balkan countries, which were under Turkish domination for a long time, but then established strong links with Western legal culture.

It was only Russia that was ascribed its own particularity of having a 'weak' legal tradition, i.e. not characterized in the sense of what is considered relevant in the context of Western law. That country was in fact 'backward' from a technical point of view, as well as from the point of view of the autonomy of law from politics. In the Russian Empire, lawyers were 'the servants of the Tsar and the State, rather than of the law', and were furthermore lacking in an 'esprit de corps'.[85]

If we emphasise legal pluralism, and in particular what we have observed on the subject of legal stratification (I.2.3), we can understand how the advent of socialism and the relative detachment of the Soviet Union from the Western legal tradition was not a complete break with the past. Although brought about by a revolutionary act aimed at wiping out all continuity with the past, and notwithstanding denials by socialist lawyers, many scholars have in fact documented non-negligible traces of bourgeois law in the socialist system.

These elements, which could be called 'substrates' or 'pre-existing cultural layers', were found above all in private law, which, somewhat questionably, was considered less exposed to political change than public law. In other words, it was in the private law of the socialist countries that one could find the indelible signs of the circulation of Western models and thus the persistence of Romanist constructions. This was, of course, clear from the analysis of pre-socialist codes, based as we have said on the Austrian, French, and German examples. However, even socialist scholars, who were after all trained in the Pandectist school, retained in their practice unmistakable traces of the past, even if they had to harmonise it with the new regime.[86]

One could therefore ask whether all this implies a lack of harmony with the socialist experiment; in other words, whether the identification of a Romanist substratum at the basis of socialist law, apart from the narrative level, gives the image of an unsuccessful experiment.[87] It is not, however, on the terrain of technical-legal continuities, emphasised in an ideological key in order to deny a specificity to socialist law,[88] that one can find answers to the question. Pandectism, and civil dogmatics in general, with its desire to provide instruments for ordering social relations regardless of their coordinates, has been able to place itself at the service of the most diverse political constructions (III.2.2). Continuities on the technical level can therefore coexist with ruptures on the ideological level, as can be deduced by taking what

83 For instance. G. De Vergottini, *Diritto costituzionale comparato*, 2nd ed., Padova, 1987, p. 579 ff.
84 P. Arminjon, B. Nolde and M. Wolff, *Traité de droit comparé*, vol. 3, Paris, 1951, p. 227.
85 R. David and J.E.C. Brierley, *Major Legal Systems in the World Today* (1966), cit., p. 137 f.
86 Already R. Sacco, *Il sustrato romanistico del diritto civile dei Paesi socialisti*, in *Rivista di diritto civile*, 1969, I, p. 115 ff.
87 For instance, I. Markovits, *Sozialistisches und bürgerliches Zivilrechtsdenken in der DDR*, Köln, 1969, part. p. 105 ff.
88 See U. Mattei, *The Cold War and Comparative Law. A Reflection on the Politics of Intellectual Discipline*, in *American Journal of Comparative Law*, 65, 2017, p. 583 ff.

we have described as the external viewpoint on law (I.1.4), and as we shall specify in more detail when dealing with the dissociation between techniques and values (IV.3.1).

Of course, continuity can and has also been spoken of with reference to the phase following the dissolution of the Soviet bloc, this time in favour of socialist law. The dissolution, although it did not take place through particularly violent events, was inspired by a revolutionary mindset, namely, the will to erase continuity with the recent past. And yet there is no real discontinuity, at least if we look at the system of sources in the former socialist countries a few years after the fall of the Wall. There are quite a few sources from the socialist period, or possibly from the even earlier period, that have been adapted to the new reality but preserved only in their formal characteristics.[89] More generally, it may be said that the end of the socialist countries as a 'family of systems' does not coincide with their end as a 'legal tradition',[90] or alternatively that the persistence of models inherited from the past alongside those imposed later may well indicate the presence of 'hybrid systems'.[91]

The German Democratic Republic deserves its own treatment because when it ceased to exist, it was merged with the Federal Republic of Germany, whose system of rules and legal institutions it took over en bloc. And these were implemented by lawyers trained at West German universities and who moved to the east,[92] which distinguishes the German experience from that of other former socialist countries, where it was impossible to replace the ruling class linked to the fallen regime.

But let us return to the overall continuities found in the countries of the former Soviet bloc. In recalling them, we certainly do not wish to downplay the considerable transformations in the legal sphere that accompanied the transition to the new order, which can be seen above all in the legal documents with a more immediate political significance, and above all in the constitutions. Important transformations relate to the abandonment of one-party regimes, the reform of the system of citizens' rights and obligations, or the overcoming of planned economies. Nor should we forget the role played in this respect by the international credit system, which to some extent acted as a catalyst for the reforms required in return for the loans needed to finance the transition, within the framework of the so-called legal aid initiatives.

Mention should be made of the initiatives undertaken in particular by the World Bank and the International Monetary Fund, which the former socialist countries joined immediately after the collapse of the Soviet bloc, and thus gained access to the so-called Structural Adjustment Plans (II.2.2). Also worth mentioning is the action of the European Bank for Reconstruction and Development, set up in the early 1990s with the stated objective of financing the transition from socialism to capitalism in the countries of Central and Eastern Europe and Central Asia. We shall return to this point at a later point (III.2.5).[93]

The reforms promoted by the international credit system were in line with the rules of countries with neo-American capitalism or, in any case, with liberal market economies. In this way, the full return of the former socialist countries to the Western legal tradition did not mean a return to a past marked by their Romanist imprint. On the contrary, it reflects the current rebalancing of power between the civil and common law models, the former destined to undergo subtle but inexorable changes to reflect the predominance of the latter.

89 G. Ajani, *Il modello post-socialista*, 3rd ed., Torino, 2008, p. 40 f.
90 R. Mańko, *Survival of the Socialist Legal Tradition? A Polish Perspective*, in *Comparative Law Review*, 4, 2013, p. 1 ff.
91 P. De Cruz, *Comparative law in a Changing World*, 3rd ed., London and New York NY, 2008, p. 185 ff.
92 See I. Markowits, *Die Abwicklung. Ein Tagebuch zum Ende der DDR-Justiz*, München, 1993.
93 See G. Ajani, *Diritto dell'Europa orientale*, in *Trattato di diritto comparato*, dir. R. Sacco, Torino, 1996, p. 115 ff.

As we know, this continues to orient the European project away from Rhine capitalism or the coordinated market economy (II.2.8). We will return to this point shortly when we discuss the restructuring of public debt that is currently affecting some European countries and which, not coincidentally, is also being set up and directed by the International Monetary Fund (III.2.7).

It should be noted here, however, that the collapse of the Soviet Union did not result in the disappearance of the family of socialist countries, within which three subgroups can possibly be highlighted: countries 'not fully westernised after the collapse of the Soviet Union', such as Russia and Bulgaria, countries 'insisting on the pure version of real socialism', among which North Korea stands out, and countries 'in transition from the traditional religiously-based hegemonic law to a proto-capitalist organisation still imperfectly translated into professional rules', such as China in particular.[94]

Those who advocate the end of the socialist family aim in particular to erase Chinese law in geopolitical terms. In so doing, they reproduce the entirely ideological rhetoric of the end of history (II.2.2), or worse, they show themselves to believe that socialist law coincides with Soviet law, and thus overlook the fact that Chinese law constitutes a reality with its own identity, mixing elements of the Confucian tradition and a reinterpretation of Marxism-Leninism in the light of what constitutes the New State Capitalism (II.2.11).[95] This is very similar to those analyses which, in the past, denied the specificity of Soviet law, claiming that its most peculiar features, such as collectivism, communitarianism and even 'one-party-system and industrialisation controlled directly by the state', were inherited from the Russian tradition.[96] Or, alternatively, which believed that Soviet communism was just 'formal communism, heavily influenced by western ideas and western concepts of law'.[97]

9 LATIN AMERICAN LAW AS THE PERIPHERY OF WESTERN LAW

Current classifications mainly neglect Latin American law as a family of systems with its own identity. This law is supposed to belong to the Western legal tradition, but occupying a minor position: the one reserved for poor imitators of models arbitrarily chosen as the benchmark and measure of centrality.

Private lawyers base this conclusion on the analysis of civil law codifications: Latin American countries were inspired in particular by the French Civil Code, emulated at the time of decolonisation, or alternatively by the German Civil Code.[98] In this way, a kind of hierarchy was skilfully constructed between national legal systems reflecting the dynamics of the circulation of the original model. This is also claimed by many Latin American scholars, who thus contribute to reproducing the distorted image of a law reduced to the periphery of the Western legal experience.[99] Even when the passage of time should at least have blurred it, the image 'rules from the grave' just like the forms of action for common lawyers.[100]

94 G.F. Ferrari, *Civil Law e Common Law*, cit., p. 781.
95 On this G. Sabatino, *Contraddizione e conflitto nella teoria del diritto cinese*, cit., p. 364.
96 On this M. Losano, *I grandi sistemi giuridici*, Roma and Bari, 2000, p. 140 ff.
97 H.P. Glenn, *Legal Traditions of the World*, 5th ed., Oxford, 2014, p. 348.
98 Alreay P. Arminjon, B. Nolde and M. Wolff, *Traité de droit comparé*, vol. 1, Paris, 1950, p. 50. Later, for instance, K. Zweigert and H. Kötz, *An Introduction to Comparative Law* (1996), cit., p. 113 ff.
99 J.L. Esquirol, *The Fictions of Latin American Law*, in *Utah Law Review*, 1997, p. 425 ff. and J.L. Esquirol, *Continuing Fictions of Latin American Law*, in *Florida Law Review*, 55, 2003, p. 41 ff.
100 M.C. Mirow, *The Code Napoléon. Buried but Ruling in Latin America*, in *Journal of International Law and Policy*, 33, 2005, p. 180.

Basically, this is the concept recently expressed by legal origin theorists, who consider Latin American countries economically backward above all because they were inspired by the civil law model, and in particular by French law. This would not have been the case if they had turned to common law countries, whose law would have ensured them prosperity and in any case better economic performance (II.3.4). Identical, however, would have been their compression into a hierarchical relationship, i.e. their labelling as the periphery of a centre from which they would passively borrow rules and institutions.

This was the private lawyers' view of the classification of Latin American countries, designed to draw them into the orbit of the civil law family. Those who use the point of view of public law instead point out that those countries are indebted to the common law family, in particular the United States. Here, the system of sources clearly does not matter, but rather the spread of solutions such as federalism and presidentialism, both modelled precisely on the example of the US constitution.[101] Even if the point of view used to observe Latin American countries changes, the aim pursued, however, is identical: to promote fictions artfully conceived to safeguard the hegemonic role of the West in geopolitical terms.[102]

The qualification of Latin American law as a periphery of the Western centre is only apparently overcome by those who classify systems on the basis of the modes of social control or incentive. In fact, we know that in such a context law loses its character of periphery of the Western legal tradition, and yet ends up being identified with features destined to place it in a subordinate position with respect to that tradition. This is the consequence of the inclusion of Latin American countries in the political hegemony systems – although those countries are in transition to professional hegemony systems – motivated by the fact that they have not yet realised the divorce between the law and political sphere, which is regarded as the founding character of the systems of professional hegemony (II.2.7). This is tantamount to saying that, while Latin American does not constitute the periphery of a model, it does represent the centre of a different model that is considered on the whole peripheral, because it is backward compared to Western experiences.

The classifications based on legal tradition (II.2.8) do not escape the same pattern. The choice of that point of reference for taxonomies does not in itself lead to questioning the hierarchical relationship between the European centre and the Latin American periphery, and with it the weight given to the characteristics traditionally invoked to support that relationship. This relates to the role of civil codification as the expression of an ideology developed in Europe and transposed to the South American continent.[103]

Similar schemes are drawn by other theorists of legal tradition, who stress the symbolic value of French codification, born of a revolution and thus able to resonate with the sentiments of those recently liberated from their colonisers.[104] All of this can also draw on the US Constitution, the fundamental law of a country that has also freed itself from colonisers, which is the basis for the special focus on federalism and presidentialism.[105] Of course, by invoking the symbolic value of a legal construction as the driving force behind its circulation, one does not directly establish a hierarchical relationship with the importing legal order, which may well give new content to that construction. And yet that content is devalued or in any case placed in the background with respect to the container: its origin ends up determining the peripheral and subordinate position of the importing legal order.

101 In particular R.B. Schlesinger et al., *Comparative Law*, 6th ed., New York NY, 1998, p. 291.
102 J.L. Esquirol, *Ruling the Law. Legitimacy and Failure in Latin American Legal Systems*, Cambridge etc., 2019, pp. 21 s and 137 ff.
103 J.H. Merryman, *The Civil Law Tradition*, cit., p. 27 ff.
104 M.A. Glendon, M.W. Gordon and P.G. Carozza, *Comparative Legal Traditions*, St. Paul MN, 1999, p. 45.
105 A. Negri, *America centro-meridionale*, in L. Acquarone et al., *Sistemi giuridici nel mondo*, Torino, 2012, p. 39.

After all, this classification is fuelled also by looking at the contents. Comparative law scholars have generally created groupings of national laws that consider Western laws as somehow oriented towards the construction of capitalist and democratic societies. Narratives have thus been conceived by reference to the tendentially global character of modernity, which elevates Europe and the US to the productive centre of models of social engineering, destined to be imitated in a flawed way by the peripheries of the planet. In this perspective, Latin American law has ended up finding itself in a sort of limbo populated by legal scholars capable at best of a 'partial and poor reading of authors that can only be mastered in rich interpretative contexts'. As stated by the Colombian scholar López Medina:

> Latin America is part of the Western world, albeit a developing part. We are embedded in Western legal culture and do not possess a philosophy or law distinctly our own. . . . Latin America, on the contrary, is right in the middle between the Western world, normalised and hegemonic, and the Eastern world, exotic and subaltern: not enough of a membership of either the colonisers or the colonised. We were less than all that: we were simply mimetic reproductions of the advanced West, pale shadows and, thus, we became very uninteresting places. We were imitations of Europeans, first, and now, perhaps, imitations of Americans.[106]

The evidence of the Latin American inability to imitate accurately is said to be numerous, starting with the professional standing of legal scholars. Particularly widespread is criticism of the formalism of scholars, their cult for the 'purity of legal science', as a result of which law becomes 'less and less relevant to social needs'.[107] This is seen as confirmation of the error made by Latin Americans in imitating the French model, which was only initially devoted to formalism: at the stage when homage was paid to legislative positivism, from which French scholarship has moved away since the Scientific School, which was affirmed precisely in order to adapt the law to its context (I.1.2).

10 THE IDENTITY OF LATIN AMERICAN LAW

As we have anticipated, not all classifications follow these ethnocentric patterns. There are, in fact, some designed to emphasise or at least make visible the Latin American identity. There are not many of those classifications, but in recent decades it is nevertheless possible to record a slight reversal of a tradition whereby 'the attention paid to Latin America in the analysis of legal systems has been almost nil'.[108]

Before dealing with this, however, we must return to the scholarship that emphasised the democratic character of Latin American law during the 1930s (II.2.1). Democracy was spoken of in order to emphasise that in the New World there were no inequalities based on class, race or nationality,[109] i.e. to indicate the 'very important universalist component' as a peculiar trait of the 'mentality of Latin American lawyers' and to contrast it with the 'legal nationalisms of so many European countries'.[110] On closer inspection, it was not the first time that such characteristics were invoked as distinctive elements of Latin American law. It had already been done at the end of the 19th century,[111] but now the reference to democracy took

106 D.E. López Medina, *La teoria impura del diritto*, in *Rivista critica del diritto privato*, 2011, pp. 198 f. and 213.
107 J.H. Merryman, *The Civil Law Tradition*, cit., p. 155.
108 S. Lanni, *Il diritto dell'America latina*, Napoli, 2017, p. 24.
109 D.F. Esborraz, *La individualización del Subsistema jurídico latinoamericano como desarrollo interno propio del Sistema jurídico romanista. II La contribución de la Ciencia Jurídica argentina en la primera mitad del siglo XX*, in *Roma e America*, 2007, p. 82 nt. 214.
110 G. Lombardi, *Premesse al corso di diritto pubblico comparato*, cit., p. 54.
111 C. Bevilaqua, *Lições de Legislação Comparada*, Bahia, 1897.

on a strong meaning: in the 1930s much of Europe was dominated by fascism. This might not have been a decisive element from the point of view of private law (II.1.3), but it marked an unbridgeable gap from the point of view of public law.

The attempt to construct the identity of Latin American law from its democratic inspiration has left its mark on Western scholarship. It was even valorised by René David who was committed above all to identifying in geopolitical terms a space for French law, crushed by the opposition between the capitalist bloc and the socialist bloc (II.2.1). At the beginning of the 1950s, he considered on the one hand that Latin American law belonged 'without possible contestation to western systems of law' and in particular to the 'French group of these systems'. On the other hand, however, he recognised 'the democratic character' of that law, even though 'it is certain that the word democracy is not understood in the same way in Western Europe' insofar as it relates to the way of understanding 'the feeling of equality'. More precisely, following David:

> In Latin American countries, democracy, rather than political or economic, is eminently social, made up of feelings of equality that exist between all men, regardless of their economic condition, origin or racial affiliation. The men of European descent who constitute or have until recent times constituted the politically dominant class are immigrants or descendants of immigrants, and the qualities and personalities of individuals count more in their eyes than nobility or seniority of lineage. Differences of origin, whether ethnic or social, are attenuated in countries where the most extensive possibilities are open to individuals regardless of this origin, and where success is essentially a function of each individual's qualities, his strength, cunning or daring, or of factors that make up his good or bad fortune. The universalist spirit has spread to these countries with their often artificial borders, opposing the nationalism manifested in Europe.[112]

Spanish literature was more daring, and in the 1950s and 1960s was far more concerned with Latin American identity and its democratic aspirations than many European countries. It is surprising, however, that this attention did not come from authors animated by tendencies of the same kind. This can be seen by considering in particular José Castán Tobeñas: a jurist associated with Francoism. It was he who carved out for the 'Ibero-American legal systems' an autonomous space within the sphere of Western legal systems of the Latin type and more precisely of 'Iberian filiation'. It was a space designed to emphasise the 'universalist' vocation of Ibero-American legal systems, in some way traceable to their democratic inspiration in the sense just clarified, which thus marked their distance from Western legal systems of the Latin type and more generally from the nationalist tendencies that 'enslaved Europe'.[113]

José María Castán also claimed an autonomy for Ibero-American law, which he traced back to Western law and in particular to its Romanist and Latin part. No characteristics concerning the democratic tendencies of that law are evoked in this regard, apart from the observation that 'the juridical equality of the foreigner and the citizen' constitutes a 'glorious peculiarity of Ibero-American legislation'. The emphasis is on features of a more strictly legal nature: it is said that Ibero-American law has an obvious and predominant Iberian origin, depending on the transplantation of Castilian models to the New World, but at the same time it is specified that in order to solve 'problems unknown in Castile', the colonies had to 'equip themselves with a new law'. All this survived the upheavals that led to the independence of the Latin American countries because 'emancipation did not presuppose the breaking up of

112 R. David, *Traité élémentaire de droit civil comparé*, Paris, 1950, p. 260.
113 J. Castán Tobeñas, *Los sistemas jurídicos contemporáneos del mundo occidental*, Madrid, 1964, p. 61 ff.

the legal community of the American peoples among themselves or even with the mother country'.[114]

On closer inspection, this description of Latin American law does not suffice as a claim for an autonomous identity. Castán Vázquez emphasises the importance of developing an 'Ibero-American private law', but then explains that it can draw its foundations from the common matrix of Latin American codifications, that is, from the imprint of European codifications as a model.[115] This ends up denying Latin American identity or at least representing it in terms of the periphery of the Western legal tradition. Original contributions are not denied, but these are overshadowed by the overall representation of Ibero-American private law as borrowed from Spanish law, or worse, French law mediated by Spanish law. In other words, this is as if the underlying theme was not the identity of a non-European law, but rather the struggle between European laws to accredit themselves as model-exporting centres.

But let us return to the most recent attempts to construct the identity of Latin American law and first consider those that rely on its historical evolution.

This approach characterises Mario Losano's reflections in particular, who insists first of all on the ways in which Latin America was colonised from the 16th century onwards, or rather on the 'ideological assumptions of the conquest, which allowed the assimilation of the indigenous populations. Those assumptions concern the religious motives that formed the backdrop to colonisation, which were different in this respect from those of 'the merchant imperialism of the 19th century supported by the gunboats', at the basis of a colonialism for which 'the indigenous populations were formally placed in a condition of inferiority with respect to the coloniser'. As Losano states:

> European law – in the specific form of Castilian-Lusitan law – spread to South America from the 16th century onwards, thus almost three centuries before the expansion of European colonialism imposed its law on other continents. This legal transplantation in South America therefore took place according to political conceptions and by means of technical instruments that were completely different from those that accompanied the imposition of European laws, for example, in India or in the Arab countries on the southern shore of the Mediterranean. For the very Catholic Crown of Castile, in fact, that unexpected territorial expansion was felt as a divine gift that also entailed a duty of evangelisation.[116]

This reading is not shared by those who, not without reason, stigmatise the violence of the conquest and therefore do not admit the idea of its assimilationist inspiration.[117] Nevertheless, this interpretation allows Latin American law to be described as peculiar with respect to Western law since it is presented as the product of a mixture of identifying features including elements of the indigenous tradition. Latin American law, in this way, 'incorporates into the formal Western container and alongside the substantive institutions of its legal tradition the pillars of the indigenous tradition'.[118] And it does so in ways that sometimes appear so accentuated that it is impossible to differentiate the Western component from the indigenous one.[119]

114 J.M. Castán Vázquez, *El sistema jurídico iberoamericano*, in *Revista de estudio politicos*, 1968, p. 215 f.

115 J. M. Castán Vázquez, *El sistema de derecho privado iberoamericano*, in Universidad de Navarra (Ed.), *Estudios de derecho civil en honor del profesor José Castán Tobeñas*, vol. 6, Pamplona, 1969, p. 155 ff.

116 M. Losano, *I grandi sistemi giuridici*, cit., p. 176 f.

117 In particular A. Alvarado Velloso, Art. *Diritto dei Paesi latino-americani*, in *Enciclopedia giuridica*, vol. 6, Roma, 1989, p. 1.

118 L. Pegoraro, *Blows against the Empire. Contro la iper-Costituzione coloniale dei diritti fondamentali, per la ricerca di un nucleo interculturale condiviso*, in *Annuario di diritto comparato e di studi legislativi*, 2020, p. 476 f.

119 Th. Duve, *Indigenous Rights in Latin America: A Legal Historical Perspective*, Max Planck Institute for European Legal History Research Papers Series, 2017, p. 2.

For some it is precisely this characteristic that justifies the consideration of Latin American law as periphery: if Western modernity is essentially defined as the overcoming of the traditional or in any case pre-modern element, the indigenous component restores the level of backwardness of Latin American law. Instead, it is possible to overturn this scheme, that is, to discuss modernity in the plural, and to consider the intertwining of indigenous law and the development of democracy and capitalism as the distinguishing feature of Latin American modernity with respect to Western modernity.

To deal with these aspects, we shall refer to the classification proposed by the theorist of legal traditions and especially of sustainable legal diversity (II.2.6). Glenn does not elevate Latin American law to an autonomous juridical tradition, but states that the chthonic tradition stands out among its peculiar traits, highlighted precisely by what is considered constitutive of the identity of indigenous law: the cult of harmony among the members of the human group, as well as between the latter and the natural environment. Glenn then discusses the civil law tradition, stating that its influence in the world appears unmistakable, but also that it is not solely due to 'simple admiration'. The civil law tradition, like Western religions, is dedicated to evangelising, and is thus portrayed as associated with the idea of domination, so much so that one wonders if Westerners are 'essentially fundamentalists, such that their ways are so true that they have to be followed elsewhere'.[120]

These clarifications seem to hint to the impossibility of combining the two traditions, civil law and Latin American, into a new form of modernity: the latter is simply perceived as unmodern, if not premodern or anti-modern. But on closer inspection, things cannot be represented as such a radical opposition, or at least this is what emerges from attempts to remedy an obvious drift of Western modernity. Although it is portrayed as a synthesis of democracy and capitalism (II.2.2), it is characterised by a growing limitation of the former through the latter. And attempts to reverse these tendencies, i.e. to allow democracy to catch up with capitalism, look with interest precisely at the indigenous tradition. The latter, as a chthonic tradition, is in fact animated by a holistic pull towards the construction of harmonious relationships within the community, as well as between the community and the natural order. In doing so, the chthonic tradition overcomes Western individualism and authoritarianism, and fosters the democratisation of the sphere of the economy.[121]

Reflecting on the identity of Latin American law emphasises the importance of considering modernity in a pluralistic manner. This is the only way to identify multiple centres from which it takes shape, perhaps precisely where the traditional approach claims to recognise a simple periphery.

Scholars resort to the concepts of 'alternative', 'parallel', or even 'multiple' modernities for this purpose. The former has been developed to emphasise that modernity does not identify a unitary evolutionist path, and that it therefore cannot feed into a theory of the convergence of cultures; rather, different starting points for the transition to capitalism and democracy can only lead to different outcomes.[122] Those who speak of parallel modernities then highlight the essence of such diversity, in a certain sense traceable to the way pluralism manifests itself as relating to the coexistence in space and time of 'multiple economic, religious, and cultural flows'.[123] And this leads one to see modernity as a multiple phenomenon that results from the succession of 'continual constitution and reconstitution of a multiplicity of cultural programs',

120 H.P. Glenn, *Legal Traditions of the World*, cit., p. 175.
121 See A. Somma, *Le parole della modernizzazione latinoamericana*, in M.R. Polotto, T. Keiser and Th. Duve (Eds.), *América Latina y Europa en la primera mitad del siglo XX*, Frankfurt M., 2015, p. 11 ff.
122 In particular D.P. Gaonkar, *On Alternative Modernities*, in *Public Culture*, 11, 1999, p. 1 ff.
123 B. Larkin, *Indian Films and Nigerian Lovers. Media and the Creation of Parallel Modernities*, in *Africa*, 67, 1997, p. 407 ff.

the outcome of which is dependent on the characteristics of the contexts in which such constitutions and reconstitutions occur.[124]

From this perspective, the spread of modernity no longer coincides with the Westernisation of the contexts in which it manifests itself. This would presuppose the possibility of mere transpositions, which is not what the circulation of models produces: rather reinventions and contaminations.

In the light of all this, we can consider another aspect concerning Latin American identity – the unification of the national laws and in particular of private law[125] – because of its centrality in power dynamics between countries since colonial times.[126]

It must be said that the theme of the unification of Latin American private law, particularly in the area of obligations, has long been on the agenda, and has long inspired more or less ambitious projects,[127] which have until now remained on paper. For the most part, however, those projects do not redeem Latin American law from its peripheral position, at the very least because they are captured in the logic of the clash between models of capitalism: they reproduce a way of interpreting the economic order according to Western canons (II.2.9).

From such a point of view, the emphasis on the Romanist origin of Latin American private law may be considered an expedient for protecting the unification process from the neoliberal ideology embodied by common law[128] (III.1.4). This, however, fuels the subordination to civil law, which can only be countered by highlighting the creative contribution of the imitating legal system. It is therefore crucial to emphasise that Latin American law has incorporated the Romanist tradition, reworking it in the form of 'American common law' and above all interweaving it with 'pre-Columbian indigenous institutions'.[129] Only under these conditions is it possible to speak of a 'pre-Columbian Iberian Roman bloc' capable of representing a reference point for the 'resistance of Latin American laws' to the 'penetration not only economic but also juridical-political of the United States of America', and at the same time a bulwark against other hegemonic projects.[130]

Public law, too, however, offers elements highlighting a convergence in various aspects, starting with those that characterised post-colonial constitutionalism. It is conceived as the bearer of a libertarian and egalitarian ethos, possibly modified in order to provide answers to the social question, expressive of 'common strong ideas'.[131]

It is precisely this ethos that has fed the traditional understanding of democracy as a common feature of Latin American laws and the foundation of their identity. But the same applies to more recent developments, such as those concerning the overcoming of the welfare state in favour of the caring state, in the wake of a counter-hegemonic path plotted with respect to that which characterises the West.[132] While in the old continent we have long witnessed 'in a regressive sense the dismantling of the guarantees of social rights', in the new continent the

124 S.N. Eisenstadt, *Multiple Modernities*, in Id. (Ed.), *Multiple Modernities*, New Brunswick NJ, 2002, p. 1 ff.

125 M. Grondona, *L'armonizzazione del diritto contrattuale latinoamericano: premesse per una discussione*, in M. Foglia (Ed.), *Il contratto apolide. La contrattazione transnazionale nel mercato globale*, Pisa, 2019, p. 175 ff.

126 M.C. Mirow, *Latin American Law. A History of Private Law and Institutions in Spanish America*, Austin TX, 2004, p. 239.

127 For instance, R. Momberg, *Harmonization of Contract Law in Latina America: Past and Present Initiatives*, in *Uniform Law Review*, 2014, p. 411 ff.

128 See S. Schipani, *Codici civili nel sistema latinoamericano*, in *Digesto delle Discipline privatistiche – Sezione civile*, Aggiornamento n. 5, Torino, 2010, p. 286 ff.

129 G. Lombardi, *Premesse al corso di diritto pubblico comparato*, cit., p. 54 f.

130 P. Catalano, *Diritto romano attuale, sistemi giuridici e diritto latinoamericano*, in *Acta juridica et politica Universitatis Szegediensis*, 1985, pp. 180 and 184.

131 A. Alvarado Velloso, Art. *Diritto dei Paesi latino-americani*, cit., p. 11.

132 S. Baldin, *Il buen vivir nel costituzionalismo andino. Profili comparativi*, Torino, 2019, p. 67 ff.

overcoming of the welfare state is being realised 'in a progressive sense' towards a new form of state. This is at least what is happening with reference to Andean constitutionalism (II.1.10), otherwise known as *buen vivir* constitutionalism, as a result of the overcoming of an individualist conception of being together as a society in favour of a communitarianism aimed at promoting balanced relations between people and between people and nature. As Bagni states:

> Individual rights are complemented by rights based on group membership and collective rights, held by indigenous groups or the community as a whole, and even new legal subjects such as Nature appear. . . . This is firmly connected both to a new relationship between man and the environment, which on the basis of indigenous cultural traditions is inspired by the search for harmony between the individual, the community in which he lives, and other living beings, and to the proposal for a new economic model, which considers as decisive development indexes based on a holistic assessment of human life that promote the idea of a good life or a worthy life and contrast that of Western welfare.[133]

On closer inspection, the opposition that emerges from this attempt to construct the identity of Latin American law vis-à-vis Western law, namely, the opposition between individualism and communitarianism, is in many respects misleading. It is the same opposition that is invoked in order to draw a distinction between the chthonic tradition and the Western legal tradition, which needs to be downplayed, or rather rethought. Indeed, we know that the Western economic order is inspired by neoliberalism, and that it aims to dissolve the individual in the economic order to isolate him within the market and force him to behave in ways that can be described as automatic reactions to the stimuli of competition (II.2.9). Western law of neoliberal inspiration is thus not an individualist law: it promotes a communitarianism designed to preside over an economic order centred on the free interaction of supply and demand.

If this is the case, the main contrast between Western and Latin American law is played out on the battlefield of values that justify limiting the individual sphere: the functioning of the market in the first case, and harmony between people and between people and nature in the second.

11 NEXT: A LAND OF TRANSITIONS IN THE CLASH OF MODELS OF CAPITALISM

Latin American law has its own identity, even if this includes elements from Western law whether they be continental European in the private law dimension or American in the public law aspects. Such a presentation is undoubtedly to be welcomed, as it finally breaks with the classifications in which this law appears as a peripheral part of the Western legal tradition. It has some imperfections, however, since it does not make sense of the dynamics relating to the ongoing clash between models of capitalism, the outcome of which we have analysed at length in terms of a spread of neo-American capitalism at the expense of Rhine capitalism (II.2.9).

This clash has not spared Latin America, where it is actually jeopardising the survival of those elements that make up its identity. However, this is not the first time this happens, as can be seen from a quick review of the transitions that have affected this region of the planet. At least three main transitions have characterised the last few decades: first the advance of democracy, then the imposition of the neoliberal agenda summarised in the so-called

133 S. Bagni, *Dal Welfare State al Caring State?*, in Ead. (Ed.), *Dallo Stato del bienestar allo Stato del buen vivir. Innovazione e tradizione nel costituzionalismo latino-americano*, Bologna, 2013, p. 20 f.

Washington consensus, and finally the attempt to overcome it or at least limit it through what has been called the *giro a la izquierda*: a turn to the left. Meanwhile, a new phase seems to be emerging, characterised on the one hand by the return of neoliberal theories and practices, and on the other by the attempt to combat it by resorting to innovative solutions.

The 1980s were marked by the advance of democracy. This followed a decade in which Latin America was a hotbed of dictatorship: most notably, the Chilean dictatorship of Augusto Pinochet, whose economic policies were dictated by the 'Chicago Boys', so called because they had been trained at the US university where Milton Friedman, the noble father of neoliberalism, taught. Friedman finally managed to find an audience for his ideas, after attempts undertaken since the 1950s with the support of the US government and funding from the Ford and Rockefeller Foundations.[134] This provides further evidence of how the reform in the neoliberal sense of economic freedoms can combine with the suppression of political freedoms (II.1.3).

In many cases, the 1980s in Latin America marked not so much the advance of democracy as its tentative resurgence, or perhaps its tentative emergence, often the result of compromises with military elites.[135] Moreover, in the same period, neoliberalism emerged from its experimental phase and began its triumphal march sponsored by Ronald Reagan and Margaret Thatcher, who inspired the action of the institutions in charge of governing the international economic order. The International Monetary Fund and the World Bank provided financial assistance as part of a kind of reform market, whereby loans were granted in return for alignment with neoliberal orthodoxy. In short, loan conditionalities required cuts in social spending, liberalisation, and privatisation, as well as the precarisation and devaluation of labour (III.2.2). After all, this was the motive behind the Washington consensus, which was the set of structural reforms aimed at remedying the indebtedness of the countries that would adopt them.[136]

This brings us to the 1990s, the era in which neoliberal orthodoxy became so pervasive that it took on the connotations of a *pensée unique*, capable of irrevocably discrediting the Keynesian approaches that had prevailed until then. This has happened at least in Europe, where we know that the European Union has made and is making a fundamental contribution to the spread of neo-American capitalism (II.2.9). In contrast, the fate of neoliberalism has been different in the Latin American context, where awareness of the consequences of this ideology has contributed to the aforementioned left turn.[137]

The 'left turn' is the term used to describe an admittedly diverse set of experiences, but which, on the whole, represent a sufficiently homogeneous tendency, at least as a reaction to the policies envisaged by the Washington Consensus. For this reason, it has been referred to as 'post-neoliberalism' or '21st century socialism'.[138] It all took shape with the coming to power of Hugo Chávez in Venezuela (1998) at a time when the Latin American left was only in power in Cuba. And it continues with the election of Ricardo Lagos in Chile (2000), of Lula da Silva in Brazil (2002), of Néstor Kirchner in Argentina (2003), of Tabaré Vázquez in Uruguay (2005), of Evo Morales in Bolivia (2006), of Daniel Ortega in Nicaragua (2007), of

134 More recently S. Edwards, *The Chile Project. The Story of the Chicago Boys and the Downfall of Neoliberalism*, Princeton NJ, 2023.

135 For instance. V. Castronovo, *Piazze e caserme. I dilemmi dell'America latina dal Novecento a oggi*, Roma and Bari, 2007, p. 148 ff.

136 In particular J. Williamson, *The Strange History of the Washington Consensus*, in *Journal of Post Keynesian Economics*, 27, 2004–05, p. 195 ff.

137 M. Carducci, *Costituzionalismo emancipatorio e ciclo progressista in America latina*, in *Diritto pubblico comparato ed europeo*, 2018, p. 107 ff.

138 Citations in S. Stoessel, *Giro a la izquierda en la América Latina del siglo XXI. Revisitando los debates académicos*, in *Polis Revista Latinoamericana*, 39, 2014, p. 8 ff.

Rafael Correa in Ecuador (2007), of Álvaro Colom in Guatemala (2007), of Fernando Lugo in Paraguay (2008), and of Mauricio Funes in El Salvador (2009).

As we said, the set of experiences in which the left turn took place was multiform. This is why in the West a distinction was made between a 'modern, open-minded, reformist' left, such as that of Chile, Uruguay, and Brazil, and a 'nationalist, strident, and closed-minded' left, whose main exponents sat in Bolivia, Ecuador, and Venezuela.[139] However, these and other definitions are inevitably imbued with the meanings widespread in the context in which they were created. More precisely, as they are typically used in Western public discourse, they express a standard of judgement that is inevitably ethnocentric.[140] This prevents one from seeing the common traits of the *giro a la izquierda*, all of which relate to the reaction to neoliberal orthodoxy and the related restoration of an active role of the state in shaping the economic order, aimed in particular at holding together growth and fair redistribution of resources.[141]

The restoration we are talking about, however, did not imply a return to the Glorious Thirties, i.e. the Keynesian compromise (II.2.9). Indeed, the limitations on economic power derive not only from the redefinition of the relationship between capital and labour, but also and above all from the subordination of the latter to the relationship between the economic order and the order of nature. This is the sense of Andean constitutionalism (II.1.10) and of the mixture of Western models and the chthonic tradition we have indicated as the essence of Latin American identity (II.3.10).

The political order, too, needs to be rethought in the light of a different way of conceiving the economic order, i.e. one that valorises populism, which is a founding trait of the *giro a la izquierda*.

In the Western context, the term 'populism' has a negative connotation and is used as the point of reference for differentiating between the advocates of the turning point we are talking about: some are considered nationalist and therefore 'populist', others democratic[142] or responsible and therefore unaffected by populism.[143]

What's more, Latin America is considered a 'paradise of populism': the ideology according to which the people form a homogeneous and harmonious community, based on the sharing of pre-modern values, and rally around a leader who is called upon to defend them against an external enemy. The Latin American political system is therefore a corporatist one, which degrades the institutions of liberal democracy to mere 'channels of clientelist recruitment of family political networks', and which ignores the mechanisms that 'in representative democracies' protect against the 'tyranny of the majority'. This is why populists are criticised for being revolutionary when it comes to replacing political elites, but not when it comes to innovating the overall social order, which on the contrary must be recomposed holistically, implementing collaboration between classes to pursue the common good.[144]

The same scholars who describe populism in these terms dwell on the reasons that it is particularly rooted in Latin America. They all view it as a symptom of the inability of representative democracy to produce emancipation. In Latin America, they say, the rules

139 J. Castañeda, *Latin America's Left Turn*, in *Foreign Affairs*, 85, 2006, p. 28 ff.

140 In particular A. Escobar, *Latin America at a Crossroads. Alternative Modernizations, Postliberalism, or Post-Development?*, in *Cultural Studies*, 24, 2010, p. 1 ff.

141 J. Grugel and P. Riggirozzi, *Post-Neoliberalism in Latin America: Rebuilding and Reclaiming the State after Crisis*, in *Development and Change*, 43, 1, 2012, p. 1 ff.

142 A. Touraine, *Entre Bachelet y Morales, ¿existe una izquierda en América Latina?*, in *Nueva Sociedad*, 205, 2006, p. 46 ff.

143 K. Weyland, *The Rise of Latin America's Two Lefts: Insights from Rentier State Theory*, in *Comparative Politics*, 41, 2009, p. 145 ff.

144 L. Zanatta, *Il populismo in America latina. Il volto moderno di un immaginario antico*, in *Filosofia politica*, 2004, p. 377 ff.

on rights and the functioning of institutions remain dead letter or at least show a considerable gap between form and substance.[145] This explanation represents the two main vices that characterise mainstream reflections on Latin America. On the one hand, its identification as a land of unfinished imitations, namely, its inability to make the institutions of democracy and capitalism work, and on the other hand, the self-representation of the latter as engines of social emancipation. As if the imitated model was not necessarily something different from the original, which therefore cannot provide points of reference for assessing the qualities of the imitator – and as if Western democracy and capitalism were not constantly in precarious equilibrium, with the latter always ready to sacrifice the former (II.1.3).

Western criticism of Latin American populism does not take into account that in the new continent social emancipation could not be achieved through the recipes developed for the old continent. In Latin America, the forces of the left could not pin hopes of social salvation on the action of any one social class, especially the working class, which was a distinct minority in a highly fragmented context. This is why they necessarily had to reinvent themselves as post-Marxist forces, capable of involving more heterogeneous or perhaps interclass groupings, and in this sense more in line with a populist discourse. However, such populism does not refer, as its critics believe, to pre-modern constructions of a corporative nature, as such dedicated to the repression of conflict. On the contrary, it alludes to the construction of a political space capable of encompassing the multiplicity of the social, dedicated to synthesis but also to the recognition of identities: it does not refer to a homogeneous society, nor to a people conceived as a pre-constituted reality.[146]

In short, populism as conceived in Latin America does not lead to the ousting of traditional representation, but rather to complementing it with forms of radical and direct democracy, indispensable to prevent corporative deteriorations,[147] and thereby rethinking the development model and stabilising the left turn. This is also necessary in order to prevent indigenous culture from being degraded to a mere 'politicised ethnicity' capable of modernity only when it is adaptable to 'the organisational models of state, nation, people and citizenship that have spread throughout the world in the last two centuries'.[148]

Nonetheless, the turn to the left appears to be in question at the moment, albeit within a scenario with blurred contours and therefore not sufficiently defined to lead one to identify a new transition. One is led to discuss a return to neoliberalism considering, for example, the recent victory in Argentina of Javier Milei (2024), who explicitly defined himself as an anarcho-capitalist. However, a defence of the turn to the left emerges from what happened in Chile with Gabriel Boric's triumph (2022), despite the failed attempt to rewrite the constitution dating back to Pinochet's time, and in Lula's Brazil, which returned to power after defeating Jair Bolsonaro (2023).[149] Then there is the US interference in Latin American affairs, which in the wake of the so-called Monroe doctrine still considers the region as the United States' backyard.[150]

If this is the case, the recent developments in Latin American can be read in the light of the ongoing clash between models of capitalism, for the description of which particularly

145 *Ivi*, p. 388 f.
146 E. Laclau, *On Populist Reason*, London and New York NY, 2005.
147 S. Ellner, *The Distinguishing Features of Latin America's New Left in Power: The Chávez, Morales, and Correa Governments*, in *Latin American Perspectives*, 39, 2012, p. 96 ff.
148 R. Brubaker, *Nazionalismo, etnicità e modernità*, in C. Corradi and D. Pacelli (Eds.), *Dalla modernità alle modernità multiple. Percorsi di studio su società e culture*, Soveria Mannelli, 2011, p. 93.
149 For instance, G. La Bella, *L'America Latina tra giro all'izquierda, ola populista e nuova destra*, in *Dpce online*, 2024, p. 2037 ff.
150 See, for instance, N. Chomsky, *Hegemony o Survival. America's Quest for Global Dominance*, New York NY, 2003.

effective images have been used: in Latin America, a process of 'de-Europeanisation' accompanied by an incisive 'Americanisation' is supposed to be underway.[151] We know that Latin America is mentioned by those who discuss the new state capitalism that could prevail over those inherited from the past. We also know, however, that the latter simply refers to the intervention of the state in the economic order conceived to support and not to oppose the functioning of the market (II.2.9).

12 THE LAW OF THE NORDIC COUNTRIES

We have already mentioned the criticism of taxonomies that tend not to differentiate between continental European laws, or more precisely to emphasise French law as the hegemonic and representative system of the civil law model, thus neglecting the contribution of German law. The same discourse can be repeated for the law of the Nordic countries, also improperly called Scandinavian law: the former include Denmark, Finland, Iceland, Norway, and Sweden, whereas the Scandinavian Peninsula, strictly speaking, only includes Finland, Norway, and Sweden.

On closer inspection, the law of the Nordic countries has not been neglected by the German literature. We know, for instance, that in the early 1950s, Pierre Arminjon, Boris Nolde, and Martin Wolff saw them as a family (II.2.1), emphasising how it had emerged around the codification efforts of Denmark and Norway in the late 17th century and Sweden in the first half of the 18th century. In the course of time, a unifying aspiration also reached Finland and Iceland and produced 'happy and original solutions to many legal problems of primordial importance'.[152]

We also know that Konrad Zweigert and Hein Kötz took up this classification and identified Scandinavian law as a civil law system, but qualifying it as autonomous (II.2.2). Two characteristics were invoked to support such a classification, both relating to private law matters: the limited importance of Roman law and the presence of codifications not in line with German or French models.[153]

In the years that followed, attention to the law of Nordic countries did not seem to increase significantly, curiously enough not even among those who resorted to taxonomies that paid more attention to extra-legal elements, such as those based on legal tradition (I.2.4). Not so, however, those who resort to the concept of legal culture (I.2.6), which identifies the Nordic legal culture on the basis of a 'common social-political basis' founded in particular on the desire to 'level off social inequality by means of intervention by public authorities'.[154]

Those who study Scandinavian law emphasise above all that the region in question shared a common historical development, with events affecting both the western and the eastern parts of the area. In the east, Sweden was the hegemonic country, and Finland was for a long time one of its provinces, maintaining Swedish law as a point of reference both in the years when it was under Tsarist Russia (1809) and after gaining independence (1917). In the West, Denmark exerted a particular influence: on Norway, which was a Danish province (from 1536) before being ceded to Sweden (1814) and finally gaining independence (1905), and

151 L. Zanatta, *Storia dell'America latina contemporanea*, Roma and Bari, 2017, p. 12.
152 P. Arminjon, B. Nolde and M. Wolff, *Traité de droit comparé*, cit., p. 50 f.
153 K. Zweigert and H. Kötz, *An Introduction to Comparative Law* (1969–71), cit., p. 285 ff. See now Iid., *An Introduction to Comparative Law* (1996), cit., p. 277 ff.
154 J. Husa, *A New Introduction to Comparative Law*, cit., p. 134.

on Iceland, which belonged to Norway (from 1262) before passing to Denmark (from 1380), of which it was a province until independence (1944).

A central element in the consideration of the Nordic countries as an autonomous grouping is then the linguistic element: Danish, Norwegian, and Swedish are very similar languages and do not represent an obstacle to mutual communication, while in Iceland and Finland knowledge of at least one of these three languages is widespread.[155]

No wonder then that the circulation of models between the Nordic countries has a long history. It has its roots in the Middle Ages, when it was based on the dissemination of Germanic law, and has not known a break in continuity since.[156] It includes a considerable production of uniform laws, through which entire sectors of the legal system are now shared in common: first of all, the sectors relevant to the functioning of the economic order, such as contract or insurance law,[157] but also those in which cultural differences usually play a greater role, such as family law.[158]

Obviously, the circulation of models also affects public and constitutional law, for example, with regard to the welfare state model, which is also relevant from the point of view just mentioned: that of legal culture as a yardstick for understanding the identity of Nordic law. In other words, one can speak of a specifically Scandinavian welfare state, which is used as an instrument of social emancipation through a strong redistribution of wealth and, as such, requires a high tax burden. All this, however, considering that that welfare state also fulfils the function of producing social pacification and even, in paternalistic terms, a 'highly integrated society in which the citizen is supported from cradle to grave'.[159] It must be noted, however, that the Scandinavian model of the welfare state, which was outlined independently of the Nordic social democracies, is at least partly in crisis, first with the marginalisation of the latter and then with the profound changes their programmes have undergone: 'of the Nordic social democracies today remains the wrapping, the content of which may turn out to be very different from the label'.[160] This is further evidence of how even Scandinavia is suffering the consequences of the conflict between models of capitalism, and above all how it has been resolved to the benefit of the neo-American and at the expense the Rhine model.

Public law is, however, also the area of law that shows sometimes significant differences within the Scandinavian area. Paradigmatic, in this respect, is the form of state and government: Denmark, Norway, and Sweden are monarchies, while Iceland and Norway are republics.

That said, the trend that emerges in the Scandinavian area is one of increased circulation of models and processes of legislative unification, which is reinforced by the fact that such dynamics have long been institutionalised. At the beginning of the 1950s, the Nordic Council was created, which is a collaboration between parliaments aimed at drafting uniform articles on matters of common interest, in the private sphere just as much as in public matters.[161] At the beginning of the 1970s, the Nordic Council of Ministers was created, a body whose

155 A. Simoni, *La tradizione giuridica dei Paesi nordici*, in V. Varano and V. Barsotti, *La tradizione giuridica occidentale*, 7th ed., Torino, 2021, p. 466.
156 For instance, K.H. Ebert, *Rechtsvergleichung. Einführung in die Grundlagen*, Bern, 1978, p. 65.
157 P. Huber, *Comparative Sales Law*, in M. Reimann and R. Zimmermann (Eds.), *The Oxford Handbook of Comparative Law*, cit., p. 946 ff.
158 D. Bradley, *Family Law*, in J.-M. Smits (Ed.), *Elgar Encyclopedia of Comparative Law*, cit., p. 319 f.
159 P. Bianchi, *Parlamentarismi nordici*, Napoli, 2022, p. 66.
160 P. Bianchi, *I socialdemocratici nuovamente al governo in Scandinavia: onda lunga o fuoco di paglia?*, in *Diritto pubblico comparato ed europeo*, 2022, p. xvii.
161 T. Rambaud, *Introduction au droit comparé. Les grandes traditions juridiques dans le monde*, 2nd ed., Paris, 2017, p. 93 f.

functioning follows the pattern of the EU Council of Ministers.[162] Currently, the legal basis for the two bodies is the Helsinki Treaty of 1962, in whose preamble the signatory parties solemnly state that they wish to 'attain uniformity of regulation throughout the Nordic countries in as many respects as possible'. Evidently, however, these aspects do not include a common striving towards the European Union: Finland, Denmark, and Sweden belong to it, but only Finland is a member of the Eurozone. Iceland, on the other hand, has withdrawn its membership application, while Norway has never submitted it.

SUMMARY

1. Representations of non-Western law are often designed to feed the self-representation of Western law, and thus, the fruit of what can be seen as legal orientalism. They are undoubtedly difficult due to the considerable amount of data that needs to be taken into account, and yet the failure to take them into account or their erroneous consideration may also stem from ethnocentrism. Alternatively, that failure may indicate an exoticist approach, i.e. a caricatured depiction of non-Western law disinterested in its real characteristics. In both cases, taxonomies are the more or less obvious expression of hegemonic and thus geopolitical projects. In particular, classifications according to legal traditions are equipped to avoid such tendencies, at least because non-Western laws are represented in a structured manner.
2. Western legal tradition includes civil law and common law systems, which have both achieved the divorce between law on the one hand and politics and religion on the other. The divorce of law from politics is traced back to the time of Edward Coke, who founded the right of the courts to scrutinise the acts of Parliament and the sovereign, a forerunner of the US Supreme Court judicial review. On the other hand, the divorce between law and religion dates back to the 11th century, when the Gregorian Reformation decreed the separation of temporal and spiritual power and codified canon law according to patterns inherited from Roman law. Hence, the technical and sapiential legitimisation of the jurist, a typical feature of the Western legal tradition.
3. It is customary to contrast common law and civil law systems by emphasising differences in the system of sources: dominated by case law in the first case and by legislation in the second. Over time, this distinction has been downplayed: in civil law countries, case law is becoming increasingly important in the source system, whereas in common law countries the same is happening with legislation. That said, the emphasis on the commonalities or differences between the two poles of the Western legal tradition depends on the point of view used by the scholar, and in particular on his sensitivity as a private or public lawyer. It also depends on his broader cultural strategies, as the debate on the construction of European private law best documents.
4. Public comparative lawyers do not focus the comparison between civil law and common law on the characteristics of the sources of law. One topic of particular interest concerns the spread of administrative law as a branch of the legal system that accompanied the process of political centralisation in France. In the past, it

162 U. Kischel, *Rechtsvergleichung*, München, 2015, p. 604 ff.

was considered that in the United Kingdom the rule of law prevented the development of a *droit administratif.* Over time, the development of a common law administrative law was recognised, with differences between the UK and the US models. Also the study of administrative law in civil law systems was enriched, highlighting a distinction between the French and German models.

5. In the past, common lawyers recognised that their model was inferior to the civil law model from a technical point of view, but superior from an ideological one: capitalism as implemented in the US context in particular produced levels of economic growth unknown in continental Europe. Subsequently, a link was established between the successful model of capitalism and the related model of democracy, which was preferred because it subdivided legislative power: vested in the courts when it came to producing private rules, and in parliament when it came to producing public rules. Hence, the superiority of common law as an efficient system insofar as it limits the interference of the state in economic activity.

6. Evidence of the superiority of common has been provided by the New Institutional Economics, claiming that state intervention beyond the limits permitted by neoliberalism leads to market failure. More recently, this argument has been re-proposed by the New Comparative Economics, which has also taken up the public choice theory. According to it, interventionist national laws feed bureaucracy and corruption, while discrete national laws benefit markets and fuel economic growth.

7. According to the New Comparative Economics, common law systems are efficient because they achieve an optimal balance between dictatorship and private disorder. The same does not happen in civil law systems, which produce private rules from above and implement them through scarcely independent courts: a situation that was understandable at the time when political power had to counteract the action of centrifugal forces, but not in the present time. Therefore, countries that imitate civil law are condemned to inefficiency, as argued within the framework of legal origin theory to support the circulation of common law models.

8. Socialist countries have traditionally been placed in the same family because of their adherence to the principles of Marxism-Leninism, as the basis of a law aimed at founding the economy on planification and the political order on the supremacy of the single party. Before the advent of socialism, those countries belonged, with the exception of tsarist Russia, to the Western legal tradition, which, moreover, remained influential at least under the radar despite the change of regime. The return to the Western legal tradition after the collapse of socialism did not prevent a certain after-effect of socialist law. In Europe, however, this return took place under the influence of neo-American capitalism, destined to quickly erase the traces of the recent past. Having said that, the family of socialist countries has certainly not disappeared, and those who claim this usually aim to deny the identity of Chinese law: a combination of Confucianism and Marxism-Leninism in the light of the New State Capitalism.

9. For the most part, classifications overlook Latin American law as an experience with its own identity: it would simply constitute a poor imitation of Western law, of which it would represent the periphery. Private lawyers refer to the imitation of French and German civil codes, while public lawyers refer to the spread of federalism and presidentialism of US origin. Identical is the aim pursued by both: to promote fictions artfully conceived to geopolitically safeguard the hegemonic role of the West. This is not limited to traditional taxonomies since a similar purpose also characterises those centred on forms of social control and legal traditions.

10. In order to challenge the representation of Latin American law as the periphery of Western law, reference has in the past been made to its democratic character: while Europe was in the grip of fascism, Latin America stood out for its universalist and egalitarian inspiration. More recently, reference has been made to the characteristics of colonialism, which in the 16th century was assimilationist. This is a reading that is lenient towards the colonisers but at least useful in bringing out the Latin American identity as a mixture of indigenous and Western traits. Other attempts to identify Latin American identity have focused on the process of unification of private law in the area, which appears, however, to be dominated by the opposition between models of capitalism and thus expressive of ethnocentric dynamics. These dynamics also underlie references to Roman law, which can only represent an element of Latin resistance on the condition of emphasising contaminations with chthonic elements. Latin American identity is emphasised also celebrating Andean constitutionalism as a holist model opposed to Western individualism, or rather as a holist model designed to dissolve the individual in the order of nature opposed to a holist model designed to annul the individual in the market.

11. Since the 1980s Latin America has undergone several transitions on the political and economic level, with considerable impacts in the legal sphere: first the advance of democracy, then the imposition of the neoliberal agenda summarised in the so-called Washington consensus, and finally the attempt to overcome this with a *giro a la izquierda*. However, a new phase is emerging, whose connotations are related to the clash between models of capitalism. It is indeed a phase characterised on the one hand by a return of neoliberal theories and practices, and on the other by the attempt to prevent this by resorting to innovative solutions, and for this stigmatised in Western literature. This is shown by the debate around populism as a founding element of the turn to the left.

12. The law of the Nordic countries is often neglected within taxonomies that compress the civil law model on French law. Authors who consider that law ascribe it to the civil law model and yet with a more or less pronounced level of autonomy, based above all on the historical relations between the Nordic countries and the de facto absence of language barriers. Indeed, the circulation of legal models is rooted in time and institutionalised. It encompasses uniform disciplines in all areas of private law and relevant areas of public law: first and foremost, the welfare state, based on interventions aimed on the one hand at achieving incisive redistribution and on the other at pacifying society in a paternalistic manner. The crisis of the Scandinavian model of the welfare state indicates that in this area, too, the conflict between models of capitalism sees a prevalence of the neo-American one.

PART III

Why compare

Legal change

TABLE OF CONTENTS

DOI: 10.4324/9781032684499-8

CHAPTER 6

EXPLAINING AND PROMOTING LEGAL CHANGE

1 COMPARATIVE LAW AND THE DYNAMIC PERSPECTIVE IN THE STUDY OF SYSTEMS

It is often claimed that 'legal systems never are, but always become',[1] for law 'always changes', and it always do so 'without interruption'.[2] This is why, when observed from a historical perspective, the law inevitably reveals objects that are never identical to themselves, whose particularities emerge not only through synchronic comparison but also and above all through diachronic comparison.[3]

We have indirectly referred to legal change when discussing the taxonomy of legal systems, which are classified into families insofar as they have certain special features. For if law changes incessantly, belonging to a family cannot constitute an immutable fact: this explains the reasons for the principle of temporal relativity as the basis of classifications (II.2.3). This applies first and foremost to legal orders considered to be in the periphery of a family, like in the case of African and Latin American countries, which experienced changes that are often sudden and so radical as to affect their classification. However, it can also apply to legal orders which are hegemonic within a family, like those which set the identity traits of the family itself: we have seen this when we considered the birth and dissolution of the group of socialist countries (II.3.8).

We then considered changes that do not affect the traditional classification of a system, but which can nevertheless lead to a new placing if only observed from new points of view. This is the case of the changes undergone by civil law countries as a result of the decline of the model of capitalism to which they have historically referred, and the contextual imposition of a model borrowed from the US legal experience (II.2.9).

If one takes into account what is said about comparison in the field of historical studies, one might believe that comparison is not equipped to shed light on (legal) change. Comparison, in fact, has a limited horizon: it would devote itself to the identification of commonalities and differences between the objects it compares, and thus, it observes them from a merely static point of view. The perspective chosen by those who deal with the 'history of relations' or 'history of transfers' (*Transfergeschichte*), on the other hand, is different. This looks at the dynamic dimension, the relationship of exchange between legal experiences and the ways in which this exchange develops, while the analysis of similarities and differences between those experiences takes a back seat and is sometimes removed.[4]

1 U. Mattei and A. di Robilant, *The Art and Science of Critical Scholarship: Postmodernism and International Style in the Legal Architecture of Europe*, in *Tulane Law Review*, 75, 2001, p. 1076.
2 A. Gambaro, R. Sacco and M. Graziadei, *Sistemi giuridici comparati*, in *Trattato di diritto comparato*, dir. R. Sacco, 5th ed., Torino, 2024, p. 25.
3 In particular, A. Pizzorusso, *Sistemi giuridici comparati*, 2nd ed., Milano, 1998, p. 29 ff.
4 H.-G. Haupt and J. Kocka, *Historischer Vergleich*, in Iid. (Eds.), *Geschichte und Vergleich*, Frankfurt M., 1996, p. 9 f.

DOI: 10.4324/9781032684499-9

A limitation of the field of enquiry entrusted to comparisons is also to be found in the literature committed to so-called global history, a trend that arose at the end of the last century to overcome what was seen as a shortcoming of world history, i.e. its Eurocentric or at the very least ethnocentric approach to the study of the past.[5] Global history is also a history of the world, observed, however, from a perspective freed from the centre-periphery dimension. It focuses its attention, instead, on the interconnections between human communities, rather than on their civilisation. This is why some advocates of global history neglect comparisons aimed first at classifying, and then even composing rankings.

Among legal historians, Thomas Duve has suggested combining global history and legal history, in particular the history of European law, thus transforming it into a history viewed from a global perspective. Global legal history is tasked with overcoming the ethnocentric perspective, typical of the era in which the history of law, just like comparative law, was at the service of the European unification processes, and for which it had to provide a kind of unifying narrative. The global perspective brings about a paradigm shift insofar as it focuses on the normative flows through the various legal experiences and thus takes a dynamic point of view. And this would put comparison out of play, unable to grasp those flows because it is irreversibly anchored to methodologies and classification criteria suited only to the static point of view.[6]

On closer inspection, the qualification and delimitation of the field of investigation of comparative law, as outlined by the advocates of global history, is not to be found in the debates of comparative lawyers. Certainly, many of them, and not only in the past, have conceived of their field in a way which is consistent with Duve's objections. This is not to say, however, that comparative law typically adopts a static perspective. On the contrary, comparativists believe that the comparison of laws implies a diachronic point of view, evident by the way they link comparison and legal history, which is necessary to highlight 'the evolutionary trajectories of individual traditions and phenomena of contagion'.[7]

In other words, the analysis of legal change is part and parcel of taxonomical research and indeed constitutes its foundation. When taxonomy resorts to classifications, and upstream comparisons, it does not do so in order to limit itself to observations from a static point of view. This point of view derives from the method used to classify, but not from the activity of classifying as such. Moreover, it is precisely the focus on the dynamic moment that has led some to reject taxonomies, which, they say, leads to an intolerable crystallisation of the legal phenomenon (II.2.10).

After all, the same attention to the dynamic dimension is shown by historians who, while sensitive to the need of renewal of their discipline, are committed to breaking down and not reinforcing the barriers that one would like to erect between comparison and transfer analysis. These historians point out that the latter cannot do without the former, whether the transfer is imposed or autonomous. In the case of autonomous transfers, in fact, the receiving legal order will adopt the solutions of others if it considers them as superior. Such a judgement can only come from comparison. The same applies in the case of imposed transfer, which is also necessarily preceded by a comparison, this time made by the exporting legal order.[8]

It should be added that if legal historians feel the need to go beyond the comparative approach, perceived as a static observation of the phenomena studied, this is probably due to

5 In particular B. Mazlish, *Comparing Global History to World History*, in *Journal of Interdisciplinary History*, 28, 1998, p. 385 ff.

6 Th. Duve, *Von der Europäischen Rechtsgeschichte zu einer Rechtsgeschichte Europas in globalhistorischer Perspektive*, in *Rechtsgeschichte*, 12, 2010, pp. 34 s. and 56. For a more nuanced view, Id., *Storia giuridica globale e storia giuridica comparata. Osservazioni sul loro rapporto dalla prospettiva della storia giuridica globale*, in M. Brutti and A. Somma (Eds.), *Diritto: storia e comparazione. Nuovi propositi per un binomio antico*, Frankfurt M., 2018, p. 149 ff.

7 L. Mezzetti, *Tradizioni giuridiche e fonti del diritto*, Torino, 2020, p. 2.

8 J. Osterhammel, *Transferanalyse und Vergleich im Fernverhältnis*, in H. Kaelbe and J. Schriever (Eds.), *Vergleich und Transfer*, Frankfurt M., 2003, p. 463.

a certain use of comparison with which they come more easily into contact: the comparative historical analysis practised by the Neopandectists, who have for some time been engaged in the construction of a European private law derived from Roman law (II.1.1).

This type of analysis is characterised as a synchronic comparison of objects observed in their historical evolution, which must necessarily go back 'at least to classical Roman law' and devote itself solely to law as a 'science': 'nothing is further from the comparative historical perspective than a history of institutions and social facts'.[9] So conceived, the interweaving of legal history and comparison does indeed involve an analysis of the dynamic dimension and thus of data useful for the study of legal change. However, this is done in a way that serves the limited purpose of constructing a history of dogmas and thus identifying artificial continuities that are instrumental to concealing the existence of ruptures that would be otherwise incompatible with the invention of traditions. These approaches force the study of transfers within pre-constituted schemes, designed to document the a priori conclusion that everything derives from Roman law, and that the study of legal change can be reduced to the reconstruction of the chain of evolutionary stages of that law within a hierarchical relationship between model-exporting and model-importing legal orders.

These observations document the bias of Neopandectism's comparative historical approach. Moreover, they also highlight the fact that the ability to explain legal change is not the exclusive prerogative of a particular discipline, but rather derives from the methodological framework of that discipline. We will now turn to these aspects, starting with a brief preliminary overview of the schemes traditionally used by legal comparativists to reflect on the ways in which law changes.

2 EXPLAINING LEGAL CHANGE: EVOLUTIONISM VS DIFFUSIONISM

At first, comparativists explained legal change in the light of evolutionist paradigms, whereby law is naturally destined to develop according to a pattern in which progress represents a universal value, and tradition is an indication of backwardness. This is in line with the rhetoric of modernity, which tends to identify progress with the development of capitalism and democracy, albeit with a particular emphasis on the former at the expense of the latter.

It follows from what was discussed at the Paris Congress of Comparative Law in 1900 that the evolutionist approach accompanied the birth of the subject (II.1.2). At the time, there was a widespread belief that law evolved unilaterally according to a pattern in which one can at most admit 'insignificant variants' corresponding to 'the series of embryonic states of living beings'. If, however, this is the basis of legal change, then the function of comparative law is somewhat delimited, and above all plagued by simplifications designed to pre-constitute the desired result. Per Tarde:

> What is the theoretical benefit – I am not talking about very obvious practical benefit – to be expected from comparative law? This depends on the idea that will have dominated and directed the research. If this guiding and dominant idea is the hypothesis, accredited by the notion of organismic society, that the evolution of law is a regulated, uniform and inevitable concatenation of successive stages . . . comparative law will have the sole purpose of tracing the trajectory. The only interest served by its collection of different customs and laws, which increases unceasingly, is therefore to fill the gaps in this curve with new points. Completing

9 C.A. Cannata, *Il diritto romano e gli attuali problemi d'unificazione del diritto europeo*, in *Studi Impallomeni*, Milano, 1999, pp. 53 and 70.

> this collection in this way, however, is an unattainable ideal. It is apparently achieved on the condition of neglecting the importance of the many differences between the compared laws.[10]

Of course, it would be possible to imagine a weak evolutionism, capable of grasping unilinear lines of development within a plurality of 'social forms', thus assigning less degraded tasks, as it were, to comparative law.[11] Nevertheless, evolutionism confirmed its tendency to use history as a 'vector of meaning for the present'.[12] This corresponds to a sense of superiority that led it to perceive the expressions of modernity as manifestations of progress, and thus the evolution of Western law as an indication of the direction to be taken.

It was precisely this motivation that lay behind Henry Sumner Maine's celebrated image, according to which societies would progress by following the movement 'from status to contract'. In Maine's conception, progress came from abandoning the idea that social relations are family-like or in any case shaped by their place within a social order perceived as natural and therefore immobile, and taking up a new conception according to which those social relations arise out of free agreement.[13] This image, moreover, was fundamentally adopted by the historical and dialectical materialism underlying the law of the socialist countries (II.3.8), which had overcome feudalism and capitalism and were now preparing for the inevitable transition to communism.

On closer inspection, there was no lack of awareness among the founders of comparative law of the limits of an analysis of legal change centred entirely on the evolutionist paradigm. This emerges from the description of the tasks attributed to the comparative history of institutions as a science distinct from comparative law. The comparative history of institutions devoted itself to describing the development of institutions on the basis of the commonalities found among peoples whose social conditions were considered similar, while comparative law set itself the task of identifying in a prescriptive key the features of the common law of civilised humanity (II.1.2). In this context, it was doubted whether those commonalities were 'purely spontaneous' and not instead dependent on the 'relations of assimilation between peoples' and in particular on the 'reciprocal borrowing that may occur as a consequence of international exchanges'.[14]

However, full awareness of the limitations of evolutionism was yet to come. Only relatively recently has it been recognised that evolutionism fuels now discredited paradigms, such as those in which 'the end point of evolution', whether unilinear or plural, indicates 'an intrinsic superiority over the starting point'. This is also the reason for the affirmation of a different explanation of legal change, which is ultimately seen as the result of contacts between cultures rather than of original innovation, albeit naturally or inexorably unidirectional. As Gambaro et al. argue:

> The evolutionary mechanism is not sufficient to explain the changes of law. Cultural expressions (religion, language, economic behaviour, law, art) can be imitated. Any human group, as long as it knows the language and law of its neighbour, can make its neighbour's linguistic structures and legal solutions its own. The phenomenon under consideration, called diffusion, counterbalances the effects of evolution. The law in a given area can also change as a result of the diffusion of an external model in the area.[15]

10 G. Tarde, *Le droit comparé et la sociologie*, in Société de législation comparée (Ed.), *Congrès international de droit comparé*, vol. 1, Paris, 1900, p. 438 f.
11 *Ivi*, p. 531.
12 N. Rouland, *Introduction historique au droit*, Paris, 1998, p. 184.
13 H. Sumner Maine, *Ancient Law: Its Connection to the Early History of Society, and Its Relation to Modern Ideas*, London, 1861, p. 169 f.
14 R. Saleilles, *Conception et objet de la science du droit comparé*, in Société de législation comparée (Ed.), *Congrès international de droit comparé*, cit., p. 169.
15 A. Gambaro, R. Sacco and M. Graziadei, *Sistemi giuridici comparati*, cit., pp. 26 and 28.

Evolutionism has thus been replaced by diffusionism as the paradigm used to explain legal change, which thus becomes an analysis concentrated on how models circulate. However, it is not enough to invoke imitation as the driving force behind the circulation of models if it is to avoid the flaws of the evolutionist creed. In fact, diffusionists claim that the creation of an original model constitutes a rare occurrence, thus fuelling visions of legal change as essentially due to the mere transposition of the exported model, without any creative contribution on the part of the receiving order. In other words, legal change ends up being constrained within a hierarchical relationship between a centre devoted to the exportation of models, and a periphery destined, or rather condemned, to their reception. We shall see this in greater detail when discussing legal transplants (III.1.3).

Moreover, in scholarship, it is usually said that the choice of the model to be imitated depends mainly on 'a quality that we do not know what to call, except by the name of prestige'.[16] Those who express themselves in these terms do not necessarily intend to conceal the fact that, alongside a circulation of models *imperio rationis*, there is also one *ratione imperii*, and that the latter manifests itself as an imposition 'made possible by military conquest or political domination'.[17] Then there is the distinction made between imitation and borrowing, namely, between the situation in which the order receiving the model aims at 'replicating the same purposes' and the situation in which it only wants 'the adoption of certain means'. In the latter case, the identity of that order would in a certain sense be preserved and one could therefore not speak of imposition.[18]

However, we must not overlook the risk that the adoption of a diffusionist point of view may downplay the role of power relations in the reception of models. If overlooked, our observations would then inevitably end up feeding discourses of an evolutionist nature since it could be concluded that the prestige of a model derives from its ability to build a 'more advanced society in terms of legal civilisation'.[19]

There are, indeed, numerous indications of a circulation of models *ratione imperii*. Think of the circulation of the French civil code as an effect of Napoleon's conquests,[20] and of the consequences at the taxonomical level of colonisation: from the New World, initiated by the so-called discovery of America, to the European and US-American division of the African continent between the 19th and 20th centuries, both preceded by the English penetration of India and Australia. Then, from the end of the Second World War and through the years of the Cold War, the imposition of the socialist model in Eastern Europe.[21]

Not to mention, finally, the processes of globalisation, i.e. the planetary spread of the Western political order and economic order, or more precisely that of the United States (II.1.9) as the country that, more than others, has used law as an instrument of hegemony.[22] The spread of the political order has been the backdrop to what was summarised as exportation of democracy using weapons or human rights imperialism.[23] The spread of the economic order, instead, went hand in hand with the imposition of neo-American capitalism (II.2.9) through

16 R. Sacco and P. Rossi, *Introduzione al diritto comparato*, in *Trattato di diritto comparato*, dir. R. Sacco, 7th ed., Torino, 2019, p. 135.
17 R. Sacco, *Antropologia giuridica*, Bologna, 2007, p. 47.
18 See M. Graziadei, *What Does Globalisation Mean for the Comparative Study of Law?*, in *Journal of Comparative Law*, 16, 2021, p. 527.
19 E. Grande, *Imitazione e diritto. Ipotesi sulla circolazione dei modelli*, Torino, 2000, pp. 44 s. and 149.
20 G. Cuniberti, *Grands systèmes de droit contemporains. Introduction au droit comparé*, 4th ed., Paris, 2019, p. 48.
21 L. Pegoraro and A. Rinella, *Introduzione al diritto pubblico comparato*, Padova, 2002, p. 69.
22 U. Mattei, *A Theory of Imperial Law: A Study on U.S. Hegemony and the Latin Resistance*, in *Indiana Journal of Global Legal Studies*, 10, 2003, p. 407 ff.
23 Following A. Gambino, *L'imperialismo dei diritti umani. Caos o giustizia nella società globale*, Roma, 2001.

the market of reforms: first, in the so-called developing countries (III.2.2), then also in the Old Continent and especially in the countries affected by the sovereign debt crisis (III.2.5).

Moreover, the diffusionist approach is not only objectionable because it conceals imposition as the engine of legal change. It is also unconvincing because of the terminology it is associated with, namely, the scheme of the circulation of models, which is not by chance used to identify the centre and the periphery of a grouping of systems. In fact, discussing the circulation of models means imagining their faithful transposition, unmediated by the creative contribution of the imitating subject, which presupposes a vision of law as divorced from its context.

To illustrate this aspect, we can return to the classification that identifies Western law as consisting of a centre, of European or US-American origin, and a periphery, mainly Latin American (II.3.9). This is not to criticise the idea of a Westernisation of the region, which in itself does not indicate a hierarchical approach to the classification of legal systems. It does, however, become so if one wishes to assert that Latin America, lagging behind Western development, has passively assimilated models produced elsewhere. This overlooks the fact that imitation implies, above all, a necessarily arbitrary selection of what is considered appropriate to imitate. And that the imitation of models necessarily involves their manipulation, to be considered in our case 'a peripheral reinvention of the law of the centre'.[24] The diffusionist view, just like the evolutionist, risks misrepresenting the reinvention as bad imitation, on the assumption that 'the savage does not copy anything without distorting it through clumsiness, just as children are wont to draw'.[25]

The latter words were uttered more than a century ago at the oft-mentioned Paris Congress of Comparative Law (II.1.2). Over time, the language has changed, and, in any case, it does not resort to formulas to which one feels an instinctive disgust. And yet the substance of the diffusionist discourse has not changed, for it is still too often intertwined with explanations of legal change based on hierarchical and thus evolutionist schemes. If one wants to overcome this, i.e. if one wants to finally acknowledge the essentially creative character of the imitation of legal models and, more fundamentally, the complexity of the processes of legal diffusion, then one must first avoid using terms that suggest a passive role for the imitator.

3 MORE ON THE CIRCULATION OF MODELS: TRANSPLANTS, BORROWING, AND MIGRATIONS

One of the most problematic terms in the discussion of the circulation of models is undoubtedly the phrase 'legal transplant'. This term is used extensively by Alan Watson to explain legal change over the centuries as a chain of more or less faithful imitations of rules and institutions, all largely modelled on Roman law, as well as on English common law.

It must be said that this theory appears innovative above all in that it breaks with the theories of 'law as a mirror',[26] according to which the rules and institutions of a society reflect its political and economic structure, ultimately shared by the Marxist approaches to the phenomenon of law: we know that in socialist countries law was considered a superstructure reflecting the economic structure (II.3.8). This scheme has been questioned by those who

24 G. Marini, *La costruzione delle tradizioni giuridiche e il diritto latinoamericano*, in *Rivista critica del diritto privato*, 2011, p. 168.
25 G. Tarde, *Le droit comparé et la sociologie*, cit., p. 444.
26 W. Ewald, *Comparative Jurisprudence (II): The Logic of Legal Transplant*, in *American Journal of Comparative Law*, 43, 1995, p. 492 ff.

have pointed out that 'an unprejudiced examination of the Marxian hypothesis leads to the conclusion that there is not always a biunivocal correlation between the class and power situation and the solution of the individual legal problem'.[27] Mirror theories are directly challenged by transplant theory, which talks down the role of political power as the engine of legal change, while emphasising the role of legal scholars who, based on their technical expertise, legitimate the foundation of the Western legal tradition (II.3.2).

In fact, Watson argues that imitations are rarely the work of the political power, which as a rule has 'little interest in producing law', but rather the autonomous initiative of the class of jurists of the imitating legal system, in particular judges and scholars. The latter, Watson argues, operate according to merely technical criteria, being conditioned solely by their specific 'legal culture'. It is to this that we owe, among other things, the recognition that a certain legal system is prestigious and authoritative, which is why it is identified as the reference system for the transplant,[28] while imposition is not invoked as the driving force behind the circulation of models. This would then be reflected in the first fundamental characteristic of legal rules, namely, the ease with which they circulate. In Watson's words:

> To indicate the scale of transplanting it is enough at this stage to call attention to the reception – in the widest sense – of Roman law and the spread of English common law. The system of private law which was set out in the 6th century by Justinian's compilers for the early Byzantine Empire could be, and was, taken over in very large measure and made to operate in most of the countries of Mediaeval, Renaissance and even 19th century Europe: in Catholic, Calvinist and Lutheran territories, in agricultural nations, in trading cities ruled by a merchant oligarchy, in monarchies and republics alike. From Europe this received law in turn could be, and was, transplanted directly or through the influence of a European code, notably the French *Code civil*, to Quebec, Louisiana, South America, much of Africa (notably South Africa), Ceylon, Japan and elsewhere. . . . England's own common law became in its turn another great legal export; to the larger part of Canada and the United States, to Australia, New Zealand, India and elsewhere. One can claim without fear of contradiction that at least in the Western world transplanting has been the major feature in legal change for the last thousand years.[29]

The longevity of legal rules then also contributes to proving the validity of the legal transplant theory:

> The second characteristic, longevity, is equally striking. The contract of sale, the most common and important contract, in all countries of the contemporary Western world is very obviously the Roman contract of the 2nd century A.D. The individual contracts as they are set out in modern civil codes are recognisably the contracts of Gaius' *Institutes* written also in the 2nd century. The distinction to be found in common law countries between written and oral defamation – libel and slander – results from particular conditions in England in the 16th century, and survives despite numerous attacks from the 19th century onwards.[30]

The transplant theory can be criticised from many points of view and first because, as even its proponents claim, it denies or at least underestimates the direct connection between law and society (IV.3.1). Its advocates not surprisingly avoid defining law, or even worse, they appear to define law in the same way as legal positivists do. Similarly, they do not appear to consider law to be a merely instrumental phenomenon with respect to the aims pursued by the lawmaker. In other words, they overlook the fact that 'law is rather ideological, symbolic, expressive, and mystifying'.[31]

27 R. Sacco and P. Rossi, *Introduzione al diritto comparato*, cit., p. 130.
28 A. Watson, *Legal Transplants. An Approach to Comparative Law*, 2nd ed., Athens GA, 1993, p. 107 ff.
29 A. Watson, *Comparative Law and Legal Change*, in *Cambridge Law Journal*, 37, 1978, p. 313 f.
30 *Ivi*, p. 314.
31 R.L. Abel, *Law as Lag: Inertia as a Social Theory of Law*, in *Michigan Law Review*, 80, 1982, p. 807 f.

Many then point out that the theory of legal transplants is based on an unacceptable simplification as it does not consider that legal models have a hermeneutic heritage that cannot be transposed without alteration: texts may well circulate, but 'meaning simply does not lend itself to transplantation'.[32] Similarly, others argue that transplantation can be spoken of only in cases in which an entire human group moves, taking its law with it. This circumstance is conceivable only in legal experiences in which the principle of the personality of law is allowed to operate, or in cases in which the movement takes place over a portion of territory not subject to any constituted authority.[33] In all other cases, one should not speak of transplants – which as a rule presuppose the death of the donor organism – but of 'grafts' that take place by 'fusing the lives of two different living organisms', the donor and the recipient, or alternatively by the 'covering of one by the other'.[34]

In short, transplantation generates a circulation of models destined to be contaminated. It constitutes a phenomenon to be analysed with the sensitivity of those concerned with legal pluralism.[35] No wonder then that transplantation theory has met with hostility from legal scholars who entrust comparative law with the task of indicating reference models to the legislature for implementing reforms (II.1.4). From such a point of view, the context in which the models to be imitated are placed clearly takes on an absolute centrality: circulation is only permissible between legal experiences that are politically, economically, and socially similar. Or, to put it more precisely, the outcome of the circulation can be predicted on the basis of an analysis of the exporting system only if the latter shows a certain degree of similarity with the importing system.[36] All this is to be assessed by resorting to an external point of view on the law (I.2.1), which is attentive to the dynamics underlying the interaction between the various actors within the political and economic order.[37]

On closer inspection, the theory of legal transplants could be rescued, and the criticisms just summarised deemed irrelevant, if one emphasises the fact that Watson understands the independence of law from society as the non-existence of a two-way correspondence between technical-juridical constructions and the purpose of their use. The theory would then ultimately support the idea of a dissociation between legal techniques and the values conveyed by those techniques (IV.3.1). What makes such a reading impossible, however, is the fact that Watson reserves too narrow a role for political power: not only does he say that it is for the most part uninterested in producing law, but also that when it produces rules intended to last in time, such as codes, it does so attributing 'no specific social message' to them. And since Watson recognises that transplants do not result in a faithful transposition of the rule, which on the contrary 'frequently, perhaps always, involves legal transformation',[38] this implies that the role assumed by the class of legal scholars is based on a usurpation of political power. This may be valid as a general observation, referring to anyone who uses legal discourse in social conflict, but not as something reserved for a particular category of subjects (I.1.4).

Finally, the way in which the theory of transplants has been elaborated, with only a cursory attention to empirical data, is unconvincing. Its supporters, rather than devoting

32 P. Legrand, *What 'Legal Transplants'?*, in D. Nelken and J. Feest (Eds.), *Adapting Legal Cultures*, Oxford and Portland OR, 2001, p. 55 ff.
33 M. Rheinstein, *Einführung in die Rechtsvergleichung*, 2nd ed., München, 1987, p. 126.
34 E.A. Feldman, *Patients' Rights, Citizens' Movements and Japanese Legal Culture*, in D. Nelken (Ed.), *Comparing Legal Cultures*, Aldershot etc., 1997, p. 220 f.
35 M. Graziadei, *Frontiere, Legal Transplants, comparazioni: le vie del diritto e l'incontro con il pluralismo*, in P. Cappellini and G. Cazzetta (Eds.), *Pluralismo giuridico. Itinerari contemporanei*, Milano, 2023, p. 24 ff.
36 Following O. Kahn Freund, *On Uses and Misuses of Comparative Law*, in *Modern Law Review*, 1974, p. 1 ff.
37 R. Cotterrell, *Is There a Logic of Legal Transplants?*, in D. Nelken and J. Feest (Eds.), *Adapting Legal Cultures*, cit., p. 71 ff.
38 A. Watson, *Legal Transplants*, cit., p. 116 f.

themselves to comprehensive general analyses, concentrate on the reconstruction of numerous and specific conceptual points, believing them all to be irrefutable proofs of the theory. On closer inspection, however, these findings have weak probative force. They are for the most part drawn from areas which are irrelevant to society, in which 'it is important to have a rule, but it does not matter what the rule is: for example, whether the cars drive on the right or the left'.[39]

We can observe at this point that reflection on legal transplants, its theorisation as well as its criticism, has particularly concerned comparativists with a private law sensibility. The scholars of comparative public law have indeed not been fascinated by a theory they consider 'mechanical'[40] – that is, incapable of appreciating the context in which the legal phenomenon is immerged. Hence, their conclusion that legal transplant theory is unsuitable for describing the circulation of public law models.[41]

From such a point of view, one prefers to use the concept of 'legal borrowing', which we have already encountered to describe the situation in which the circulation of models takes place due to the willingness of the importing legal system to transpose the instruments and not the aims pursued by the exporting legal system (III.1.2). Still others resort to the concept of 'legal migration', deemed more suitable for observing the circulation of models, considering that it may concern the texts but not also their hermeneutical heritage.[42]

4 PROMOTING LEGAL CHANGE: LAW AND DEVELOPMENT

That imposition is to be considered the main cause of legal change by imitation was emphasised in the context of the comparison between common law and civil law carried out for primarily classificatory purposes.[43] Things clearly remained the same even when the focus shifted to creating rankings – after classifications – based on parameters now valued by the New Comparative Economics. In fact, the theory of legal origin is explicitly based on the recognition that the current economic performance of non-European countries stems from their colonial past, when they received the law of the colonisers, which was often maintained even after liberation (II.3.6).

As we know, the relationship between law and development has not always been accompanied by a desire to demonstrate that common law countries offer the best models for promoting development. For a long time, the claim to the economic superiority of common law coexisted with the recognition of the technical-legal superiority of civil law countries (II.3.5). What has remained constant, however, is the more or less explicit identification of economic development with development as such, which ultimately appears as one of the driving forces of legal change.

The emphasis on economic development is illustrated through the activities of the institutions created at Bretton Woods: the World Bank and the International Monetary Fund. Their work testifies to the persistence of the conviction that development is provided by economic

39 P.G. Monateri, *Critica dell'ideologia e analisi antagonista*, in *Rivista critica del diritto privato*, 2000, p. 709.

40 V. Perju, *Constitutional Transplants, Borrowing, and Migrations*, in M. Rosenfeld and A. Sajó (Eds.), *Oxford Handbook of Comparative Constitutional Law*, Oxford, 2012, p. 1307.

41 G. Halmai, *Constitutional Transplants*, in R. Masterman and R. Schütze (Eds.), *The Cambridge Companion to Comparative Constitutional Law*, Cambridge, 2019, p. 582.

42 A. Di Martino, *Circolazione delle soluzioni giuridiche e delle idee costituzionali. Questioni di metodo comparativo e prassi tra culture costituzionali e spazi globali*, in *Dpce Online*, 2021, p. 743 s.

43 J.H. Merryman, *The Civil Law Tradition. An Introduction to the Legal Systems of Europe and Latin America*, Stanford CA, 1969, p. 5.

growth, and that this derives from the spread of capitalism, particularly as manifested in the US legal experience. Moreover, capitalism does not necessarily presuppose democracy, so much so that the latter may well prevail as a result of the expansion of the former.[44] Moreover, this is precisely what the events of the first half of the 20th century testify to, when fascism accredited itself as the political order called upon to resolve the impasse of the economic order (II.1.3).

In other words, while the Bretton Woods institutions promoted and promote both foundations of the Western legal tradition, democracy and capitalism, it is on the beneficial effects of the latter that the emphasis has been, and continues to be, placed. This is obviously due to the adherence to neoliberal visions of development, which have also influenced the political order, even though the competences of these institutions were and are limited to economic matters. Indeed, the World Bank oversteps its bounds when it claims an interest in the good governance of states, and, more particularly, involves itself in prescribing the outcome of government action. This has affected 'the processes by which authority is exercised in the management of a country's economic and social resources', as well as 'the capacity of governments to design, formulate, and implement policies, and, in general, to discharge government functions'.[45]

The World Bank puts these intentions into practice in the framework of a kind of market for reforms. This was achieved by making its loans conditional on the implementation of so-called Structural Adjustment Programs (III.2.2), which focused on the functioning of the economic order but also aimed to promote the rule of law. The latter was understood as a driving force for the spread of democracy and human rights, but also and above all for the political reforms fundamental to the neo-American capitalism – in particular, those concerning the protection of individual property rights and their effective enforcement through a system of independent courts. All this in order to implement the plan drawn up by the International Monetary Fund to impose the Washington Consensus (III.2.2). The latter is a scheme that is now being used as a point of reference for the restructuring of the public debt of even the so-called developed countries, as well as the market for reforms, which can be the leitmotif for describing the origins and development of the European project (III.2.3–6).

The same faith in the development of capitalism as an engine for the affirmation of democracy was the background to the birth, between the 1950s and 1960s, of the Law and Development movement, which arose to deepen the terms of a relationship that was somewhat problematic and, in any case, difficult to conceptualise. However, the movement's interest was not only scientific: it aimed at promoting the spread of Western legal models as the best catalysts for economic growth and, through it, for wellbeing and social justice.[46] Jurists from colonising countries took part to the movement with an ethnocentric impetus sometimes inspired by a genuine missionary spirit, nevertheless indicative of a 'legal imperialism',[47] as well as of imperialism as such since the promotion of the development of non-Western countries aimed at ensuring their continued dependence on Western countries, i.e. at safeguarding their development.[48]

This conclusion seems in many ways inevitable when one considers the movement's sources of funding. It was institutions such as the Agency for International Development, a US government agency, and the Ford Foundation, also from the US, that sponsored legal assistance schemes for so-called developing countries. They did so at a time when Western

44 A. Somma, *Diritto e capitalismo. Leggi dello Stato e leggi del mercato nella costruzione della soggettività neoliberale*, in M.G. Bernardini and O. Giolo (Eds.), *Teorie critiche del diritto*, Pisa, 2017, in particular p. 311 ff.
45 See World Bank, *Managing Development: The Governance Dimension*, Washington DC, 1991, p. 23, n. 2.
46 In this regard S. Adelman and A. Paliwala, *Introduction*, in Iid. (Eds.), *The Limits of Law and Development. Neoliberalism, Governance and Social Justice*, Abingdon and New York NY, 2021, p. 1 ff.
47 J.A. Gardner, *Legal Imperialism. American Lawyers and Foreign Aid in Latin America*, Madison WI, 1980.
48 In particular A. Gunder Frank, *América Latina: subdesarrollo o revolucion*, Ciudad de México, 1973.

countries were still promoting the Keynesian compromise (II.2.9), thus sponsoring first and foremost the building of state institutions capable of promoting orderly capitalist development, as well as the training of jurists equipped to set them up and make them work. The institutions just mentioned were the same ones that gave their financial support to the Chicago boys,[49] i.e. the Chilean economists later involved in supporting Pinochet's dictatorship and in particular in defining its economic policy (II.3.11).

In its first phase, the Law and Development movement was inspired by an over-estimation of the role of law and legal education,[50] which can be traced back to a conviction opposite to that shared by the proponents of the theory of law as mirror (III.1.3). While the latter viewed law as reflecting defined political and economic arrangements, the Law and Development movement regarded the state and its rules as 'the primary agent of social control and change' and exalted the legal professions as 'representative of the public interest'. Moreover, their supporters were convinced, in an openly evolutionist key, that there was 'some natural tendency for legal systems in the Third World to evolve in the direction of the ideal model of liberal legalism'. Under these conditions, the movement's failure is not surprising at all. As Trubek and Galanter observed:

> Law and development studies are in crisis because some scholars have come seriously to doubt the liberal legalist assumptions that 'legal development' can be equated with exporting United States institutions or that any improvement of legal institutions in the Third World will be potent and good. They have come to see that legal change may have little or no effect on social economic conditions in Third World societies and, conversely, that many legal 'reforms' can deepen inequality, curb participation, restrict individual freedom, and hamper efforts to increase material well-being.[51]

Soon, however, in the 1980s, a second phase of the movement returned to the scene. In the meantime, the Keynesian compromise entered in a crisis, while the model of neo-American capitalism was gaining ground, starting with the Chilean experiment just mentioned. And this model included an alternative ideology to the one implicitly shared by the exponents of the first phase: a decisive downsizing of the role of public powers in regulating the market was now being promoted, hence the development of private institutions to protect individual economic rights, to the detriment of the public institutions to which the promotion of economic development had previously been entrusted.[52] In order to disseminate these programmes, a much greater effort was made in terms of legal aid than in the era when the Keynesian compromise was still respected. This involved a more substantial and, if possible, more focused, and manifestly ethnocentric, effort to promote the common law model, which was identified with US law as the natural foundation of the neo-American capitalism. (II.2.9).

From such a point of view, the New Comparative Economics merely amplifies the efforts of the second phase of the Law and Development movement, combining them with a more explicit use of practices aimed at enforcing the circulation of the common law model, while at the same time opposing the civil law model, particularly in its French manifestation (II.3.6). All this reflects the conviction, common to both phases of the movement, that law is a useful instrument of social engineering whose effectiveness depends on the quality of the rules adopted or imposed, rather than on the context in which they are applied. This is a naïve

49 V. Brender, *Economic Transformations in Chile: The Formation of the Chicago Boys*, in *American economist*, 55, 2010, p. 113.
50 M. Bussani, *Introduzione al diritto comparato. Un breviario della globalità*, Milano, 2022, p. 60 f.
51 See D.M. Trubek and M. Galanter, *Scholars in Self-Estrangement. Some Reflections on the Crisis in Law and Development Studies in the United States*, in *Wisconsin Law Review*, 4, 1974, p. 1078 ff.
52 In this regard, for instance, L. Nader, *Promise or Plunder? A Past and Future Look at Law and Development*, in *Global Jurist Frontiers*, 7, 2007, p. 1 ff.

belief also shared by those who witnessed the transition to capitalism of the countries that formerly belonged to the Soviet bloc due to a lack of attention to the complex and changing relationships between law and society.[53]

It is astonishing that all this happened after the United Nations had conceived the human development index,[54] as an alternative measuring tool to gross domestic product (GNP), in order to value parameters such as the level of social services and the diffusion of environmental awareness. It is also surprising how little consideration was given to the views of some of the main supporters of the Law and Development movement who had broken away from equating development with freeing markets from public powers, i.e. from the dominant beliefs during its second phase, now discredited as the result of an erroneous premise. In its place, they recognised that development must consider its human aspect, in addition to the economic one, and thereby must be conceived as an engine of emancipation. As Trubek and Santos summarised:

> As the last century came to an end, reactions to the neoliberal program in development economics grew stronger. . . . People recognized that unrestricted markets were often inefficient and that state intervention was necessary to correct such market failures as transaction costs or information asymmetries. Critics charged neoliberal policymakers for not having paid attention to existing local institutions and to timing of reforms. . . . Development economists no longer insist on 'deregulation' of internal markets, but rather focus on introducing 'appropriate regulation'. . . . There is an appeal for a reconceptualization of development that would decenter the focus on economic growth. Advocates of this view argue that development policies should broaden their scope in the pursuit of human development, of which income is only an aspect, and equal consideration should be paid to political, social, and legal development. Taken together, these multiple aspects of development aim at promoting development as freedom: the goal is to enhance people's capabilities and to enable individuals to lead the life they choose to live.[55]

Similar intentions inspired a third phase of the law and development movement, which is referred to as the post–Washington Consensus phase.[56] This was the backdrop to the initiatives taken by the World Bank and the International Monetary Fund in reaction to the criticism provoked by their support, in the last decade of the last century, for the circulation of neoliberal models. The result was the elaboration of a 'holistic approach to development', taking into account its social and human aspects, which had to be addressed in agreements that did not follow the approach of structural adjustment plans. Hence, the idea of a 'comprehensive development strategy', i.e. a participatory definition of the ways in which the objectives set out in the structural adjustment plans could be pursued, taking into account their social and environmental implications. This required the involvement of civil society to ensure that the views of the poorest sections of the population were adequately represented, thus facilitating the provision of appropriate measures to achieve what is considered, in the aforementioned human development index, a social security system aimed, in particular, at guaranteeing the right to health and the right to education.[57]

We shall see that this did not affect the intrinsically neoliberal nature of the Bretton Woods institutions' action (III.2.2.). We will thus obtain further evidence of the tendentially

53 J.H. Merryman, *Comparative Law and Social Change*, in *American Journal of Comparative Law*, 25, 1977, p. 481 f.
54 See United Nations Development Programme, *Human Development Report 1990*, Oxford, 1990, p. 9 ff.
55 D.M. Trubek and A. Santos, *The Third Moment in Law and Development Theory*, in Iid. (Ed.), *The New Law and Development. A Critical Appraisal*, Cambridge MA, 2006, p. 6 ff.
56 See M. Siems, *Comparative Law*, 2nd ed., Cambridge, 2018, p. 336 ff.
57 See N. Hanna and R. Agarwala, *Toward a Comprehensive Development Strategy*, World Bank Oed Working Papers Series n. 16/2000.

evolutionist and ethnocentric inspiration of the Law and Development movement, and its sharing of the same ideals promoted by these institutions.[58]

The same tendency has not been significantly undermined in the most recent studies aimed at revitalising the movement, which recognise the mistakes made in the first and second phases and the opportunity to remedy them by amplifying certain aspects of the third. Those studies indeed certify that development is not the prerogative of common law systems, not least because 'a civil law system, based on state-sponsored codes, appears more adaptable than a common law system' and because in countries with a weak private sector, public intervention in the economic order is 'essential'. The same studies then recognise the desirability of adopting a holistic notion of development, thus different from that promoted by neoliberals due to its emphasis on 'non-market values', but point out that even these latter values presuppose an institutional architecture requiring 'considerable economic and technical resources'.[59]

Under these conditions, no significant progress has been made since the time when the debate on law and development was squeezed between those who did their utmost to add adjectives to the word development and those who instead condemned it regardless of those adjectives, including its combination with the concept of sustainability. The latter was also criticised for its inability to emancipate itself from the economicist imaginary and finally to challenge the unsustainable myth of 'infinite development'.[60]

5 THE DOING BUSINESS REPORTS OF THE WORLD BANK

The initiatives undertaken by the World Bank to dissociate the concept of development from its economic dimension have only produced ephemeral or mere cosmetic effects. Therefore, the overall development framework has produced results in line with those supported by openly neoliberal initiatives.[61] The latter were, moreover, numerous in the period we are talking about, which in many respects is characterised by an unchallenged spread of the foundations of neo-American capitalism. This was not seriously questioned even after a wave of crises, from the sovereign debt crisis to the pandemic crisis, which made all its limitations evident (III.2. 7–8).

Emblematic among the initiatives we refer to is the case of the Doing Business Reports, which the World Bank produced annually between 2004 and 2020 to measure the economic costs of regulation borne by businesses over their lifetime: from start-up to possible insolvency proceedings. All this has been done to identify, in addition to the most attractive national legal systems from an investor's point of view, the virtuous legal models that should be promoted in order to allow businesses to create wealth and the market to produce economic development or, more broadly, development as such.[62]

That this is the underlying inspiration of the Reports is hardly surprising as they were conceived and directed by the initiators of the New Comparative Economics (II.3.6). More precisely, their research was used as the background for the rankings that demonstrate the Reports' finding: the superiority of common law systems over civil law systems, and more fundamentally of neo-American capitalism over Rhine capitalism. All this because common law

58 L.G. Pes, *Diritto e sviluppo neoliberale: il dibattito sul New law and development*, in *Politica del diritto*, 2007, p. 611 ff.
59 Y.-S. Lee, *General Theory of Law and Development*, in *Cornell International Law Journal*, 50, 2017, p. 415 ff. As well as Id., *Law and Development. Theory and Practice*, 2nd ed., London, 2022.
60 S. Latouche, *Le pari de la décroissance*, Paris, 2006, p. 113 ff.
61 U. Mattei and L. Nader, *Plunder. When the Rule of Law is Illegal*, Malden etc., 2008, p. 53 ff.
62 All Reports and materials related to their drafting are freely accessible: https://archive.doingbusiness.org/en/doingbusiness.

systems show a restrained intervention of the public authorities, whose main task is to protect individual economic rights and to promote their enforcement.

The first Report was published in 2004.[63] It considers more than 130 countries, whose legal systems are analysed by reference to five topics that exemplify the activity of companies with similar characteristics: limited liability companies with a maximum of 50 employees, operating in the most populous or economically important city, whose shareholders are non-foreign natural persons. The topics are then analysed by means of a series of indicators expressed in numerical form, in order to enable a comparison to be made between national laws and, finally, to establish a ranking of the laws considered to be the most virtuous.

The first topic is 'starting a business'. In order to allow for a comparison, the reports considered a number of indicators. These included 'all procedures officially required for an entrepreneur to operate an industrial or commercial business legally', the 'time of fulfilling each procedure', the related costs expressed as a 'percentage of income per capita', and 'the minimum capital requirements to operate'.[64] It goes without saying that the regulation of these aspects is assessed positively when the number of procedures is limited, and the time devoted to fulfilling them is short; similarly, the same 'less is more' logic applies to the costs and the minimum capital requirements, if any. The latter are not normally present in common law countries, where other means of protecting corporate creditors are used (III.1.8), thus giving those systems a considerable advantage.

The second topic considered by the Reports is the regulation of the employment relationship, with indicators concerning the modalities of its establishment and termination ('hiring and firing workers'). Here, to facilitate comparison, a relatively precise identikit of the worker is drawn: he is employed full-time, has been employed by the same company for at least 20 years, has a spouse who is not employed and two children, and is 'not a member of a labor union (unless membership is mandatory)'. It then goes on to state that the most virtuous law, and therefore the one to be indicated as a reference model, is the one that entrusts the definition of the main terms of the employment relationship to the autonomy of the parties. In short, the Reports endorse the law of flexible employment, not only with regard to hiring and dismissal, but also from the point of view of the overall discipline of the relationship.[65] This, as we shall shortly say, produces noticeable friction with what is required at the level of labour law within the United Nations.

Let us turn to the third topic, that of commercial dispute resolution, or in the language of the Reports, 'enforcing contracts'. The typical dispute considered for comparison is one between a party that has fulfilled its obligation and the defaulting party, which is also interested in slowing down the proceedings, for the value of half the per capita income and only considering first instance proceedings. Here, the indicators used to assess the most virtuous legal order concern the number of procedures requiring 'interaction between the parties or between them and the judge or a court officer', then the duration of the dispute, its costs including the lawyer's fee, and finally its 'procedural complexity' from the point of view of 'how heavily dispute resolution is regulated'. Systems which, in addition to lower time and cost, are characterised by a simplified procedure that favours orality, limits formalities e.g. regarding notifications or evidence, reduces the possibility of appeals, and perhaps establishes 'specialized commercial courts' are considered as models to be followed.[66] This evidently

63 World Bank, *Doing Business in 2004. Understanding Regulation*, Washington DC, 2004.
64 *Ivi*, pp. 3 ff. and 17 ff.
65 *Ivi*, pp. 5 s. and 29 ff.
66 *Ivi*, pp. 6 and 41 ff.

gives common law jurisdictions a special place, and conversely disqualifies civil law jurisdictions characterised by a certain procedural formalism.[67]

However, this has considerable implications. The discipline of the civil process in common law systems is devoted to the 'pure and simple settlement of the dispute', whereas in civil law systems the fundamental value is the 'application of the law at the occasion of the dispute' and thus the 'protection of rights'. In short, the Doing Business Reports promote the safeguarding of contractual freedom, which is its explicitly aspiration. However, in doing so, it does not take sufficient account of the fact that the disputes decided by the courts are also and above all relevant as points of emergence of a social conflict which, as such, must be linked to the fundamental values of the legal system, unless one considers that the latter only concern the 'active preservation of the current financial economic system'.[68]

The fourth and fifth topics considered by the Doing Business Reports concern access to credit ('getting credit') and insolvency proceedings ('closing a business'), which are related. In assessing access to credit, consideration is given to those information systems that measure the reliability of prospective borrowers, but also to the system of protection available to creditors in the event of a debtor's insolvency: in particular, the regulation of security.[69] Regarding insolvency proceedings, account is taken not only of security, but also of the time and costs of the proceedings and the powers of the courts. The reports highlight as a positive model those systems in which the powers of the courts are limited in favour of the powers of creditors and the legislator refrains from tightening procedures[70] – for example, by identifying categories of privileged creditors to be given priority over secured creditors.[71] This again gives a considerable advantage to common law countries and disfavours civil law countries, where it is customary to consider workers and the Treasury as privileged creditors.

Thus, the conclusion drawn by the first Doing Business Report, that accompanied the summary ranking of data on the various topics, obviously aligned with the dictates of the New Comparative Economics and, more fundamentally, the theory of legal origin (II.3.7). The message was clear: in countries that have imitated the common law, the ability to create a suitable environment for the development of entrepreneurial activities, and thus high levels of prosperity, is superior because they 'regulate the least'. The opposite is the case in countries that have embraced civil law solutions which 'regulate the most' by using expensive processes and bogging disputes down in 'the highest number of procedures'. More precisely, as the 2004 Report states:

> The regulatory regimes of most developing countries are not indigenous – they are shaped by their colonial heritage. When the English, French, Spaniards, Dutch, Germans, and Portuguese colonized much of the world, they brought with them their laws and institutions. After independence, many countries revised legislation, but in only a few cases have they strayed far from the original. . . . Common law countries regulate the least. Countries in the French civil law tradition the most. . . . Heavier regulation is generally associated with more inefficiency in public institutions – longer delays and higher cost – and more unemployed people, corruption, less productivity and investment, but not with better quality of private or public goods.[72]

67 S. Djankov et al., *Courts*, in *Quarterly Journal of Economics*, 118, 2003, p. 453 ff.
68 R. Caponi, *Processo civile e conflitto sociale*, in A. Somma (Ed.), *Diritti fondamentali e conflitto sociale. Un dialogo tra le discipline*, Roma, 2024, p. 116 ff.
69 World Bank, *Doing Business in 2004*, cit., pp. 6 s. and 55 ff.
70 *Ivi*, pp. 7 and 71 ff.
71 G. McCormack, *Why Doing Business with the World Bank May Be Bad for You*, in *European Business Organization Law Review*, 19, 2018, p. 669 f.
72 World Bank, *Doing Business in 2004*, cit., pp. xiv and 48.

It is therefore not surprising that the first Report provoked disparate reactions. The most piquant ones are those of French legal scholars, who are among other things committed to documenting the positive traits of their system as representative of the civil law model. It is in this perspective that codification, considered by the New Comparative Economics as a drift towards inefficient planning tendencies, is instead exalted as an instrument to bring people 'closer to their law' at least because this makes it democratic and rational. As one riposte put it:

> French law is an eminently democratic law. This cannot be emphasised enough: a law is democratic on the double condition that it is drafted by national representatives and that it is accessible to all citizens, including non-specialists. . . . In an age in which the law is becoming more and more complex due to the proliferation of its sources (domestic, European, international) and the instability of its content, but in which the avenues of knowledge are widening to become information highways, a written and ordered law offers the advantage of being more easily networked and more easily consulted.[73]

French law is also celebrated for its remarkable adaptability. Indeed, one of the characteristics of codification is its flexibility since it is constantly manipulated by the activity of the courts, whose work cannot be described in terms of the old and anachronistic image of the 'mouth of the law': the judiciary properly exercises its role as a source of law endowed with 'pragmatism and imagination'. This indicates an element of superiority of the civil law model over the common law model: 'thanks to the audacity of judges who integrate the law, adapt it and sometimes even circumvent it, French law evolves, despite the immobility of the text, without the rigidity of the rule of precedent'. The economic efficiency of French law is also documented with particular reference to the law of contracts, expressive of a 'liberal and individualistic morality', albeit mediated by equitable considerations. It is also an efficient law because, being contained in simple and clear rules, it allows the parties to conclude contracts whose text is decidedly less complex than the typical 'troublesome Anglo-Saxon-inspired contracts'.[74]

Also worth mentioning, against the backdrop of a long-standing competition with France, is the reaction from the associations of the legal professions in Germany, which, after the publication of the first Doing Business Report, set up the Alliance for German Law (*Bündnis für das deutsche Recht*) in conjunction with the Federal Ministry of Justice. Of course, we should not confuse it with the Academy of German Law (*Akademie für deutsches Recht*), which arose between the two world wars to promote the development and dissemination of German law. And yet some parallels come to mind when thinking of a publication promoted by the Alliance dedicated to the marketing of German law: an expression chosen not by chance since the title of that publication, which is constantly updated, is *Law made in Germany*.[75]

There, it is emphasised that German law constitutes a model to be imitated, or at least chosen for the resolution of disputes between private parties, because it is 'cost-effective' and 'predictable', as well as enforced by a 'low-cost' judicial system. It is, in short, a law that 'ensures the optimum framework for your company', and which demonstrates that '*made in Germany* is not just a quality seal reserved for German cars or machinery, it is equally applicable to German law'. We are not at the level of imperialism typical of the inter-war period, but we are not far from a similar tendency, albeit articulated from economicist paradigms: the degradation of the law to a product that must be distributed as widely as possible.[76]

73 See Association Henri Capitant, *Les droits de la tradition civiliste en question. À propos des Rapports Doing business de la Banque mondiale*, vol. 1, Paris, 2006, p. 87 f.
74 *Ivi*, p. 91 ff.
75 Bundesnotarkammer et al., *Law – Made in Germany*, 3rd ed., Berlin, 2020.
76 J. Maxeiner, *Law Made in Germany: Global Standort or Global Standard?*, in S. Hülshörster and D. Mirow (Eds.), *Deutsche Beratung bei Rechts- und Justizreformen im Ausland*, Berlin, 2012, p. 43 ff.

It should be noted here that comparisons carried out within the framework of the New Comparative Economics could be motivated by purposes opposite to those related to the celebration of common law efficiency; for example, they could emphasise the social benefits that flow from private costs. In order to reach such a conclusion, however, one would have to choose appropriate benchmarks for highlighting these benefits, which are obviously different from those used instead to discredit systems in which private costs are considered excessive. In particular, one could refer to the degree of social pacification brought about by state interventionism, or to its ability to prevent destabilising market failures, or even to its capacity to determine general welfare levels. These are all aspects from which economic operators can obviously also benefit, directly or indirectly. By recasting the reports in this way, the advantages of civil law model could be revealed. This conclusion was reached by the critics of the Doing Business Reports, who do not question the reliability of the method used, but rather its concrete application.[77] We shall see, however, that quantitative comparison is normally used to promote neoliberal sensibilities: the evidence of its use for other purposes is decidedly limited (IV.2.5).

6 NEXT: FROM CRITICISM TO AN IGNOMINIOUS END

The Doing Business Reports have kept appearing over the years and have become the World Bank's most popular publication. Over time, the number of countries covered has increased to 190 in the latest edition, covering the entire planet with the exception of North Korea and some Pacific islands. At the same time, the range of issues used as benchmarks to assess the efficiency of their laws has increased.

Since 2005, the regulation of the transfer of real estate ('registering property') has been added, with an examination of the procedures and their time and cost, as well as the quality of the land administration system: its reliability, transparency, and dissemination. The 'protection of minority investors' has also been considered, in particular to reward those jurisdictions that require transparency in certain transactions and provide for extensive liability of directors.[78]

Since 2006, the building permit system ('dealing with construction permits') has been assessed, using the example of building a shed. This analyses the number of procedures required, the time and cost involved, and the quality of the building regulations. The tax system ('paying taxes') was then considered, assessing the overall burden and collection methods. 'Trading across borders' was then considered, looking at the cost and time involved in exporting and importing.[79]

In 2011, it was the turn of electricity supply ('getting electricity'), for which the same parameters were considered as for obtaining building permits, in addition to reliability of the energy network and costs.[80] Finally, in 2020, the regulation of public procurement ('contracting with the government'), or more generally the mechanisms through which 'governments purchase goods and services from private firms', was considered. All of this is to reward the systems that provide for limited procedures,[81] i.e. to celebrate a foundation of the public

77 R. Michaels, *Comparative Law by Numbers? Legal Origins Thesis, Doing Business Reports, and the Silence of Traditional Comparative Law*, in *American Journal of Comparative Law*, 57, 2009, p. 778.

78 World Bank, *Doing Business 2005. Removing Obstacles to Growth*, Washington DC, 2005, pp. 33 ff. and 49 ff.

79 World Bank, *Doing Business 2006. Creating Jobs*, Washington DC, 2006, pp. 15 ff. and 45 ff.

80 World Bank, *Doing Business 2011. Making a difference for Entrepreneurs*, Washington DC, 2011, p. 84 ff.

81 World Bank, *Doing Business 2020. Comparing Business Regulation in 190 Economies*, Washington DC, 2020, p. 67 ff.

choice theory (II.3.6): the interference of public powers fuels corruption, while limited interference benefits the markets and thus stimulates economic growth and therefore economic development, which is equated, of course, with development tout court.

In short, development is a prerogative of the common law model, the circulation of which should then be promoted as a point of reference for the countless reforms that the Doing Business Reports have in fact stimulated and conditioned over time at the national level.[82] Even the European Union holds them in high and constant regard in order to identify the areas in which to intervene to foster the development of the single market, and above all to do so in compliance with the principles of neo-American capitalism.[83] Not to mention the impact that the Reports had among the scientific community, which devoted over 13,000 contributions to them,[84] and above all in the public discourse also thanks to the widespread involvement of mass media.

Of course, the interest aroused by the Reports does not only testify to a benevolent reception of the data reported and, more fundamentally, of the methodology and ideology of which they are an obvious expression.

As for the ideology, there is widespread criticism of their neoliberal inspiration. This criticism homes in on the fact that economic efficiency and 'market facilitation' constitute the 'sole metrics for evaluating legal institutions',[85] which is the impetus for the liberalisation and deregulation of markets.[86] The criticism is so well-founded and widespread that it has even inspired the World Bank to establish a commission of independent experts, which was charged with the task of countering its complete identification with the ideology inspiring the Doing Business Reports.

The commission has acknowledged that while the Doing Business Reports 'have been highly effective in drawing attention to the burdens of business regulation', they overlook the overall effects of that regulation, i.e. the macro-economic datum: 'What is good for a firm (or firms) may not be good for firms at large, or the economy and society as a whole'. In particular, the Reports ignore the social and environmental benefits that, alongside the private costs, are generated by the regulation of entrepreneurial activity. More precisely, they conceal policies that are attentive to the social and human implications of development. This leads to a conflict with international law, for example, with the spirit of important conventions drawn up within the International Labour Organization, where the protection of wage labour, which necessarily implies a considerable interference in entrepreneurial activity, is highly valued and considered positive.[87]

It should be noted that the commission of experts also dwelt on the limits of the legal origin thesis, from which the Doing Business Reports derived the superiority of the systems in which the common law model was transposed. The criticism on this point is radical because it strikes at the indicators used to evaluate the rules concerning various aspects of the lifespan of a firm, which are deemed artfully selected to promote neoliberal orthodoxy. This can be seen, for example, in the regulation of labour relations, as measured by the rigidity of rules on hiring, working hours and dismissals: those indicators are inevitably destined to document the

82 *Ivi*, p. iv, around 3500 reforms since the year of the first Report (2004) are recorded.
83 For instance: *Identifying and addressing barriers to the Single Market* of 10 March 2020, Com/2020/93 fin.
84 World Bank, *Doing Business 2020*, cit., p. 27 n. 8.
85 For instance, T. Krever, *The Legal Turn in Late Development Theory. The Rule of Law and the World Bank's Development Model*, in *Harvard International Law Journal*, 52, 2017, pp. 311 ff. and p. 315.
86 For instance, N. Garoupa and C. Gómez Ligüerre, *The Syndrome of the Efficiency of the Common Law*, in *Boston University International Law Journal*, 29, 2011, p. 204 f.
87 Independent Evaluation Group, *Doing Business: An Independent Evaluation. Taking the Measure of the World Bank-Ifc Doing Business Indicators*, Washington DC, 2008, pp. xi ff. and 51 ff.

superiority of the law of neo-American capitalism. All this while indicators that could have led to the opposite result are neglected; for example, indicators that would require consideration of the quality of welfare and social security.[88]

In short, the thesis of the superiority of the common law is ideologically connoted also and above all because it is the result of a biased selection of the data from which it claims to be based. This leads to the criticism centred on the methodology of the Doing Business Reports, to which we will return (IV.2.5). Here, we will merely highlight aspects we have dealt with in dealing with legal transplants (II.1.3), which are relevant because they are related to the lack of consideration for the macroeconomic context. We mean the aspects summarised in the slogan in the opening volume of the Reports: 'one size fits all', i.e. 'many times what works in developed countries works well in developing countries, too'.[89] The slogan is in line with the doctrine of the New Comparative Economics, which, as we have repeatedly said, inspired the Reports, and thus with a 'universalist, quasi-imperialist vision' that exalts the role of rules and legal systems and neglects that of 'non-legal factors'. As McCormack argues:

> The DB project appears to embody a top-down formalistic logic assuming that if certain reforms are enacted the intended consequences will more or less automatically follow. Assessing 'success' also becomes a self-referential process which is judged in terms of how the legal system is changed instead of on how social realities have been affected. The DB project has a formalist tendency that appears to overestimate the closeness of the link between legal rules and structures and economic outputs in the 'real' world. . . . The question becomes not whether legal rules have been transplanted from one country to another but whether the legal institutions in a particular country as a whole function in such a way as to support rather than to obstruct economic growth. Addressing this question calls more for a process of continuous adjustment and learning from experience rather than a simple 'big bang' solution which the Doing Business set of indicators appears implicitly to endorse.[90]

It cannot be said that the criticisms levelled at the Doing Business Reports and their underlying philosophy have gone completely unheeded, and yet the reactions of their authors have indicated a willingness to change nothing,[91] or possibly to carry out mere window-dressing operations which give the appearance of change. A good example is the choice to revise certain evaluation criteria in the employment relationship in order to 'recognize minimum levels of protection in line with relevant conventions of the International Labour Organization'.[92] This choice has not really affected the basic approach and, above all, the final outcome of the Reports: the data on labour law are still published and simply not taken into account in the ranking measuring the overall attractiveness of the countries assessed.

It is also worth mentioning a second independent evaluation commissioned by the World Bank in 2012 which went largely unheeded. The evaluation criticised the 'one size fits all' approach and the neoliberal interpretation of the relationship between law and development: it does not authorise the establishment of 'a causal relationship between such variables at country level'. Moreover, the evaluation stressed that 'the real business world is very different to the one "on paper"', especially if one claims to represent it through a ranking inevitably based on an arbitrary and opaque aggregation of data: concealing the fact that it 'explicitly or implicitly involves a value judgment'.[93]

88 *Ivi*, p. 69 f.
89 World Bank, *Doing Business in 2004*, cit., p. xvi.
90 G. McCormack, *Why Doing Business with the World Bank May Be Bad for You*, cit., p. 671 f.
91 M. Anozie et al., *Re-Examining the World Bank's Doing Business Report in Light of Its Pro-Deregulation Bias*, in *Hong Kong Law Journal*, 50, 2020, p. 1017.
92 World Bank, *Doing Business 2011. Making a Difference for Entrepreneurs*, Washington DC, 2011, p. 10.
93 *Independent Panel Review of the Doing Business Report* of 24 June 2013.

That said, the *coup de grâce* to the Doing Business Reports was not dealt by its critics and above all had nothing to do with the ideology and methodology of which they are an expression. Indeed, the World Bank suspended their publication following an internal investigation which revealed 'data irregularities' for the years 2018 and 2020: in particular, data that harmed Azerbaijan and favoured Saudi Arabia, China, and the United Arab Emirates.[94]

After all, it was not the first time that the accuracy of the Reports had been called into question, or that it had been assumed that they had been manipulated maliciously or for political ends. There had already been controversy over the data on Chile, suspected of being altered to damage the country during the progressive presidency of Michelle Bachelet and instead favour it during the conservative presidency of Sebastián Piñera.[95] This time, however, an external investigation has yielded some certainties: the manipulation of the data came from pressure from senior World Bank executives with the complicity of the main experts responsible for drafting the Reports, and was also motivated by economic advantages secured by the beneficiary countries.[96]

The consequence was the decision to discontinue the publication of the Doing Business Reports and to replace them with a new project called Business Ready (B-Ready), which we will deal with (IV.2.5).

7 LAW AS A COMMODITY: COMPETITION BETWEEN LEGAL SYSTEMS

We presented law and development as a movement committed to promoting legal change and in particular the spread of common law as the law of neo-American capitalism. We then dwelt on the Doing Business Reports as an effective expression of that movement, capable of conditioning numerous reforms on a planetary level and above all of determining the circulation of solutions from common law systems. All this without producing any particular consequences from the point of view of traditional classifications of national legal systems, and yet notable for the progressive marginalisation of civil law as the law of Rhine capitalism or in any case as an alternative law to neo-American capitalism.

We shall now focus on another expedient used to promote legal change, which ultimately aims at the same result pursued within the Law and Development movement. The reference is to the competition between legal systems, which, while not promoting the spread of common law, at least not openly, ends up stimulating its circulation as the reference law of neo-American capitalism.

On closer inspection, competition between legal systems has a long-standing tradition and it is no coincidence that it is linked to events of a certain importance in the evolution of US law. It was in the United States that the idea was born and developed that competition is an optimal method of selection of not only consumer goods but also legal rules: if a product is rewarded through the consumers' choice, the legal rules can also be rewarded through the decision of the citizens to indicate them as the source of the regulation of their relations. All of this is the outcome of evaluations similar to those carried out for the choice of a consumer good: they concern the costs and benefits of the application of the rule, understood in its

94 World Bank Group, *Review of Data Irregularities in Doing Business Prepared by Management of the Development Economics Vice-Presidency* of 16 December 2020.

95 See M. Anozie et al., *Re-Examining the World Bank's Doing Business Report in Light of Its Pro-Deregulation Bias*, cit., p. 1019 f.

96 R.C. Machen et al., *Investigation of Data Irregularities in Doing Business 2018 and 2020* of 15 September 2021.

essence as an incentive or disincentive to behave in a certain way,[97] following what has been highlighted in particular by the economic analysis of law (IV.2.4).

It all began in the late 19th century, when most US companies were incorporated in New Jersey. It was the state in which optimal conditions were ensured with regard to the costs and requirements of incorporation and the level of taxation; moreover, there was favourable discipline for shareholders and directors with regard to their liability, and there was ample room for manoeuvre in the governance of the company.[98] This situation stimulated other states to provide better conditions and this started a competition that also involved favouring cartels between companies or 'trusts'. These were widespread at the time and sources of considerable distortions in market dynamics, and yet they were encouraged as they were considered by many to increase the quality of production, lower the final price for consumers and even protect workers.[99]

The competition eventually eroded New Jersey's position. It was undermined by other states that gave rise to a competition between jurisdictions, which by the beginning of the 20th century had a clear winner: Delaware. Hence, the formula used to describe the benefits of competition between jurisdictions, i.e. the 'Delaware effect': the mechanism whereby it results in a 'race to the top',[100] not least from the point of view of the presence in that context of courts and law firms particularly well-equipped to deal with corporate litigation.[101]

Obviously, the mechanism can also be described as a 'race to the bottom'[102]: the assessment cannot be unequivocal since it depends on the point of view chosen. From the point of view of directors and shareholders, the emergence and development of competition between jurisdictions is welcomed. Things change, however, if we choose the point of view of other corporate stakeholders. For workers, or consumers, or creditors in general, or the public as a whole, it is easy to see how competition between legal systems leads to a downgrading of their rights.

The different points of views and observations have been replicated in the discussion of competition between legal systems at the global level. For those who regard law as a commodity which should be subjected to market forces neo-American capitalism is promoted, or if you prefer, deployed to undermine the foundations of Rhine capitalism (II.2.9). We will look at this aspect by turning first to the prerequisites for there to be competition between legal systems.

The first prerequisite is obviously that there are different rules, i.e. that legal systems pursue the goal of diversity and not harmonisation or a fortiori unification,[103] even though competition between systems does not aim to promote their diversity. The ultimate goal is indeed the standardisation resulting from the free encounter of supply and demand for rules: the 'mimesis of rules' and the 'uniform regulation of the market' is supposed to be a natural consequence of the market for rules.[104] This, however, is the result of a process dictated by the laws of economics and not of politics; that is, it does not require the mediation of the democratic

97 In particular U. Mattei, *Comparative Law and Economics*, Ann Arbor MI, 1997, p. 101 ff.

98 M. Yablon, *The Historical Race Competition for Corporate Charters and the Rise and Decline of New Jersey: 1880–1910*, in *Journal of Corporation Law*, 32, 2007, p. 323 ff.

99 E. Mostacci and A. Somma, *Gli Stati Uniti e il loro diritto*, Torino, 2024, p. 48 ff.

100 R.K. Winter Jr., *State Law, Shareholder Protection, and the Theory of the Corporation*, in *Journal of Legal Studies*, 6, 1977, p. 251 ff.

101 See R. Romano, *The Genius of America Corporate Law*, Washington DC, 1993, p. 28 ff.

102 W.L. Cary, *Federalism and Corporate Law: Reflections upon Delaware*, in *Yale Law Journal*, 83, 1974, p. 663 ff.

103 For instance, M. Dreher, *Wettbewerb oder Vereinheitlichung der Rechtsordnungen in Europa?*, in *Juristen Zeitung*, 1999, p. 105 ff.

104 A. Zoppini, *La concorrenza tra ordinamenti giuridici*, in Id. (Ed.), *La concorrenza tra ordinamenti giuridici*, Roma and Bari, 2004, pp. 17 and 26.

sphere, where the allocation of resources takes place according to alternative criteria to those fuelled by the principle of competition. All this, while the advocates of competition between legal systems claim that it 'rectifies and counteracts the structural bias of the domestic democratic process'. However, the opposite is true: the compression of the democratic dimension also results in the debasement of the social dimension. As Peters puts it:

> First, there is the risk that legal competition, rather than breaking up the political process, may again give preference to special interests. Those players who can 'vote with their feet' more than others are exactly those who are the better lobbyists anyway. The more credible an actor's (for example an industry's) threat of emigration is, the louder is its voice in the political process, too. This applies to capital, in particular financial capital, which is much more mobile than labour forces and whose voice as a result becomes more influential. Seen in such terms, competition between legal systems greatly accentuates the deficiencies of the democratic process rather than compensating for them. . . . It even risks damaging the principle of democracy because the 'customers' of the law do not enjoy formally equal standing in the process of competition. . . . The 'consumers'' de-facto-inequality of influence poses a democratic problem because the individual choices of law made by some players almost always have an impact on outsiders who will be subjected to the laws which result from the 'competition'. . . .
>
> In addition, competition does not allow for any, or only a small degree of, social redistribution. This is particularly obvious in tax competition. In order to remove the incentive for wealthy taxpayers to migrate to low-tax jurisdictions, States are inclined to cut taxes, as a result of which the finances available for redistribution shrink. The policy-shift from direct to indirect taxation – which has taken place in response to the risk of emigration – also reduces options for redistribution.[105]

Let us move on to the second prerequisite of competition between legal systems, namely, the possibility of freely choosing between competing laws, i.e. not regulating relations between citizens on the basis of mandatory provisions that cannot be derogated from. This evidently implies the recognition of free movement and of the possibility of migrating to the legal order deemed most favourable. More precisely, this can be done physically, but also and above all, it can be done virtually,[106] i.e. on the basis of merely formal criteria of connection to a legal order. That is to say, it implies that the national legislator relinquishes its monopoly on the production of rules as an expression of sovereignty and, ultimately, as the foundation of the distinction between the market as the place of freedom and the state, in its very essence, as the place of coercion.[107]

It is only when this condition is met that free competition between legal systems is fully realised, and this leads to the desired outcome: an optimal selection of rules, obviously from the point of view of the subjects for which one speaks of a race to the top, and ultimately a legal change consisting in the diffusion of these rules. If, in fact, individuals cannot independently decide on the rules applicable to their relations, then the diversity of those rules does not constitute a value. Competition between market participants is indeed distorted by the different burdens imposed by the rules to which they are subject by virtue of their substantial connection to a national legal system.

A third prerequisite relates to the environment in which free choice takes place, or rather the environment which makes such a choice possible. For competition between legal systems

105 A. Peters, *The Competition between Legal Orders*, in *International Law Research*, 3, 2014, p. 53 s.

106 A. Ogus, *Competition Between Legal Systems: A Contribution of Economic Analysis to Comparative Law*, in *International and Comparative Law Quarterly*, 48, 1999, p. 408.

107 B. Grzeszick, *Hoheitskonzept – Wettbewerbskonzept*, in J. Isensee and P. Kirchhof (Eds.), *Handbuch des Staatsrechts*, 3rd ed., vol. 3, Karlsruhe, 2006, p. 367 ff.

to function, it is necessary to have a system of private property rights and, above all, to create the conditions for the principle of competition to operate.[108] This further emphasises the ideological character of this way of promoting legal change, in line with what we have suggested is the closely related approach of economic analysis of law.

A final prerequisite concerns the way in which the law is conceived. This must necessarily be valorised in its essence as a technocratic construction dissociated from the context in which it came into existence and is used: the reduction of law to a commodity can only take place in disregard of its broader cultural dimension.[109] This is yet another example of how competition between legal systems is functional in promoting neo-American capitalism and its foundations. It, in particular, exalts the market as an instrument of redistribution of values and resources whose functioning requires the removal of any obstacle to the free encounter of supply and demand.

In short, the circulation of legal models is only conceivable in a context shaped by free choice and free movement: of goods, services, capital, and persons. And in such a context it emerges as the fifth freedom called upon to complete the 'traditional' ones: the 'free circulation of rules'.[110]

8 NEXT: CENTROS AND EUROPEAN COMPANY LAW

We have already mentioned the implications of legal diversity as a prerequisite for competition between legal systems, and observed that its aim is not to promote pluralism but rather to prevent the production of rules through democratic participation. The consequences of the freedom of choice of law, which is the further precondition of competition between systems, can best be illustrated by considering the rules of this way of promoting legal change in the European Union, in particular with reference to the founding mechanism of the single market, i.e. the one centred on the mentioned four freedoms.

In this context, there is generally no application for the principle of territorial competence in the setting of the quality standards of the goods and services. This principle according to which the country of destination retains the power to establish criteria for the movement of goods and services, is, in fact, considered to be an obstacle to competition. Instead, the opposite principle of home country control applies, according to which those criteria are established in the country of origin of the good or service, and are recognised in the country of destination. In this situation, and in the absence of harmonised rules, there will be competition between legal systems, the outcome of which will depend on their diversity.

It is precisely the latter situation that has arisen with the movement of legal persons. In this respect, the Treaty on the Functioning of the European Union states that 'companies or firms formed in accordance with the law of a Member State and having their registered office, central administration or principal place of business within the Union shall, for the purposes of this Chapter, be treated in the same way as natural persons who are nationals of Member States' (Article 54). They cannot therefore be restricted in their 'freedom of establishment' (Article 49), although the aim is not to promote competition between legal systems: the Treaty itself establishes that a series of directives shall harmonise company law and in particular the

108 L. Antoniolli Deflorian, *La struttura istituzionale del nuovo diritto contrattuale europeo: competizione e circolazione dei modelli giuridici*, Trento, 1996, p. 336 ff.

109 Y.-M. Laithier, *Droit comparé*, Paris, 2024, p. 182.

110 R. van den Bergh, *Subsidiarity as an Economic Demarcation Principle*, in *Maastricht Journal of European and Comparative Law*, 5, 1998, p. 152.

forms of 'the protection of the interests of members and others' (Article 50). It also excludes situations in which diversity and therefore special provisions are justified 'on grounds of public policy, public security or public health' (Article 52).

This model, however, has not been fully implemented. European company law is full of gaps and awaiting a decision as to whether it should be based on the principle of harmonisation or on that of competition between legal systems.[111] The latter thus prevails in this situation of uncertainty, which, moreover, is fuelled by the case law of the Court of Justice, according to which the link between the legal person and the national legal system is established based on purely formal criteria.

The Court arrived at this conclusion in the well-known *Centros* case.[112] Centros was a company registered by a Danish citizen in the United Kingdom, but which had no presence there. The owners by registering in the UK, but trading in Denmark, sought to circumvent the application of Danish law on the registration of companies. In Danish law, like other in civil law systems, proposers are required to pay-up a fixed sum of share capital on registration, which is designed as an ultimate guarantee of creditors' claims. In common law, proposers pay a nominal sum on registration, and creditor protection is, instead, based on transparency rules in relation to management of the corporate entity.[113] Having incorporated Centros in the UK, the Danish directors sought to have a subsidiary company registered in Denmark. The relevant public authority, the Danish Trade and Companies Board, rejected their application because, in essence, they regarded the request to register a subsidiary as an attempt to circumvent Danish law's protections of corporate creditors and, additionally, to guard against the risk of fraudulent insolvencies. In other words, they regarded the scheme as an abuse of freedom of establishment.

The shareholders of Centros then turned to the Danish Supreme Court, which stayed the proceedings and raised a preliminary question before the Court of Justice. The Danish authorities resisted, reaffirming that the refusal of registration served the protection of creditors and therefore had to be permitted under European law. As we have seen, the latter in fact permits derogations from the rules on the movement of persons in order to protect the public interest.

The Court of Justice rejected this interpretation and underlined that the connection of a legal person with a national system is to be established according to a merely formal criterion. In other words, only the statutory seat is relevant, that is to say, the seat indicated in the articles of association of the entity, and not that based on substantive criteria outlined by national law, such as, for instance, the actual exercise of a business activity. Nor could the fight against fraud justify the refusal to register a branch of a company that has its seat, even if only on paper, in a member state. Per the Court of Justice:

> The refusal of a Member State to register a branch of a company formed in accordance with the law of another Member State in which it has its registered office on the grounds that the branch is intended to enable the company to carry on all its economic activity in the host State, with the result that the secondary establishment escapes national rules on the provision for and the paying-up of a minimum capital, is incompatible with Articles 52 and 58 of the Treaty, in so far as it prevents any exercise of the right freely to set up a secondary establishment which Articles 52 and 58 are specifically intended to guarantee. . . .

111 For instance, P. Montalenti, *Il diritto societario europeo*, in Id. (Ed.), *Profili di diritto societario europeo*, Torino, 2023, p. 1 ff.

112 CJEU, *Centros Ltd v Erhvervs- og Selskabsstyrelsen* of 9 March 1999 (C-212/97). In the same direction, *Überseering BV v Nordic Construction Company Baumanagement GmbH* of 5 November 2002 (C-208/00) and *Kamer van Koophandel en Fabrieken voor Amsterdam v Inspire Art Ltd.* of 30 September 2003 (C-167/01).

113 For instance, D. Corapi, *Le società per azioni*, in G. Alpa et al., *Diritto privato comparato. Istituti e problemi*, new ed., Roma and Bari, 2012, p. 457 ff.

> The fact that a Member State may not refuse to register a branch of a company formed in accordance with the law of another Member State in which it has its registered office does not preclude that first State from adopting any appropriate measure for preventing or penalising fraud, either in relation to the company itself, if need be in cooperation with the Member State in which it was formed, or in relation to its members, where it has been established that they are in fact attempting, by means of the formation of the company, to evade their obligations towards private or public creditors established on the territory of a Member State concerned. In any event, combating fraud cannot justify a practice of refusing to register a branch of a company which has its registered office in another Member State.[114]

More explicit was the advocate general, who clarified that in regulating business activity, the aim of promoting free enterprise must be pursued above all else: 'it is the opportunity to exercise business activities that is protected, and with it the contractual freedom to make use of the instruments provided for that purpose in the legal systems of the Member States', while 'the motives, calculations and particular personal interests underlying the choice do not come into consideration'.[115]

It follows that, if a national legal system prefers other objectives, it is the task of European company law to act to severely restrict the interference of public authorities in freedom of contract – thus certifying that the social function of the company is 'definitively obsolete', replaced by 'that entirely private, entrepreneurial dimension in which it was born and in which it should better remain'.[116]

In other words, anyone wishing to set up a company on the basis of rules with a clear entrepreneurial and private inspiration will be able to do so from any European country. He will only have to take care to write in the articles of association of the firm that it has its head office in the United Kingdom, even if it is a fictitious head office, and even if the secondary office is in fact the main one. This forces other countries to either lose their attractiveness to investors, or to change their company law as well, making its social dimension definitively disappear.

This scheme can therefore only work if freedom of movement is ensured not only in real terms, but above all in virtual terms by recourse to the connecting criteria of a national law of a formal order to which we have just referred. This is the only reason that competition between jurisdictions in corporate matters does not produce a race to the bottom from the point of view of consumers and employees: the regulation on the law applicable to contractual obligations provides for the use of substantive connecting factors for them.[117] Problems remain, however, with regard to the relationship between capital and labour, in particular with reference to the German system of codetermination (*Mitbestimmung*), concerning the participation of workers in the decision-making processes of the company.[118]

The rules governing codetermination pertain indeed to company law so that it is affected by the same mechanisms as the protection of creditors other than employees and consumers. In this way, before Brexit competition between legal systems has led an increasing number of German companies to formally set themselves up as branch offices of English companies, which as such are not obliged to resort to codetermination. This has had considerable

114 CJEU, *Centros Ltd v Erhvervs- og Selskabsstyrelsen* of 9 March 1999, cit., nn. 30 and 38.
115 As per Advocate General La Pergola in his *Opinion* of 16 July 1998, n. 20.
116 G.M. Flick, *Gli obiettivi della Commissione per la riforma del diritto societario*, in *Rivista delle società*, 2000, p. 7.
117 Artt. 6 and 8 EU Regulation n. 593 of 17 June 2008.
118 See A. Somma, *Giustizia o pacificazione sociale? La codeterminazione nello scontro tra modelli di capitalismo*, in *Politica del diritto*, 2015, p. 549 ff.

implications for a system of industrial relations whose foundations date back to the first half of the 20th century, and whose underlying philosophy is that constitutive of Rhine capitalism centred, as we know, on social pacification and on the collaboration between capital and labour (II.2.9).

The purpose of the legal change promoted through the competition between legal systems is thus in all respects similar to that promoted within the Law and Development movement. Both aim at the diffusion, if not directly of common law, then certainly of the economic order which it is traditionally associated with, i.e. the one in line with neo-American capitalism.

SUMMARY

1. In the social sciences other than law, comparison is considered to be anchored in methodologies and classification criteria suited only to a static dimension. In reality, comparative law is equipped to grasp the dynamic dimension and thus the interaction of legal experiences as the basis of their change. This, moreover, constitutes an indispensable point of view for taxonomy since classifications must be observed bearing in mind their temporal relativity as well.
2. At first, legal change was explained by recourse to evolutionist paradigms: law changes according to the same pattern based on the expressions of Western modernity, elevated to manifestations of progress. Later, diffusionist paradigms became dominant, whereby legal change was held to be the consequence of contact between cultures and thus circulation of models. An evolutionist attitude survives, however, when circulation is constrained within a relationship between a centre devoted to the exportation of models and a periphery devoted to their importation. The same applies to the assertion that the engine of circulation is prestige, or to the concealment of imposition as the cause of legal change. One think, for instance, of the link between the spread of common law and civil law models and the colonial expansion of the countries exporting those models, but also of the spread of US models as a result of globalisation processes.
3. The theory of legal transplants has an evolutionist flavour, which explains legal change over the centuries as a chain of imitations of rules largely modelled on Roman law realised autonomously by the class of jurists, i.e. in the absence of any connection between law and the political and economic order of the societies to which those rules are addressed. Additionally, the theory overlooks the fact that rules cannot circulate together with their hermeneutic heritage, so it cannot be used to explain legal change. This is also why it is neglected by scholars of comparative public law, who prefer to speak of legal borrowings or possibly legal migrations precisely to emphasise the incompatibility of transplant theory with the external viewpoint on law.
4. The pursuit of economic development in the sense widespread in the West undoubtedly constitutes a driving force for legal change, as can be seen in exemplary fashion from the activities of the World Bank and the International Monetary Fund, most of which are committed to promoting the spread of neo-American capitalism. Expressed in this way, the nexus between law and development has

been deepened in the Law and Development movement, which arose to promote the dissemination of the rules considered to be the foundation of the Western economic order: rules of public law when Keynesian models prevailed, and rules of private law in the years when neoliberal orthodoxy was established. Ultimately, the movement intended to adopt a holistic approach to development, i.e. to value it as human development, yet there were no actions consistent with these intentions on the part of the Bretton Woods institutions. Even the legal literature shows only cosmetic attention to a different idea of development: however adjectival it is, it appears little more than a rhetorical device incapable of breaking free from the economist imaginary.

5. Prominent among the initiatives to promote the spread of neo-American capitalism are the Doing Business Reports, produced by the World Bank between 2004 and 2020 to measure the costs of regulation borne by companies over their lifetime: from incorporation to liquidation. Those Reports purport to document what has been argued in the New Comparative Economics in line with the legal origin theory: that the circulation of common law models produces economic growth, while impoverishment is the perspective of countries that imitate civil law models. The Reports were criticised first and foremost by French law scholars as representatives of the civil law world, who also celebrated the democratic and rational character of codified law.

6. Other criticisms of the Doing Business Reports have targeted their intimately neoliberal inspiration, which was even stigmatised on the occasion of an independent survey commissioned by the World Bank. There, among other things, the underlying purpose of the Reports was denounced, namely, their desire to document the superiority of common law, in particular by avoiding a macroeconomic view of market dynamics: by failing to assess private costs in light of the related public benefits. Other criticisms concerned the methodology of the Reports, which ultimately feed a universalist and imperialist vision combined with a marked legal formalism. However, it was not these criticisms that led to the end of the Reports, which followed the discovery that the data on which they were based had been manipulated to favour some countries at the expense of others.

7. Among the expedients used to promote legal change, the competition between legal systems stands out: a mechanism that, while not openly promoting the spread of common law, ends up stimulating its circulation as the law of reference of neo-American capitalism. The mechanism takes shape in the United States, where Delaware is credited as the place to set up companies with favourable rules for directors and shareholders. Hence, the conclusion that competition between legal systems fuels a race to the top, which, however, turns into a race to the bottom when assessed from the perspective of workers and consumers in particular. Anyway, competition between legal systems presupposes that diversity in law is considered a higher value than convergence. It is then necessary that proprietary rights are recognised and effectively protected, and that the same applies to the principle of competition. Finally, there must be the possibility of choosing between several laws also from a virtual point of view, i.e. through formal criteria of connection to national legal systems. This is not to promote pluralism but to achieve choices mediated more by the market than by democratic participation.

8. Competition between jurisdictions has been promoted in the European context using the principle of home country control. Its implications can be verified by considering the development of European company law at the instigation of the Court of Justice in the famous Centros case. The case had no implications for cases where the control criteria are uniform or where there are substantive criteria connecting the business activity and the applicable law. There were, however, important consequences with German co-determination, which competition between jurisdictions made it possible to circumvent, thereby sinking a foundation of the Federal Republic's industrial relations system. This is clear evidence of its use as a tool to reaffirm the corporate dimension of the enterprise to the detriment of the social one, and upstream to propagate neo-American capitalism to the detriment of Rhine capitalism.

CHAPTER 7

THE MARKET FOR REFORMS

1 COERCIVE AND PUNITIVE FEDERALISM

Legal change is the outcome of an imitative process whereby the circulation of models is either determined by their prestige or, more often, their imposition (II.1.2). In the second case, and besides colonial imposition through violence, the imposition of models may also be the result of more subtle forms of coercion. These include, claiming and propagating the superiority of a legal order from the point of view of its capacity to generate wealth through the market. Emblematic from such a point of view are the World Bank's Doing Business Reports, designed to promote the spread of common law as the law of neo-American capitalism (II.1.5).

The cases of ostensibly non-violent imposition of legal models are, moreover, as numerous as they are insidious. Perhaps the most widespread is a practice we have already mentioned (III.1.4) which we can define as the market for reforms: reforms are requested in consideration for the granting of financial assistance or at least economic and other benefits.

Recourse to such a market ultimately takes on the form that first developed in the evolution of federalism, or rather from the federalising process, which in the course of the 20th century was realised within states. That process can be characterised as the emancipation from the 19th-century liberal state federalist model, which distinguished the centre from the periphery.

In that model, there were two distinct sovereignties, i.e. at national and state level, corresponding to a rigid distinction of competences.[1] The process of the redistribution of powers was underpinned by the 20th-century affirmation of an interventionist state, which sought to rebalance the emphasis on market rationality towards other criteria of value, and required central coordination to achieve the redistribution of wealth. The same state then became active in civil rights and thus redistribution was supplemented by policies on recognition and, gradually, identity in its multiple manifestations. Hence, gradually, a different kind of 'cooperative' federalism based on shared sovereignty came to be affirmed. This form of federalism requires a coordination of competences of the centre and the periphery, without which the state would not be able to perform the new tasks.[2]

In the United States, the collapse of New York Stock Exchange at the end of the 1920s and the ensuing Great Depression, provoked the New Deal, a vast programme of federal intervention. In these years, the public powers finally took on the contradictions of the economic order which had hitherto been tolerated if not tacitly supported by the political order. More precisely, the federal government tackled the contradictions linked to the market's failures to redistribute wealth, as well as those linked to racism as a founding trait of US-American society.[3]

1 E. Mostacci, *Commerce power e federalizing process. Il governo dell'economia nell'evoluzione dei federalismi di common law*, Milano, 2018, p. 7 ff.
2 G. Bognetti, *Lo spirito del costituzionalismo americano* (*La Costituzione democratica*), vol. 2, Torino, 2000, p. 203 ff.
3 E. Mostacci and A. Somma, *Gli Stati Uniti e il loro diritto*, Torino, 2024, pp. 78 ff. and 87 ff.

DOI: 10.4324/9781032684499-10

While this evolution of federal competence has not followed a straight line, there has been a gradual expansion of those competences, which ended up legitimising actions of the federal state that were not contemplated by the formal distribution of tasks between it and the federated states. Forms of financial assistance to the states, conditional on the commitment to use the funds in pursuit of specific purposes (grants-in-aid), was an important tool used to realise this 'competence creep'. All this in line with a centuries-old practice: as early as the end of the 18th century, the states received federal land for sale, and then used the proceeds for purposes such as assisting the poor or building public infrastructure.[4]

The recourse to conditional financial assistance has understandably fuelled conflicts in the US between the centre and the periphery, or rather between those who wish to preserve the prerogatives of the federated states and those who wish to promote the interventionism of the federal state and who endorse its policy programme. The navigation of this conflict requires identifying the limits of federal power, i.e. to decide what is meant by the US Constitution stating that 'the Congress shall have Power . . . to provide for . . . the general Welfare of the United States' (Art. 1 sec. 8). All this in the light of an evolutionary interpretation of the provision attributing to Congress itself the 'power to lay and collect taxes on incomes' (16th amendment), according to which the power may be exercised not only to finance activities directly related to its own competences, but also for initiatives pursuing the general welfare.[5]

The use of conditional financial assistance provided by the centre is not, however, without more or less defined limits, which over the years have been identified in an attempt to balance the expectations of the periphery, or rather of those who wished to defend the prerogatives of the federated states from the interventionism of the federal state. In particular, assistance must follow the model of incentive and not also of coercion: i.e. it must be designed in such a way that the periphery is free to refuse the incentive, or in other words that the situation does not arise in which 'the political cost of foregoing a significant federal contribution would be too high for the state administration'.[6] On the other hand, the conditionalities do not have to be related to the management of the assistance received, as they can be cross-cutting as they relate to other aspects of state action (crosscutting requirement): one can, for example, tie the disbursement of funds for road construction to the adoption of restrictive measures on alcohol consumption.[7]

It must be said, however, that distinguishing between incentive and coercion is, in practice, often difficult. While recipients may formally refuse to accept conditional financial assistance by so doing they may face considerable budgetary problems. In such a case, we may speak of a further evolution of federalism, which turns from cooperative federalism to coercive federalism or regulatory federalism: it becomes an instrument through which the centre imposes choices on the periphery over which the latter cannot exercise any kind of resistance.[8] And this is precisely what happened in the United States from the 1960s onwards and more markedly in the 1970s, when a growing recourse to 'specific purpose grants' ended up transforming conditional financial assistance into a tool 'to concentrate decision-making powers in the hands of the national government'.[9]

4 A. Baraggia, *La condizionalità come strumento di governo negli Stati compositi. Una comparazione tra Stati Uniti, Canada e Unione europea*, Torino, 2023, p. 47 ff.
5 *United States v. Butler*, 297 U.S. 1 (1936).
6 M. Comba, *Gli Stati Uniti d'America*, in P. Carrozza, A. Di Giovine and G.F. Ferrari (Eds.), *Diritto costituzionale comparato*, 2nd ed., Roma and Bari, 2014, p. 84.
7 *South Dakota v. Dole*, 483 U.S. 203 (1987).
8 J. Kincaid, *From Cooperative to Coercive Federalism*, in *Annals of the American Academy of Political and Social Science*, 509, 1990, p. 139 ff.
9 R. Cranston, *From Co-Operative to Coercive Federalism and Back?*, in *Federal Law Review*, 10, 1979, p. 121 ff.

At least all this intended to promote policies in line with the aims traditionally pursued through cooperative federalism, i.e. redistributive and social policies in general, as well as policies of recognition and anti-discrimination in particular. The Civil Rights Act of 1964 is exemplary: it prohibits discrimination on the basis of race, skin colour, and national origin and reinforces the prohibition by specifying that it applies to participation in 'any program receiving Federal financial assistance'.[10]

Having said this, US federalism is an ongoing process and its coercive version is but its latest iteration. Indeed, there has been a further evolution that has led to talk of punitive federalism: federalism that includes a sanctioning apparatus, whereby subsidies are suspended when the recipient of financial assistance fails to comply with the relevant conditions. This development, too, has a certain tradition, as can be seen from a measure from the 1970s, where sanctions can also apply in a different sphere from that to which conditional financial assistance refers. In other words, in addition to cross-cutting conditions, cross-cutting sanctions are possible. For example, the 1974 Highway Energy Conservation Act, adopted as a response to the oil crisis, limited the granting of funds for road construction to those states which agreed to lower the speed limit.[11]

More recently, punitive federalism has been transformed more in terms of its content than in terms of the manner in which it is implemented. It has, in fact, moved away from a progressive policy agenda. This is particularly evident when considering the Trump administration's migration policy. The administration has, in particular, suspended federal funds to so-called sanctuary cities, i.e. that refuse to align themselves with the federal administration's policy to deport irregular migrants.[12]

We shall see how this punitive pattern of US-American federalism has been exported to the world. It is precisely this model of coercion and punishment that underpins the forms of conditional financial assistance devised by the Bretton Woods institutions. They are evidenced by the International Monetary Fund's approach to the heavily indebted countries when attempting to restore balance of payments equilibrium, and by the World Bank as conditions for granting development aid (III.2.2).

The same applies to the financial assistance provided by the European Union (EU) to third states, which is a central plank of its external policy. More precisely, relations between the EU and third states are typically conditioned by compliance with requirements concerning the most diverse aspects.[13] The same consideration also applies to internal relations, but with one caveat: while in its external relations conditionalities concerning respect for human rights or democratic principles prevail, its internal relations mainly impose financial and macroeconomic policies.[14] This market for reforms concerns not only the period following the sovereign debt crisis (III.2.7), as most believe, but may very well be the reference point for charting an alternative history of a united Europe from its beginnings (III.2.3).

Conditionality in internal European relations, just like financial assistance from the World Bank and the International Monetary Fund, is conceived in a similar way and inspired by a shared purpose. Both are for the most part coercive and punitive, and unlike earlier progressive iterations in the US, both aim to implement neoliberal reforms.

10 See Advisory Commission on Intergovernmental Relations, *Regulatory Federalism: Policy, Process, Impact and Reform*, Washington DC, 1984, p. 71 f.

11 *Ivi*, p. 9 f.

12 A. Baraggia, *La condizionalità come strumento di governo negli Stati compositi*, cit., p. 75 ff.

13 In particular E. Cannizzaro, *Il diritto dell'integrazione europea. L'ordinamento dell'Unione*, 2nd ed., Torino, 2018, p. 361 ff.

14 C. Pinelli, *I temi della condizionalità nel negoziato sul Quadro finanziario pluriennale 2021–2027*, in *Documenti IAI*, 2018, 7, p. 1 ff.

2 THE FINANCIAL ASSISTANCE OF THE WORLD BANK AND THE INTERNATIONAL MONETARY FUND

We have already evoked the market for reforms in connection with the activities of the Bretton Woods institutions. Indeed, we know that, in the years when neoliberalism was spreading, they made their financial assistance to Latin American countries conditional on the implementation of reforms in line with that creed (II.3.11). After the implosion of the Soviet bloc, and without hesitation, the same conditionalities were imposed on former socialist countries (II.3.8). We then spoke of the Structural Adjustment Plans, through which the World Bank and the International Monetary Fund imposed reforms on developing countries in exchange for financial assistance. These reforms reflected the underlying philosophy of the Washington consensus, namely, that development is, in essence, to be equated with economic growth (III.1.4).

The Washington consensus was a term coined at the end of the 1980s to emphasise how Washington-based institutions shared a common approach to economic policy and a singular view on the path to economic development. These institutions included the International Monetary Fund and World Bank, but also the US Treasury Department and all the main US political and economic institutions, all advocates of neoliberalism and neo-American capitalism (II.2.9). The 1980s, after all, witnessed a change in the approach to development, abandoning the idea that public authorities are its driving forces (II.1.4). All this, while the belief was spreading that economic recipes suitable for rich countries should be the point of reference for poor countries: these had to follow them in order to set themselves on the road to economic growth and escape a destiny of poverty and irrelevance.[15]

The Washington Consensus was summarised in a contribution written having the Latin American debt crisis in mind, and in particular the type of 'reforms' the affected countries had to carry out as 'strong conditionalities' linked to the financial assistance. The contribution takes up the main indication that emerged during the second phase of the Law and Development movement: reserving for the market the role of engine of development (II.1.4). Following this indication, the state has to fulfil the limited task of providing 'budgetary discipline', understood as a tendency to balance the budget, to be pursued by 'reducing expenditures rather than increasing tax revenues' and in any case within the framework of a tax system focused on moderation. For the rest, the public authorities are called upon to deregulate and liberalise the markets, and in particular to remove obstacles to the movement of goods and capital. They must in fact eliminate barriers to international trade and thereby abolish competition-limiting measures aimed at 'protecting domestic industries'. And the same applies to barriers to 'foreign direct investment', which is to be favoured as it brings 'capital, skills, and know-how', thereby 'producing goods needed for the domestic market or contributing new exports'.[16]

Obviously, the state must also take a step back in its role as entrepreneur. It must protect private property as an element of 'fundamental importance for the satisfactory operation of the capitalist system'. And it must proceed without delay to the privatisation of public enterprises, which are stigmatised for the usual neoliberal reasons. Indeed, the entrepreneurial state is considered to be a source of corruption without economic growth and ultimately the manifestation of economic nationalism. As Williamson states:

> More generally, privatization may help relieve the pressure on the government budget, both in the short run by the revenue produced by the sale of the enterprise and in the longer run

15 See J.E. Stiglitz, *Globalization and Its Discontents*, New York NY and London, 2002, p. 13 ff.
16 J. Williamson, *What Washington Means by Policy Reform*, in Id. (Ed.), *Latin American Adjustment: How Much Has Happened?*, Washington DC, 1990, p. 5 ff.

> inasmuch as investment need no longer be financed by the government. However, the main rationale for privatization is the belief that private industry is managed more efficiently than state enterprises, because of the more direct incentives faced by a manager who either has a direct personal stake in the profits of an enterprise or else is accountable to those who do. . . .
>
> The lack of a strong indigenous private sector is one reason that has motivated some countries to promote state enterprises. This is again a nationalistic motivation and hence commands little respect in Washington.[17]

We have argued that the motivations and aims just listed inspired the conditional financial assistance of the Bretton Woods institutions, and that these were detailed in the Structural Adjustment Plans. No wonder that the results obtained were very different from those imagined by the advocates of development understood as mere economic growth, i.e. entrusted to the beneficial virtues of the market and its liberation from state interventionism.[18] While the Plans may have produced an increase in growth, this was mainly to the advantage of Western companies ready to invest in countries with low labour costs and substantially lacking in environmental protection regulations. All this had negative repercussions on the possibility for the recipient countries to escape the spiral of marginality and to improve the quality of life of the populations involved.[19]

We know that in the 1990s, in response to the criticism that its policies were neoliberal, the World Bank and the International Monetary Fund created a new 'comprehensive development framework'. This framework was meant to embody a more holistic concept of development. The goals pursued by Structural Adjustment Plans were, additionally, meant to be the outcome of participatory engagement with stakeholders through which the social and environmental repercussions of development would be taken into account. (III.1.4). We can now see, with the benefit of hindsight, that such intentions have not been translated into effective action, and indeed have produced negative effects. The participatory definition of reforms has, if anything, allowed the Bank to increase its influence on government action in assisted countries and thus to strengthen its control over compliance with conditionalities. From the outset, it became clear that this cooperation concerned countries lacking a lively civil society: in its absence, economic growth and development continue to be equated.[20]

More recently, the Bretton Woods institutions have modified their loan agreements in the light of the non-economic impacts of development. The inspiration for this change has been the recognition of the UN's Millennium Development Goals, and a particular emphasis is placed on poverty reduction. Thus, conditional financial assistance is now tapered by reference to Poverty Reduction Strategy Papers, which can be submitted by recipient country. These documents are conceived as action plans aimed at better integrating social and environmental development expectations within a growth-oriented macroeconomic framework. There is also a greater focus on participation in the pursuit of that goal,[21] which is meant to lead to local 'ownership' of conditional financial assistance, whatever that means, and its articulation by its recipients.[22]

17 *Ibid.*

18 For instance, E. Stern, *World Bank Financing of Structural Adjustment*, in J. Williamson (Ed.), *Imf Conditionality*, Washington DC, 1983, p. 87 ff.

19 S. McGregor, *Structural Adjustment Programmes and Human Well-Being*, in *International Journal of Consumer Studies*, 29, 2005, p. 170 ff.

20 See R. Cameron Blake, *The World Bank's Draft Comprehensive Development Framework*, in *Yale Human Rights and Development Law Journal*, 3, 2000, p. 159 ff.

21 See, for instance, R. Klump and C. A. Miralies Cabrera, *Pro-Poor Growth: Theory, Measurement and Policy Implications*, in L. Menkhoff (Ed.), *Pro-Poor Growth: Policy and Evidence*, Berlin, 2006, p. 11 ff.

22 W.H. Buiter, *Country Ownership: A Term Whose Time Has Gone*, in S. Koeberle et al. (Eds.), *Conditionality Revisited. Concepts, Experiences and Lessons*, Washington DC, 2005, p. 27 ff.

From the point of view of the World Bank and the International Monetary Fund, the new approach has succeeded in introducing a new concept of development and in promoting human rights as a central aspect of development. One could speak of a post-Washington Consensus, as was done with regard to the demands made during the third phase of the Law and Development movement. (III.1.4). After all, this expression is born within the World Bank to promote a new adjectivization of development: sustainable, equitable, and democratic.[23]

However, the same criticisms that we have already encountered in respect of the general development framework have also been levelled at the Poverty Reduction Strategy Papers. The first criticism is that much-heralded participatory processes have not led to 'ownership of conditionality' by the recipient countries. On the contrary, those processes turned out to be harmful because of the role assumed by the Western actors involved, in particular donors and non-governmental organisations. They turned participation into 'a technology of social control, which seeks to shape domestic political space' and ultimately aims to 'securing consent to liberal systems of political and economic management'.[24]

In other words, the fact that the Bretton Woods institutions have taken poverty reduction as the reference point for formulating conditional financial assistance has not led them to innovate in their approach to development. Poverty, the reduction of which conditional financial assistance is aimed at, is understood as a mere material condition, neglecting the historical and political foundation of the condition of destitution, i.e. with criteria functional to make economic growth appear as the only antidote.[25]

This amounts to saying that the post-Washington consensus is nothing but 're-invention of global neoliberalism under the guise of an 'augmented Washington consensus'.[26] Efforts to justify the conditionality mechanism as such have been to no avail,[27] as have attempts within the Bretton Woods institutions to refine it[28] and even overcome it.[29] Thus, market for reforms marches on, and it has, if anything, been deployed to new theatres beyond so-called developing countries. This is illustrated very clearly by the International Monetary Fund 'bail outs' of European Union member states during the sovereign debt crisis (III.2.5). In the first case, as in the second, it is coercive and punitive at the same time: financial aid is a necessity from which the countries receiving it cannot escape, just as they cannot escape the punitive nature of the conditions attached to it.

3 THE BIRTH OF A UNITED EUROPE: THE MARSHALL PLAN

The market for reforms may be the point of reference for reconstructing a kind of alternative history of the united Europe from the moment it was conceived and in all the salient phases of its development.

The beginning of the European adventure conventionally coincides with a declaration made on 9 May 1950 by the then French Foreign Minister Robert Schuman, in which

23 J.E. Stiglitz, *More Instruments and Broader Goals: Moving toward the Post-Washington Consensus*, Helsinki, 1998, p. 31 ff.
24 A. Fraser, *Poverty Reduction Strategy Papers: Now Who Calls the Shots?*, in *Review of African Political Economy*, 32, 2005, p. 317 ff.
25 A. Saeed et al., *The Politics of Poverty Reduction Strategy Papers*, in *Journal of Political Studies*, 22, 2015, p. 595 ff.
26 M. Beeson and I. Islam, *Neo-liberalism and East Asia: resisting the Washington Consensus*, in *Journal of Development Studies*, 41, 2005, p. 199.
27 In this regard, A. Dreher, *Imf Conditionality: Theory and Evidence*, in *Public Choice*, 141, 2009, p. 233 ff.
28 International Monetary Fund, *Imf Policy Paper. 2018 Review of Program Design and Conditionality*, Washington DC, 2019.
29 W.S. Koeberle et al. (Eds.), *Conditionality Revisited*, cit.

he called for the pooling of coal and steel production as an instrument through which peace could be secured. Its material impetus was that control over the Ruhr, a rich mining basin, had often been the basis of conflicts between France and Germany. For many, this declaration, which was the basis for the birth of the European Coal and Steel Community shortly afterwards, marks the birthday of unified Europe.

The perspective of the market for reforms, however, leads one to back to 5 June 1947. It was on that date that the so-called Marshall Plan was inaugurated at Harvard University by the eponymous US secretary of state. The Marshall Plan was, as it is well known, a recovery plan for Western Europe. It was conceived not so much and not only to prevent yet another continental war, but to close ranks in view of the confrontation between the United States and the Soviet Union that would result in the Cold War.

Through the Marshall Plan, the United States made massive use of the conditionality mechanism in order to pursue its foreign policy objectives, and in particular to promote the spread of its political and economic order. Human rights were used as 'ideological weapons' in order to denounce the socialist countries' violations and at the same time conceal their violations and those of their allies.[30]

The Marshall Plan also had strong ideological overtones. While the loans and grants it provided aimed to enable the European economy to recover, its motivation was as much about ideas as it was about material wellbeing. There was a fundamental, even existential, concern that capitalism was incapable of generating growth and prosperity, and that this inability was leading impoverished populations to turn their eyes to socialism. At the same time, the political forces that referred to communism were enjoying great electoral success and were gaining a growing audience in the trade union movement. For many, this was a sign that the market economy was not the answer to the demand for work and welfare and, above all, that the planned economy had gained credibility as an alternative.[31]

Therefore, as we have said, it was deemed necessary to tighten the ranks of the capitalist West and, in particular, to stave off those within the West who were sympathetic to the planned economy. At the same time, the US was also concerned about the fate of its own economy. Europe's weakness destabilised international markets and, above all, prevented it from absorbing goods produced overseas. This led to the creation of the European Organisation for Economic Co-operation, a body in which the United States and the countries receiving its financial aid participated and which was designed as an instrument for coordinating their economic policies.[32]

The organisation was entrusted with tasks that in many respects can be considered preparatory to a closer communitarian bond. The founding treaty, signed in Paris on 16 April 1948, deals first of all with the construction of a common market when it calls to 'continue the study of Customs Unions or analogous arrangements such as free trade areas', and in the future to achieve the free movement of goods and workers: 'a multilateral trade system' and a system whereby each party may 'have recourse to manpower available in the territory of any other Contracting Party'. The same treaty also provided for the coordination of economic policies, stipulating that each party will undertake 'avoiding or countering the dangers of inflation' and promote 'the stability of its currency and of its internal financial position, sound rates of exchange and, generally, confidence in its monetary system'. Finally, one should not overlook the reference to an embryonic monetary union when it provides for the creation of a

30 C. Pinelli, Art. *Conditionality*, in *Max Planck Encyclopedias of International Law*, Oxford, 2013, n. 17.
31 In particular G. Mammarella and P. Cacace, *Storia e politica dell'unione europea*, Roma and Bari, 2008, p. 25 ff.
32 K. Loewenstein, *The Union of Western Europe: Illusion and Reality. An Appraisal of the Methods*, in *Columbia Law Review*, 52, 1952, p. 81 ff.

'multilateral system of payments', i.e. an area within which national currencies can be freely exchanged.

Thus far, we have considered the reforms referred to in the Marshall Plan. We must now focus on how they were implemented through a mechanism that would later be defined by federalism scholars as coercive and punitive. That is to say, capable of imposing reforms with conditionalities that might be disconnected from the management of the assistance received, and with sanctioning mechanisms for their non-implementation (III.2.2). The Economic Cooperation Administration, a US government agency, has all these hallmarks. It was entrusted with the supervision of assistance through verification of compliance with the Economic Reconstruction Plans submitted by each assisted country.[33] The plans specified the conditionalities attached to the use of grants and loans. These conditionalities related to the reinvigoration of the national economy, but also to the objectives set out in the Treaty establishing the European Economic Cooperation Organisation. Where it ascertained that the beneficiaries did not comply with those conditionalities – and this is the key point – the administration could suspend or interrupt the financial assistance, or sanction the behaviour of the non-performing country.[34]

Of course, the Economic Cooperation Administration did not apply the same criteria everywhere. In countries such as France and Italy, where communist-inspired parties had made considerable electoral gains, it was content to keep them out of government. In other cases, a more decisive alignment with neoliberal orthodoxy was demanded in return for financial aid. In Germany, for instance, neoliberalism took root with greater intensity as a result of US intervention far beyond that envisaged by the Marshall Plan.[35] Elsewhere, like in the UK, the implementation of the Marshall Plan led to the abandonment of plans considered incompatible with the neoliberal creed. Clement Attlee's Labour government's attempt to limit private ownership of the means of production foundered under US pressure.[36]

On the whole, however, it can be agreed that one outcome of the market for reforms stimulated by the Marshall Plan was common to all recipients of financial assistance: it favoured the affirmation of an approach to the economic order that anticipated the founding approach of European integration and did so 'without being undermined by mass labor and social unrest'.[37] In short, the Marshall Plan functioned as an instrument to neutralise social conflict, thus confirming itself as the starting point of the process of European unification, which undoubtedly includes among its aims the pacification of the economic order. We shall return to this aspect at length (III.2.8).

4 THE DEVELOPMENT OF A UNITED EUROPE: THE INTERNATIONAL MONETARY FUND AND THE ENLARGEMENT TO THE SOUTH

In the years that followed, the exchange of financial aid in return for the adoption of capitalist reforms remained the main driving force of European project, which was activated at all the decisive stages of its development. We will now look at the main enlargements through this

33 A. Pera, *Comparing the Marshall Plan and the European Next Generation Eu. Models and Legal Tools of International and Supernational Cooperation to Promote Economic Development*, in *Cardozo Electronic Law Bulletin*, 22, 2022, p. 10 ff.
34 F. Salmoni, *Piano Marshall, Recovery fund e il containment americano verso la Cina. Condizionalità, debito e potere*, in *Costituzionalismo.it*, 2021, 2, p. 52 ff.
35 A. Somma, *La dittatura dello spread. Germania, Europa e crisi del debito*, Roma, 2014, p. 35 ff.
36 B. Steil, *The Marshall Plan. Dawn of the Cold War*, Oxford, 2018, p. 339 ff.
37 *Ibid.*

lens. These enlargements have all drawn on the same justification for the original ideal of uniting Europe; that is to say, they invoked the ideal of creating a garrison of peace and a barrier against the threat of totalitarianism. More precisely, the enlargement to the south following the collapse of the fascist regimes that had survived the Second World War, and the enlargement to the East following the implosion of the socialist bloc.

Let us begin with the first enlargement, which involved Greece, Portugal, and Spain. In Greece, fascism had not survived the Second World War, but this was followed by a period of political instability interrupted in 1967 by the dictatorship of the colonels, which then fell in 1974 as a consequence of the failed attempt to annex Cyprus. In Portugal, a military dictatorship took over as early as 1926, leading to a regime led by António de Oliveira Salazar and for a short period by Marcello Caetano, whose end was marked in 1974 by the Carnation Revolution. In Spain, fascism took power in 1939, lasting until the death of dictator Francisco Franco in 1975, when the return to democracy was ensured by the monarchy.

As a result of these events, all three countries applied for membership of the then European Economic Community on the basis of the aforementioned founding reasons for the construction, explicitly referred to in the documents of the time: Brussels certainly could not reject the request to provide 'protection against the return of dictatorship'.[38] But nor could it accept that accession should challenge the foundations of the economic order, which at the time was in the process of moving away from anything incompatible with the neoliberal approach that was destined to prevail in the conflict between capitalist models (II.2.9).

It was precisely neoliberalism, however, that was rejected by the Greek, Portuguese, and Spanish fundamental charters, which adopted post-war constitutionalism as summarised in the principle of substantive equality (I.2.1). All this was seen by the European authorities as the cause of the conditions in which the candidate countries found themselves, conditions which were obviously not due to the newborn democracy, but which were nevertheless blamed on it. For Brussels, if those countries were plagued by high levels of unemployment, a severely depressed balance of payments and low levels of industrialisation, it was because they had chosen to favour economic policies that were considered out of line with the principles expressed in the Treaties.[39]

Portugal was especially in Brussels' crosshairs because its constitution was born in a climate still conditioned by the events that led to the defeat of the fascist dictatorship. The Carnation Revolution was a bloodless event directed by the army, but, intellectually, it was fuelled by anti-imperialist and socialist ideals.[40] These ideas carried over into the 1976 Constitution, which mentioned the will of the people to 'open up a path towards a socialist society' (preamble), to promote the transformation of the Republic into a 'classless society' (art. 1), which shall 'socialize the means of production and wealth' and shall 'abolish the exploitation and oppression of man by man' (art. 9).

However, the political climate quickly changed with the victory of conservative forces in the 1971 elections, which allowed the rewriting of the most controversial articles from a neoliberal point of view. Nevertheless, economic policy choices that were unwelcome at the European level persisted. For example, the Portuguese government embarked on a programme of nationalisation in industry and services, which was, for Brussels, a clear sign that the country needed 'radical economic and social reforms'.[41] These reforms were needed, it

38 *General considerations on the problems of enlargement* of 20 April 1978, Com/78/120 fin.
39 *The transitional period and the institutional implications of enlargement* of 24 April 1978, Com/78/190 fin.
40 R. Villares, *Transizioni iberiche alla democrazia: tra rivoluzione e riforma*, in F. Bertagna and L. Tedoldi (Eds.), *Transizioni in Europa e in America latina (1945–1995)*, Milano, 2018, p. 97 ff.
41 *Opinion on Portuguese application for membership* of 19 May 1978, Com/78/220 fin.

was said, because Portugal had a particularly high public debt, resulting from, among other things, the costs associated with granting independence to its colonies: in particular the cost of absorbing citizens who had returned from Angola and Mozambique into the public administration (II.2.9).

It was at this point that the market for reforms came into play: preparing Portugal for accession was the job of the International Monetary Fund, which was given a sort of tacit mandate by the European authorities to take charge of the issue.[42] Thus, the granting of two IMF loans: the first, in 1976, a year after the first free elections won by the Mario Soares' socialist party, and coinciding with the request for accession to the European Economic Community, and the second, between 1983 and 1985, when the socialist party had returned to power after a conservative interlude.

This second loan was particularly effective at obtaining reforms in line with neoliberal orthodoxy, and thus paved the road to future entry into the EEC. The privatisation of publicly owned enterprises was not directly imposed, but rather their activities were restricted. This was achieved by a 'substantial reduction in investment in public enterprises', which were thus forced to sustain themselves out-of-pocket, and thus were unable to practise a regime of administered prices for the goods produced and services provided: from basic necessities, to the supply of electricity and water, to transport, to which 'realistic prices' would now have to be applied.[43]

Portugal also accepted 'the freezing of the investment programme in the public sector' and pledged to contain expenditure through 'the revision of the system of social benefits'. This had repercussions also on the functioning of the Supply Fund *(Fundo de abastecimento)*, a body in charge of the sale of imported essential goods sold at reduced prices, to which it was decided to apply 'a significant increase'. Last but not least, in order to help contain inflation, as well as to fuel supply-side policies, labour reforms were announced aimed at 'moderating labour costs' in the public sector, called to 'serve as an example for wage negotiations in the private sector'. The same effort was made to increase precariousness in employment as an inevitable consequence of measures to 'increase labour mobility' and 'flexibility in the use of labour'.[44]

It is little wonder, then, that the International Monetary Fund's coercive and punitive neoliberal intervention in Portugal, was considered the test-bed for the development of what was later defined in terms as the Washington consensus (III.2.2).[45] Given the complicity of the European institutions, it could well be called the Washington and Brussels Consensus.

5 NEXT: THE EUROPEAN BANK FOR RECONSTRUCTION AND DEVELOPMENT AND THE ENLARGEMENT TO THE EAST

If enlargement to the south posed a number of problems for the European agenda, enlargement to the East was no less problematic. As we have said, it had to be pursued for the same reasons as enlargement to the south, namely, because it would guard against the return of totalitarianism and thus affected the *raison d'être* of European integration. Moreover, unlike the fascist dictatorships, the socialist dictatorships had not repudiated political liberalism

42 See J.S. Lopes, *Imf Conditionality: The Stand-By Arrangement with Portugal 1978*, in J. Williamson (Ed.), *Imf Conditionality*, cit., p. 475 ff.
43 *Carta de Intenções dirigida ao Fundo Monetário Internacional* of 9 September 1983.
44 *Ibid.*
45 A.B. Nunes, *The International Monetary Fund's Standby Arrangements with Portugal*, Gabinete de História Económica e Social – Documentos de Trabalho 44/2011.

simply to allow a reform of economic liberalism (II.1.3). Socialist countries had intended to overcome the proprietary order in order to build a new one based on the rejection of both cornerstones of the Western tradition: of democracy but also of capitalism. This is the context for the considerable number of problems posed by enlargement to the East, which the European institutions decided to tackle by resorting to the market for reforms.

Enlargement was first discussed at the Copenhagen European Council in 1993, shortly before the countries concerned formally applied for membership. On that occasion, the criteria to be met by the candidate countries in order to become part of the Union were identified based on the foundations of the political and economic order laid down in the Treaties: the former, summed up in the reference to respect for human rights, fundamental freedoms and the rule of law (now Article 2 of the Treaty on European Union), and the latter expressed in the formula 'open market economy with free competition', corresponding to the current 'highly competitive social market economy' (now Article 3 of the EU Treaty).[46]

As can be seen, these criteria concern democracy and capitalism. However, the attention was focused mainly on capitalism consistent with the neoliberal way of conceiving European integration. Thus, trade relations between the Union and the countries of the East were emphasised, which were considered the 'engine of integration' as well as 'a new saving impulse in the face of stagnating growth in the West'.[47] The path to accession would involve creating a free trade area in which 'restrictive practices, abuse of dominant positions and public aid which distort or threaten to distort conditions of competition' would be banned – all this while the European Union would support the Eastern countries in their efforts to 'modernize their economies, which have been weakened by 40 years of central planning'. These economic reforms would become the main, almost exclusive, way in which the constitutive aims of a united Europe would be achieved: 'Peace and security in Europe depend on the success of those efforts'.[48]

In all of this, the market for reforms took centre stage, as the transformation of a planned economy into a market economy was elevated to conditionality in the context of the financial assistance provided by the European Investment Bank and especially the European Bank for Reconstruction and Development. The latter had been set up hastily to assist the transition to capitalism of the former Soviet bloc countries. It was celebrated as the sign of the final victory of capitalism over socialism, or as a product of the end of history (II.2.2), and in this sense as the 'first institution of the new world order'.[49]

The Bank's founding agreement is dated 29 May 1990. It contains very clear indications about its tasks: 'to promote private and entrepreneurial initiative in the Central and Eastern European countries committed to and applying the principles of... market economics' (Art. 1). This meant:

> (i) to promote, through private and other interested investors, the establishment, improvement and expansion of productive, competitive and private sector activity . . . (ii) to mobilize domestic and foreign capital . . . (iii) to foster productive investment, including in the service and financial sectors, and in related infrastructure where that is necessary to support private and entrepreneurial initiatives, thereby assisting in making a competitive environment and raising productivity . . . (v) to stimulate and encourage the development of capital markets.
>
> (Art. 2)

46 T. Beichelt, *Die Europäische Union nach der Osterweiterung*, Wiesbaden, 2004, p. 38.
47 J.-D. Giuliani, *L'élargissement de l'europe*, Paris, 2004, p. 43 f.
48 Copenhagen European Council of 21 and 22 June 1993, *Presidency Conclusions*.
49 P.A. Menkveld, *Origin and Role of the European Bank for Reconstruction and Development*, Berlin, 1991, p. 96.

References are also made in the Agreement to the 'fundamental principles of multiparty democracy' and 'pluralism', as well as to the 'rule of law' and 'respect for human rights', which, however, do not undermine the centrality attributed to the foundations of the capitalist economic order. Those references must indeed be read in the light of another document immediately adopted by the Bank to define the 'political aspects of the mandate'. The document stated that political freedoms are a function of economic freedoms in the neoliberal sense. It stressed, in particular, the 'critical link between the political and economic aspects of the Agreement', so that social rights simply 'can be taken into account', but not 'considered when evaluating a country's progress'.[50]

The Agreement then regulates the market for reforms by stressing the purposes and modalities of financial assistance. Indeed, it specifies that 'the resources and facilities of the Bank shall be used exclusively to implement the purpose and carry out the functions set forth, respectively, in Articles 1 and 2'. Above all, it specifies that if an assisted country implements 'inconsistent' policies, the Bank reserves the right to suspend or modify access to its resources. (Art. 8). We are thus faced with a conditionality regime that is both coercive and punitive: it constitutes a necessity from which the assisted countries cannot escape and whose effectiveness is fuelled by a regime of sanctions.

The market for reforms is present at all stages of the path leading to the formal opening of accession negotiations. This accession was decided in the second half of the 1990s, together with the 'enhanced pre-accession strategy' and 'increased pre-accession aid',[51] aimed at supporting the investments required by specific national programmes for the adaptation to the *acquis communautaire*. Shortly afterwards, in view of enlargement, the Treaty of Nice signed in February 2001 made some changes to the institutional structure of the Union, which were considered indispensable to facilitate decision-making within an organisation that would soon grow quite large. In 2004, Estonia, Latvia, Lithuania, Poland, the Czech Republic, Slovakia, Slovenia, and Hungary acceded to the European Union, while the accession of Bulgaria and Romania occurred in 2007.

The point here is not to describe the chaotic transition from a planned economy to a market economy that has affected the countries of the former Soviet bloc at all levels of the legal system, including the constitutional one. It suffices to highlight the markedly neoliberal inspiration of the reforms linked to the loans granted to favour the accession to the European Union.[52] These have the same flavour as the International Monetary Fund's intervention in Portugal: both processes of accession were implementations of the Washington consensus (III.2.2). Indeed, the reforms are intended to cut down the public administration, reduce social spending, promote privatisation and liberalisation plans, and transform the labour market to make it more flexible. All this to redeem countries in which 'there was no concept of private property, and profit was immoral'.[53]

In this context, it is illustrative to recall the furore surrounding the Slovak Labour Code of 2001, prepared by the Slovak Ministry of Labour and Social Affairs to achieve harmonisation with the *acquis communautaire*. Initial criticism was levelled at the Labour Ministry as a whole, which was considered to be 'strongly resistant to change' and 'lacking in professional skills to prepare modern legislation'. It was the Bank's view that it was 'reminiscent of the communist era in its physical appearance and work practice'. The real reason for the

50 *Political Aspects of the Mandate of the European Bank for Reconstruction and Development*, www.ebrd.com/downloads/about/aspects.pdf.
51 European Council of 12 and 13 December 1997 in Luxembourg, *Conclusions of the Presidency*.
52 See G. Ajani, *Diritto dell'Europa orientale*, in *Trattato di diritto comparato*, dir. R. Sacco, Torino, 1996, p. 115 ff.
53 A. Newburg, *Eastern Europe and the European Bank for Reconstruction and Development*, in *The International Lawyer*, 28, 1994, p. 435.

Bank's displeasure was the Labour Ministry's failure to share an analysis of the relationship between unemployment and the labour market, or, more precisely, their failure to conduct that analysis through a neoliberal lens: the Slovak authorities allegedly failed to recognise that 'the rigidity of the Slovak labour market and insufficient labour mobility are among the main causes of high unemployment'. Hence, for the Bank, the resulting Code was flawed, held guilty of having even further diminished 'labour flexibility', increased labour costs, placed limits on working hours, and discouraged dismissal and, above all, because it 'significantly increases the role of trade unions'.[54]

Notwithstanding these isolated setbacks, the Bank has more often than not gotten its way and Eastern states, and institutions, have been submitted to their neoliberal agenda. This agenda has been pursued with a zeal which is incompatible with post-war constitutionalism. This leads to a different interpretation of the current situation in many of the countries that once belonged to the socialist bloc, where a fervour for economic freedoms coexists with a repressive attitude towards political freedoms. This is usually considered a consequence of unfamiliarity with democracy. On the contrary it follows the pattern that fascism took between the two world wars: societies threatened by the market turn to the state for social security, which the state provides in return for renouncing political liberties (II.1.9). Put another way, the problem is not caused by unfamiliarity with democracy but is the result of neoliberalism which is the source of unbearable social imbalances.

6 THE EUROPEAN STRUCTURAL AND INVESTMENT FUNDS AND MACROECONOMIC CONDITIONALITIES

The market for reforms has affected the discipline of the European Structural and Investment Funds. This refers not so much to conditionalities relating to the use of resources in compliance with the purposes for which the funds were created, but to conditionalities that we have called cross-cutting because they relate to other aspects of state action (III.2.1): first and foremost, macroeconomic conditionalities.

On closer inspection, such conditionalities are new. Structural funds were first established as solidaristic measures in the 1950s, alongside the emergence of the EEC, and it was not until the 1980s they began to be conceived through a neoliberal lens.[55] At that time solidarity gave way, and the structural funds began to be seen as a sign of a 'loveless marriage' between member states or, similarly 'conditional solidarity'.[56]

In order to document such a transformation, we will reconstruct the stages that have marked the evolution of the European Structural and Investment Funds.[57] Let us therefore begin with the provisions contained in the Treaty establishing the European Economic Community, which introduced the European Social Fund and also mentioned various agricultural funds.

The European Social Fund was given an employment-oriented purpose; its aim was to increase the 'geographical and occupational mobility' of workers and above all 'improve employment opportunities for workers in the internal market and to contribute thereby to

54 K. Mathernová, *A Reformer's Lessons Learned: The Case of the Slovak Republic*, in *Law in Transition*, 2002, 2, p. 53.

55 A. Somma, *Quando l'Europa tradì sé stessa e come continua a tradirsi nonostante la pandemia*, Roma and Bari, 2021, p. 79 ff.

56 In this regard M. Fisicaro, *Condizionalità macroeconomica e politica di coesione: la solidarietà europea alla prova dei vincoli economico finanziari*, in *Rivista giuridica del Mezzogiorno*, 2019, p. 416 f.

57 For instance, R. Adam and A. Tizzano, *Manuale di diritto dell'unione europea*, 4th ed., Torino, 2017, p. 830 ff.

raising the standard of living' (Art. 123). Currently, the Treaty on the Functioning of the EU also gives the Social Fund the task 'to facilitate their adaptation to industrial changes and to changes in production systems, in particular through vocational training and retraining' (Art. 162).

The establishment of agricultural funds, which the Treaty merely defined as 'guidance and guarantee funds' (Art. 40), took place in the early 1960s. It was at that time that the European Agricultural Guidance and Guarantee Fund was created 'to enable the common organisation of agricultural markets to attain its objectives' (Regulation No. 25 of 4 April 1962). These objectives included advancing what the Treaty summarised as follows: 'to increase agricultural productivity', thus ensuring 'availability of supplies', as well as 'reasonable prices' and 'a fair standard of living for the agricultural community' (Art. 39). This Fund has since been replaced by the European Agricultural Guarantee Fund, which is responsible for financing market and other measures, and the European Agricultural Fund for Rural Development, both of which have been in operation since 2007 (Regulation No. 1290 of 21 June 2005).

Then, in the mid-1970s, the European Regional Development Fund was established, with the purpose of assisting the most underdeveloped regions within member states. More precisely, it aimed to correct imbalances 'resulting from the preponderance of agriculture and from industrial change and structural unemployment' (Regulation No. 724 of 18 March 1975). The Treaty on the Functioning of the EU summarised its functions in a somewhat different way, specifying that it participates 'in the development and structural adjustment of regions whose development is lagging behind and in the conversion of declining industrial regions' (Art. 176 TFEU).

An important step in the regulation of structural funds occurred with the Single European Act of 1986. This inserted in the then EEC Treaty a title dedicated to 'economic and social cohesion', which in the Treaty on the Functioning of the EU also includes the 'territorial' aspect, conceived to promote 'harmonious development' and, in particular, to 'reducing disparities between the levels of development of the various regions and the backwardness of the least-favoured regions' (Art. 130A). Here the European Social Fund, the European Agricultural Guidance and Guarantee Fund, and the European Regional Development Fund are mentioned, and initiatives to define their tasks are called for (Art. 130D). As a result, a number of regulatory measures have been taken to promote the coordination of funds, most notably a regulation in the late 1980s which gives an overview of the objectives to be achieved through financial assistance: 'promoting the development and structural adjustment of the regions whose development is lagging behind', reconverting those 'seriously affected by industrial decline', then 'combating long-term unemployment' and 'facilitating the occupational integration of young people', and finally 'speeding up the adjustment of agricultural structures' and 'promoting the development of rural areas' (Regulation 24 June 1988 no. 2052).

A well-known policy document, the White Paper on the Completion of the Internal Market, which preceded the Single European Act and ultimately anticipated the path towards the single currency, also devotes special attention to the European Structural and Investment Funds. The White Paper was prepared by the Commission chaired by Jacques Delors at the beginning of his term of office. More than any other document, it marks the definitive alignment of the European project with the neoliberal way of conceiving the functioning of the economic order. Most pointedly, it dealt with the possible consequences of a measure introduced to pave the way for Economic and Monetary Union, namely, the realisation of the free movement of capital: a measure envisaged by the Treaty of Rome but not implemented, on the grounds that if goods can and must move freely, the same does not apply to capital.

This latter principle became established at the end of the Second World War, when there was a Keynesian sensitivity, even if declining, to the discipline of the economic order. It is based on the assumption that if capital is free to circulate, states are obliged to adopt policies to attract international investors. This would inevitably encourage the lowering of wages and the tax burden on firms, and thus make the Keynesian compromise unworkable (II.3.9). All this is codified in the by-laws of the International Monetary Fund, which provides for state control over the movement of capital, and completed by the founding of the World Bank, which was charged with providing resources to countries in need at low interest rates and thus on the basis of political criteria sheltered from the rules of the financial markets.[58]

The White Paper shows awareness of the effects of the free movement of capital, which is seen as the key to economic growth in European integration. Indeed, it states that it can aggravate the condition of disadvantaged areas, and that such an effect must be counteracted by strengthening the structural and investment funds:

> The Commission is firmly convinced that the completion of the Internal Market will provide an indispensable base for increasing the prosperity of the Community as a whole. The Commission is, however, conscious that there may be risks that, by increasing the possibilities for human, material and financial services to move without obstacle to the areas of greatest economic advantage, existing discrepancies between regions could be exacerbated and therefore the objective of convergence jeopardized. This means that full and imaginative use will need to be made of the resources available through the structural funds. The importance of the funds will therefore be enhanced.[59]

Such clarifications invite a reflection on the European Structural and Investment Funds as fundamental components of a neoliberal approach to the economic order, without denying that as originally conceived they had clear solidaristic motivations. The paradigm shift becomes clear shortly after the White Paper's publication, in a document concerning the path towards the Economic and Monetary Union hinted at the development of a conditionality regime for the funds related to state action in areas other than those to which the various funds refer. Indeed, it is said that the funds were no longer to be understood as devices designed to redistribute wealth: 'Community instruments must cease to be seen as mere elements in a system of offsetting payments', their central role instead being 'one of bringing about the convergence of national economies alongside and in harmony with national and regional policies'.[60]

These very principles ended up inspiring the transformation of the European Structural and Investment Funds, which were deprived of their solidaristic connotation and became a catalyst for neoliberal economic policies. The spirit of the times led to this, and that spirit was embodied in the Maastricht Treaty. There, the path towards Economic and Monetary Union was defined, as well as the criteria that member states must meet in order to be part of it: first and foremost, to keep the deficit and public debt within a 'reference value', set at 3% and 60% of the gross domestic product respectively. All of this is complemented by corrective procedures aimed at eliminating excessive deficits (current Art. 126 of the Treaty on the Functioning of the EU), and fundamentally by preventive mechanisms concerning coordination of national economic policies and above all 'surveillance': on the one hand, of 'economic development in each of the Member States', and on the other of compliance with the 'broad guidelines' formulated to bring it into line with the fundamentals of Economic and Monetary Union (current Art. 121 of the Treaty on the Functioning of the EU).[61]

58 M.A. Clemens and M. Kremer, *The New Role for the World Bank*, in *Journal of Economic Perspectives*, 30, 2016, p. 53 ff.
59 *Completing the internal market: White Paper from the Commission to the European Council*, 14 June 1985, Com/85/310 fin.
60 *The Single Act: A new frontier for Europe* of 15 February 1987, Com/87/100 fin.
61 For instance, A. Somma, *La dittatura dello spread*, cit., p. 220 ff.

The philosophy behind the Maastricht Treaty, did not impact each and every Structural and Investment Fund. There is, for instance, no impact on the Financial Instrument for Fisheries Guidance (Regulation No. 2080 of 20 July 1993),[62] tasked with the promotion of the balanced exploitation and improvement of the supply of fishery resources.

The Maastricht philosophy is instead evident in the discipline of the Cohesion Fund, designed to support projects 'in the fields of environment and trans-European networks in the area of transport infrastructure'. Its use is reserved for member countries that meet two requirements: a per capita gross domestic product below a certain threshold, and above all having implemented 'a programme leading to the fulfilment of the conditions of economic convergence' and thus the debt and deficit limits. Therefore, in the event that the requirements are no longer met during the period of utilization and the funded projects are to be implemented in multiple phases, assistance from the Fund will be suspended (Regulation No. 1164 of 16 May 1994).[63] There is thus an explicit reference to the use of the structural funds being conditional on government action in areas other than those that are functional to the purposes originally covered by the Fund. It also highlights the dual nature of the macroeconomic conditionality to which the Fund rules refer: coercive because it often concerns projects that cannot otherwise be financed, and punitive because the EU reserves the right to suspend midstream funding for a failure to comply with conditionalities.

These rules were tightened following the adoption of the Stability and Growth Pact in 1997, which included a set of measures aimed at hardening of the neoliberal foundations of the Economic and Monetary Union. These measures include a deeper coordination and surveillance of member states' economic policies and more effective corrective procedures for dealing with excessive deficits.[64] Further, a slightly later measure specifies that recourse to the Cohesion Fund is reserved for countries that have drawn up the stability programme provided for by the Stability Pact with regard to the coordination and surveillance of national economic policies (Regulation No. 1466 of 7 July 1997). Thus, the states requesting assistance from the Fund are eligible for support only if they have indicated the measures intended to pursue the 'medium-term objective' (Regulation No. 1264 of 21 June 1999), i.e. the achievement of a budget balance close to balance or in surplus, as a value that will make it possible 'to deal with normal cyclical fluctuations while keeping the government deficit within the 3 percent of GDP reference value'.[65]

All the later developments of the European Structural and Investment Funds reinforce these coercive and punitive tendencies with respect to conditionalities imposed. In order to document them, we shall refer to the measures that have defined its basic features in the European Union's multiannual financial frameworks. In addition, we will examine partnership agreements governing the overall allocation of funds to each member state covering the same period.

The framework for the years 2014 to 2020, the first to follow the sovereign debt crisis, is neoliberal all the way through. It is characterised by the massive use of macroeconomic conditionalities, which are imposed in exchange for access to financial assistance (III.2.7). In line with this trend, the macroeconomic conditionality regime has been extended to all types of funds and beyond the Cohesion Fund. The conditionalities are now aligned with the so-called European semester: a complex procedure introduced in 2011, aimed at coordinating national economic policies, which provides for European-level assessment of fiscal and

62 Now called the European Maritime, Fisheries and Aquaculture Fund.
63 Regulation No 1084 of 11 July 2006 made suspension non-mandatory.
64 G. Contaldi, *Diritto europeo dell'economia*, Torino, 2019, p. 274 ff.
65 European Council of 16 and 17 June 1997 in Amsterdam, *Conclusions of the Presidency*.

budgetary policy.[66] This reaffirms the desire to create 'a closer link' between the funds and 'the economic governance of the Union . . . in order to ensure that the effectiveness of expenditure . . . is underpinned by sound economic policies'. Thus, a number of provisions were enacted which were aimed at producing the desired result. These included the revision of the aforementioned partnership agreements to correspond to the broad guidelines formulated in the surveillance of national economic policies, and above all the suspension of assistance if 'a Member State has not taken effective action to correct its excessive deficit' (Regulation No. 1303 of 17 December 2013).

The provisions of the financial framework for the years 2021 to 2027 (Regulation No. 1060 of 24 June 2021) are similar. While they have some notable differences, like the removal of automatic suspension of assistance in the mentioned cases, they do not affect the basic tenor of the system of macroeconomic conditionalities.[67] Overall, these various measures amount to the definitive transformation of economic, social, and territorial cohesion policies into instruments aimed at consolidating Economic and Monetary Union and, more precisely, aimed at encasing it within a neoliberal ideology.

If this is the case, the regulation of European Structural and Investment Funds manifestly leads to the distortion of instruments that were created to promote solidarity-based policies. But there is more: it also and above all ends up altering the character of European fiscal and budgetary policy, which unlike monetary policy, is not a supranational competence. Rather, it is a member states' competence, and insofar as they are under a legal obligation it is an obligation to coordinate them only (Article 5 of the Treaty on the Functioning of the EU). In other words, the EU has used soft law instruments to coordinate and surveil national economic policies, which, de facto, has had the same effects as if it were imposed by a hard law enactment. We are thus faced with an alteration of the European institutional architecture of considerable proportions and implications.[68]

7 THE DEBT CRISIS AND THE INTERVENTION OF THE INTERNATIONAL MONETARY FUND

We have seen that the system of macroeconomic conditionalities linked to the use of European Structural and Investment Funds was generalised and intensified during the sovereign debt crisis, and that the latter was also tackled with instruments largely characterised by this type of conditionality. We shall now turn to that crisis, after a brief reconstruction of its origin, which is intimately linked to two characteristics of neo-American capitalism, namely, its marked tendency to encourage financialization[69] and its reluctance to redistribute wealth through an extensive social security system (II.2.9).

This last characteristic has led to the abnormal development of a practice used as a substitute for welfare, namely, consumer credit, which has characterised the United States in particular. There, a model effectively described in terms of 'privatised Keynesianism' has been realised.[70] Primary goods, such as education or housing or even health, are not provided

66 Regulation No. 1175 of 16 November 2011. See G. Contaldi, *Diritto europeo dell'economia*, cit., p. 296 f.
67 I. Ottaviano, *Politica di coesione e governance economica europea: prospettive giuridiche di un'integrazione in evoluzione*, in *Eurojus*, 2023, p. 117.
68 V. Vita, *Revisiting the Dominant Discourse on Conditionality in the Eu: The Case of Eu Spending Conditionality*, in *Cambridge Yearbook of European Legal Studies*, 19, 2017, p. 116 ff.
69 L. Gallino, *Finanzcapitalismo. La civiltà del denaro in crisi*, Torino, 2011.
70 C. Crouch, *Privatised Keynesianism: An Unacknowledged Policy Regime*, in *British Journal of Politics and International Relations*, 11, 2009, p. 382 ff.

by the state, but by the credit system. In other words, they are funded by massive private debt in circumstances in which the ability of debtors to repay their debts is to be doubted. This private indebtedness, roughly the mirror image to the public indebtedness that has exploded in European countries, can be traced back to the attempt to preserve welfare despite the US's adherence to neoliberal orthodoxy.[71]

At the beginning of the new millennium, the use of consumer credit was stimulated by the US Central Bank's decision to contain the cost of money, which inevitably translated into a credit boom. Hence, there was an increase in demand for housing by those who wanted to shelter themselves from rising rents or possibly speculate on a future sale. Consequently, house prices also rose, which led to an increasing risk for lending institutions, who wanted to mitigate this by resorting to mortgage security.

As a rule, mortgages were granted at variable or mixed rates and were therefore perceived as particularly advantageous by borrowers while the cost of money was low. However, the cost of money was destined to rise as soon as the Central Bank intervened to elevate it, which happened from 2004 onwards. This rate hike was in line with the US economy's recovery as it moved beyond two recent shocks: first, the aftershocks of dot-com bubble collapse and, secondly, the attacks on the World Trade Centre.[72]

Subprime debtors who were at an elevated risk of insolvency, ended up finding themselves unable to repay their loans and thus losing ownership of the real estate they had granted as collateral. For their part, the lending institutions had no other recourse than to claim on properties whose market value had dropped considerably, to the point of being considerably lower than the value of the loan granted. These effects were multiplied by the securitisation of the mortgages, whereby mortgages were transformed into negotiable securities. These securities had been purchased without the knowledge of their high financial risk, i.e. of the fact that the insolvency of the subprime borrower would have caused their value to collapse. Hence, the contagion transmitted to the banking system as a whole, radiating far beyond the circle of institutions that had issued the high-risk mortgages.[73] The latter effect was then increased by the use of derivatives, i.e. financial products whose value depends on the performance of other products, in particular securitised mortgages, traded in deregulated markets.

The result was the global spread of the US credit system's distress, and ultimately the sovereign debt crisis caused by the bailout with public money of major banks otherwise doomed to fail. All this happened while unemployment and impoverishment reached worrying and, in some cases, dramatic levels. The Europe Union responded with austerity: the neoliberal creed prohibited counter-cyclical measures like spending on welfare and pro-employment policies (II.2.9).

Not even the instruments normally used in the Glorious Thirties, when states following the Keynesian compromise (II.2.9) monetised debt, by requiring the Central Bank to buy debt securities and thus issue money, could be permitted to consolidate public budgets: in the Europe Union the National Central Banks, as well as the European Central Bank, are indeed independent of political power and furthermore cannot grant credit facilities or purchase debt securities directly (Art. 123 Treaty on the Functioning of the EU). For their part, the European Union and the member states 'shall not be liable for or assume the commitments of central governments' and thus intervene to rescue them (Art. 125 Treaty on the Functioning of the EU).[74] All this follows a clear design of giving power over to financial markets to regu-

71 W. Streeck, *Tempo guadagnato. La crisi rinviata del capitalismo democratico*, Milano, 2013, p. 94 ff.
72 In particular A. Tooze, *Crashed: How a Decade of Financial Crise Changed the World*, New York NY, 2018, p. 37 ff.
73 For instance, C. Peicuti, *Securitization and the Subprime Mortgage Crisis*, in *Journal of Post Keynesian Economics*, 35, 2013, p. 443 ff.
74 See G. Contaldi, *Diritto europeo dell'economia*, cit., p. 269 ff.

late the member states and, in this sense, is consistent with the neoliberal creed: it forces member states to obtain resources from financial markets and, thus, subjects their economic policies in market discipline.

In short, a united Europe was founded on a creed incompatible with policies required to steer itself through the crisis it was experiencing. This could have been an opportunity to revise those policies, but that opportunity was not taken. On the contrary, the crisis, once again, reinforced the market for reforms.[75]

Such a solution could not rest on a solid legal foundation. Or rather, the market for reforms was foreseen, but only with reference to non-Eurozone countries. For the latter, the Maastricht Treaty had stipulated that, in the event in which a member state is in 'difficulties or is seriously threatened with difficulties as regards its balance of payments' detrimental to 'the functioning of the internal market or the implementation of the common commercial policy', then 'mutual assistance', i.e. medium-term financial support, could be granted (current Art. 143 of the Treaty on the Functioning of the EU). A regulation was then added that a loan or credit line could only be extended by agreeing 'economic policy conditions attaching to the medium-term financial assistance with a view to re-establishing or ensuring a sustainable balance of payments situation'. Any loan or credit line would be constantly monitored since the disbursement or drawdown was conditioned on 'successive instalments, the release of each instalment being subject to verification of the results achieved in implementing the programme in terms of the objectives set' (Regulation No. 332 of 18 February 2002).

For the Eurozone countries, too, the intention was to proceed in the same way, i.e. to provide financial assistance conditional on the implementation of structural reforms. However, nothing of the sort was provided for in the Maastricht Treaty. There was, in fact, a provision dedicated to situations where 'a Member State is in difficulties or is seriously threatened with severe difficulties caused by natural disasters or exceptional occurrences beyond its control', to which financial assistance could be granted 'under certain conditions' (Art. 122 of the Treaty on the Functioning of the EU). However, it was widely felt that this provision was not a sufficiently solid legal basis for sweeping conditionalities, which is why it was decided to strengthen it by involving the International Monetary Fund. As we know, the latter had gained considerable experience in the restructuring of the sovereign debt of so-called developing countries, where financial assistance was conceived as given in return for the implementation of neoliberal structural reforms (III.2.2). And it could now be put at the disposal of the European authorities engaged in sovereign debt restructuring, which in fact resorted to it extensively; moreover, as we know, it was not the first time (III.2.4).

Against this backdrop, and on the basis of the Treaty provision just mentioned, the European Financial Stabilisation Mechanism and the European Financial Stability Facility were created. The Mechanism operated within the framework of support linked to 'strong economic policy conditions' (Regulation No. 407 of 11 May 2010) and provided conditional financial assistance to Ireland and Portugal between 2011 and 2014 and to Greece in 2015. The Fund provided financing to states which had concluded a memorandum with the European Commission 'including conditions such as budgetary discipline and economic policy guidelines' (Preamble of the EFSF Framework Agreement) and operated in Ireland from 2011 to 2013, in Portugal between 2011 and 2014 and in Greece between 2012 and 2014.

The matter was finally put in order by a decision of the European Council (of 25 March 2011 No. 199), which amended the provision of the Treaty on the Functioning of the Union

75 V. Vita, *In Conditionality We Trust: What Scope for Conditionality in the Emerging European Economic Constitution?*, in H.C.H. Hofman, K. Pantazatou and G. Zaccaroni (Eds.), *The Metamorphosis of the European Economic Constitution*, Cheltenham, 2019, p. 199 ff.

dedicated to the Eurozone countries (Art. 136). In that decision, a clarification was included according to which the latter 'may establish a stability mechanism to be activated if indispensable to safeguard the stability of the euro area as a whole and stating that the granting of any required financial assistance under the mechanism will be made subject to strict conditionality'. Thus, the European Stability Mechanism was established to replace the aforementioned European Financial Stabilisation Mechanism and European Financial Stability Facility.[76] All of this was endorsed by the EU Court of Justice, which legitimised the solution as being in line with the 'logic of the market'[77]: it is justified by the need to preserve the balance of the Eurozone – i.e. the purpose is not to assist a state in difficulty – and in this perspective it does not undermine the aforementioned role attributed to the markets in conditioning the conduct of States. As stated by the Court of Justice:

> The prohibition laid down in Article 125 TFEU ensures that the Member States remain subject to the logic of the market when they enter into debt, since that ought to prompt them to maintain budgetary discipline. Compliance with such discipline contributes at Union level to the attainment of a higher objective, namely maintaining the financial stability of the monetary union. Given that that is the objective pursued by Article 125 TFEU, it must be held that that provision prohibits the Union and the Member States from granting financial assistance as a result of which the incentive of the recipient Member State to conduct a sound budgetary policy is diminished. . . . The activation of financial assistance by means of a stability mechanism such as the ESM is not compatible with Article 125 TFEU unless it is indispensable for the safeguarding of the financial stability of the euro area as a whole and subject to strict conditions.[78]

The conditions imposed in return for financial assistance all follow the same pattern. This concerns first and foremost the International Monetary Fund, which was used before the Treaty explicitly referred to conditionality.[79] And it is all the more true for financial assistance based on what the Treaty later stipulated, i.e. the activities of the European Stability Mechanism, as well as its predecessor institutions.[80]

In both cases, the financial assistance is provided in return for measures to reduce expenditure and, in particular, to curb pension and social spending, including, of course, health and education spending, to freeze or reduce civil servants' salaries, and in general to downsize the public administration. In addition, there are indications on how to increase revenue, especially through privatisation and liberalisation programmes in the energy, telecommunications, insurance, and local public services sectors.

There are also widespread conditionalities concerning the reform of the labour market, conceived in such a way as to restore higher levels of contract freedom, useful, among other things, to remove the obstacles to the flexibilisation and precariousness of the employment relationship. This assimilates labour more and more to any other kind of market relationship, relating to the mere exchange of human activity for money, purified of any accessory obligation to protect the weaker party. All this while the EU encourages the development of industrial relations in which the power of workers' trade unions is limited: for example, by promoting the possibility for agreements at the level of the individual company, where the employer's bargaining power is strongest, in derogation from agreements concluded at the

76 *Treaty establishing the European Stability Mechanism* of 2 February 2012.

77 H. Schepel, *The Bank, the Bond and the Bail-out: On the Legal Construction of Market Discipline in the Eurozone*, in *Journal of Law and Society*, 44, 2017, p. 79 ff.

78 Case *Pringle* of 27 November 2012 (C-370/12), n. 135 s.

79 Activities documented on the website of the Fund: www.imf.org/external/country/index.htm.

80 Documented in www.esm.europa.eu/financial-assistance.

central level, where it is easier for trade unions to counter that power. Finally, note the favourable view of the introduction of a wage component linked to company profits, encouraged as a measure capable of inducing cooperation and collaboration between capital and labour.[81]

What is more, this financial assistance is provided on a piecemeal basis, i.e. in instalments, the payment of which depends on the implementation of the reforms set out in the roadmap agreed with the assisted country. We are thus confronted with a coercive instrument since it provides resources that would otherwise be accessible only under unacceptable conditions, and punitive since it is destined to be suspended if the reforms are not implemented. In short, the market for reforms within the framework of the financial assistance provided to member states whose indebtedness endangers European integration is also used to propagate neo-American capitalism (II.2.9). This confirms the role of the European Union as a catalyst for this model of capitalism to the detriment of the one that once prevailed on the Old Continent.

8 THE PANDEMIC CRISIS AND THE RECOVERY AND RESILIENCE FACILITY

The European Union tackled the debt crisis by imposing austerity policies on the assumption that this would restore the ability of states to raise funds and of companies to produce wealth. In other words, it did not question the centrality of the market as main tool for wealth redistribution and the focus on the support of business as the foundation of growth at the expense of workers.

Even in neoliberal circles it is admitted that these are flawed principles, at least when applied in the adverse phases of the economic cycle, which not surprisingly require countercyclical measures. This is what the proponents of the New Comparative Economics claim, for example, when they extol the virtues of common law as the law of neo-American capitalism, recognising, however, that in adverse phases one can and indeed must resort to a civil law solution or at least to forms of marked interventionism. It is therefore not surprising that during the economic crisis caused by the recent pandemic, there was a desire expressed for change of approach. The pandemic crisis should, it was said, be addressed by recourse to alternative instruments to those used only a few years earlier. It is surprising, however, that words have not been followed by deeds, as can be seen from the fact that financial assistance has been coupled with macroeconomic conditionalities similar to those seen so far. The market for reforms has once again been brought into play as a catalyst for solutions firmly aligned to the neoliberal creed.

We derive the main evidence for this from the measures taken to support economic recovery, and in particular from the rules governing the main funds created for this purpose under the umbrella of Next Generation EU.[82] One such fund, the Recovery and Resilience Facility, is an instrument with an original budget of approximately EUR 672.5 billion, provided partly as a loan and partly as a grant within the financial framework for the years 2021 to 2027.[83]

The Facility has its legal basis in the provision of the Treaty on the Functioning of the EU that allows for 'specific actions' in the field of cohesion policy in cases where the

81 Citations in A. Somma, *Giustizia o pacificazione sociale? La codeterminazione nello scontro tra modelli di capitalismo*, in *Politica del diritto*, 2015, p. 549 ff.

82 For instance, F. Cerquozzi, *Pnrr e democrazia rappresentativa. Responsabilità di bilancio o responsabilità sociale?*, in L. Cestaro and G. Comazzetto (Eds.), *Dialoghi giuspubblicistici sulla ripresa*, Naples, 2022, p. 17 ff.

83 In particular O. Chessa, *Dall'ordine di Maastricht al Next Generation Eu*, in G.P. Dolso (Ed.), *Governare la ripresa. La Pubblica amministrazione alla prova del Recovery plan*, Trieste, 2022, p. 27 ff.

existing Structural and Investment Funds cannot be used (Art. 175) (II.2.6). It aims at enabling the overcoming of the economic crisis caused by the pandemic and preventing its recurrence in case of future events. More particularly, it aims to 'promote the Union's economic, social and territorial cohesion by improving the resilience, crisis preparedness, adjustment capacity and growth potential of the Member States . . . by supporting the green transition' and the 'digital transition', promoting 'sustainable growth', and by 'fostering high quality employment creation'. This is to be achieved by 'investing in green and digital technologies, in innovation and research in a knowledge-based economy, in the clean energy transition, and in boosting energy efficiency in housing'. Also, 'reforms based on solidarity, integration, social justice and a fair distribution of wealth should be introduced with the aim of creating quality employment and sustainable growth, ensuring equality of, and access to, opportunities and social protection' (Regulation No. 241 12 February 2021).[84]

The objectives of the Recovery and Resilience Facility are thus multifaceted and the conditionalities designed to oversee them relate largely to the issue of economic and social cohesion. However, macroeconomic conditionalities are not absent, firstly because there is an explicit reference to 'measures that strengthen the competitiveness, growth potential and sustainable public finances'. They are, secondly, linked with to the Maastricht parameters and, in particular, the deficit and debt limits. There is also provision for the total or partial 'suspension of commitments or payments' if a member state 'has not taken effective action to correct its excessive deficit'. Finally, there is a reminder of the indications formulated in the context of the European Semester (II.2.6), which must be taken into account in the National Recovery and Resilience Plans: the plans containing a detailed list of the investments that the states receiving assistance commit themselves to make, together with the reforms on which it is conditional (Regulation No. 241 of 12 February 2021).

Initially, the reference to the European semester was not particularly penalising. The activation of the general safeguard clause of the Stability and Growth Pact 'to allow for a coordinated and orderly temporary deviation from the normal requirements' was among the first measures taken in response to the pandemic.[85] The point of reference for this decision are the provisions governing the functioning of the preventive and corrective arms of the Pact in the event of a 'severe economic downturn'. These provide that national budgets may deviate from the adjustment path towards the medium-term objective, and therefore that multilateral surveillance may be suspended, but only 'temporarily' and only 'provided that this does not endanger fiscal sustainability in the medium term' (Regulation No. 1175 of 16 November 2011). The same condition is then envisaged to allow the relaxation, but not the suspension, of the excessive deficit procedure (Regulation No. 1177 of 8 November 2011).

In the meantime, the Stability and Growth Pact has not only been reactivated, but its content has undergone changes that have tightened its function as a guardian of the neoliberal way of conceiving economic policies in the European Union.[86] Not only the Maastricht parameters on debt and deficit limits have been maintained, despite being denounced by many as anachronistic approaches to the economic policy of European states. Automaticity has also been established with reference to debt and deficit reduction, which must progress annually by a predefined percentage and therefore cannot be reconsidered in

84 See A. Conzutti, *In conditionality we trust. Riflessioni sulle condizionalità macroeconomiche introdotto dal Recovery and resilience facility*, in *Ambientediritto*, 2022, 3, p. 1 ff.
85 *On the activation of the general escape clause of the Stability and Growth Pact* of 20 March 2020, Com/2020/123 fin.
86 F. Salmoni, *La riforma del patto di stabilità e crescita: un'occasione per trasformare l'Europa o un maquillage per l'austerity che verrà?*, in *Costituzionalismo.it*, 2021, 3, p. 46 ff.

the light of political criteria.[87] In particular, if the ratio of public debt to gross domestic product exceeds 90%, an annual decrease of one percentage point must be made, whereas if the ratio is below that value, a decrease of half a percentage point will suffice. As for the deficit, it is to be reduced below the 3 per cent threshold over a four-year adjustment period extendable to seven years, with a 'reference trajectory' and a horizon that 'provides a common resilience margin in structural terms of 1,5 % of GDP'. And this is to be done with an annual improvement in the structural primary balance of 0.4 per cent of gross domestic product or 0.25 per cent if the adjustment period is extended to seven years. This is set out in 'national medium-term fiscal-structural plans' along the lines of the national recovery and resilience plans. They must contain 'the fiscal, reform and investment commitments of a Member State' (Regulation No. 1263 of 29 April 2024).[88]

But let us return to the Recovery and Resilience Facility and its macroeconomic conditionalities, in particular those stemming from the reforms that the recipient countries undertake to implement in return for the financial assistance. In order to assess them, we will refer to the Italian National Recovery and Resilience Plan and, by way of example, to two reforms that were immediately implemented to promote simplification in the areas of public procurement and the environment, and more specifically to streamline anti-mafia controls and environmental impact assessments (Decree-Law No. 77 of 31 May 2021). In both cases, the intention was to embed the neoliberal public choice theory (II.3.6). In that theory, public intervention that goes beyond mere support for the functioning of the market through 'regulatory simplification' produces 'the multiplication of corruptive phenomena'.[89]

Particularly significant is the commitment to implement a measure of 2009 that entrusted the executive with the task of preparing 'yearly laws for the market and competition' in order to 'remove regulatory obstacles of a legislative or administrative nature to the opening of markets' and 'promote the development of competition' (Article 47 of Law No. 99 of 23 July 2009). The provision has indeed been largely disregarded and the economic crisis caused by the pandemic has provided the occasion to reiterate its importance also and above all when adopting counter-cyclical measures. That is to say, the latter must not undermine competition in its essence as a mechanism of resource allocation and selection of economic players, as is claimed from a questionable reconstruction by the Italian Competition and Market Authority of the crises of recent decades:

> The great recession of the 1930s, the crisis in Japan in the 1990s and the more recent financial crises have taught us that even when the economic system is in trouble, competition is not a luxury. There is ample literature confirming how the loosening of competition rules prolonged the recession of the 1930s; how leniency in merger control did not foster efficiency gains and greater financial stability during the global financial crisis of 2009 and the experience of the Japanese economy in the 1990s; how, finally, the sectors characterised by a more intense competitive dynamic were those that grew and regained competitiveness sooner than others, while the sectors protected by competition-restricting measures were those where the negative impact on productivity was more pronounced. In this perspective, there emerges the need for economic policy decisions and public intervention to support the economy . . . to be designed in full awareness of the effects on competition, especially the medium-term effects that can jeopardise the recovery of productivity of the economic system and the possibility of growth. . . . Competition promotes productivity and job creation, induces enterprises to be

87 A. Francescangeli and G. Gioia, *Il nuovo Patto di stabilità e crescita. Much ado about (almost) nothing?*, in *Diritti comparati*, 27 maggio 2024.
88 A. Guazzarotti, *Debito e democrazia. Per una critica del vincolo esterno*, Milano, 2024, p. 159 ff.
89 *Piano nazionale di ripresa e resilienza* (30 April 2021), p. 73.

> more productive and innovative, favours a better allocation of resources between economic activities, and allows the most innovative and efficient enterprises to enter the market and grow.[90]

The call to prepare a Market and Competition Law annually was largely disregarded, and in fact it had only been done once (Law No. 124 of 4 August 2017). The macroeconomic conditionalities attached to the National Recovery and Resilience Plan intended to enhance that law, stating that 'its annual cadence should be ensured, as it is essential to continuously review the status of legislation in order to verify whether there remain regulatory constraints to the competitive game and efficient market functioning'.[91] Hence, the change of course that in light of recent history appears truly epochal: annual laws have been issued for 2021 (Law No. 118 of 5 August 2022), 2022 (Law No. 214 of 30 December 2023) and 2023 (Law No. 193 of 16 December 2024).

9 POLITICAL CONDITIONALITIES AND THE PROTECTION OF THE UNION BUDGET

So far, we have focused on how macroeconomic conditionalities are used as instruments of the market for reforms to align the European project with neoliberalism. We have suggested, however, that the conditionalities attached to financial aid may well aim to produce results other than those directly related to the nature of the economic order. That is, they may focus on a foundation of the Western legal tradition other than that of market discipline; they may, in short, affect the ways of being of the political order and, in particular, the way of conceiving democracy.

These latter conditionalities may pursue different goals from those aimed at by macroeconomic conditionalities by promoting values that are not related to the neoliberal way of conceiving the European project.[92] We will see, however, that even what we might call political conditionalities can be aligned with macroeconomic ones. That is to say, they can contribute to the construction of neo-American capitalism to the extent that they feed an institutional framework that is about freedom rather than equality.

Conditionalities not directly linked to macroeconomic schemes not only stand out in the external relations of the united Europe, where they take into account the most diverse aspects (III.2.1): they are also particularly widespread in cohesion policy and thus in the regulation of the various European structural and investment funds. We derive this from analysing the Union's multiannual financial frameworks, which are acts in which the conditionalities to which financial assistance is subject are set out (II.2.6). They specify, in particular, horizontal conditionalities, relating to all funds, and conditionalities linked to specific funds.

With regard to horizontal conditionalities, we will consider by way of example the latest multiannual financial plan which covers the period between 2021 and 2027. Its stand out feature are conditionalities concerning the 'effective application and implementation of the Charter of Fundamental Rights' (Regulation No. 1060 of 24 June 2021), which has been recognised as having the same legal value as the Treaties (Art. 6 EU Treaty). It is certainly significant that financial aid is subordinated to respect for rights, and values, that do not directly concern the preservation of the Maastricht parameters. It is equally significant, however, that

90 Autorità garante della concorrenza e del mercato, *Proposte di riforme concorrenziale ai fini della Legge annuale per il mercato e la concorrenza anno 2021*, AS1730 of 22 March 2021.

91 *Piano nazionale di ripresa e resilienza* (30 April 2021), p. 79.

92 See M. Fisicaro, *Condizionalità macroeconomica e politica di coesione*, cit., p. 441.

unlike post-war constitutionalism there is no emphasis on the principle of substantive equality, which would assign the redistribution of resources primarily to public authorities (I.2.1).

In other words, the Charter of Fundamental Rights refers to aspects that are not directly macroeconomic in nature, but nevertheless assigns to the market a central role in the redistribution of resources, protected by the codification of the principle of formal equality (Art. 21),[93] as well as by the lack of reference to social rights. Indeed, the Charter imposes the 'respect' of rights, but only to 'observe' the principles it contains (Art. 51), and as the preparatory work shows, that the principles are those relating to social rights, which differ from other rights insofar as their implementation may require a legislative or executive act.[94] Consistently, the Charter devotes ample space to the positions indispensable to the protection of the competitive mechanism: the freedom to conduct a business (Art. 16) and the right to property, including intellectual property (Art. 17). It should be also noted that, in defining the latter, reference is made to the general interest, but in order to limit the intervention of the public authorities and not, as is instead the case in post-war constitutionalism, to limit the exercise of the right. Nor can this be the case with the provisions on the protection of the environment (Art. 37) and consumers (Art. 38), which carefully avoid recognising rights and therefore do not allow the prerogatives of the entrepreneur and owner to be effectively affected.

But let us return to the conditionalities that are not directly linked to macroeconomic concerns and focus on those that have been used for a relatively long time, in particular those related to employment and environmental policies. With regard to conditionalities of the first type, we can, for instance, recall what was established by the regulation establishing the European Regional Development Fund, according to which investments in industrial agricultural or service activities could only be financed if they were able to create jobs or at least maintain them (Regulation No. 724 of 18 March 1975). Conditionalities of the second type include those linked to the disbursement of agricultural funds, whose beneficiaries are required to maintain the land in 'good agricultural and environmental condition' (Regulation No. 1306 of 17 December 2013).[95]

If the conditionalities we have just referred to are indeed not closely related to neoliberalism, the same cannot be said for the conditionality relating to the defence of the rule of law which is a horizontal type of conditionality that has recently become central in the European context.

The rule of law is elevated to a founding value of European integration along with respect for human dignity, freedom, democracy, equality, and human rights (Art. 2 TEU). The defence of the rule of law is the aim of the procedure laid down in the event of a 'serious and persistent breach by a Member State', which can lead 'to suspend certain of the rights deriving from the application of the Treaties to the Member State in question, including the voting rights of the representative of the government of that Member State in the Council' (Art. 7 TEU). However, the procedure is complex and above all requires a unanimous finding of breach by the European Council, which is why it has never been initiated.[96]

Hence, the approval of a specific regulation on the protection of the Union budget 'in the event of breaches of the principles of the rule of law' in the member states (Regulation No. 2092 of 16 December 2020). It was created in anticipation of the financial framework for the years 2021 to 2027, which as we know includes the funds to be disbursed under Next

93 See S. Rodotà, *La Carta come atto politico e documento giuridico*, in A. Manzella et al., *Riscrivere i diritti in Europa. Introduzione alla Carta dei diritti fondamentali dell'unione europea*, Bologna, 2001, p. 81.
94 The European convention – WG II – Working doc. 23, p. 4 s.
95 V. Vita, *Revisiting the Dominant Discourse on Conditionality in the Eu*, cit., p. 131 ff.
96 See C. Pinelli, *Common Values, Rule of law Conditionality and the State of Democracy in Europe*, in *Liber amicorum Besselink*, Amsterdam, 2021, p. 6 f.

Generation EU (III.2.8). This has led the Europe Union to value the use of conditionalities as a particularly effective tool in inducing member states to behave in ways they would otherwise have avoided.[97]

The provision first of all provides a definition of the rule of law, to be understood in the light of the founding values of the European Union, borrowed from the jurisprudence of the EU Court of Justice and widely taken up by the Commission.[98] The rule of law includes 'legality, which implies a transparent, accountable, democratic and pluralistic process for enacting laws; legal certainty; prohibition of arbitrariness of the executive powers; independent and impartial courts; effective judicial review including respect for fundamental rights; and equality before the law'. This is followed by the clarification that violations of the rule of law, including threats to the 'independence or impartiality of the judiciary', are relevant insofar as this 'affects or seriously risks affecting the sound financial management of the Union budget or the protection of the financial interests of the Union'. This is the case, by way of example, when they affect the proper functioning of the authorities implementing the Union budget' or 'carrying out financial control, monitoring and audit', or dealing with 'fraud, including tax fraud', 'corruption or any other illegal activity affecting the financial interests of the Union', or where the infringement relates to 'a situation or conduct of authorities that are relevant for the sound financial management of the Union budget or for the protection of the Union's financial interests'.[99] In these cases, the outcome of a particularly complex procedure may lead to the suspension of planned or ongoing financial assistance, including, of course, that provided for by the various funds we have mentioned.[100]

As can be guessed, rule of law mechanism constitutes a compromise between positions that are in many respects irreconcilable. On the one hand, the positions of those who wished to use conditionality in order to achieve an overall promotion of the founding values of European construction. On the other hand, those who wished to defer to national sovereignty in aspects for which the supranational level does not have competence.[101] It is on this compromise, moreover, that the legal basis of the regulation on the protection of the Union's budget was conceived: the provision of the Treaty on the Functioning of the EU concerning the protection of the Union budget (Art. 317), linked to the provision according to which 'the Commission shall implement the budget in cooperation with the Member States' and may adopt 'financial rules which determine in particular the procedure to be adopted for establishing and implementing the budget and for presenting and auditing accounts' (Art. 322).

Moreover, the reference to the rule of law as a decisive element in the protection of the European budget is not only an expedient aimed at circumventing the problems posed by the distribution of competences between centre and periphery, in the wake of what happened in the Bretton Woods institutions (II.1.4). That reference also and above all points to a neoliberal ideological inspiration: restricting the political sphere to prevent it from acting against the market. As certified by the EU Court of Justice:

> Member States can only ensure sound financial management if public authorities act in accordance with the law, if breaches of the law are effectively pursued and if arbitrary or

97 M. Coli, *Stato di diritto e condizionalità finanziaria: un binomio ormai inscindibile per la tutela dei valori dell'unione europea?*, in M. Guglielmi, S. Cocchi and L. Marini (Eds.), *Democrazia e rule of law in Europa. Criticità e sfide aperte alla vigilia delle elezioni per il Parlamento europeo*, Speciale *Questione giustizia*, 2024, p. 46 f.

98 *A new EU Framework to strengthen the Rule of Law* of 11 March 2014, Com/2014/158 fin.

99 *Guidelines on the application of the Regulation (EU, EURATOM) 2020/2092 on a general regime of conditionality for the protection of the Union budget* of 2 March 2022, C/2022/1382 fin.

100 N. Kirst, *Rule of Law Conditionality: The Long-awaited Step Towards a Solution of the Rule of Law Crisis in the European Union?*, in *European Papers*, 6, 2021, p. 101 ff.

101 A. Baraggia, *La condizionalità a protezione dello Stato di diritto: tra potenzialità costituzionali e limiti applicativi*, in *Diritto pubblico comparato ed europeo*, 2023, p. 291 ff.

> unlawful decisions of public authorities can be subject to effective judicial review. . . . The independence and impartiality of the judiciary and investigation and prosecution services are required as a minimum guarantee against unlawful and arbitrary decisions of public authorities that could harm the financial interests of the Union.[102]

In short, the rule of law rhetoric constitutes a device to be used to nullify democratic and social constitutionalism (I.2.1), admitting only that which is functional to support a neoliberal order. That order is founded on 'the mantras of economic efficiency and entrepreneurial activity as a *raison d'être* for law itself'.[103]

In the name of the rule of law, therefore, there will be no recourse to gimmicks to interfere in other areas of national competence and to make up for the lack of supranational competence, such as those relating to the social dimension of European integration: a dimension that the neoliberal creed reduces to an economic dimension, equating social inclusion with market inclusion (II.2.9). Or, alternatively, the conditionalities concerning the social dimension – which are present just as other conditionalities of a non-macroeconomic character although ineffective[104] – will be thwarted by other conditionalities: at least because of the narrowness of resources imposed on national budgets by the observance of the Maastricht parameters.

SUMMARY

1. Legal change produced by imposition can take place by resorting to practices that are not overtly violent, such as the market for reforms: the situation in which reforms are demanded in return for financial assistance. The United States provides the blueprint for this market in the context of the development of cooperative federalism, i.e. the coordination of the actions of the centre and the periphery in such a way as to alter the distribution of competences by force. This is what is happening with the transition to coercive federalism, which includes conditional financial support to the states, i.e. the obligation to use the support for specific purposes, which is allowed to the extent that it manifests itself in the form of an incentive. Moreover, from a substantive point of view, this is often transformed into a constraint, so much so that one can speak of coercive or regulatory federalism, or even punitive federalism: a scenario that is realised when sanctions are envisaged for non-compliance with conditionalities. At the same time, the aims pursued concern less and less the promotion of progressive policies, as has traditionally been the case, and more and more the spread of neoliberalism.

2. The framework of the market for reforms also underpins the financial assistance provided by the World Bank and the International Monetary Fund, articulated in the Structural Adjustment Plans and conditional on the implementation of the reforms in line with the Washington Consensus: on the one hand deregulation of markets, liberalisation, and privatisation, and on the other budgetary discipline and fiscal moderation. In order to take into account demands that were not merely

102 CJEU, *Hungary v European Parliament and Council of the European Union* of 16 February 2022 (C-156/21), n. 116.

103 T. Krever, *The Legal Turn in Late Development Theory. The Rule of Law and the World Bank's Development Model*, in *Harvard International Law Journal*, 52, 2017, p. 317.

104 M. Fisicaro, *Beyond the Rule of Law Conditionality: Exploiting the Eu Spending Power to Foster the Union's Values*, in *European Papers*, 2022, p. 697 ff.

economic, the Bretton Woods institutions first elaborated the concept of a comprehensive development framework, with which to promote a participatory definition of reforms attentive to their social and environmental implications. Subsequently, they sought to contribute to the reduction of extreme poverty within the framework of initiatives undertaken by the United Nations by including conditionalities in Poverty Reduction Strategy Papers. On the whole, these innovations were supposed to nurture a holistic notion of development attentive to human rights. However, they have not altered the system of conditionality in its underlying philosophy, which in many respects is actually tightened.

3. The European Union is the product of a huge market for reforms and indeed its birth and the main stages of its evolution can be seen through a similar scheme. The start of the unification process can indeed be traced back to the launch of the Marshall Plan: the financial assistance provided by the United States to European countries in order to close the ranks of the capitalist West. The Plan led to the birth of the European Organisation for Economic Co-operation, aimed at creating an embryonic common market and monetary union based on currency stability and financial equilibrium. It was accompanied by the Economic Cooperation Administration, charged with verifying compliance with the conditions of financial assistance, including those relating to the achievement of the aims of the European Economic Cooperation Organisation. It is also in charge of penalising defaulting countries with the interruption or suspension of financial assistance.

4. The market for reforms also accompanies the major enlargements of the European Union. The one to the south followed the collapse of fascist regimes in Greece, Portugal, and Spain in the mid-1970s. Problems arose particularly in Portugal, where the return to democracy was accompanied by the seizure of power by socialist forces, whose ideals were neutralised by the intervention of the International Monetary Fund. The IMF granted financial aid to the country on condition that it reformed its economic system. So much so that this intervention was seen as a testing ground for the definition of the Washington Consensus.

5. Enlargement to the East followed the collapse of the socialist bloc and was accompanied by the definition of the so-called Copenhagen criteria: the criteria that countries wishing to join a united Europe had to fulfil in order to be considered. These concerned the re-establishment of democracy and capitalism, but it was on the latter that the focus was placed: the path to membership was set in motion by the creation of a free trade zone and political freedoms were only taken into consideration if they were functional to nurturing economic freedoms understood in the neoliberal sense. All this was accompanied by the activities of the European Bank for Reconstruction and Development, which was set up to provide financial assistance to the countries that had belonged to the socialist bloc and to foster their transition through the market for reforms.

6. The European Structural and Investment Funds originated as a solidaristic instrument for the redistribution of resources. Over time, however, they ended up serving the opposite purpose in many respects, namely, to promote first the construction and later the consolidation of the Economic and Monetary Union. The instrument used for this purpose are macroeconomic conditionalities, whereby financial assistance is reserved for those countries that follow the guidelines formulated at the European level mainly in order to pursue the so-called Maastricht parameters: in particular, debt and deficit limits. These conditionalities are coercive and punitive in nature: they provide otherwise unavailable funding, which is suspended if the recipient country does not meet the conditions. In this way, macroeconomic indications, formally acts of soft law as they relate to matters of exclusive competence of the national level, are transformed into acts of hard law, thereby profoundly altering the character of European construction.

7. The European Union also resorted to the market for reforms to deal with the consequences of the sovereign debt crisis produced by the private debt crisis: the one that broke out in the United States as the subprime crisis. After all, there was no alternative: in line with the neoliberal creed, states can only finance themselves by resorting to the financial markets, which in this way obtain a disciplining function on states' behaviour. Unless the Eurozone as a whole is put at risk: in such latter case the EU can provide assistance, but subject to strict conditionalities. These all follow the same pattern, designed to accommodate the spread of the neo-American model of capitalism. In fact, measures are imposed to reduce expenditure and in particular welfare spending. Reforms are then prescribed to increase revenues, especially through privatisation and liberalisation programmes. Finally, the reorganisation of the labour market is promoted in order to increase the flexibilisation and precariousness of the employment relationship.

8. The economic crisis caused by the pandemic was supposed to be an opportunity to highlight a change of course on the part of a united Europe, and in particular to affirm that it had to be tackled by promoting the centrality of redistribution achieved by the public authorities over that decided by the market. The solutions that were eventually adopted, however, followed traditional patterns, which were reaffirmed through the market for reforms. More precisely, the united Europe allocated resources to support states' efforts to tackle the crisis and equip themselves to withstand future ones. The related financial assistance was, however, conditional on the implementation of neoliberal reforms, or in any case aimed at reaffirming the centrality of the market as an instrument of wealth redistribution. All this while compliance with the Maastricht parameters was elevated to the status of criterion to be used in deciding on the possible suspension of assistance and thus to affirm the intimate neoliberal inspiration of European construction in this way too.

9. Alongside the macroeconomic conditionalities, designed to directly guard the neoliberal foundation of the European economic order, there are conditionalities relating to the promotion of foundations of the political order whose underlying inspiration does not appear to be connected to that foundation. These are, however, conditionalities for the most part aimed at building an institutional architecture suitable for the development of the economic order and, in any case, focused on freedom rather than equality: in particular, the freedom functional to preserving the functioning of the competitive market. The same applies to the recent conditionality aimed at protecting the rule of law, emphasised in particular as it concerns limits on the action of public authorities that could hinder the functioning of the competitive market.

PART IV

How to compare

The methods of comparative law

TABLE OF CONTENTS

DOI: 10.4324/9781032684499-11

CHAPTER 8

COMPARATIVE LAW BETWEEN SCIENCE AND METHOD

1 COMPARISON AS A METHOD

This introduction to comparative law has highlighted that it focuses on fundamental issues such as the notion of law and the legal system, the ways of classifying them and the dynamics of legal change. From this point of view, the question is not whether it constitutes a simple method or an autonomous science, but rather to recognise that comparative law has become one and the same 'with its object, that is with law as such'.[1] Nevertheless, the dispute between those who consider legal comparison to be a simple method and those who recognise its status as a science continues to dominate the debate, which is why it is necessary to address it here.

Comparative law scholars used to argue that their discipline does not constitute an autonomous field of knowledge since it cannot be described as a 'body of rules and principles'. They considered it a 'method, a way of looking at legal problems, legal institutions, and entire legal systems' through which it becomes possible 'to gain insights, which would be denied to one who limits his study to the law of a single country'.[2] Following this line of thought, some have considered comparative law to be a variant of historical knowledge of law, others of sociological knowledge, in both cases stressing that it 'cannot be constrained within national borders'.[3]

Those who invoke the link between comparative law and legal history emphasise that the former broadens the horizon of the latter by producing research extended to 'parallel legal manifestations'. In short, legal history when joined to comparative law creates a horizontal comparative law that accompany the vertical study of law. However, these insights are not considered enough to edify comparative law as an autonomous science: it remains a method, or rather a particular method that can be used in the field of legal history. In other words, as Messineo states:

> It is always implied in any dispute on the subject that, by comparative law, one wants to express a mode of essentially historical knowledge of laws. . . . It must be made clear that this is a special attitude of historical knowledge, marked by the fact that it does not restrict itself to the confines of a specific law and that, without wanting to be super-history or even universal history . . . it aims to explain (explain historically, that is, referring to given particular situations) the parallel legal manifestations: the concrete reasons for the emergence, development, decay or resistance of individual institutions among various peoples, considered in their twofold substantive (content or subject matter) and formal (technical structure) aspects. There is no qualitative difference, therefore, from the common history of law, except this: that comparative law aims at the simultaneous knowledge of as many legal systems as possible and to shed more light on the history of single laws'.[4]

1 Y.-M. Laithier, *Droit comparé*, Paris, 2024, p. 44 f.
2 R.B. Schlesinger et al., *Comparative Law. Cases Texts Materials*, 6th ed., New York NY, 1998, p. 2 (1st edition 1950).
3 J. Ghestin and G. Goubeaux, *Introduction générale*, in *Traité de droit civil*, dir. J. Ghestin, 3rd ed., Paris, 1990, p. 78.
4 F. Messineo, *L'indagine comparativa negli studi giuridici*, in *Archivio giuridico F. Serafini*, 1931, p. 14 f.

DOI: 10.4324/9781032684499-12

Others have traced comparative law, always understood as a method, to the sociological, as well as historical, study of law, which they distinguish from 'studies of legal dogmatics'. The latter aims 'to reconstruct a given system' or, more precisely, to discover the 'legal rule that would be applicable to a given case according to a given system'. Comparative law, by contrast, is interested in the law's effectiveness instead of its validity (I.2.1). In short, comparison considers 'not only compliance but also non-compliance with the law' and in this way goes beyond rules and principles formally considered to be the foundation of the legal system. As Ascarelli states:

> Rather than comparative law, however, one should speak of a comparative method in the study of legal problems, since in reality, by its very nature, there is not and cannot be comparative law, but only the comparison of the various institutions and problems. The purpose of comparison is to ascertain the legal discipline in force in a given system and not to ascertain what the solution to an unsolved case or problem might be in a given system. . . . The study of comparative law thus falls within the realm of historical and sociological studies and is opposed to the methodology that the jurist must resort to when studying a given system.[5]

We find in this description of comparative law an implicit distinction between an internal and an external point of view on law: the former typical of the scholar who reproduces the intent of the legislator in prescriptive terms, the latter adopted by those who instead seek to describe the state of the art (I.2.1).

In these pages, too, we have repeatedly asserted the common origin of comparative law on the one hand, and of legal history and sociology on the other. And we have shown how the agenda common to those disciplines includes overcoming the approach whereby the scholar only considers the validity of precepts, turning his attention to their effectiveness instead. However, interest in the law's effectiveness cannot be reduced to a purely methodological perspective, as is the case with the history and sociology of law: both are considered sciences.

The same must be true of comparative law, which can be practised using a variety of methods, all of which can be used profitably. Indeed, there are no correct or incorrect methods, but rather methods that are more or less appropriate to the objectives pursued (IV.1.3). And exactly the existence of several methods confirms that a certain discipline constitutes a science,[6] while its reduction to a method entails its downgrading to a 'mere technicality' or 'legal engineering'[7]: to a 'mechanical process by which we juxtapose different cultural objects'.[8] Worse, the reduction of a science to a method implies a certain methodological poverty, precluding the possibility of comparisons that are 'structurally more complex than those of the man in the street'.[9]

Having said this, one cannot overlook the academic consequences of considering comparative law as a science, after years in which its scholars were kept at the margins of university teaching[10]: a fate that has not yet been fully overcome, as well as the reasons for it.[11] Indeed, the elevation of comparative law to a science implies its place on an equal footing to any other legal subject, which is as such entrusted to a cadre of professors specifically called upon to teach it. These then form a scientific community, identified through the sharing of

5 T. Ascarelli, *Studi di diritto comparato e in tema di interpretazione*, Milano, 1952, pp. 12 and 41 f.

6 G. Samuel, *An Introduction to Comparative Law Theory and Method*, Oxford and Portland OR, 2014, p. 13 f.

7 G. Frankenberg, *Comparative Law as Critique* (2016), Cheltenham e Northampton MA, 2019, p. 40.

8 F. Bertoni, *La letteratura comparata*, in G. Resta, A. Somma and V. Zeno-Zencovich (Eds.), *Comparare. Una riflessione tra le discipline*, Sesto San Giovanni, 2020, p. 105.

9 A. Marradi, *Concetti e metodo per la ricerca sociale*, Firenze, 1987, p. 115.

10 R. Sacco, *Introduzione al diritto comparato. Sommario delle lezioni di diritto privato comparato tenute nell'Università di Torino nell'anno accademico 1979–1980*, Torino, 1980, p. 8.

11 G. Resta, *L'albero e l'onda. Il discorso della comparazione al crocevia delle discipline*, in Id., A. Somma and V. Zeno-Zencovich (Eds.), *Comparare*, cit., p. 37.

epistemological paradigms, i.e. of 'a set of recurrent and quasi-standard illustrations of various theories in their conceptual, observational, and instrumental applications'.[12] All this leads to the development of power relations within the community of comparative law scholars conditioning the selection of those who gets admitted to it and are able to control the paradigms around which it develops its activity.

These power dynamics are common to all disciplines and always have an impact on their academic recognition. Only the intention to subject them to the logic of the market can lead us to consider these dynamics as abnormal: scientific communities do debate and give rise to disputes, even heated ones, but they are cooperative contexts incompatible with competitive mechanisms and individualistic approaches. There is no point in hiding this reality under the smokescreen of discourses centred on merit and excellence, or on other empty buzzwords and formulae, no matter how impactful they may be in the public discourse.[13]

But let us return to comparison as a method. We shall see that such a framing occurs widely in the social sciences other than law, where comparison is considered a substitute for experiment. However, this does not imply that comparison identifies a method and not an autonomous field of knowledge. That is to say, it does not reveal an intention to support a technocratic viewpoint, nor does it disavow methodological pluralism (IV.1.4). If, on the one hand, comparative law is spoken of as a method, on the other hand, several ways of interpreting the data acquired through recourse to that method are used, which is tantamount to recognising the existence of several methods of comparison.

We will then look at the methodological reflections of positive law scholars and see that their reflections are linked to a view of the purposes of comparison that differs considerably from those of comparative lawyers. In fact, this reflection does not consider the mere cognitive purposes claimed by the comparative law scholars (II.1.1): it focuses on the specific purposes to which comparisons are directed, in the light of which one has to consider methodological approaches of their authors. We shall see that this discourse tends to reduce comparative law to a method, but also that this method is combined with several ways of interpreting the data obtained through it. We thus reach the same conclusion as that just formulated for the social sciences other than law: we are faced with more than one method of comparison, so that comparative law can be considered as a science.

Be that as it may, the framework of analyses in the literature on the nature of comparative law appears to be rather fragmented and based on a notion of method that is not shared by all and in many respects not well thought out. In order to navigate the field, it is essential to identify cross-disciplinary points of reference between the various disciplines. To that aim, we will begin by examining the logical framework of comparison, i.e. its being a comparison between objects around the state of a given property, in order to highlight its main goal: to identify either the similarities or the differences between those objects. This approach will guide our analysis of comparative legal methods, introducing a discourse on the methodological pluralism that characterises the field, followed by an account of the methods most favoured by its scholars.

2 A SUBSTITUTE FOR THE EXPERIMENT: COMPARISON IN THE SOCIAL SCIENCES

According to a prevailing view in the social sciences other than law, comparison is just a method. We mentioned that this view does not imply a technocratic approach to comparison.

12 T.S. Kuhn, *The Structure of Scientific Revolutions* (1962), Chicago IL, 2012, p. 43.
13 In particular, F. Bertoni, *Universitaly. La cultura in scatola*, Roma and Bari, 2016, especially p. 55 ff.

We can now be more precise: scholars of social sciences other than law who claim that comparison is a method do not mean to assert that there is only one way to compare. Their statements must therefore be viewed in context.

But let us proceed in an orderly fashion. In social sciences there is a widespread belief that comparison, without being elevated to the level of a science, 'does not occupy the same place as other methods'; rather, it is a 'research strategy', which poses the same methodological problems that social research does in general. Therefore, no clear indications are possible as to how this should be carried out and how its results should be understood. Indeed, to compare means to adopt a point of view that imposes an extension of the space-time dimension, thus bringing to light a multiplicity of issues that are otherwise hardly visible because they are concealed by the parochial dimension of research.[14] It follows that comparison does not simplify research, rather it highlights its problematic nature and prevents an artificial reduction of complexity.

The fact that comparison is merely a method in the social sciences is based on a trivial observation: that in social sciences it is not possible to carry out experiments as it is possible in hard sciences. From the latter it is therefore possible to draw conclusions that are considered universally valid: one can record the behaviour of a body subject to the law of gravity in a given space-time context and conclude that the same behaviour will occur in different space-time contexts. In social sciences something like this is inconceivable: one cannot test the functioning of a rule in a given community of people and draw directly valid conclusions about how the same rule will function in other communities.

To overcome such shortcomings, methods are developed to 'establish general empirical relationships between two or more variables'.[15] Some use the statistical method, which 'relies on a large number of empirical cases to establish significant correlations between variables'.[16] Most turn instead to comparison as an expedient that 'reproduces the phenomenology to be studied'. As Pirni states:

> The comparative method . . . systematically explains – according to the canons of scientific observation, measurement and inference – the variants of social phenomena found in clearly different social units. The comparative method of analysis assumes the existence of different variants for some phenomena, tries to formulate concepts and schemes to understand and describe these phenomena, tries to isolate and control possible explanatory variables in order to determine the precise causal relevance of each one.[17]

In the past, such an understanding of comparison was widespread among legal scholars. We found it at the beginning of the 20th century, at the time when national legislators analysed foreign law in order to obtain a guide as to the concrete functioning of the reforms they wished to introduce (II.1.3). And also in more recent years we can find scholars who believe that 'comparative law offers, to some extent, a substitute for experiments in a laboratory'.[18]

In the social sciences other than law, this idea goes back even further and is still present in the reflections of their scholars. An example of this is the approach of comparative linguistics, which emerged in the 19th century to compare Indo-European languages, highlighting not only lexical but also grammatical and morphological connections. In this way, researchers

14 C. Vigour, *La comparaison dans les sciences sociales*, Paris, 2005, p. 16 ff.

15 G. Delli Zotti, *Il metodo comparato in sociologia*, in A. Gasparini and R. Strassoldo (Eds.), *Tipi ideali e società*, Milano, 1996, p. 153.

16 A. Martinelli, *La comparazione in scienza politica e sociologia*, in G. Resta, A. Somma and V. Zeno-Zencovich (Eds.), *Comparare*, cit., p. 144.

17 A. Pirni, *Sociologia e comparazione: alla ricerca dello spazio istituzionalizzato*, in G. Resta, A. Somma and V. Zeno-Zencovich (Eds.), *Comparare*, cit., p. 160.

18 R.B. Schlesinger et al., *Comparative Law*, cit., p. 48.

began to reconstruct the protolanguage of the Indo-European languages, a prehistoric language that had disappeared without leaving any trace.[19]

When comparison is a mere substitute for experiment, as in the cases just reported, it may well be degraded to a method. This, however, implies a scientistic approach to the discipline, which has characterised the social sciences in the past, but which is no longer tenable. Neither is the evolutionist assumption on which comparative linguistics is based. The latter allows the use of comparison as a substitute for experiment, but requires that the comparative method be distinguished from the interpretation of the results obtained through it. It also specifies that interpretation must rectify the errors produced by the distorted view of linguistic mutation that the comparative method provides.[20] This is tantamount to admitting that this method must be combined with other approaches, thus generating a plurality of methods, all derived from the practice of comparison, but carried out according to schemes that cannot be reduced to unity.

A similar conclusion is made explicit in other social sciences that use comparison. Political science, for example, speaks of the comparative method as a tool for 'identifying cause-effect mechanisms' and then 'explaining observed phenomena in terms of the factors that influence them with a certain regularity'.[21] The comparative method is nonetheless extensively employed in combination with other methods, resulting in a kind of catalogue of comparative methods linked to the different approaches to the subject.[22]

Similarly, comparative economics regards comparison as a method that must be applied to the various 'criteria for evaluating economies'.[23] Those criteria concern the study of specific aspects, such as macroeconomic stability, the degree of economic freedom or the human development index (II.1.4). As one might expect, these are aspects that can be studied through a variety of lenses, which in turn means that there is a wide range of methodological options. This is, moreover, what we found in the analysis of models of capitalism, which were identified as the result of comparisons carried out within a clear ideological framework (II.2.9).

In any case, disciplines do not always consider comparison as a method only for them to downplay it. This is true at least, where the discipline is constitutively linked to a comparative approach. An example is sociology,[24] where the belief is widespread that 'comparison is the tacit foundation of contemporary social sciences', so much so that it is 'almost impossible to carry out any cognitive activity without making comparisons'.[25]

Similar assertions can be found among anthropologists, who see comparison not as 'one method among many that can be used' in anthropology, but rather as 'an epistemic attitude that grounds its very possibility of existence'. Certainly, it is described as the method without which 'a specific cultural trait' cannot emerge, but this does not imply a kind of methodological monism: 'the history of anthropological studies could be read in the form of a history of comparative methods'.[26]

Then, there is comparative literature, whose scholars, on the one hand, liken comparison to a method and, on the other hand, point out that it is rather 'an approach, a point of view,

19 Among others, J. Clackson, *Indo-European linguistics: An Introduction*, Cambridge, 2007, p. 1ff.
20 A. Fox, *Linguistic Reconstruction. An Introduction to Theory and Method*, Oxford, 1995, p. 137 ff.
21 S. Vassallo, *Politica comparata*, in Id. (Ed.), *Sistemi politici comparati*, 2nd ed., Bologna, 2016, p. 23.
22 For instance, D.-L. Seiler, *La méthode comparative en science politique*, Paris, 2004, p. 45 ff.
23 J.B. Rosser jr. and M.V. Rosser, *Comparative Economics in a Transforming World Economy*, 3rd ed., Cambridge MA, 2018, p. 17 ff.
24 Among others, F. De Nardis, *Sociologia comparata. Appunti sulle strutture logiche della ricerca sociopolitica*, Milano, 2011, p. 13 ff.
25 A. Pirni, *Sociologia e comparazione: alla ricerca dello spazio istituzionalizzato*, cit., p. 155.
26 F. Dei, *La comparazione in antropologia*, in G. Resta, A. Somma and V. Zeno-Zencovich (Eds.), *Comparare*, cit., p. 69.

a heuristic and cognitive attitude that offers us a different way of looking at the phenomena we study'. They then conclude that 'the methods and instruments of comparison are numerous and subject to constant evolutionary pressure throughout history'.[27] In other words, we are faced with the same recurring paradigm among anthropological scholars, namely, the implicit recognition that we are in the presence of a science to be considered as such insofar as it can be practised on the base of a methodological pluralism (IV.1.5).

This last conclusion sums up a widespread sentiment in the social sciences. We can conclude our survey by quoting the words of historians who are committed to recalling that comparison should be seen as 'a form of consciousness of the researcher, which guides him in the choice of objects of research, in the elaboration of the questions to be asked of the past, in the definition of the criteria of relevance'.[28] In short, comparison constitutes a connecting factor between the scholar or legal professional and the part of reality he dedicates his attention to[29]; it is therefore inevitably linked to the most diverse purposes and can only be practised by resorting to a plurality of methods.[30]

3 COMPARISON AND POSITIVE LAW: PRIVATE LAW SUBJECTS

We have already considered the opinion of those who consider comparative law as a method linked either to legal history or legal sociology. This framework has characterised the thinking of positive law scholars, and in particular civil and commercial lawyers, who have used comparative law as a means by which to undermine positivism and its corollaries, and above all the idea that law coincides with legislation (I.1.1).

This general aim, as well as those concerning the will to counter 'our very clear tendency to consider our legal categories as universal',[31] ultimately relate to the acquisition of knowledge as the purpose of comparative law. We know that, according to most comparative law scholars, this should be the only purpose invoked to justify the recognition of the discipline as an autonomous science. We also know that, nevertheless, some of them devote a great deal of attention to identifying the specific aims of comparative law, fearing that its absence would call its legitimacy into question (I.1.1).

Among positive lawyers, this approach is widespread, consistent with the assertion that the 'normative' function prevails over the 'documentary' function,[32] and with the understanding of comparative law as a method. However, as in the social sciences other than law (IV.1.2), this does not imply that there is only one way to compare, and methodological pluralism is not denied. What is lacking, however, is an in-depth analysis of the different ways of making comparisons, as well as of the background taxonomic categories: micro-comparison has become widespread, but not macro-comparison (II.2.2), which is the only area in which comparative law scholars can claim a kind of exclusivity.

But let us return to the specific aims pursued by positive law scholars who make comparisons, and the consequences of regarding comparative law as a method. An overview of the main subjects they occupy themselves with will provide evidence of what we have just stated.

27 F. Bertoni, *La letteratura comparata*, cit., pp. 100 and 105.

28 L. Baldissara, *Della comparazione in storia. Prospettive della storia comparata sull'epoca contemporanea*, in G. Resta, A. Somma and V. Zeno-Zencovich (Eds.), *Comparare*, cit., p. 115.

29 J. Basedow, *Comparative Law and Its Clients*, in *American Journal of Comparative Law*, 62, 2014, p. 856.

30 P. Rossi, *Introduzione*, in Id. (Ed.), *La storia comparata. Approcci e prospettive*, Milano, 1998, p. xvi.

31 M. Fabre-Magnan, *Droits des obligations (Contrat et engagement unilatéral)*, vol. 1, Paris, 2008, p. 72.

32 F. Terré, *Introduction générale au droit*, 4th ed., Paris, 1998, p. 400.

Let us start with commercial law, the discipline in which comparative law is considered as a variant of the method used by sociologists of law. The same author who expressed this view entrusts comparative law with the task of contributing to the interpretation of law by reference to the canons typical of the hermeneutic approach. More precisely, Ascarelli emphasises that the contribution of the interpreter is a creative one since he is called upon to 'grasp a scope' of the text that was 'unforeseeable at the moment of its historical positing', and that comparison contributes to achieve a similar result. However, this does not give rise to a critical hermeneutics or a reflection on the hermeneutic approach (I.1.4): the interpreter is committed to the 'strict observance of that continuity and legality which are the basis of legal certainty and the guarantee of individual freedom'.[33]

On closer examination, this approach is to a large extent influenced by the post-war intellectual climate in which it matured. At that point, comparative law was entrusted with the task of contributing to peace and understanding between peoples (II.1.1). This does not detract from the fact that it was precisely comparative law that was considered to be the instrument by which the interpreter would critically examine the premises 'taken for granted' by the scholar of national law, thus contributing to a reinterpretation of the legal system in the spirit of 'a democratic legal consciousness outside of which any constitution falls into a vacuum'.[34]

This interpretation of the role of comparative law has a long tradition. Already at the beginning of the 20th century its use was proposed as an instrument for the development of national law, or more precisely for its 'enrichment . . . outside the legislative route': an operation that would not be feasible by recourse to traditional canons, given the 'impotence of the rigidly logical system to solve problems'.[35] Yet the same approach continues to characterise the thinking of commercial law scholars, who are still committed to illustrating the potential of comparative law as an interpretative method[36] and of private law scholars in general. In the latter case, however, legal comparison is no longer linked to social prophylactic objectives but instead contributes to the promotion of neoliberalism.[37]

Remaining in the private law sphere, we can examine the relationship between comparative law and labour law. This discipline emerged between the 19th and 20th centuries distinguishing itself from civil law and had the particular aim of preventing the principles applicable to general market relationship from being applied to the labour relationship.[38] And comparative law could contribute to that aim since it helped to 'interpret civil law with a certain social imprint': in particular, to develop protection against accidents at work or to define a regulation of the labour contract that strengthened its collective dimension.[39]

Over the years, labour law has not ceased to attribute the mentioned purpose to comparative law, but it has at least become aware of its limits, or at least of the need to use comparison wisely. This turning point marked the same years in which the theory of legal transplants was formulated (III.1.3), distinguishing between the correct use of the 'comparative method in lawmaking' and its 'abuse'. The point of reference was the assertion, attributed

33 T. Ascarelli, *Studi di diritto comparato e in tema di interpretazione*, cit., p. xxxii.

34 *Ivi*, p. lii.

35 F. Gény, *Méthode et sources en droit privé positif. Essai critique* (1919), 2nd ed., vol. 2, Paris, 1954, p. 269.

36 In particular V. Cariello, *Comparazioni e interpretazioni*, Torino, 2020.

37 Among others, M. Grondona, *La giurisprudenza quale strumento di trasformazione ordinamentale: tra l'ermeneutica e la comparazione*, in M. Graziadei and A. Somma (Eds.), *Esperienze giuridiche in dialogo. Il ruolo della comparazione*, Roma, 2024, p. 29 ff.

38 Among others, G. Cazzetta, *Scienza giuridica e trasformazioni sociali. Diritto del lavoro in Italia tra Otto e Novecento*, Milano, 2007, especially p. 69 ff.

39 L. Gaeta, *La comparazione nel diritto del lavoro italiano*, in A. Somma and V. Zeno-Zencovich (Eds.), *Comparazione e diritto positivo. Un dialogo tra saperi giuridici*, Roma, 2020, p. 184 ff.

to Montesquieu (II.1.2), that the rules and institutions of one country can be profitably used in another only if there are converging environmental factors, but coupled with the observation that the political factor is central among them. Per Kahn-Freund:

> The process of economic, social, cultural assimilation or integration among the developed countries (and also the dominant classes of the developing countries) has been accompanied by a process of political differentiation. It is this dual development of cultural and social assimilation and political differentiation which compels us to shift the emphasis of Montesquieu's test in order to find some workable criterion that can be used to determine how far a legal institution is transplantable.[40]

It is telling that the use of comparative law by labour lawyers is ultimately seen as merely aimed at illustrating the state of the art of foreign law and, from this narrow point of view, 'not very academically rewarding'.[41] However, the recent uses of comparative law as a method to promote the development of labour law are certainly no more satisfactory than those of mere speculative nature. In fact, they are functional to supporting the processes of globalisation and thus undermining state control over labour relations and the system of industrial relations[42]; that is, they are aimed at promoting the adoption of common law solutions,[43] and in this perspective at contributing to the spread of neo-American capitalism or at any rate to the overcoming of the Rhine model.

A similar trend characterises agricultural law. Like labour law, it emerged as a remedy to civil law's unsuitability to regulating market relations characterised by differences in power, with legal comparison playing a central role in this regard. And like labour law, recent uses of comparative law have overshadowed the original function of the discipline. Agricultural law no longer serves agricultural producers and the rural territory: it supports the needs of the food industry.[44]

However, in labour and agricultural law, as in commercial law, this is not, at least for our purposes, the aspect to which the attention needs to be drawn. It is more useful to point out that the reference to legal comparison as a method does not mean that it cannot be recognised as an autonomous science. It is clear, in other words, that it can also be practised with different methods.

More precisely, in labour law as in agricultural law, what is presented as a method concerns the purpose typically privileged in both areas. That is to say, it concerns the way of understanding the relationship between the political order and the economic order, an aspect that can be explored from radically different perspective.[45] This leads to the same conclusions as for the use of the comparative method in social sciences other than law: it shows that the method, combined with different interpretative approaches for the data collected, ultimately highlights how these sciences can be practised by resorting to a plurality of methods.

4 NEXT: PUBLIC LAW SUBJECTS

So far, we have considered the use of comparisons by positive law scholars in private law. We will now look at how it is used in public law, where a more cautious use of comparisons is to be expected. Indeed, private law regulates the market and is therefore more prone to

40 O. Kahn-Freund, *On Uses and Misuses of Comparative Law*, in *Modern Law Review*, 37, 1974, p. 8.
41 L. Gaeta, *La comparazione nel diritto del lavoro italiano*, cit., p. 203.
42 M.W. Finkin, *Comparative Labour Law*, in M. Reimann and R. Zimmermann (Eds.), *The Oxford Handbook of Comparative Law*, 2nd ed., Oxford and New York NY, 2019, p. 1130 ff.
43 Following P. Ichino, *Il diritto del lavoro e i modelli economici*, in *Lavoro e diritto*, 1998, p. 309 ff.
44 A. Iannarelli, *Comparazione e diritto agrario*, in A. Somma and V. Zeno-Zencovich (Eds.), *Comparazione e diritto positivo*, cit., p. 7 ff.
45 U. Kischel, *Rechtsvergleichung*, München, 2015, p. 38.

trespassing borders, while public law traditionally deals with identity traits that are unknown to the economic.

We shall see, however, that legal comparison does not occupy a marginal position, at the very least because of the transformations that globalisation has brought about in public law (II.1.9). These transformations have in fact fuelled a movement towards the progressive elimination of national identities incompatible with the spread of neo-American capitalism (II.2.9). And this movement has survived the recent crises, which have nonetheless led, if not to deglobalisation tendencies, at least to a reconstitution of the relationship between law and space. This proves that the idea that took root at the end of the last millennium, according to which 'law is destined to become increasingly detached from territory', certainly 'partially captured a real process, but also had an ideological core'.[46]

Obviously, we will not be dealing here with comparative public law, which, like comparative private law, is a science whose boundaries have now been defined, and which has developed a sophisticated methodology. We will, instead, examine administrative law and criminal law, as well as civil procedural law and criminal procedural law. In these disciplines, as in private law, comparative law is largely regarded as a method. But here too, this does not imply a rejection of methodological pluralism (IV.1.5).

Let us begin with comparative administrative law, which has a certain tradition of comparative studies (II.3.4), even if it is mainly carried on by public law and administrative law scholars. Comparative public law scholars do not call into question the qualification of comparative administrative law as a science, therefore practicable by resorting to several methods, assessed only from the point of view of their suitability to the objectives pursued by the author of the comparison.[47] On the contrary, administrative lawyers regard comparison largely as a method. For some, it coincides with functional analysis (IV.2.2),[48] while others offer less narrow views: they do speak of a 'comparative method' but conceive of it 'in combination with different methods and approaches'. In doing this, they recall the limits of the traditional taxonomies, namely, the distinction by families of systems (II.2.1), as well as the most accredited methods of analysing legal change, and in particular the theory of legal transplants (III.1.3). As Napolitano states:

> While the theory of legal families has the historical merit of being the first attempt to move away from legal nationalism, its artificiality and almost exclusively Western perspective severely undermine its credibility and reliability. . . . The idea of transplants is often misleading because it is based on two implicit assumptions, both of which are false. The first is that there is a lead country that can influence the institutional legal choices of other countries. . . . The second is that legal systems are compact and coherent entities and that scientific knowledge about them is based on the logic of non-contradiction.[49]

Furthermore, administrative law scholars, while they search for 'a common understanding of increasingly similar legal institutions', also conceive administrative comparative law as an alternative to European or global administrative law. The latter indeed leads to comparative administrative law being regarded as 'a merely temporary if not a belated guest destined to be overtaken by supranational legal harmonisation'. Comparison is, in short, the tool to understand that 'even the most intense degree of legal harmonisation . . . may favour convergence and increase similarities, but is not capable of generating homogeneity'.[50] In other

46 G. Preterossi, *L'Odissea dello spazio*, in *Rivista di filosofia del diritto*, 2019, p. 327.
47 R. Scarciglia, *Diritto amministrativo comparato*, Torino, 2020, p. 24.
48 H.P. Nehl, *Administrative Law*, in J.M. Smits (Ed.), *Elgar Encyclopedia of Comparative Law*, 2nd ed., Cheltenham and Northampton MA, 2012, p. 23.
49 G. Napolitano, *Introduzione al diritto amministrativo comparato*, Bologna, 2020, pp. 21 and 28.
50 *Ivi*, pp. 22 ff.

words, comparison of national administrative laws only makes sense if they share underlying values, such as the rule of law and the protection of fundamental rights.[51]

If, in administrative law, comparison as a method is intended to promote the convergence of national systems, or possibly to define the limits of such a project without calling it into question, in criminal law the same method is conceived with reference to more heterogeneous aims. The convergence of national legal systems is not neglected, but it is not the primary concern of criminal lawyers, whose discipline is traditionally, and to a certain degree inevitably, characterised by a considerable dose of 'parochialism' that in some respects is unavoidable.[52] Indeed, criminal law concerns the deprivation of freedom for persons deemed to be a danger to society, which implies the harmony between the discipline and the values with which society identifies. All this eventually concealed by recourse to the 'dogmatic exegetical' method, which is good to promote or rather simulate the autonomy of the discipline from the political power.[53]

To be more precise, criminal law scholars speak of a 'descriptive-recognitive' comparison, although they are aware of the impossibility of a 'descriptive and apolitical knowledge', but they favour a comparison with 'a theoretical-practical or dogmatic or reform function'.[54] They also add that the latter function is the main motive for comparing national laws, although perhaps only to rhetorically reinforce a choice made independently of that comparison.[55]

In criminal law the reference to the national dimension, or rather the link with the values with which society identifies, makes it difficult the use of comparison to promote the convergence of systems. Indeed, its scholars make a distinction between comparison and harmonisation of law in the European context, which is also emerging as an autonomous discipline,[56] with greater clarity than that in administrative law. As Donini states:

> It is in fact doubtful . . . that criminal lawyers specialised in European law, and in any case researchers who can no longer separate national law from EU law in so many areas now crossed by supranational sources in a continuous stream, are comparative lawyers only because of this European dimension of the sources: the national expansion of EU law does not at all imply that comparative law is really cultivated, since EU sources can be considered as quasi-internal positive law, alongside the national one, according to the schemes of a single multilevel system. Here lies the suspicion or possibility that various Europeanist scholars are not comparative lawyer: neither in a descriptive sense, nor in an evaluative sense.[57]

Nevertheless, it cannot be denied that the use of comparison to promote reform is unlikely to lead to an exaggeration of the differences between the systems being compared or, in any case, to the promotion of the reasons for their uniqueness (II.1.8): taking a foreign solution as a point of reference for legislative reform, obviously presupposes the belief that convergence between systems is possible. Nor can it be denied that this use of comparison requires an appreciation of the context of the rule whose adoption is proposed. In other words, if

51 J.S. Bell, *Comparative Administrative Law*, in M. Reimann and R. Zimmermann (Eds.), *The Oxford Handbook of Comparative Law*, cit., p. 1262 f.

52 M.D. Dubber, *Comparative Criminal Law*, in M. Reimann and R. Zimmermann (Eds.), *The Oxford Handbook of Comparative Law*, cit., p. 1277.

53 G. Fornasari, *L'evoluzione della comparazione giuridica in ambito penalistico*, in A. Somma and V. Zeno-Zencovich (Eds.), *Comparazione e diritto positivo*, cit., p. 319 ff.

54 M. Donini, *I due paradigmi fondamentali della comparazione penalistica*, in A. Somma and V. Zeno-Zencovich (Eds.), *Comparazione e diritto positivo*, cit., p. 284 f.

55 T. Weigend, *Criminal Law and Criminal Procedure*, in J.M. Smits (Ed.), *Elgar Encyclopedia of Comparative Law*, cit., p. 262.

56 For instance, K. Ambos and P. Rackow (Eds.), *The Cambridge Companion to European Criminal Law*, Cambridge and New York NY, 2023.

57 M. Donini, *I due paradigmi fondamentali della comparazione penalistica*, cit., p. 285.

convergence is practicable, it is because there is a certain proximity between the system from which the rule is taken as a model and that which is the candidate for its importation, not so much and not only from a technical legal point of view, but above all from that of the innumerable extra-legal factors usually considered by the legislator.

All this was highlighted in a long-standing dispute about the purposes of comparative law between a father of the discipline and a well-known scholar of civil procedure. The former, Sacco, was prepared to accept only that comparative law had a cognitive purpose, believing that the desire to identify specific objectives was proof of the weakness of a science in search of legitimacy (II.1.1).[58] The latter, Denti, by contrast, presented the reform perspective as central; i.e. he emphasised 'the legal-political aspect of comparative research'. More precisely, he argued, on the one hand, that a 'politically neutral' comparison – as claimed by the advocates of the structural method (IV.2.1) – was impossible, and, on the other hand, that it was necessary to operate 'within the framework of homogeneous political systems'.[59]

The same perspective is still a point of reference for scholars of civil procedure, who continue to consider legal comparison as 'more than a field of law . . . a powerful research methodology'.[60] This, however, must be combined with the various methods of interpreting data obtained through comparisons and with the choice of the objects of comparison. Thus, from this point of view, it can be considered a science. Here too, as in administrative law and criminal law, this science is called upon to deal with the search for a European or international law. However, such law is not stigmatised as an alternative to comparative law: European civil procedural law and comparative civil procedural law are considered to be related disciplines.[61]

The usefulness of comparison as a method for guiding the work of the legislature was demonstrated in the case of the reform of the Italian Code of Criminal Procedure. Its reform was also a good opportunity to see how references to a foreign model can inspire appealing rhetoric, even in the absence of an effective circulation of models (II.1.4). Among scholars of criminal procedural law, however, more than in other disciplines, there is a recurrent emphasis on the national dimension of the discipline. Hence, the call to avoid a 'broad comparison' and therefore to 'consciously choose the system or systems to which one refers for a fruitful comparison'.[62] This is understandable because of the centrality of criminal procedure to personal freedom, which is undoubtedly put at risk by substantive law, but also threatened by the mechanisms chosen to ascertain its violation.

In any case, criminal procedure scholars point out that the focus on the reform perspective is complemented by objectives that are more familiar to comparative lawyers. Indeed, they express a desire to analyse the context in which different criminal procedural laws have evolved and operate,[63] which is consistent with cognitive concerns, albeit linked to practical aims. If this is the case, references to comparison as a method are quite misleading: the analysis of the context can be carried out by resorting to a variety of methods. In short, we

58 R. Sacco, *Comparazione giuridica e metodo casistico*, in Id. (Ed.), *L'apporto della comparazione alla scienza giuridica*, Milano, 1980, p. 243 ff.

59 V. Denti, *Diritto comparato e scienza del processo*, in R. Sacco (Ed.), *L'apporto della comparazione alla scienza giuridica*, cit., p. 204 ff.

60 A. Dondi, *Comparazione oggi. Brevi (e molto limitate) impressioni dal côté processuale*, in A. Somma and V. Zeno-Zencovich (Eds.), *Comparazione e diritto positivo*, cit., p. 333.

61 J. Zekoll, *Comparative Civil Procedure*, in M. Reimann and R. Zimmermann (Eds.), *The Oxford Handbook of Comparative Law*, cit., p. 1313 ff.

62 R. Orlandi, *L'approccio comparatistico nelle dottrine processualpenalistiche. Spunti di riflessione in ordine al contesto italiano*, in A. Somma and V. Zeno-Zencovich (Eds.), *Comparazione e diritto positivo*, cit., p. 361.

63 E. Grande, *Comparative Criminal Justice*, in M. Bussani and U. Mattei (Eds.), *Cambridge Companion to Comparative Law*, Cambridge and New York NY, 2012, p. 202.

are faced with the confirmation that the combination of criminal procedure and comparison produces a science.

5 FROM THE LOGICAL STRUCTURE OF COMPARISON TO METHODOLOGICAL PLURALISM

The previous overview has provided much evidence that the encounter between positive law and comparative law produces a plurality of methods and for this reason it can be accurately described as a science. However, such a conclusion is not accompanied by a precise identification of those methods, even if some clues can be deduced from the purposes assigned to the comparison. Since these clues remain in the background and in any case are not the subject of an in-depth examination, we find ourselves in an area that is almost exclusively the domain of comparative law scholars: positive law scholars practise comparative law but avoid delving into the theoretical aspects of how to do so.[64]

In order to deal with this aspect, we must resort to categories which are suitable to the peculiarities of the disciplines considered earlier. However, when doing so, we should be mindful not to disregard that the methods of comparison cannot be judged as more or less suitable in absolute terms. If an assessment can be made, it must be based on the strategies pursued by the author of the comparison,[65] which must be taken into account on the basis of a fundamental dichotomy: the author's interest in highlighting the differences or, on the contrary, in emphasising the similarities of the objects compared. In fact, there are methods suitable for a comparison that emphasises the individuality of the laws being compared and thus divides them, and methods more suitable for a comparison that emphasises convergence and thus unites them. This is why the comparative legal scholar must adopt the standpoint of methodological pluralism, that is, 'tolerance of a variety of research methods, each of which must be considered as part of the research as a whole'.[66]

Such a conclusion confirms the 'in principle contextualised character of all research and scientific knowledge'.[67] It is foundational in comparative history, whose scholars assume that research can be conducted by resorting to several modalities, all of which can be traced back to the aim of obtaining 'generalising', or alternatively 'individualising' reconstructions.[68] The same is not explicit in comparative law, at least not beyond the circle of scholars who emphasise that the discipline inevitably expresses the cultural orientation of those who practice it: 'even if the task of the comparative lawyer is not to judge, to compare is always to judge'.[69]

In order to document the usefulness of discussing the methods of comparison in relation to its aims, and in particular the aim of promoting the assimilation or differentiation of the compared objects, we can start from the literature that has examined these aspects in general terms, i.e. with reference to comparison as such. That is to say, we can look to authors who

64 A. Somma, *Per un dialogo tra comparazione e diritto positivo*, in Id. and V. Zeno-Zencovich (Eds.), *Comparazione e diritto positivo*, cit., p. 377 ff.
65 See T. Amico di Meane, *Metodologia e diritto comparato alla ricerca della creatività. Verso un approccio flessibile*, in *Annuario di diritto comparato e di studi legislativi*, 2019, pp. 191 and 193.
66 R. Scarciglia, *Metodi e comparazione giuridica*, 3rd ed., Milano, 2021, pp. 177 and 179.
67 E. Mostacci, *Schemi di classificazione e comparazione giuridica: un regno immenso e anonimo*, in *Diritto pubblico comparato ed europeo*, 2017, p. 1176.
68 For instance, H. Kaelble, *Der historische Vergleich. Eine Einführung zum 19. und 20. Jahrhundert*, Frankfurt M. and New York NY, 1999, p. 25 ff.
69 P. Legrand, *Le droit comparé*, Paris, 1999, p. 56 f.

analyse the logical structure of comparison, understood as 'the comparison of the states of two objects in relation to a property'. Marradi points in this direction when he states:

> In the sentence 'Mario is taller than Lucia', Mario and Lucia are the objects; the specific heights of Mario and Lucia are their states in relation to the property 'height'. The result of the comparison in this case was a judgement of greater-lesser. In other cases – if the property has unordered categories – it may be a judgement of equal-different ('Luigi is a surveyor, Giulia is a lawyer') or a judgement of the presence-absence of the property ('Antonio is a union member, Teresa is not'). Objects are never compared directly and globally, but always on their states (in relation to one or more properties). The judgement 'Mario is different from Lucia' is either tautological (because each object is, by definition, different from any other) or elliptical (because it implies 'in character' or 'in behaviour', i.e. a property whose states are being compared).[70]

Enhancing the profile of properties will easily produce a comparison that unites: one may say, for example, that Mario and Lucia are similar in that their height differs by a few inches. If, on the other hand, one focuses attention on the profile of the objects, one is more likely to produce a comparison that divides: one may add that while Mario and Lucia are similar in height, they are different nonetheless because the former is a clergyman, while the latter is an unruly rock musician.

Among the methods that lead to a unifying comparison, following the main strands of comparative law (II.1.1), we will look first at structuralism and functional analysis. Both have been perfected with objectives that can ultimately be traced back to what we have called the subversive function of comparative law: its mission to challenge legal positivism (I.1.2). Structuralism emerged mainly in Italy to counter the reduction of law to legislation and, more generally, to place the substantive sources of law at the centre of comparative research. German comparative lawyers, by contrast, were particularly devoted to functional analysis, which, for the same purposes, focused more on 'what the law is for' than on 'how the law is made'.[71] We shall see, however, that structuralism and functional analysis are not as clearly distinguishable as they might at first glance appear and, above all, they both conceal the context in which the law develops. In this sense, they both produce comparisons aimed, above all, at highlighting convergence.

The examination of the methods of comparative law will then focus on the intertwining of comparative law and the economic analysis of law, before turning to the role of quantitative methodology when making comparisons.

We will conclude our review of the methods of comparative law by focusing on those used by comparative public law scholars. Although the in-depth study of methodology has traditionally been the prerogative of comparative lawyers with a private law background, this does not detract from the fact that comparative public lawyers have produced reflections of considerable interest.

We will conclude our reflections with a methodological proposal, which emphasises the dissociation between techniques and values. This will be the opportunity to return to a theme that has formed the background to this introduction to comparative law, and in particular to reflect once again on the relationship between law and society.

70 A. Marradi, *Introduzione all'edizione italiana*, in N.J. Smelser, *La comparazione nelle scienze sociali* (1976), Bologna, 1982, p. 13.
71 N. Bobbio, *Dalla struttura alla funzione. Nuovi studi di teoria del diritto* (1977), Roma and Bari, 2007, p. 48.

SUMMARY

1. It was customary for scholars of comparative law to regard it as a method, close to legal history or legal sociology. The latter are nonetheless considered sciences because they can be carried out using several methods, as is now recognised for comparative law itself. The different methods are to be assessed solely on the basis of their suitability for the objectives pursued by the author of the comparison.
2. In the social sciences other than law, causal relations cannot be established with the same tools as in the hard sciences, and in particular with experiments. General empirical relationships must be established between two or more variables, using statistics or comparison as a means of reproducing the phenomenon under examination. Comparison is seen as a method whose results must be interpreted on the basis of different techniques and approaches. This is tantamount to admitting that there are several methods of comparison and that it therefore constitutes a science, including in the field of law.
3. Positive law scholars consider legal comparison a method and use it for specific purposes. In commercial law, comparison is used to promote a reading of rules in the light of the canons of hermeneutics. In labour and agricultural law, comparison has served to emancipate the disciplines from the principles of civil law, thus allowing for the consideration of social issues. More recently, however, it has become a vehicle for neoliberal demands due to the ultra-national origin of the sources.
4. Comparison is seen as a method also in public law subjects, which are more inclined than private law subjects to consider national rootedness. On the other hand, public and private law subjects are equally interested in the specific purposes of comparison, which are mostly related to the promotion of reforms: in administrative law also to support the movement towards the harmonisation of national systems, which is more cautiously contemplated in criminal law and procedural law.
5. Comparative law, even in its combination with the various positive laws, is a science in the sense that it can be practised using various methods. These methods can only be evaluated in terms of their suitability to the underlying strategies of the author of the comparison, who may be interested in promoting convergence or conversely divergence of the objects of comparison. This is why methodological pluralism has to be the basis of comparative law.

CHAPTER 9

STRUCTURALISM AND FUNCTIONAL ANALYSIS

1 STRUCTURALISM AND THE THEORY OF FORMANTS

We have just recalled that comparative law asserts itself as a science critical of the dogmas promoted by legal positivism as the founding ideology of Western law. We also know that legal positivism has been subjected to revisionist accounts in order to dilute its original significance, and that, nevertheless, the legitimation strategies of the Western lawyer have not changed significantly (I.1.5). In Italy, the continued reverberations of legal positivism have been brought to light, to a large extent, by Rodolfo Sacco's theory of formants, based on concepts from the field of acoustics: the study of the physical consistency of vocal sounds and their diffusion through a medium such as air.

In acoustics, the formant indicates the resonance frequency of the sounds produced in the oral cavity, which characterises their timbre. This allows these sounds to be broken down and, above all, their different components to be highlighted and identified.[1] Similarly, among comparative lawyers, the formant identifies sets of rules that are 'kept separate in the discourse of the jurist': in particular, legislative, doctrinal, and judicial rules.[2] These sets are not disregarded by domestic law scholars but are analysed in accordance with the principle of the uniqueness of the rule, i.e. by preserving the internal coherence of the system and thus concealing the existence of antinomies and gaps (I.1.2).

By speaking of formants, comparative law scholars intend to emphasise their different approach to the analysis of sets of rules, in line with their desire to adopt an empirical approach[3]: to take an external point of view on the law. They will then note possible inconsistencies between formants, stressing the dissonance between the legislative formant, i.e. the set of rules produced by the legislator, the doctrinal formant, consisting of the precepts formulated by the scholars, and the judicial formant, coinciding with the law as declared by courts. In this sense, he will focus his attention on the 'dissociation of formants'. In Sacco's words:

> Comparison, therefore, offers us a vast terrain where, having decomposed each legal system and reduced it to a series of distinct formants, we can determine the degree of dissociation of the formants and, above all, the extent to which the formal sources of a country, the law applied there, and the lawyers' knowledge of their own system match. We have seen that the lawyer of a system explains these asymmetries as possible errors of the interpreter. But the opposition between right and wrong interpretation is a luxury the comparative lawyer cannot afford. The lawyer of a single system bridges the gap between the idea (the law, which entails a single exact interpretation) and the fact (the existence of numerous interpretations)

1 B. Malmberg, *La phonétique*, 19th ed., Paris, 2002, p. 12 f.
2 R. Sacco and P. Rossi, *Introduzione al diritto comparato*, in *Trattato di diritto comparato*, dir. R. Sacco, 7th ed., Torino, 2019, p. 57.
3 M. Graziadei, *Rodolfo Sacco's Theoretical Contribution to Comparative Law: A Personal Account*, in *International Journal for the Semiotics of Law*, 37, 2024, p. 1475.

DOI: 10.4324/9781032684499-13

> by choosing an interpretation which his personal preferences lead him to regard as exact. . . . Just as he has no preference for one system over another, neither does the comparative lawyer have a preference for this or that formant of a given system, nor for this or that element he finds within a given formant.[4]

The rupture caused by the theory of formants with regard to what constitutes the ideal foundation of legal positivism is thus evident. For this and many other reasons the theory has received deserved and ample recognition. Nevertheless, it cannot be exempt from criticism, since in many respects it cultivates a scientistic approach typical of the currents of thought it seeks to combat. Indeed, while the theory of formants is accompanied by the recognition of the importance of history for comparative law, and more precisely by the demanding affirmation that 'the comparative perspective is *par excellence* a historicist perspective',[5] it ultimately neglects it and thus devalues the context in which the objects of comparison are placed. It ends up being a unifying vehicle of comparison, or at least easily destined to produce such a result.

For a better understanding of this criticism, we need to reflect on the theoretical background of formant theory in linguistic structuralism. There, it undermined the empiricist orientation of those who regarded the individual as a *tabula rasa* and therefore believed that learning the mother tongue happened through simply listening to its speakers. Structuralists argued, instead, that learning occurs through the presence in the child of a pre-existing system capable of receiving and using the information provided by the senses: precisely, the structures. In short, the child is capable of organising empirical data since 'the mind already possesses the basic principles', i.e. an 'innate biological endowment' implanted by 'the original hand of nature'.[6]

Sacco himself established a connection between formant theory and structuralist linguistics.[7] He emphasised that 'visible language' adapts to 'latent linguistic patterns which are more permanent than the visible ones', and then went on to say that the same thing happens in law. Here, too, there are 'implicit rules of a system', called 'cryptotypes', which can be brought to light through comparison. When the dissociation between formants is revealed, this can in fact 'put us in direct contact with the effective data of a legal system, without the mediation of the traditional categories customary to the jurists of the system in question'.[8]

In other words, the theory of formants, with its strong structuralist inspiration, suggests that even legal orders are animated by structures which, if they cannot be said to be innate, at least appear identical to themselves despite the passage of time – which, in practice, is the same thing. In short, structures are such insofar as they pass unscathed through different historical contexts, which, as we have said, are in fact taken into account but only at the outset. This then means that 'if fundamental rules and principles and structures survived in very different, economic, social, and political conditions, they could hardly reflect in any adequate way the power or economic base'.[9]

These last words are taken from a work by Alan Watson, the legal transplant theorist (III.1.3), who emphasised the convergence of his approach with that of Sacco[10] and thus prompted discussion of 'transoceanic assonances'.[11] After all, both comparative lawyers of a

4 R. Sacco and P. Rossi, *Introduzione al diritto comparato*, cit., p. 61.
5 For instance, R. Scarciglia, *Introduzione al diritto pubblico comparato*, Bologna, 2006, p. 56 ff.
6 N. Chomsky, *New Horizons in the Study of Language and Mind*, Cambridge, 2000, pp. 2 and 4.
7 See S. Ferreri, *The Language Issue in Law. A Recollection of Rodolfo Sacco Contribution to Interpretation*, in *International Journal for the Semiotics of Law*, 37, 2024, p. 1521 ff.
8 R. Sacco, *Comparazione giuridica e conoscenza del dato giuridico*, in Id. (Ed.), *L'apporto della comparazione alla scienza giuridica*, Milano, 1980, p. 248 f.
9 A. Watson, *Legal Transplants*, 2nd ed., Athens GA, 1993, p. 107.
10 A. Watson, *From Legal Transplants to Legal Formants*, in *American Journal of Comparative Law*, 43, 1995, p. 469 ff.
11 S. Ferreri, *Assonanze transoceaniche: tendenze a confronto*, in *Quadrimestre*, 1993, p. 172 ff.

structuralist persuasion and theorists of legal transplants accept the idea of an apolitical law. This idea is acceptable only if it implies that there is no one-to-one correspondence between legal techniques and the values that techniques are supposed to convey (IV.3.1). However, it is not in this sense that the idea of an apolitical law is formulated, but rather in the sense that law constitutes an aspect effectively dissociated from the strategies of political power. And dissociable, moreover, from the strategies of the comparative law scholar, who would even be able to 'choose between science and politics', i.e. to distinguish between 'impartial comparison' and 'committed comparison'.[12]

It is not only the devaluation of context that makes the structuralist method problematic. It may also be criticised for its scientism, exemplified by the conviction that by identifying the structures of legal orders and thus establishing their insensitivity to context, comparative lawyer are able to provide precise indications of the states of objects in relation to a given property. Indeed, '*verum ipsum factum* is the criterion prepared by Vico that inspires the comparative lawyer in his analysis' and he can 'measure' without resorting to data 'coming from a science of a political or ethical nature or, in any case, extraneous to the study of linguistic data'.[13]

Scientistic, then, is the reference to the possibility of faithfully reconstructing the content of the different formants, implicit in the quotation of the Vichian maxim, which leads one to see in structuralism a way of multiplying rather than overcoming the defects of positivism. Indeed, structuralists do not believe in the uniqueness of the legal rule, and yet they show that they trust in the possibility of identifying the structures and fundamentally the components of law from which they can derive the dissociation between formants, whose internal coherence they thus end up supporting. In doing so, they behave like the advocates of traditional hermeneutics: they reduce themselves to constructing a theory of the multiplicity of conceptual schemes (I.1.4). This is, in fact, the natural consequence of the mentioned idea that it is possible to measure the dissociation between formants, and thus the distance between the reality of the law and the image provided by its interpreters.

It is no wonder, at this point, that Hans Kelsen, whose teaching finds authoritative supporters among contemporary comparative law scholars,[14] may be considered an *ante litteram* structuralist.[15] Indeed, he believed that it was precisely comparison that made it possible to identify the essence of law as a phenomenon dissociated from its coordinates of space and time, that is, that it led to the 'pure theory of law':

> The pure theory of law is a theory of positive law; a general theory of law, not a presentation or interpretation of a special legal order. From a comparison of all the phenomena which go under the name of law, it seeks to discover the nature of law itself, to determine its structure and its typical forms, independent of the changing content which it exhibits at different times and among different peoples. In this manner it derives the fundamental principles by means of which any legal order can be comprehended. As a theory, its sole purpose is to know its subject. It answers the question of what the law is, not what it ought to be. The latter question is one of politics, while the pure theory of law is science.[16]

Having listed, alongside the merits, the shortcomings of the structuralist method, we must not, however, forget that all methods of comparison cannot be evaluated in absolute terms. It

12 R. Sacco, in P. Legrand, *Questions à Rodolfo Sacco*, in *Revue internationale de droit comparé*, 1995, pp. 949 and 959.

13 R. Sacco and P. Rossi, *Introduzione al diritto comparato*, cit., pp. 10 and 60.

14 Among many O. Pfersmann, *Le droit comparé comme interprétation et comme théorie du droit*, in *Revue internationale de droit comparé*, 2001, p. 287.

15 T.E. Frosini, *Hans Kelsen comparatista*, in *Percorsi costituzionali*, 2023, p. 625 ff.

16 H. Kelsen, *The Pure Theory of Law and Analytical Jurisprudence*, in *Harvard Law Review*, 55, 1941, p. 44.

is always essential to relate them to the strategies of the scholar practising them, and then to consider them in the light of the aims of his research (IV.1.5). This leads one to admit that the dissociation between formants is nevertheless useful in many cases, particularly if one intends to produce a unifying comparison.

To mention a concrete and fruitful application of the dissociation between formants, we can briefly turn to the analysis of the notion of contract in the German and Italian legal systems. In the former, there is no codified definition and therefore, in the silence of the legislative formant, legal scholarship affirms that the contract is a bilateral legal act, thus taking up the well-known scheme made famous by Savigny. In this scheme, legal facts may be casual circumstances or voluntary acts, which take the name of declarations of will or legal acts if they are immediately intended for the creation or extinction of a legal relationship, and of contracts or bilateral legal transactions if brought about by several parties to realise a common intention (IV.3.7).

This definition of a contract is consistent with data from the German Civil Code. On the one hand, the Code does not define the word 'contract' (I.1.2), but on the other it regulates contracting in such a way as to lead the scholarship to emphasise that it constitutes an institution which is present in all areas of civil law. Indeed, alongside contracts under the law of obligations (*schuldrechtlicher Vertrag*), and due to the absence of the consensualistic principle according to which ownership is transferred by consent, there are also contracts relevant to property law only (*dinglicher Vertrag*): those that record consent around the mere transfer of ownership, either by delivery of a movable property or registration of immovable property. What is more, German civil law also knows of family law contracts (*familienrechtlicher Vertrag*), such as marriage or prenuptial agreements, and inheritance law contracts (*Erbvertrag*), which are permitted due to the lack of an absolute prohibition of agreements as to succession.[17]

Seen in these terms, the German notion of contract appears to be very different from the Italian one, at least according to the legislative formant. The Civil Code, more precisely, limits the notion of contract to the law of obligations, requiring that it must be of a pecuniary nature (art. 1321). This conclusion, however, is not reflected in German case law which distinguishes between legally relevant obligations and merely socially relevant obligations: courts apply contract law and not tort law if they recognise a pecuniary interest in the performance.[18]

In other words, the dissociation between formants makes it possible to point out that, in spite of the silence of the German civil code and of what scholarship supports, the courts have even more restrictive requirements for identifying a contract than those mentioned by the Italian legislative formant: the latter mentions the pecuniary nature of the legal relationship, but not also the interest in performance. Evidently the comparative lawyer who notes this state of the art is not interested, as in the case of traditional civil law scholarship, in remedying the inconsistency of the system by identifying the notion of contract to be considered correct, and the one which must be rejected as erroneous. Those who shed light on the dissociation between formants intend more simply to descriptively reconstruct the framework of a certain discipline and to disregard the prescriptive point of view typically assumed by legal positivists.

It is a fact, however, that in this way the context in which legal constructions operate is overlooked and one often ends up with a comparison that unites. It is precisely this fact that must be taken into account in the choice of method, which, as we have repeatedly pointed out, cannot be fixed once and for all but must be linked to the objectives pursued by the author of the comparison.

17 See A. Somma, *La nozione di Vertrag e la patrimonialità del rapporto giuridico*, in *Rivista trimestrale di diritto e procedura civile*, 1996, p. 1230 f.
18 Among many, BGH, 22 June 1956, I ZR 198/54.

2 FUNCTIONAL ANALYSIS AND THE PRESUMPTION OF SIMILARITY OF PRACTICAL SOLUTIONS

While in Italy comparative analysis has used structuralism to disrupt the traditional approach to the study of law, in other countries the same role has been played by the use of functional analysis.[19] This was particularly the case in Germany and in the US, in the latter case due to the influence of Ernst Rabel,[20] an academic of Jewish heritage who was forced to leave Nazi Germany.

As a scholar of private international law, Rabel was concerned with characterisation, i.e. the way of understanding the terms used in the conflict of law rules to determine their material scope of application, and thus, the national law called upon to settle a dispute. If the national courts understood those concepts according to the canons of national law, they would probably arrive at erroneous results from the point of view of the foreign system to which the conflict rule refers and would in any case lead to a situation characterised by confusion and disparity. For this reason, Rabel argued, the characterisation should not follow the conceptualism typical of national laws, but rather the meaning that can be derived from the factual situation to which the conflict rule refers.[21] In doing so, confusion and disparities are avoided since that factual situation is identified by using a language that tends to be insensitive to cultural differences.

Rabel's theory had a scientific basis, but it ran up against the expectations of the national legal orders interested in deciding independently on the methods for determining cases with a connection or link to other national legal orders. We have covered this aspect in our discussion of competition between legal systems, showing that it is not only nationalist claims that are at stake, but also questions of the protection of weak subjects (III.1.7). For these reasons, Rabel's theory was not accepted; rather, the thesis prevailed that the qualification should be made according to the canons of the order to which the conflict rule belongs. Nonetheless, Rabel's theory had considerable success, and is considered seminal for functional analysis: a polysemic concept,[22] which, among comparative law scholars, is understood mainly in the sense given to it by Konrad Zweigert and Hein Kötz, the two German authors who also proposed the classification of systems according to their style (II.2.3). Zweigert and Kötz observe that while, on the one hand, law is used in every society to solve similar problems, on the other hand, the solutions adopted at the technical legal level often diverge. This is why the comparative lawyer must start his research from questions posed in factual rather than conceptual terms. If, for example, he comes from a jurisdiction in which the protection against improvident contracts is centred on formal requirements, he will not compare his own jurisdiction with the foreign one by searching there for the regulation of formal requirements of the contract. Instead, he will need to take care to identify the technical-legal solutions adopted to protect the improvident, e.g. certain applications of the doctrine of consideration in common law systems.[23] That is to say, the technical-legal solutions may be different from those contemplated by 'the concepts of one's own national system', and indeed they often are. In this sense, 'one must focus on the concrete problem'.[24]

19 G. Samuel, *An Introduction to Comparative Law Theory and Method*, Oxford and Portland OR, 2014, p. 67.
20 G. Capuzzo, *Modernismo giuridico e uniformazione del diritto. Ascesa e declino di un paradigma*, Napoli, 2018, p. 63 ff.
21 E. Rabel, *The Conflict of Laws. A Comparative Study*, vol. 1, Ann Arbor MI, 1945, p. 49 f.
22 See R. Michaels, *The Functional Method of Comparative Law*, in M. Reimann and R. Zimmermann (Eds.), *The Oxford Handbook of Comparative Law*, 2nd ed., Oxford and New York NY, 2019, p. 345 ff.
23 K. Zweigert and H. Kötz, *An Introduction to Comparative Law* (1996), 3rd ed., Oxford, 1998, pp. 365 ff. and 388 ff.
24 *Ivi*, p. 34 f.

While analysing foreign law, the comparative lawyer will have to become aware of the particularities of the foreign legal system. That is to say, he will have to turn his attention to 'whatever moulds or affects the living law in his chosen system, whatever the lawyers there would treat as a source of law, and he must accord to those sources the same weight and value as they do'. The comparison could thus involve solutions that, from the point of view of the comparative lawyer's system of origin, are not technical legal solutions: the 'function performed' by a rule of law could well be found in 'an extralegal phenomenon'.[25]

This last clarification is noteworthy because it points to the external point of view on law (I.1.4). More problematic, however, is the suggestion that the comparative lawyer must adopt the perspective of the foreign lawyer, which is not consistent with the proposition that functional analysis is a tool by which comparison overcomes conceptualism (I.1.3). In fact, as the structuralists have rightly pointed out, precisely by overlooking the foreign lawyer's perspective, one is able to go beyond the verbalised or explicit formants, and to identify what we have called 'cryptotypes' (IV.2.1): the rules that govern the imperative distribution of values and resources without their addressees being fully aware of them.[26]

However, this is not the most obvious flaw in the functional analysis. Instead, the major problem is the conclusion to be drawn from the observation that, even if they present 'differences in historical development, in their theoretical systematic structure and in the style of their practical applications', different legal systems adopt solutions that are in every respect similar. For Zweigert and Kötz, this leads to the view that the comparative lawyer, while noting considerable differences at the technical legal level, relies on a 'presumption of similarity of practical solutions', which is valid at least in all areas which are not compromised by cultural preferences. This leads to the assertion that, outside of family, personal, and inheritance law, there is an 'apolitical private law' that in essence coincides with economic or market law. In this vein, Zweigert states:

> Despite their different historical development, theoretical-systemic structure and style of practical application, different legal systems reach identical or very similar solutions in practice. Certainly, many areas of human life are affected by strong moral and customary values rooted in different religious approaches, historical traditions, climate, development, and popular traditions. These values can differ so markedly that it is only possible to speak of a coincidence of the rules governing them to a very small extent. However, if we leave aside issues that are particularly affected by value judgements and moral commands – issues mostly concerning family and inheritance law – and turn to apolitical private law, we constantly find confirmation that identical or very similar solutions are found to identical needs in all legal systems worldwide.[27]

These assertions can easily be challenged by recalling, for example, the strong differences that characterise legal systems by reference to the models of capitalism. These differences, as we know, result in violent conflicts, such as those related to the advance of neo-American capitalism at the expense of Rhine capitalism (II.2.10). From another point of view, we can observe spontaneous convergences in many legal systems on issues that are decisively linked to strong cultural preferences. This can be seen, for example, in the development of family law within the Western legal tradition since the second half of the last century.[28]

25 *Ivi*, p. 35 f. and p. 38.
26 A. Gambaro, R. Sacco and M. Graziadei, *Sistemi giuridici comparati*, in *Trattato di diritto comparato*, dir. R. Sacco, 5th ed., Torino, 2024, p. 6 f.
27 K. Zweigert, *Die "praesumptio similitudinis" als Grundsatzvermutung rechtsvergleichender Methode*, in M. Rotondi (Ed.), *Buts et méthodes du droit comparé*, Padova and New York NY, 1973, p. 737 f.
28 For instance, M. Antokolskaia, *Comparative Family Law: Moving with the Times?*, in E. Örücü and D. Nelken (Eds.), *Comparative Law. A Handbook*, Oxford and Portland OR, 2007, p. 241 ff. and J.M. Sherpe, *Comparative*

Above all, the idea of an apolitical law is unconvincing because it harks back to the image of a law produced autonomously by a caste of lawyers. This founding myth of the Western legal tradition emphasises the separation of law from politics and religion (II.3.2), and as we know, is not only common to functionalists but is shared with proponents of structuralism and in the diffusionist approach (III.1.2). The dissociation between law and society that this approach introduces would be welcome if it only aimed to highlight the absence of a one-to-one correspondence between technical legal discourse and the imperative distribution of values and resources that this discourse seeks to promote. If this were the case, it would have to be recognised that the use of legal discourse to exercise power is a prerogative of those who control it (I.2.1). But this is not what the proponents of functional analysis are aiming at; on the contrary, they show that they consider this use to be an exclusive prerogative of the legal profession (II.4.2).

Another aspect of functional analysis that needs to be critically assessed is derived by considering the limits that Zweigert and Kötz place on the activity of the comparative lawyer, who is called upon to compare only rules designed to fulfil the same function:

> The basic methodological principle of all comparative law is that of *functionality*. From this basic principle stem all the other rules which determine the choice of laws to compare, the scope of the undertaking, the creation of a system of comparative law, and so on. Incomparables cannot usefully be compared, and in law the only things which are comparable are those which fulfil the same function.[29]

It is as a result of this limitation that Zweigert and Kötz can arrive at what appears to be the self-evident and incontrovertible truth that even if national laws are different, the concrete solutions, i.e. their functions, are similar.[30] In other words: similarity is not a result of the comparison, but 'a confirmation of the validity of the comparative act'.[31]

In short, functional analysis may be understood as constituting an 'advanced approach' to comparative law, but one which fits with a 'traditional' framework. What it leaves out is the context in which the law is placed, or at any rate it considers it limited to its function.[32] This leads the functional approach into confusion because without context, it can only focus on concepts, and this conceptualism contradicts the premises from which it was conceived.[33] Under these conditions, and if limited to the boundaries of the Western tradition, functional analysis may yet produce significant results.[34] This is because in Western legal tradition it is possible to fulfil its implicit methodological assumption that all legal systems are equipped to perform the same functions.[35] If, however, the comparison involves non-Western legal systems, the most likely outcome will be their marginalisation and, in any case, will give support for the hegemony and expansion of Western legal systems.[36]

Family Law, in M. Reimann and R. Zimmermann (Eds.), *The Oxford Handbook of Comparative Law*, cit., p. 1088 ff.

29 K. Zweigert and H. Kötz, *An Introduction to Comparative Law* (1996), cit., p. 34.

30 See M. Graziadei, *The Functionalist Heritage*, in P. Legrand and R. Munday (Eds.), *Comparative Legal Studies: Traditions and Transitions*, Cambridge, 2003, p. 102.

31 V.G. Curran, *Cultural Immersion, Difference and Categories in U.S. Comparative Law*, in *American Journal of Comparative Law*, 46, 1998, p. 67.

32 M. Van Hoeck and M. Warrington, *Legal Cultures, Legal Paradigms and Legal Doctrine: Towards a New Model for Comparative Law*, in *International and Comparative Law Quarterly*, 47, 1998, p. 495.

33 G. Frankenberg, *Comparative Law as Critique* (2016), Cheltenham and Northampton MA, 2019, p. 54.

34 J. Husa, *Farewell to Functionalism or Methodological Tolerance?*, in *Rabels Zeitschrift für ausländisches und internationales Privatrecht*, 2003, p. 446.

35 See J. Husa, *A New Introduction to Comparative Law*, Oxford and Portland OR, 2015, p. 124.

36 L. Rosen, *Comparative Law and Anthropology*, in M. Bussani and U. Mattei (Eds.), *The Cambridge Companion to Comparative Law*, Cambridge, 2012, p. 75.

It is no wonder, then, that this method is conceived for a unifying comparison, and fundamentally to decree that anything that might contradict the image of an apolitical law and, as such, universal law, is not a matter of interest or concern for comparative lawyers. The upshot is that research on sectors of the legal system which are thought to have strong cultural or ideological influences is marginalised. However, as we know, one cannot assume away the influence of culture and ideology since they are pervasive features of the law.

Be that as it may, functional analysis may be used to emphasise commonalities to the detriment of differences, or convergences kept hidden by superficial differences in technical-legal constructions.

In order to test this conclusion, we can turn our attention to the issue of strict liability for risk, which we will analyse in the Italian and German experiences, obviously formulating a question in functional terms and without resorting to municipal conceptualisms: for example, how is the victim of damage caused by dangerous activities protected in the two legal systems. The comparison will need to be made only between the provisions that fulfil the task indicated and will therefore take into account, for Italian law, what the Civil Code establishes in general terms: damage caused in the exercise of dangerous activities must be compensated by means of liability without fault (art. 2050).

The situation is different in German law, which does not have a general rule on the subject, but only specific rules establishing no-fault liability for certain dangerous activities (*Gefährdungshaftung*). These include rail transport, the production of nuclear energy, the manufacture of medicines, or the use of genetic engineering. The absence of a general clause has traditionally been lamented by German scholarship, which has repeatedly proposed the inclusion of such a clause in the Civil Code.[37] However, it would be wrong to believe that the special laws dedicated to regulating these activities, which have been interpreted by the courts in a restrictive manner, prevent a general principle similar to that formulated by the Italian legislature from being found in German law. The German courts, in fact, starting from the general principle of liability for fault and relying on presumptions, have elaborated a de facto doctrine of liability without fault. In other words, while the two legal systems have adopted different technical-legal solutions, it cannot be said that the practical solutions are equally different.[38]

It goes without saying that the same result, in the sense of a comparison carried out by breaking down legal positivist dogmas, can be obtained by resorting to the theory of formants. Indeed, it can be said that in German law the legislative formant does not express a general principle of liability without fault for the exercise of dangerous activities, whereas the same principle is found in the judicial formant. It could also be added that the doctrinal formant supports the work of the courts and thus also differs from what can be derived from the legislative formant. This is not surprising: as we shall soon see, the structuralist approach and the approach of functional analysis are in many ways complementary and intertwined.

3 THE FACTUAL APPROACH AND THE CASE METHOD

At this point we must consider the factual approach, which is in many ways an application of structuralism but which also has points of contact with functional analysis.[39] This will be an

37 As done as well by H. Kötz: *Gefährdungshaftung*, in Bundesminister der Justiz (Ed.), *Gutachten und Vorschläge zur Überarbeitung des Schuldrechts*, vol. 2, Köln, 1981, p. 1779 ff.

38 See A. Somma, *Le fonti di notevole pericolo nelle esperienze italiana e tedesca*, in L. Cabella Pisu and L. Nanni (Eds.), *Clausole e principi generali nell'argomentazione giurisprudenziale degli anni Novanta*, Padova, 1998, p. 435 ff.

39 S. Goltzberg, *Le droit comparé*, Paris, 2018, p. 13.

opportunity to deepen some of the criticisms levelled at the two methods, and in particular those which address their neglecting the context of law.

The first theorisations of the factual approach are due to comparative research coordinated by Rudolf Schlesinger and carried out during the 1960s at Cornell University, which was dedicated to contract formation.[40] The research attracted the attention of Rodolfo Sacco, first of all because it sought to avoid the reduction of law to legislation and in this sense 'accept the presence of all the formants of the legal system'.[41] He then appreciated the choice to avoid 'the use of any abstract category that has not previously been recognised as universally valid', thus allowing 'the reduction of national materials to common denominators', as a technique designed to compare a large number of legal systems.[42]

The connection between the factual approach, as it was called, and Rabel's observations on qualification (IV.2.2) is hard to miss since it takes 'fact situations as the initial focus of legal comparison'. All this by means of the case method, i.e. using questions formulated on the basis of fact situations typically derived from practice. As Schlesinger states:

> It was clear from the outset that these questions had to be formulated in such a way that our colleague from India would understand them in the same way as our colleague from Italy. If the questions had been asked in abstract legal terms, each participant might have read particular notions of his own legal system into such terms, and the result would have been the complete lack of a common focus. It was decided, therefore, to ask the questions in factual terms. . . . The participants were instructed to regard each of these fact situations as an inquiry seeking to elicit an answer to the following questions: How would the legal system or systems covered by you react to this fact situation? Would the court hold in favor of the plaintiff or the defendant?[43]

The case method was not invented by Schlesinger. As is well-known, its originator was Christopher Columbus Langdell, a university professor who was dean of Harvard Law School in the second half of the 19th century. This period was characterised by the desire to emancipate the training of lawyers from the English approach, i.e. to bypass the legal profession. In fact, Langdell wanted to place academic training at the centre of legal education, giving it a scientific guise with an innovative teaching technique: the presentation of cases considered emblematic or ordered in a systematic way.[44]

The case method just described cannot be considered the same as that used in the Cornell research, not least because the context in which it was used was different. This does not detract from the fact that there are at least two points of contact, the first of which is the formalist approach, which ultimately aims to depoliticise legal experience. Consider, then, that Langdell's ultimate goal was to overcome the divisions between the orientations of state courts and to establish a federal common law.[45] Hence, the second point of contact: that goal is very similar to that of Schlesinger, who was in search of the common core of national laws.

Let us consider the formalist approach and its link to the desire to depoliticise the study of law. This approach is evident first of all in Sacco's assertion that the research carried out at Cornell was applied to a subject 'with a low coefficient of connection to its social context',

40 R.B. Schlesinger (Ed.), *Formation of Contracts. A Study of the Common Core of Legal Systems*, 2 voll., New York NY and London, 1968.

41 R. Sacco, *Comparazione giuridica e conoscenza del dato giuridico*, cit., p, 251 f.

42 R. Sacco, *Un metodo di lavoro nuovo: il Seminario di Cornell*, in *Rivista di diritto civile*, 1972, II, p. 175 ff.

43 R.B. Schlesinger, *Formation of Contracts. A Study of the Common Core of Legal Systems: Introduction*, in *Cornell International Law Journal*, 2, 1969, p. 36 ff.

44 For instance, N. Duxbury, *Patterns of American Jurisprudence*, Oxford, 1997, p. 14 ff.

45 L. Serafinelli, *U.S. Law Schools. Una visione alternativa della formazione del giurista negli Stati Uniti*, Milano, 2023, p. 69 ff.

which allowed the researchers to avoid 'parallel sociological investigations' or 'evaluations'. Obviously, such an assertion concerning the formation of contracts, which has a central role in the functioning of the economic order, is hazardous but can be explained in the light of the principles of structuralism. Indeed, we know that its proponents try to analyse the law purified of the context in which it is immersed (IV.2.1). In other words, they attempt to make comparisons without 'stealing space from social or political sciences'. The aim is to identify the solutions capable of withstanding the passage of time, that is to say, the 'most profound and therefore most lasting reasons for decision', valuing the dissociation between formants and, in any case, denying the principle of the uniqueness of the legal rule (I.1.2). Per Sacco:

> It is clear that the researcher, in broadening the investigation to test the robustness of a rule, will have to go back, whenever possible, from the judicial decision to the statute; and sometimes from the judicial decision to the doctrinal system. But he will avoid mixing the components of his own system of sources or reducing the whole complex of legal sources to one element only.[46]

Further evidence of the formalist nature of the case method can be found in Gino Gorla, a father of Italian comparative law who participated in the research led by Schlesinger. Gorla had made extensive use of the case method in the 1950s analysing the ways in which common law and civil law systems resolve the friction between the promisor's desire to be free from an obligation and the promisee's expectation that his reliance will be protected. The study had 'a very strong political value',[47] and stigmatised the exclusive recourse to the 'logical method of abstractions and generalisations' as being focused on 'mere nominal questions' and submissive to a 'latent natural law approach'. However, the intention was not to overcome it, but rather to complete it by observing the 'legal systems . . . at work in the concrete case' in order to reconstruct the mechanism that leads to 'formulating rules and principles'. More precisely, Gorla stated:

> It is a matter of redoing or reproducing . . . the mental process that leads judges and legislators (who also proceed in this way, sometimes by long unconscious sedimentation of concrete cases) to formulate abstractions of rules and principles, to then descend again – in a continuous exchange or loop – to the problem of the concrete case. It is a matter of seeing how rules and principles (i.e. the men who use them) behave, adapt, and modify in the face of this problem, which is that of historically conditioned justice. . . . If there is therefore a novelty . . . it consists in not neglecting the merits of the systematic logic method and in combining it with the comparative historical and case methods, which have been taken as means for a better understanding of our positive law, and to correct the other method as it insists on abstractions and generalisations.[48]

It should be noted that the case method continues to be a point of reference for scholars of comparative law, who have even resurrected it as a solution to the deficiencies of taxonomy (II.2.6), or rather the 'rarefied air of taxonomic classifications of systems'.[49] All this is linked to objectives that allow us to shed light on the second point of contact between the case method and Langdell's original approach. This is the search for the common core of the national laws and, ultimately, the pursue of the ancient aspiration of comparative law of

46 R. Sacco, *Un metodo di lavoro nuovo*, cit., p. 174 ff.

47 G. Marini, *L'Italian style fra centro e periferia ovvero Gramsci, Gorla e la posta in gioco nel diritto privato*, in *Rivista italiana per le scienze giuridiche*, 2016, p. 145.

48 G. Gorla, *Il contratto. Problemi fondamentali trattati con il metodo comparativo e casistico* (*Lineamenti generali*), vol. 1, Milano, 1955, p. vii ff.

49 M. Serio, *Nuove condensate riflessioni sull'apporto della comparazione alla scienza giuridica*, in *Comparazione e diritto civile*, 2020, p. 13 ff.

identifying the law of civilised humanity (II.1.2). This last remark may sound hazardous, but it is borne out by the research carried out at Cornell, which, not coincidentally, was funded by the Ford Foundation: an organisation committed to promoting the law and development movement (III.1.4). In this context, the research was presented as part of a series of studies aimed at identifying 'general principles of law recognised by civil nations': the formula contained in the Statute of the International Court of Justice (art. 38),[50] whose evolutionary inspiration we have already highlighted (II.1.3).

In recent years, there have been several research studies, which in this vein have sought to apply the model used at Cornell to study the formation of the contract, while at the same time noting their connection with the method developed by structuralist comparative law.[51] Prominent among these is an early-'90s study by the University of Trento dedicated to the reconstruction of the 'common core of European private law'. It was explicitly conceived as a development of the research carried out at Cornell and an implementation of the structuralist approach and the related dissociation between formants.[52]

The study, which is still ongoing, aims to provide 'a very precise map' of laws in Europe, in order to highlight 'deep similarities masked by formal differences' and thus provide 'a reliable and plausible picture of existing law'. The promoters of the study make it clear that it is intended to be analytical and not prescriptive, and yet they do not fail to emphasise that the materials produced 'may become indispensable to those responsible for drafting European legislation'.[53] This is again an illustration of the limitations of structuralism and its applications as an approach that claims to be technical and neutral, yet is laden with broadly political repercussions: for example, the hiding of a hegemonic project. Furthermore, the factual approach overlooks that facts are actually artefacts: they are not found in nature but are 'socially constructed'.[54]

4 THE COMPARATIVE ECONOMIC ANALYSIS OF LAW

Some scholars drawing on the subversive function of comparative law, namely, its natural inclination to combat the orthodoxies inherited from tradition (I.1.1), have proposed combining comparative law with the economic analysis of law. The latter is a discipline that in the United States has been conceived and used for the same purposes within an approach similar to functional analysis. Both fields of knowledge are in fact considered to be 'the most formidable methodological attacks on rampant legal positivism' so that their combination would produce considerable advantages for comparative lawyers. First of all, it would allow them to 'recover theoretical breath by using functionalist analyses such as those developed by economists'. Secondly, the economic analysis of law develops models to be used as a homogeneous basis for comparisons, thus enabling the use of reliable tools to measure the similarities and

50 R.B. Schlesinger and P. Bonassies, *Le fonds commun des systèmes juridiques. Observations sur un nouveau projet de recherches*, in *Revue internationale de droit comparé*, 1963, p. 502 f.

51 U. Mattei, *The Comparative Jurisprudence of Schlesinger and Sacco*, in A. Riles (Ed.), *Rethinking the Masters of Comparative Law*, Oxford and Portland OR, 2001, p. 238 ff.

52 B. Gardella Tedeschi, *Italian Comparative: A Trait of the Legal System*, in *Florida International University Law Review*, 18, 2024, p. 816 f.

53 M. Bussani and U. Mattei, *Le fonds commun du droit européen*, in *Revue internationale de droit comparé*, 2000, pp. 31 and 40.

54 G. Frankenberg, *How to Do Projects with Comparative Law. Notes of an Expedition to the Common Core*, in *Global Jurist Advances*, 6, 2006, pp. 18 and 25.

differences between the objects compared: 'the tools of economic science, a discipline that many consider the most theoretically advanced of the social sciences'.[55]

In other words, if comparison consists in comparing the states of two objects in relation to a property, economic analysis makes it possible to represent those states accurately, i.e. to reliably describe the identities and differences between legal constructions with reference to a specific feature: the function they serve. This is the inspiring motive of a discipline called comparative economic analysis of law,[56] to which we shall turn after a brief discussion of the economic analysis of law as such: a discipline which has mainly interested comparatists with a private law background.[57]

The economic analysis of law can be defined, first and foremost, as the use of canons developed by economic science to reflect on the legal phenomenon. This practice goes back a long way and has spread in both capitalist and socialist experiences in areas where interaction between law and economics is common. However, the recourse to the same practice in other areas is more recent, and in the United States it is the specific programme of the Law and Economics movement, which emerged in the 1970s.[58] The aim was to target traditional legal theories by using economic analysis to shed light on the relationship between law and society.[59] Whether recourse to the economic analysis of law, especially by way of comparison, actually leads to results in line with such intentions, however, may be seriously doubted.

In a kind of manifesto of the movement, or at least of a prominent part of it, Richard Posner set out the conditions for the application to legal analysis of certain fundamental precepts elaborated within economic science: 'the science of human choice in a world in which resources are limited in relation to human wants', which 'explores and tests the implications of assuming that man is a rational maximizer of his ends in life, his satisfactions – what we shall call his self-interest'.[60]

The precepts developed by economic science, which can be profitably employed by law, derive from the 'proposition that people respond to incentives'. A first precept concerns 'the inverse relation between price charged and quantity demanded'. This leads one to see the law, rather than as a set of obligations and prohibitions correlated with sanctions, as the instrument by which human behaviour is given a price. The price should be set high if behaviour is to be discouraged and low if it is to be encouraged. In particular:

> Let the price of steak rise by ten cents a pound. If other prices remain unchanged, a steak will now cost the consumer more, relatively than it did before. Being rational and self-interested, the consumer will react by investigating the possibility of substituting goods that he prefers less when steak was at its old price but that are more attractive now because they are cheaper relative to steak. . . . In general, then, if the price of one product rises and all other prices remain unchanged, the quantity of the product demanded by purchasers, and hence the amount produced, will decline. . . . The 'Law of Demand' – as the negative relationship between price and quantity is called – has many applications to the legal system. The convicted criminal who has served his sentence is said to have 'paid his debt to society', and an economist would find the metaphor apt. Punishment is the price that society charges for a criminal offense.

55 U. Mattei and P.G. Monateri, *Introduzione breve al diritto comparato*, Padova, 1997, p. 99.
56 U. Mattei, *Comparative Law and Economics*, Ann Arbor MI, 1998.
57 See E. Mostacci, *La comparazione giuridica, tra diritto ed economia*, in *Diritto pubblico comparato ed europeo*, 2024, p. 754 f.
58 Among many R. Pardolesi, *Analisi economica del diritto*, in *Digesto delle discipline privatistiche – Sezione civile*, vol. 1, Torino, 1987, p. 310.
59 G. Minda, *Postmodern Legal Movements: Law and Jurisprudence at Century's End*, New York NY and London, 1995, p. 73.
60 R. Posner, *Economic Analysis of Law*, 2nd ed., Boston MA and Toronto, 1977 p. 3.

> The economist is led to predict that an increase in either the severity of the punishment or the likelihood of its imposition will raise the price of crime and therefore reduce its incidence. The criminal will be encouraged to substitute other activity.[61]

A second precept is 'the tendency of resources to gravitate toward their most valuable uses' but only under conditions of 'voluntary exchange'. Only in such cases are resources 'shifted to those uses in which the value to consumers, as measured by their willingness to pay, is highest'.[62] From this, it follows that law must favour the construction of an economic order centred on the free encounter of supply and demand without claiming to addressing market failures, i.e. without introducing transactional costs: as summarised in the celebrated Coase theorem.[63]

On closer inspection, this is not consistent with neoliberal thinking. Neoliberals take the view that public authorities should be the visible hand of the market, i.e. actively work to impose competition (II.2.10). It is also a different point of view from the one long favoured in economic literature, summarised in the theses of Arthur Cecil Pigou, according to whom market failures must be remedied by corrective state intervention.[64] However, the economic analysis of law is linked to a different conception of the relationship between the state and the market: its abstention is seen as an indispensable condition for achieving a use of resources that maximises 'the willingness to pay' and therefore ensuring 'efficiency'. In fact, 'if the transaction is involuntary, its consequences for efficiency cannot be determined'. As Posner clarifies:

> An important question in the economic analysis of law is whether and in what circumstances an involuntary exchange may be said to increase efficiency. Efficiency is, as we have said, determined by willingness to pay, and the only way in which willingness to pay can be determined with certainty is by actually observing a voluntary transaction. Where resources are shifted pursuant to a voluntary transaction, we can be reasonably confident that the shift involves a net increase in efficiency. . . . But many of the transactions either affected or effected by the legal system are involuntary. Most crimes and accidents are involuntary transactions, and so is a legal judgment to pay damages or a fine. How is one to know when such transactions increase, and when they reduce, efficiency?[65]

Defining efficiency is not an easy task, since the paradigms that are evoked in this context are often vague and contradictory. Among the more uncontentious definitions, we can mention those that stress the neutral value of the concept due to the fact that it expresses a stable parameter capable of measuring the values of different people in a satisfactory manner. If the concept traditionally used by jurists, that of justice, is arbitrary and subjective, that of efficiency is technical and universal, the only one capable of 'founding a scientific discourse on social organisation'.[66] In fact, efficient is the situation in which welfare is maximised: 'if it is impossible to change it so as to make at least one person better off without making another person worse off',[67] or at least 'if the losers are compensated by the winners'.[68]

Borrowing from the economist's method, the lawyer who argues in terms of efficiency does not believe that the evaluative aspect is absent, but he relegates it to an antecedent moment:

61 *Ivi*, p. 4 ff.
62 *Ivi*, p. 9 f.
63 R.H. Coase, *The Problem of Social Cost*, in *Journal of Law and Economics*, 3, 1960, p. 1 ff.
64 A.C. Pigou, *The Economics of Welfare*, 4th ed., London, 1952, p. 172 ff.
65 R. Posner, *Economic Analysis of Law*, cit., p. 10 f.
66 U. Mattei and P.G. Monateri, *Introduzione breve al diritto comparato*, cit., p. 86.
67 R. Cooter et al., *Il mercato delle regole*, Bologna, 1999, p. 25 citing Vilfredo Pareto.
68 U. Mattei, *Comparative Law and Economics*, cit., p. 4 with reference to Kaldor Hicks.

that of political choice made by the legislator. The economic analysis of law intervenes at a later stage in order to identify the best, i.e. the most efficient, of the various correct solutions to 'maximise the size of the pie', and 'leaving to others . . . the decision how to divide it'.[69]

One can deduce from these statements a first problematic aspect of the economic analysis of law, which ends up supporting an internal point of view on law which is very similar to that of the proponents of legal positivism (I.1.3). Indeed, it is a prescriptive point of view, for which the lawyer can identify the legislator's intention as a certain and faithful knowable element, and then share and amplify it through interpretation.

On closer inspection, the evaluative moment entrusted to the legislator is not free from conditioning. As we have seen, in order for it to be conceived as a system of incentives and disincentives, the law must first establish an economic order centred on the free meeting of supply and demand, that is, it must support what we have seen as the common law model of capitalism (II.2.9). The view of the individual as a person capable of rational self-determination is also ascribed to precise ideological schemes which are not shared by those who believe that the human type of reference for technical-legal constructions should preferably be the *homo sociologicus*, and certainly not the *homo oeconomicus* (I.1.4).

In short, the economic analysis of law aims to accredit itself as a neutral and non-evaluative approach, and yet it turns out to be undermined by a considerable ideological bias. This is regardless of the distinctions usually proposed between a so-called progressive economic analysis, often associated with Guido Calabresi, and the conservative one, often associated with Richard Posner.[70] As Procida Mirabelli di Lauro makes pointedly clear:

> The tendency to reject justice as an appropriate parameter for founding a scientific model of social organisation, the formal guarantee of equal starting opportunities at the expense of any redistributive function, the distrust of private law rules and the valorisation of the fiscal instrument (because it is less costly), the glorification of any solution that eliminates or reduces wasted costs leads to results that are sometimes comical and paradoxical – as in the case of the Posnerian analysis of sexual relations – sometimes dramatic and questionable – as in the Calabresian study on organ donation – that hide behind an apparent neutrality (as happens with legal formalism) precise choices that are often arbitrary and therefore not always acceptable. . . . The failure to perceive the social problem, for which a given rule is or should be intended as a solution, reduces the legal discourse to a sterile formal game that loses all contact with reality.[71]

If this is the case, all the presuppositions on which the comparative economic analysis of law was built fall down. The combination of economic analysis and comparison does not strengthen the subversive value of the latter, but ends up imprisoning it within the formalistic schemes of the former. In other words, we are not dealing here with a new discipline,[72] but only with the invasion of the field of a pre-existing discipline to the detriment of another pre-existing discipline. Comparative law, in this way, becomes subordinated to the aims of the economic analysis of law.

It should be noted here that the economic analysis of law has evolved over time into a more complex and less trivial science than the minimal features typical of its first phase, adumbrated earlier, would suggest. This is due to the tendencies that have

69 A.M. Polinsky, *An Introduction to Law and Economics*, Boston MA, 1983, p. 7.

70 See respectively G. Calabresi, *The Costs of Accidents. A Legal and Economic Analysis*, New Haven CT and London, 1970 and R. Posner, *The Economics of Justice*, Cambridge MA and London, 1981.

71 A. Procida Mirabelli di Lauro, *La civilistica italiana e il metodo comparativo*, in *Rivista critica del diritto privato*, 1999, p. 380 f.

72 See F. Faust, *Comparative Law and Economic Analysis of Law*, in M. Reimann and R. Zimmermann (Eds.), *The Oxford Handbook of Comparative Law*, cit., p. 848 ff.

emerged among economists, who have made the most of the insights of cognitive sciences in their research on how human preferences and choices are acquired and information processed. All this has provided an inexhaustible source of evidence of the fallacy of the paradigm of economic rationality that underpins neoclassical economics – so much so that the contours of cognitive and behavioural economics have now emerged, a new science born out of the encounter between economics and disciplines such as psychology and neuroscience.[73]

The consequences of such a turnaround for the economic analysis of law have been numerous.[74] Perhaps the best known is the one that has affected the very foundation of the subject, namely, the incentive as an instrument for influencing economic behaviour. The reference is to the 'nudge' (or 'gentle push') theory, which alludes to a certain way of conceiving incentives: 'not coercive, but based on freedom of compliance, simple, easy to understand and also low cost'.[75]

Nonetheless, this and other similar theories do not seem to have led to an effective change of course. In other words, the comparative economic analysis of law has not questioned its own foundations. This is exemplified by the lack of consideration of cultural factors, except to consider them incompatible with the evaluation of law through the lens of economics.[76] The economic analysis of law that comparative lawyers consider, in short, remains fundamentally anchored in the traditional schemes that it claims to reject when it emphasises its differences from 'traditional' economic analysis of law. As Mattei and Monateri put it:

> Economic science has bequeathed to traditional economic analysis of law a legacy that comparative scholars can only accept with reservations. These are the institutional assumptions of natural law that, used by Adam Smith, the founder of modern economics, have reached economic analysis of law without further discussion. It is easy for a comparative lawyer to observe how these naturalistic models constitute oversimplified abstractions that are unable to reflect the structural complexity that different legal notions have developed over the course of deeply distinct historical evolutions. Such comparative and historical complexity cannot be understood nor illuminated by legal models tailored to the economist's needs.[77]

Comparative economic analysis of law does not promote classical liberalism, which is based on a belief in the ability of markets to self-regulate. Indeed, the ideology underlying this belief has for decades been replaced by neoliberalism, according to which the functioning of the market is due not to the invisible hand but to the incisive intervention of the state (II.2.7). However, this does not change the terms of the question: even if comparative economic analysis values the role of public authorities and thus of the law, it nevertheless assesses their efficiency from the point of view of an economic order still based on the free meeting of supply and demand and on the defence of property rights. It is simply a question of determining which state laws are more in line with the laws of the market, i.e. more efficient in terms of their ability to facilitate the orderly interaction of economic agents in a context dominated by the principle of competition.

73 See V. Scoppa, *Economia comportamentale*, Bologna, 2014.
74 For instance, J.D. Hanson and D.A. Kysar, *Taking Behavioralism Seriously. Some Evidence of Market Manipulation*, in *Harvard Law Review*, 112, 1999, p. 1420 ff.
75 F. Vella, *Diritto ed economia comportamentale*, Bologna, 2023, p. 75 f.
76 See J. De Coninck, *Reinvigorating Comparative Law through Behavioral Economics: Cautiously Optimistic View*, in *Review of Law and Economics*, 7, 2011, p. 711 ff.
77 U. Mattei and P.G. Monateri, *Introduzione breve al diritto comparato*, cit., p. 102.

5 FROM QUANTITATIVE COMPARISON TO INDICATORS

Comparative economic analysis of law claims to use a language that is neutral, or at least transversal, with respect to the laws involved, and thus to be able to provide reliable measurements of the similarities and differences between the phenomena analysed. This conviction is obviously debatable, although it is shared by other methods of comparison – for example, the factual approach and its case method (IV.2.3), whose similarities with economic analysis have been emphasised for good reason.[78]

We also know that the same conviction is found among the proponents of the New Comparative Economics, who translate the phenomena they analyse into mere numerical data in order to produce exact assessments of the economic performance of legal rules (II.3.6). However, New Comparative Economics best intentions do not bear fruit. They have not provided reliable measurements since there is nothing more approximative and unreliable than a comparison that 'treats different legal systems as mere compilations of information which can be coded in a numerical way'.[79] Consider then that this culture of numbers, as a culture, is by definition inseparable from the context in which it is formed and develops and is therefore incapable of expressing rational parameters.[80] Lastly, consider that the numerical data, even if it were to be considered a faithful reproduction of reality, is necessarily linked to aspects lacking the character of objectivity: in particular, the way in which the data is understood and, upstream, the choice to consider a particular data at the expense of other data.[81]

The New Comparative Economics is perhaps the best-known and most controversial example of what we could call 'quantitative comparison', aimed at making comparisons between laws reduced to their numerical dimension[82]: i.e. derived from the measurement of their real or perceived impact (*counting facts about law*), or alternatively from the arbitrary attribution of numerical values to their content (*coding law*).[83] The New Comparative Economics is, however, not the first example of quantitative comparison, if only one considers the use of data within the Law and Development movement (II.4.4). Indeed, from the very beginning, its exponents believed that the comparison of numerical quantities avoided the typical flaws of research conducted according to the prevailing canons of the time, i.e. legal positivist conceptualism.[84]

It must be said at this point that quantitative comparison is not limited to scholars who wish to promote the development of the economic order in a neoliberal sense. Sometimes this type of comparison may well constitute a kind of forced choice. Particularly in cases where the comparison involves a very large number of laws (large-N), their reduction to the numerical dimension may be the only way to identify a possible common denominator for the comparison.[85]

The point, then, is not to demonise the use of quantitative methods, but rather to highlight their implications, especially their possible normative significance and the context in which this develops. Before turning to these latter aspects, however, it is useful to offer two

78 F. Parisi, *The Multifaceted Method of Comparative Law and Economics*, in *Comparative Law Review*, 12, 2021, 2, p. 25 ff.
79 M. Siems, *The End of Comparative Law*, in *Journal of Comparative Law*, 2, 2007, p. 143.
80 B. Grossfeld, *Kernfragen der Rechtsvergleichung*, Tübingen, 1996, p. 233.
81 R. Scarciglia, *Il cigno nero e il comparatista. Riflessioni su indicatori, variabili e comparazione giuridica*, in *Diritto pubblico comparato ed europeo*, 2021, p. 76.
82 See the contributions, edited by M. Graziadei, in the special issue '*Misurare il diritto*', in *Annuario di diritto comparato e studi legislativi*, 2012.
83 M. Siems, *Comparative law*, 2nd ed., Cambridge, 2018, p. 181.
84 See Y.-M. Laithier, *Droit comparé*, Paris, 2024, p. 226 f.
85 R. Hirschl, *Comparative Matters. The Renaissance of Comparative Constitutional Law*, Oxford, 2014, p. 267 ff.

examples of quantitative comparisons that are not motivated by neoliberal ideals. This will give us a more complete picture of the phenomenon we are about to analyse.

The first example is the Global Slavery Index, published by the Australian NGO Walk Free in collaboration with the International Labour Organization: the UN agency specialising in labour and social security issues. The index provides a ranking of countries based on an estimate of the percentage of people in a state of 'modern slavery': a concept that includes, in addition to actual slavery or practices similar to slavery, human trafficking, forced labour, the exploitation of prostitution, forced marriages, and forms of child labour linked to the use of violence.[86]

This publication not only stigmatises countries where these practices are most common. It also provides data to assess countries where these practices are less widespread by drawing, for example, attention to consumer behaviour that at least indirectly fuels forms of modern slavery.[87] In short, the Index promotes critical consumerism, that is not only attentive to the quality of products, but also and above all to the way in which they are produced, thereby signalling its distance from the neoliberal way of conceiving the economic order.[88]

A similar distance characterises the Indicators of Employment Protection, which we will use as our second example. These are published by the Organisation for Economic Co-operation and Development (OECD), which is certainly not hostile to the neoliberal ideology as a whole. After all, it has been concerned with promoting the capitalist order since its days as the Organisation for European Economic Co-operation (II.2.3). However, the distance from this ideology can be seen in comparison with what the Doing Business Reports have achieved on the same subject, as they promoted the freedom to terminate the employment relationship and, more generally, the tendency to view the employment relationship as no different from any other market relationship (III.1.5). The Indicators, by contrast, have the opposite objective: they take into account labour legislation, collective agreements, and the relevant case law, and then give more positive ratings to those systems that restrict employers' freedom with regard to individual and collective dismissals, in both fixed-term and open-ended contracts.[89]

Then, there are the rankings that consider aspects not directly related to the neoliberal way of conceiving the economic order, and yet at least indirectly concerning its promotion. In this regard, we can cite perhaps the best-known example, the Worldwide Governance Indicators.[90] We know that governance has long been taken into account by the World Bank as it concerns the outcome of government action, over which the World Bank would have no competence (III.1.4). It is little wonder then that the Indicators are published by the World Bank itself, which also in this way strengthens its interference in the political order.

Among other things, the Indicators focus on three aspects of governance, measured in terms of how it is perceived to work rather than how it actually works in reality. The first aspect is 'government effectiveness', i.e. the quality of public administration and the 'degree of independence from political pressure'. The second aspect is 'regulatory quality', which refers to the 'ability of the government to formulate and implement sound policies and regulations that permit and promote private sector development'. The third aspect is the 'rule of

86 See www.walkfree.org/global-slavery-index.
87 *The Global Slavery Index 2023*, p. 254 ff.
88 For instance, M.J. Carrington, D. Zwick and B. Neville, *The Ideology of the Ethical Consumption Gap*, in *Marketing Theory*, 16, 2016, p. 21 ff.
89 See www.oecd.org/en/data/datasets/oecd-indicators-of-employment-protection.html.
90 Recently, N. Karkanitsa, *Measuring the Unmeasurable: Foreign Aid and the Rule of Law*, in *American University International Law Review*, 39, 2024, p. 305 ff.

law', which includes the quality of rules governing 'contract enforcement, property rights, the police, and the courts'.[91]

We can see that the Indicators consider the political order to reward its being functional to support neo-American capitalism, i.e. that they are aligned with the Doing Business Reports (II.2.9). This very aspect was repeatedly criticised,[92] and partly considered in the context of an evaluation by a commission of independent experts. There, the flaws of the Indicators were acknowledged, but this did not prevent the conclusion that, as far as the results and the methodology are concerned, there is no 'better alternative for cross-country comparisons of governance'.[93]

Having looked at some examples of quantitative comparisons, it is now necessary to say something about their implications and, first of all, to make it clear that not all comparisons and rankings based on numerical data have the same significance. For the most part, they are merely an illustration of what is considered to be the state of the art on the subject analysed. This illustration is never purely descriptive[94] but sometimes acquires normative value, giving rise to real 'indicators', i.e. 'law-like' entities. This occurs if they are the fruit of the work of an institution that is recognised as authoritative and competent and that is sufficiently influential and established to exert a 'persuasive power'.[95]

It must also be said that the normative value of indicators is particularly insidious in that it is not expressed explicitly, but rather is a natural implication. Moreover, indicators provide a numerical and therefore simplified and even simplistic representation of complex social phenomena based on competency and are therefore perceived as neutral. In other words, indicators express a technocratic normativity and with it a more or less explicit aversion to politics and, more precisely, to democratic participation. In short, they present themselves as the result of 'objective truths' derived with the sole aid of 'knowledge', which as such legitimise themselves as a form of 'governance'. As Ajani puts it:

> As form of knowledge, indicators rely on the magic aura that numbers convey and on the appearance of impartiality and certainty that they communicate. A key aspect of their power consists in the capacity to transform complexity into clear and non-ambiguous measurements. They manage to submerge particularities and local idiosyncrasies in universal categories, generating a standardised knowledge, which is comparable among different nations and regions. As a form of governance, they are extensively used by decision-makers to adopt important decisions. . . . By replacing judgments based on politics or values with more (allegedly) rational decisions based on numbers and rankings, the use of statistical information and indicators determines a significant shift in the power dynamics of the decision-making process.[96]

If this is the case, the use of indicators produces a scenario not unrelated to legal positivist paradigms.[97] Having said that, as we noted when introducing it, quantitative comparison can produce the most diverse results, and therefore, its suitability must be assessed in the light of them. The problems it poses can, moreover, be circumvented by combining this with other

91 See www.worldbank.org/en/publication/worldwide-governance-indicators.
92 M. Infantino, *Numera et impera. Gli indicatori giuridici globali e il diritto comparato*, Milano, 2019, p. 115 ff.
93 *External Review of The Worldwide Governance Indicators* (4 September 2024), www.worldbank.org/en/publication/worldwide-governance-indicators/documentation#5.
94 See Y.-M. Laithier, *Droit comparé*, cit., p. 231.
95 M. Siems and D. Nelken, *Global Social Indicators and the Concept of Legitimacy*, in *International Journal of Law in Context*, 13, 2017, pp. 436 and 442.
96 G. Ajani, *Ruling by Indicators: How the Use of Vague Notions and Quantitative Indicators Facilitates Legal Change*, in *Cardozo Electronic Law Bulletin*, 23, 2017, p. 1 ff.
97 M. Nicolini, *Praising the World by Geometrical Terms: Legal Metrics, Science and Indicators in Swift's Voyage to Laputa*, in *Pólemos*, 13, 2019, p. 327 ff.

methodological approaches: further confirmation that 'methodological pluralism can represent a great opportunity for comparatists'.[98]

6 NEXT: FROM DOING BUSINESS TO BUSINESS READY REPORTS

We have devoted a great deal of space to the Doing Business Reports in order to illustrate their fundamentally neoliberal inspiration and, more precisely, how they constitute a stimulus for the spread of common law as the law of the neo-American capitalism to the detriment of civil law as the law of Rhine capitalism (III.1.5). We can now better understand how indicators are used and how their use carries with it a normative force when canvassing for a reform. In other words, to quote just a few indicators from the latest report, it is of normative value to note that in the system considered to be the most attractive to investors and therefore the most conducive to growth, it is possible to set up a company in one day without paying capital as a guarantee for creditors, where the tax burden on companies does not exceed 26%, and where it is possible to obtain a building permit in just 26 days.[99]

We know that the Doing Business Reports have been at the centre of bitter controversy from the outset precisely because of their neoliberal inspiration. We also know that it was not because of this that the World Bank decided to stop publishing them. That decision followed, more banally, from a history of data manipulation, which served to discredit them. Finally, we know that this decision was followed by a new World Bank publication called Business Ready (III.1.6). The latter saw the light of day in 2024 with data relating to 50 countries 'that span all income levels and geographic regions around the world', expected to reach 180 in 2026.[100]

The interest in this initiative stems from its formal departure from certain features of the previous publication. We will therefore analyse it by focusing on this aspect, to see if it is reflected in the way the comparisons have been structured.

Business Ready is primarily concerned with improving the real impact, and therefore the real operational efficiency, of not only the rules governing business activity (the regulatory framework) but also the policies and infrastructures adopted by the public authorities for the benefit of economic operators and the market (public services). This implies the recognition that the economic order requires significant heteronomous interventions,[101] which is undoubtedly a novelty compared to the Doing Business Reports. However, it does not imply a departure from their basic ideology: indeed, from a neoliberal perspective the proper functioning of the market presupposes potentially decisive actions by public authorities, at least those deemed necessary and sufficient to make capitalism historically possible (II.2.11).

Business Ready looks, then, at the impact of the law on the 'development of the private sector as a whole'. This distinguishes Business Ready from the Doing Business Reports' exclusive focus on the individual firm as the yardstick chosen to evaluate the national laws. In short, the new publication emphasises the macroeconomic dimension of the rules relevant to

98 R. Scarciglia, *Scienza della complessità e comparazione giuridica nell'età dell'asimmetria*, in *Diritto pubblico comparato ed europeo*, special issue, 2019, p. 743.

99 World Bank, *Doing Business 2020. Comparing Business Regulation in 190 Economies*, Washington DC, 2020, p. 79 f.

100 World Bank, *Business Ready 2024*, Washington DC, 2024, p. 50. Among the countries considered, seven are members of the European Union (Bulgaria, Croatia, Estonia, Greece, Portugal, Romania, and Hungary) and one is located in North America (Canada).

101 *Ivi*, p. xix ff. and *Business Ready Methodology Handbook* (October 2024), p. 11.

business life, abandoning the exclusive focus on the microeconomic dimension typical of the old publication. However, this does not imply a change in the basic approach, since taking the viewpoint of the private sector as a whole does not mean that it should take precedence over that of individual market participants: it does not mean that private costs should be accepted if they are offset by public benefits, as the critics of the Doing Business Reports have demanded. It simply means that if, as we have said, the functioning of the market requires public intervention, this can only be assessed from a macroeconomic point of view.[102]

However, Business Ready does not claim to look only at the private sector as a whole. The perspective is broadened beyond that of the individual company to draw attention, in particular, to 'the possibility that reducing the "cost of doing business" can unintentionally mean raising the costs for society at large'. Yet this statement is accompanied by concern about the low propensity to invest following the global economic and financial crisis that erupted in 2008, which is to be countered by type of private sector development that 'mobilizes private capital and maximizes the benefits for businesses'.[103] This contrasts with the intention to enhance society's point of view since the mobilisation of private capital requires its free movement and this constitutes an obstacle to collective welfare (III.2.6). Or rather, it prevents this from being derived from redistribution entrusted to the public authorities; i.e. it requires it to be the market's exclusive prerogative and, more precisely, a matter of the meeting of supply and demand in a condition of free competition. All this strives to implement schemes that maximise, as we have said, the benefits for enterprises and thus pose a further obstacle to the consideration of society's point of view.

If this is the case, the alleged distancing from the Doing Business does not seem to herald a real change of direction. Rather, it appears to be a kind of stylistic clause, somewhat necessitated by the ignominious end of the Reports (III.1.7). This clause, in the final analysis, aims to conceal a substantial continuity in terms of support for the neoliberal way of regulating the economic order and thus conceiving the role of the political order.

This impression is also confirmed by looking at the range of issues addressed by Business Ready, which are substantially the same as the Doing Business Reports. The overlap includes: the procedures associated with starting a business ('business entry'), those associated with the 'business location', access to water, electricity and web ('utility services'), the functioning of the labour market and the regulation of employment relations ('labor'), access to credit ('financial services'), the opportunities for developing 'international trade', the 'taxation' for businesses, the commercial 'disputes resolution', the regulation of 'market competition', and 'business insolvency'.

In line with the intentions of its authors, Business Ready analyses all these issues from the perspective of the overall development of the private sector and even its impact on society. Hence, the decision to assess three cross-cutting aspects: the state of digital services (digital adoption), environmental sustainability, and gender equality. This is based on indicators grouped into the three 'pillars' mentioned, namely, the rules governing business activity, the policies and infrastructures put in place by public authorities for the benefit of economic operators and the market, and the actual impact of both. In addition, there is a clear emphasis on indicators which suggest that consideration for the private sector and society stems from a neoliberal perspective. There is little doubt but that role allocated to public intervention is to ensure the functioning of the market.

102 Among many O. Chessa, *Critica del neo-costituzionalismo finanziario. Sul nesso tra scienza economica e diritto pubblico*, in *Bilancio comunità persona*, 2021, p. 103 f.
103 World Bank, *Business Ready 2024*, cit., p. xix.

Only one topic out of ten, in fact, takes other issues into account. The role of social security is emphasised with reference to labour; however, it is valued to the extent that the 'labor market that provides firms with opportunities and workers with protections can improve employment dynamics and productivity'.[104] It is then stated that 'labor regulations and labor market institutions must strive to achieve a fair balance between the need to protect workers' rights and labor market flexibility'. However, a clarification is added that hints to an unbalanced equilibrium in favour of the enterprise. It is said that in a system where 'labor regulations make hiring costs too high and rules too cumbersome' firms 'may choose to use more capital than labor or to hire informally'.[105] At the same time, the mentioned preference for the free movement of capital gives considerable bargaining power to enterprises when negotiating working conditions with state authorities.

The same goes for the tax system, which, on the one hand, is celebrated as it will 'generate revenue and reallocate resources to various social sectors, thereby fostering economic development and addressing public needs', but, on the other hand, should be informed by a basic principle that 'excessive taxation may foster tax evasion'.[106] This, in a system centred on the free movement of capital, is an invitation to severely limit the tax burden on businesses and thus further frustrate the point of view of the community.

Indications of continuity with the Doing Business Reports in Business Ready can also be derived from its general statements. This is evident from the incipit of the publication, which declares that 'a vibrant private sector is central to efforts to end extreme poverty and boost shared prosperity'.[107] This shows loyalty to a foundation of neoliberal ideology, according to which the redistribution of wealth is the task of the market, and from which it follows that social inclusion must coincide with inclusion in the market (II.2.9). All this accompanied by specific reference to the ambitious goals that the World Bank identified the mid-2010s, when it set out to 'end extreme poverty' and 'promote shared prosperity'[108]:

> Private sector development can be defined by three characteristics: it promotes economic growth through innovation and entrepreneurship; it increases equality of opportunities among market participants; and it ensures the general sustainability of the economy in the long term. Private sector development is driven by the efforts and ingenuity of private entrepreneurs but is critically affected by a range of public policies and regulations that create a conducive business environment. These policies and regulations incentivize the startup of new firms, the facilitation of existing businesses, the creation of good jobs, and the transition of informal to formal workers and firms. Through its focus on private sector development, B-READY can effectively contribute to meeting the WBG's twin goals of eliminating poverty and boosting shared prosperity. The private sector is essential to successful development because it is the primary source of employment and pathway out of poverty.[109]

The methodological framework used by their authors does not directly concern the inspiration behind Business Ready, but does help to reconstruct it. Overall, it follows the one adopted by the Doing Business Reports and is therefore characterised by the ambiguity of quantitative comparisons combined with a certain opacity with regard to the methods of data collection and assessment.[110] Here, however, there is an element that aggravates the judge-

104 *Ivi*, p. 70.
105 *Ivi*, p. 70 f.
106 *Ivi*, p. 78.
107 *Ibid.*
108 World Bank, *Global Economic Prospects. Shifting Priorities, Building for the Future*, Washington DC, 2014.
109 *Business Ready Methodology Handbook*, cit., p. 1 f.
110 G. Chiedo, *L'armonizzazione soft del diritto privato e commerciale: dai Doing business reports al B-Ready*, in *Ianus*, 2024, p. 151 ff.

ment: the attribution of a numerical value to events observed from the point of view of the private sector and the community constitutes an operation that is, if possible, more complex and therefore more in need of transparency than that concerning microeconomic aspects.

The ranking position of the countries considered so far in the classification prepared within each pillar is also in line with the Doing Business Reports. There is a noticeable emphasis on regulations related to business activity and their actual impact, less emphasis on infrastructures provided by public authorities.[111] All this while maintaining the reference to the purpose of the rankings and the indicators, which is 'to promote reforms'.[112]

7 THE DEBATE ON METHOD IN COMPARATIVE PUBLIC LAW

An overview of comparative public law shows that its scholars have not developed methodologies distinct from those of their private law colleagues. The former generally apply the methods used by the latter, while acknowledging their greater prominence in their elaboration.[113] This does not detract from the fact that there are differences in the theoretical debate and, possibly, in its translation into research work, also due to peculiarities in classifying legal systems, e.g. those related to a less emphasis placed on the distinction between civil and common law (II.2.4). Another difference seems to concern a particular awareness of the centrality of the 'methodological bases' for any 'scientific discourse' and their intimate connection with the objectives pursued by the researcher. Lombardi makes this point clearly:

> These, consciously or unconsciously, are present in any discourse, which is first and foremost an organisation of words and concepts in view of a main purpose, which is to express oneself, and of further purposes, which are those aimed at conveying emotions, ideas, convictions, principles, such as to serve to persuade the interlocutor of the existence of a problem, of its possible solutions, of the merits of one of these, of the need to follow it, of the actions that are necessary to this end.[114]

Let us concentrate on the first aspect: the recourse of comparative public lawyers to the methods developed by comparative private law scholars, which we will document by reference to the textbooks.

References to structuralism are widespread among comparative public lawyers, who take up the definition of formants as 'sets of legislative rules, doctrinal propositions, precedents',[115] which is widespread among comparative lawyers of private law background (IV.2.1). The same motivation underpins this methodology: the dissociation of formants offers useful elements to counteract the shortcomings of legal positivism and, in particular, the principle of the uniqueness of the legal rule (I.1.2).[116] In this perspective, the factual approach is alluded to by promoting comparisons 'between normative solutions adopted by different jurisdictions in response to more or less similar practical problems created by social, economic, political developments'.[117]

111 World Bank, *Business Ready 2024*, cit., pp. 1 and 38.
112 *Business Ready Methodology Handbook*, cit., p. 1.
113 A. Pizzorusso, *La comparazione giuridica e il diritto pubblico*, in *Foro italiano*, 1979, v, c. 131 ff.
114 G. Lombardi, *Premesse al corso di diritto pubblico comparato. Problemi di metodo*, Milano, 1986, p. 7.
115 A. Pizzorusso, *Sistemi giuridici comparati*, 2nd ed., Milano, 1998, p. 18.
116 L. Pegoraro and A. Rinella, *Sistemi costituzionali comparati*, Torino, 2017, p. 12.
117 G. Bognetti, *L'oggetto e il metodo*, in P. Carrozza, A. Di Giovine and G.F. Ferrari (Eds.), *Diritto costituzionale comparato*, 2nd ed., Roma and Bari, 2014, p. 727.

If one difference can be noted between comparative private lawyers and comparative public lawyers, it is that concerning the list of formants. While comparative private lawyers point out that the list is open-ended, especially comparative public lawyers make extensive use of the expression beyond the classic distinction between legislative, judicial, and doctrinal formants. In comparative public law, e.g. a reference is made to 'empty formants' to refer to 'provisions that are not or cannot be implemented due to the choice or inability of the legislators'.[118] Then, also constitutional and administrative practices and even ideology are regarded as formant,[119] while 'non-legal formants' are the 'socio-political' and 'economic' formants, i.e. the complexes of rules produced by 'the retraction of politics, the private society of intermediate bodies, the emphasis on the isolated individual, the transfer of decision-making powers to bodies lacking in representativeness and accountability'.[120] Finally, experts or technocrats also produce formants, first and foremost those concerning the 'construction of a new legal ecosystem'.[121]

However, there are also scholars of comparative public law who are critical of structuralism. For example, the factual approach, and in particular its application in the context of the Cornell research (IV.2.3), is considered perplexing. The approach is welcomed as a necessary corrective 'to the old dogmatic method', but at the same time it is said to lead to 'a real flattening into universally applied categories, which precludes consideration of differences'. Or worse, that it has led to the universalisation of the approach typical of common law systems, reducing even civil law systems to 'systems based on precedent'.[122]

Functional analysis is also more or less explicitly criticised, and this is not surprising. Proponents of such a method discuss apolitical law (IV.2.2), and this category, which does not fit private law subjects, seems even more out of place when it comes to public law.[123] There, it is difficult to dispute that the relevant provisions are not derived from 'criteria of efficiency and efficacy', but from 'a precise axiology of civil and political values in which the social group, the political community, recognises the matrix of its identity and the reasons for its unity'.[124]

In short, it is more difficult in comparative public law to carry out the same operations as in comparative private law, where a certain convergence of solutions can be presented as a spontaneous event rather than an imposed one, and therefore insensitive to the political dimension. The comparatist with a publicist background must in fact deal with the 'institutionalised political formula', defined as the essence of the 'constitutional structure' of a system consisting of 'a series of mechanisms . . . more or less highlighted in legislation and often not even at the constitutional level'.[125] Hence, the conclusion that functional analysis as a 'decontextualised' approach is simply 'impossible'.[126]

This does not detract from the fact that the 'functional approach' or, in any case, a careful comparison of the 'various ways of performing fundamental public functions' is also

118 L. Pegoraro and A. Rinella, *Sistemi costituzionali comparati*, cit., p. 14.
119 A. Di Giovine, *Diritto costituzionale comparato: lineamenti introduttivi*, in Id. et al. (Eds.), *Lezioni di diritto costituzionale comparato*, Milano, 2017, p. 30.
120 L. Pegoraro, *Blows against the Empire. Contro la iper-costituzione coloniale dei diritti fondamentali, per la ricerca di un nucleo interculturale condiviso*, in *Annuario di diritto comparato e di studi legislativi*, 2020, p. 448.
121 S. Baldin, *La sostenibilità ecologica e i principi eco-giuridici per la salvaguardia del sistema Terra*, in *Rivista di diritti comparati*, 2022, p. 268.
122 G. Lombardi, *Premesse al corso di diritto pubblico comparato*, cit., p. 31 ff.
123 U. Kischel, *Rechtsvergleichung*, München, 2015, p. 38 f.
124 L. Pegoraro and A. Rinella, *Sistemi costituzionali comparati*, cit., p. 13.
125 G. Lombardi, *Premesse al corso di diritto pubblico comparato*, cit., p. 70.
126 F. Tap, *L'apport du droit comparé à la scientificité du discours constitutionnaliste*, in *Revue internationale de droit comparé*, 2018, p. 12.

appreciated in the public law context.[127] Nor does it detract from the fact that explicit reference is made to a corollary of the functional analysis, namely, that comparisons should be limited to what is considered 'homogeneous in terms of values and ideology'.[128] Some even consider functional analysis to be the prevailing methodological approach in comparative public law, pointing out that it is used for both descriptive and prescriptive purposes and furthermore that it is subject to criticism by those who emphasise the importance of a 'contextualist' point of view.[129] It should also be noted that the advocates of functional analysis do not invoke the presumption of similarity of practical solutions (IV.2.2), an idea that we have already emphasised is hardly compatible with public law subjects because of its related conclusion that law is apolitical.

At this point, something must be said about 'critical'[130] comparison, which some comparative public lawyers have identified as a third method alongside structuralism and functional analysis. First of all, critical comparison distances itself from the latter and from the factual approach, which are seen as means to 'reduce complexity' and to hide it under a claimed 'neutrality, objectivity'. Critical comparison, on the other hand, aims to emphasise 'differencing' and, above it, 'distancing'. Frankenberg puts it in these terms:

> Distancing can be described as an attempt to break away from firmly held beliefs and settled knowledge and as an attempt to resist the power of prejudice and ignorance. . . . Mere distance, however, neither opens our eyes nor makes us see clearly. . . . By *differencing* comparatists take on the fact that they do not view the phenomena they study from 'nowhere in particular'. . . . *Distancing/differencing* calls on the comparatist to decenter her worldview and to consciously establish subjectivity and context in the comparative space, that is, to take into account the observer's perspective.[131]

The way in which critical comparison is described, and the bitter polemic with functional analysis represented by the idea that comparative enquiry should start from the '*preasumptio dissimilitudinis*',[132] shows that its advocates allude to postmodern comparison (II.1.7). This is evident because being critical ends in the exaltation of differences and because this seems to be indicated as the ultimate aim of comparisons. Prescribing a predefined outcome for the latter, no matter whether to promote the exaltation of differences or possibly of commonalities, nevertheless means denying methodological pluralism as a point of reference for comparison, which can be either as a 'science of convergence' or as a 'science of difference'.[133] In the first case, functional analysis must be used in particular, and in the second, approaches that observe law as a cultural phenomenon and thus the critical or postmodern approach with the caveat that idea of incommensurability must be avoided (II.2.8). This would inevitably end up translating into the 'impossibility of comparison'.[134]

If methodological pluralism is a value, and if the choice of method must be determined first and foremost by the aims pursued by the author of the comparison, then extreme forms of integrative comparison such as quantitative comparisons must also be allowed. They will be

127 P. Biscaretti Di Ruffia, *Introduzione al diritto costituzionale comparato. Le forme di Stato, le forme di governo, le Costituzioni moderne*, 6th ed., Milano, 1988, p. 16.
128 G. De Vergottini, *Diritto costituzionale comparato*, 11th ed., Milano, 2022, p. 37.
129 V.C. Jackson, *Comparative Constitutional Law: Methodologies*, in M. Rosenfeld and A. Sajó (Eds.), *The Oxford Handbook of Comparative Constitutional Law*, Oxford, 2012, p. 62 ff.
130 R. Scarciglia, *Metodi e comparazione giuridica*, 3nd ed., Milano, 2021, p. 124 f.
131 G. Frankenberg, *Comparative Law as Critique*, cit., pp. 52 ff. and 70 ff.
132 S. Goltzberg, *Le droit comparé*, cit., p. 14 f.
133 T. Rambaud, *Introduction au droit comparé. Les grandes traditions juridiques dans le monde*, 2nd ed., Paris, 2017, p. 41 f.
134 M.-C. Ponthoreau, *Droit(s) constitutionnel(s) comparé(s)*, 2nd ed., Paris, 2021, p. 72 ff.

of considerable help, for example, to those who wish to document the existence of global constitutionalism.[135] However, these forms of comparison can hardly be legitimised as a means of overcoming a lack of knowledge of the systems being compared. This latter, instead, appears to be the view of those who argue that quantitative comparisons finally make it possible to overcome the traditional view according to which the comparative lawyer must immerse himself in the object of study: the view according to which 'in order to know French laws, the scholar must speak and read French, live in France for a certain period of time and know the feelings of the French'.[136]

SUMMARY

1. In Italy, comparative law has contrasted legal positivism and thus fulfilled its subversive function by resorting to the theory of formants. These are sets of rules, in particular legislative, judicial and doctrinal rules, observed in their essence as formal or substantive sources whose inconsistency and hence dissociation must be emphasised. However, the theory of formants is combined with structuralism, i.e. an approach that leads to neglect the historical dimension and supports scientism, including the idea that law constitutes a creation of jurists. These are flaws of the theory, which is nevertheless a suitable method for making comparisons that unite.

2. In Germany, the subversive function of comparative law has been emphasised through recourse to functional analysis. According to this method comparisons must be conducted on the basis of questions posed in factual rather than conceptual terms, but only between rules that fulfil the same function. This limitation is untenable and makes the presumption of similarity of practical solutions, which the proponents of functional analysis elevate to an epistemological paradigm, appear as a self-referential truth. Also problematic is the notion that the presumption of similarity only applies to market law as apolitical law because it implies the image of a law produced autonomously by jurists. Functional analysis is, however, a suitable method for the scholar interested in comparison that unites.

3. While the Italian comparative lawyers opposed legal positivism with structuralism and the dissociation of formants, United States scholars developed the factual approach and the case method. The latter was theorised by Christopher Columbus Langdell in an epoch far removed from our own, with which it nevertheless has points of contact: today, as then, the aim is to promote the study of the legal phenomenon stripped of its political dimension, and thus to identify a common core of the systems analysed. This is the main implication of a recent research aimed at identifying the common core of European private law, which definitively highlights the limits of the factual approach and the case method: these involve not facts, but artefacts, i.e. parts of reality whose political value seems inescapable.

4. To strengthen the subversive function of comparative law, it has been proposed to combine it with the economic analysis of law, a discipline that emerged in the United States to combat legal positivism. Comparative economic analysis of

135 D. Law and M. Versteeg, *The Evolution and Global Constitutionalism*, in *California Law Review*, 99, 2011, p. 1163 ff.

136 A. Meuwese and M. Versteeg, *Quantitative Methods for Comparative Constitutional Law*, in M. Adams and J. Bomhoff (Eds.), *Practice and Theory in Comparative Law*, Cambridge and New York NY, 2012, p. 255.

law would benefit from the functional analysis typical of economics and would also borrow from it reliable tools for measuring the similarities and differences. However, the combination with the economic analysis of law gives comparative law a precise ideological bias: by elevating efficiency as a criterion for measuring rules, the former leads to the discrediting of state intervention in the market and is therefore a catalyst for neoliberal solutions.

5. Comparison is quantitative when it takes place between laws reduced to their numerical dimension and may be unavoidable when an extremely large number of legal systems are to be compared. It is usually used to promote a neoliberal point of view on market regulation, although there are examples of its use for other purposes. Quantitative comparison can produce indicators; i.e. it can have normative valence, but only if it is practised within institutions that are considered authoritative and internationally influential. This valence is insidious because indicators are presented as the fruit of a technocratic approach which neutralises democratic participation.

6. The Doing Business Reports produced by the World Bank are the best-known example of a quantitative comparison whose indicators are subordinated to a neoliberal project: the promotion of neo-American capitalism. Business Ready, the project that replaced them, formally sought to distinguish itself from the Reports because it departed from the point of view of the individual enterprise and takes into account that of the private sector and even of society as a whole. It additionally considers the activities and infrastructures put in place by the public authorities for the benefit of economic operators and the market. In reality, Business Ready remains anchored in the underlying philosophy of the Doing Business Reports: a vibrant private sector is seen as crucial to ending extreme poverty and promoting shared prosperity, thus reducing social inclusion to market inclusion.

7. Among scholars of comparative public law, the methodological debate largely follows that of comparative private lawyers. The former also resort to structuralism and the dissociation between formants, or on occasions criticise them as unifying forms of comparison. Comparative public lawyers also use functional analysis, although most are wary of the related idea of apolitical law, which is incompatible with their discipline. Some comparative public lawyers identify critical comparison as a third methodological approach, describing it in terms similar to those used by comparative private lawyers to describe postmodern comparative law.

CHAPTER 10

THE DISSOCIATION BETWEEN TECHNIQUES AND VALUES

1 LEGAL COMPARISON, LAW, AND SOCIETY

We have discussed how to compare, evaluating the different methods from the point of view of whether the comparison results in emphasising similarities or, on the contrary, differences. And we have added that these are the benchmarks for identifying the method best suited to the aims of the comparative lawyer (IV.1.5).

With regard to the objects of comparison – what is to be compared – it has been argued that all the rules that govern the imperative distribution of resources and values must be taken into account. This includes not only merely valid rules, but also effective rules, whether they are created by formal sources of law or by those who actually have the power to direct individual and collective behaviour (I.2.1). This has allowed us to identify a common thread or, in any case, a theme that is always present, at least in a hidden way: the ability or inability of the law – in the broad sense here explained – to condition individual behaviour and to shape society, that is, to be an 'organising force of the political community'.[1]

To affirm this ability, and thus to believe in the possibility that society is the mirror of the law, is not to reject the opposite idea that the law is the mirror of society (III.1.3). After all, a given structure of power is destined not to endure if the superstructure that supports it does not also reflect the real relations of power. Also, acknowledging the capacity of the law to direct behaviour does not mean believing in the one-to-one correspondence of technical-legal constructions and concrete modes of exercising power because, at the very least, the law is composed of rules whose meaning is obtained through interpretation. The latter is an activity that is both cognitive and creative (I.1.4), and to which one must ascribe political rather than philosophical value (I.2.1). The result is that several legal constructions can express the same mode of exercising power, and the same legal construction can coordinate with several modes of power.

In analysing the purposes of comparison, we have come across approaches that express, or at least presuppose, the conviction that law is an effective instrument for directing human behaviour. This is particularly true of the approaches cultivated by the New Institutional Economics, which was created with the precise objective of studying the influences of law on behaviour relevant to the functioning of the market (II.3.6). However, the relationship between law and society is questioned by those who reconstruct the Western legal tradition as the product of a professional class operating according to a culture that developed autonomously within the circle of its adherents. In this way, it is not denied that society reflects the law but rather that the law reflects society. It is assumed that the law can guide behaviour, but without reference to the internal power relations within society. The same is done by comparative lawyers who, from a diffusionist perspective, explain legal change as a chain of

1 L. Moccia, *Comparazione giuridica e diritto europeo*, Milano, 2005, p. 4.

DOI: 10.4324/9781032684499-14

transplants that are also the result of decisions made and controlled by legal scholars (III.1.3): a belief also shared by proponents of the structuralist method (IV.2.1).

The comparison that is carried out in the context of the New Institutional Economics, i.e. the research to which the New Comparative Economics is devoted (II.3.6), not only takes up the acceptable idea of a direct link between law and society, or rather between law and the economic order,[2] but also supports the one-to-one correspondence of technical-legal constructions and concrete modes of imperative redistribution of resources and values. This latter belief does not seem tenable, at least if one wants to overcome outdated approaches such as those inspired by legal positivism (I.1.2), which have long since been rejected by comparative lawyers.

In economics, this has been emphasised in particular by regulatory theorists. This trend emerged in France at the beginning of the 1970s also in order to emphasise the link between the economic order and society. Indeed, regulatory theorists distinguish between the 'accumulation regime' or growth model supported by the different varieties of capitalism and the associated institutional architecture or 'mode of regulation'. More precisely, they discern between patterns of production and consumption that are stable over time, and the wider discipline of market and social relations that is deemed necessary to stabilise and pacify these patterns.[3]

If we take this distinction into account, we can see, for example, that Fordism, the growth model based on mass production and consumption, which reached its crisis point in the 1970s, was fuelled by several models of capitalism, which therefore differ significantly only from the point of view of the institutional architecture considered most appropriate each time. This is particularly evident when comparing the US-American and French experiences in the post–World War II period. They both adopted the Keynesian framework (II.2.9), but did so differently with regard to the extent of state intervention in the market, and yet both were aimed at the maintenance of mass production and consumption. The same can be said of the growth model established after the crisis of Fordism, based on flexible and differentiated production and consumption, often referred to as post-Fordism.[4] Here, too, the withdrawal of public powers and the expansion of the market may present themselves in a more or less accentuated manner and thus give rise to different institutional architectures, all of which are nevertheless aimed at supporting the new growth model.[5]

A similar approach to that just described characterises many of the contributions by comparative lawyers committed to documenting the absence of a one-to-one correspondence of law and society. One think of the distinction between the technical and the ideological level, the latter corresponding to the political and cultural preferences in a given context, which underlies David's classifications of systems (II.2.1). The emphasis on the differences between concepts and solutions, or between 'the structure of an institution and its real function', recurring among advocates of the functional analysis, is another example (IV.2.2).[6]

The indication that a dissociation must be made between legal techniques and the values to whose implementation these techniques are directed is, in fact, the most important methodological recommendation regardless of the comparison one wishes to promote: whether unifying comparison or aimed at making identities emerge. It follows that a link between society and law can be identified, but only at the discursive level as an essentially unstable

2 G. Ajani, *Ruling by Indicators: How the Use of Vague Notions and Quantitative Indicators Facilitates Legal Change*, in *Cardozo Electronic Law Bulletin*, 23, 2017, p. 5.
3 Among others R. Boyer, *The Regulation School: A Critical Introduction*, New York NY, 1990.
4 For instance, V. Codeluppi, *Il biocapitalismo*, Torino, 2008, p. 21 ff.
5 For instance, R. Boyer and Y. Saillard, *A Summary of Regulation Theory*, in Iid. (Ed.), *Regulation Theory. The State of the Art* (1995), London and New York NY, 2001, p. 36 ff.
6 T. Ascarelli, *La funzione del diritto comparato e il nostro sistema di diritto privato* (1949), in Id. (Ed.), *Studi di diritto comparato e in tema di interpretazione*, Milano, 1952, p. 57 f.

relationship between the techniques used by power – of which law is only one – and the values that the power seeks to promote – including through the control over the legal discourse – in order to first assert and then perpetuate itself.

This applies, of course, to synchronic comparison or comparison between objects placed in the same temporal context. But it is also, and above all, true of diachronic comparison, which involves the historical dimension.[7] There, we are confronted with concepts that may seem timeless, but which, despite their terminological continuity, present ruptures at the semantic level. These ruptures are often cleverly concealed, as in the case of the Neopandectists, in order to suggest the existence of traditions, when the intention is simply one of legitimising power structures through their rootedness in historical experience (I.2.4).

By proposing to disassociate techniques and values, we do not wish to argue that this will result in a more faithful reconstruction of historical ruptures and continuities. Both will be more or less accentuated or diminished depending on the background aims of the comparative investigation, which also determines whether differences or similarities between the objects compared will be exalted. More simply, the dissociation between techniques and values is intended to underline the potential of analyses focusing on the discursive dimension of law, to highlight the complexity that characterises the evolution of meanings, or rather of the control over meanings, attributed to legal language.

The transition from one meaning to another has phases in which the new coexists with the old, before the new becomes dominant and finally self-evident. These are the phases in which the struggle for the imperative distribution of values and resources are more visible, in which continuities and ruptures appear in the succession of power structures, in which law reveals its essence as a technique placed at the service of the values around which social conflict occurs. This is the approach that the comparative lawyer must emphasise in his research in order to highlight the discursive dimension of law, and then show how it has no one-to-one correspondence with the values that the power seeks to promote through law.

In many respects, it appears easier to investigate the dissociation between techniques and values when addressing particularly broad concepts and even references to a legal system as a whole, whether current or from the past. That is, for instance, the case of Roman law, used to support the most different power structures, in addition to what is indicated by Neopandectism. However, the sequence of cultural aspects encompassed in legal technicism can also emerge from the use of specific concepts. We will see this, for example, when considering the concepts used to describe the structure of contractual consent.

In any case, we should not forget that the study carried out by comparative law scholars is intimately subjective: 'it is nothing but the answer to a question that he himself has formulated in a context in which his questioning leaves whole aspects in the shadows'[8] – hence, the constructivist nature of comparative law, which can aim at exalting analogies or differences, as well as continuities and ruptures: the only points of reference for evaluating the methodology applied by their scholars.

2 THE USE OF ROMAN LAW: LEGITIMISING POWER

The analysis of power and its strategies have as its fundamental point of reference the Weberian distinction between rational and traditional 'legitimate domination': the former

7 See G. Ajani, D. Francavilla and B. Pasa, *Diritto comparato* (Questioni di metodo), vol. 1, Torino, 2023, p. 1.
8 P. Legrand, *Le droit comparé*, Paris, 1999, p. 15 f.

based on the 'belief on the legality of enacted rules', the latter on the 'established belief in the sanctity' of practices rooted in time.[9] For both forms of power, the reference to Roman law has played and continues to play a prominent role. It is indeed a law that has inspired the construction of a systematics suitable for any time and place, and at the same time is endowed with a long and prestigious tradition. In this double guise, with varying emphasis on the first or the second aspect, Roman law has been used to lend prestige to the most varied political and cultural operations.

We will mention only a few emblematic cases, starting with the events of the Enlightenment. This was the era in which the old holistic certainties were deemed irrational, and replaced by scientific criteria aimed at defining man's place within the order of nature (I.1.1). Calls were then made to overcome the arbitrary classifications of medieval origin and to realise what was summed up in the formula 'property belongs to the citizen, and empire to the sovereign' (I.2.3).

The French Civil Code of 1804 implemented this scheme by invoking Roman law, primarily to justify the actions of the sovereign as the guardian of the balance referred to in that formula. Justinian was evoked, who by 'rummaging, mutilating, and recomposing old materials foreign to the society of his times', had crafted a text to be elevated as a model for those called to accomplish 'the heroic task of a unique code'.[10]

In short, codified civil law was celebrated as it realized a synthesis of Roman provisions, considered a source of 'written reason' and 'elementary rules of equity'.[11] It was the product of a rational and traditional political power, recognised by the class that emerged victorious from the French Revolution, confident in its role as protector of the individual economic sphere. In fact, the French Civil Code reflected the transition from a society where relations were based on status, to a society in which those relations were shaped by the free agreement between citizens. In other words, it reflected the movement from status to contract (III.1.2) and sheltered it from the 'awesome power of judging' precisely because the norms conformed to the coherent schemes of Roman law rather than the obscure ones of customary law. In the words of its main draftsman, Jean-Étienne-Marie Portalis:

> France, at one time divided into countries of customary law and countries of written law, was governed partly by customs, and partly by written law. . . . Written law, which is made up of Roman laws, has civilised Europe. Our forefathers' discovery of the Justinian Compilation was a kind of revelation for them. It was then that our courts assumed a more regular form, and the awesome power of judging became subject to principles. Most authors who criticise Roman law as bitterly as they do rashly, blaspheme that of which they are ignorant. One is soon convinced of this if, in the collections that have brought this law down to us, he can distinguish those laws worthy of being termed written reason, from those that concerned only specific institutions, foreign to our situation and our customs.[12]

The close correspondence between the civil law resulting from the Revolution and Justinian's Corpus Juris was explicitly highlighted in works devoted to comparing the two systems.[13] It was the political power, moreover, that organised the teaching of French Code 'by comparing it with Roman laws': laws that were considered rational in that they had been

9 M. Weber, *Economy and Society* (1922), Los Angeles CA and London, 1978, p. 215.
10 Preface, in G.B.M. Toullier, *Il diritto civile francese secondo l'ordine del codice*, 3rd ed., Napoli, 1837, p. 2.
11 A.R. Bousquet, *Explication du Code Civil*, vol. 3, Paris, 1805, p. 183.
12 J.-E.-M. Portalis, *Preliminary Address on the First Draft of the Civil Code* (1801), https://www.justice.gc.ca/eng/rp-pr/csj-sjc/ilp-pji/code/page02.html.
13 For instance, H.-J.-B., *Code civil des français avec des notes indicatives des lois romaines*, new ed., Paris, 1807.

able to realise 'the accumulation of the wisdom of two peoples, the wisest – the Greeks and the Romans – who had ever witnessed the ages of the world'.[14] The combined rational and traditional character of codified French law based on Roman law thus made it possible to transform rules based on individual self-determination, i.e. sensitive to the economic and social realities of the time, into universal rules.

References to Roman law also characterised the historicist reaction to Enlightened rationalism, and in particular the reaction within the Historical School founded by Friedrich Carl von Savigny. Law was described as a phenomenon rooted in local traditions (I.1.1): as a product of the 'popular spirit' springing from 'the essence of the nation and its history'.[15] This led to a redefinition of the foundations of political power, which could no longer be found in its ability to be the interpreter of a rational and thus timeless order.[16] Those foundations were discredited for their connection with the French Revolution and their symbols – first and foremost the codification of civil law – which was opposed in the name of the Restoration. This was so much so that the Austrian General Civil Code of 1811, while regulating the economic order in terms similar to those of the French codification, had to present itself as the product of romantic nationalist conceptions in order to resist the anti-revolutionary reaction.

These conceptions formed the backdrop for the two main currents that influenced German culture at the time: that of national and liberal inspiration, which emphasised the production of law by the popular spirit, and that of a conservative Christian inspiration, in the name of which the way was paved for the codification of civil law. The two currents produced discourses around law with articulate references to Roman law, which were thus confirmed as effective vehicles for both traditional and rational power.

These references were initially used to emphasise the temporal dimension of the legal phenomenon and thus the traditional value of the solutions proposed. In fact, the intention was to discredit the Enlightenment tendency to believe that 'law arises from the arbitrariness of the people to whom the power to legislate is entrusted' and that it is 'dictated by mere opinion and by the inspiration of the moment, regardless of the tradition of past centuries'.[17] This tendency was criticised because it led to neglecting the question of the foundations of the norms of social life, i.e. because it led to accepting that they are at the mercy of rapidly changing power relations.

Subsequently, the temporal dimension of references to Roman law, which was essentially intended as a history of doctrines, ceased to be emphasised.[18] That law became the incarnation of a system whose placement in time was not concealed, but which was nevertheless celebrated for the same characteristics recognised to the Roman era during the times of rational law by those who wondered:

> Is there any other history that has the right to capture the attention of legislators more than Roman history, that offers more varied and magnificent examples, and that, in the succession of ever great events, more imperiously commands admiration, and at the same time offers a wider range of salutary instructions either in the art of taming the enemy or in the perhaps more difficult art of governing the citizen?[19]

14 O. Taglioni, *Al lettore*, in *Codice civile di Napoleone il Grande col confronto delle Leggi romane*, Milano, 1809, p. v ff.
15 F.C. von Savigny, *Ueber den Zweck dieser Zeitschrift*, in *Zeitschrift für geschichtliche Rechtswissenschaft*, 1, 1815, p. 6.
16 See F. De Marini, *La politica del diritto di Savigny*, in *Politica del diritto*, 1979, p. 423 ff.
17 F.C. von Savigny, *Ueber den Zweck dieser Zeitschrift*, cit., p. 6.
18 A. Mazzacane, *Pandettistica*, in *Enciclopedia del diritto*, vol. 31, Milano, 1981, p. 603 ff.
19 N. Bettoni, *La storia romana di Tito Livio*, vol. 1, Brescia, 1804, p. iii f.

This is how, within the conservative-inspired historicist current, studies were devoted to 'modern Roman law',[20] which moved from 'the work accomplished by our predecessors' and had the purpose of 'removing the spurious but of appropriating to ourselves the true as a lasting possession'. All this in order to construct a system at the service of the practitioner, conceived as the 'summarizing of that which in individual cases, he is to become conscious of an apply', and also to 'prepare legislators so that legislation and case law proceed in close connection with each other'.[21]

The recovery of the nexus between Roman law and systematic approach to law, i.e. between history and logic, ended up making the former suitable for the legitimation of rational power. Indeed, the system was perceived as a 'natural' construction, as 'knowledge and exhibition of the innate connexion or of the relationship, by which the single ideas and rules of law are attached to a great unity'.[22] The rationalising potential of references to Roman law was exaggerated by those who praised the spirit of the people as a unanimous manifestation, detached from the real context, capable of producing coherent normative constructions that could only be understood through legal science (I.1.1).[23] The rational power legitimised by the discourses around Roman law thus ceased to be that of the legislator. After all, German political power at the time was characterised by a strong territorial fragmentation, thus finding itself incapable of effectively expressing the level of economic and social development of the period and meeting the related demands for the unification of law.

In this situation, Pandectists were able to accredit themselves as the source of a system of rules centred on the autonomy of the will and therefore in line with those demands. As Windscheid stated:

> Pandect law is German common private law of Roman origin. Common German private law is that German private law that applies to Germany as Germany, to Germany as a whole. This common German private law is only partly of indigenous origin. In the other parts, and these are the predominant ones, it is based on received foreign law, and among these, Roman law occupies the main place.[24]

A few years after Windscheid's words, German political unity was reached and followed by the enactment of the *Bürgerliches Gesetzbuch*, the Civil Code of 1896. In this context, the references to Roman law were clearly not intended to delegitimise the production of law by the sovereign, who was with unification finally able to centralise political power and guarantee the centralisation of economic power in the hands of the individual. The purpose of these references was merely to ensure that there would be considerable scope for legal scholarship (I.1.1), which would not be reduced to the role reserved for it by the Enlightenment: that of a pale exegete of the words of the legislator.

At the time of its adoption, it was widely believed that the German Civil Code was the last fruit of the 19th century rather than the prelude to the 20th: it was considered as the statute of a society in decline. This aspect was at the centre of the Romanist and Germanist controversy, which accompanied the drafting of the German Civil Code and which represented a split from within the Historical School.

Initially, the differences concerned only the object of study, namely, whether the popular spirit should be associated with Roman or Germanic law. Over time, the division of scholarly focus turned into an ideological opposition on the nature of private law, with Roman law being

20 J.F.L. Göschen, *Vorlesungen über das gemeine Civilrecht*, vol. 1, Göttingen, 1838, p. 6.
21 F.C. von Savigny, *System of the Modern Roman Law*, vol. 1 (1840), Madras, 1867, pp. iii and xi.
22 *Ivi*, p. xix.
23 G.F. Puchta, *Cursus der Institutionen*, 6th ed., vol. 1, Leipzig, 1865, p. 32.
24 B. Windscheid, *Lehrbuch des Pandektenrechts*, 2nd ed., vol. 1, Düsseldorf, 1867, p. 1 f.

used to support constructions with an individualist inspiration and Germanic law responding to constructions centred on the primacy of the collective interest. When the first draft of the German Civil Code was prepared in the late 1880s, the Germanists, in the words of Otto Gierke, regarded it as the product of 'a Romanist intellectual effort untouched by the Germanic spirit':

> If one considers this project as a whole, i.e. apart from a few well-executed details, if it is analysed from top to bottom in order to identify the spirit that animates it, then it may perhaps present some praiseworthy features. However, it is not German, it is not popular, it is not creative, and furthermore, the social task of a new private law system does not seem to be on its horizon. . . . Admittedly, there are ample concessions to modern and German law, many Romanist institutions in a vegetative state of existence are left out, and numerous local models are accepted, without which a law for the present age would not even be conceivable. But the soul of the entire construction, from foundation to summit, originates from a Romanist intellectual effort untouched by the Germanic spirit.[25]

The equation of Roman law with individualism, together with the negative connotation of both, thus became a constant in the discourses of the advocates of a socially sensitive German private law. This equation also made it possible to expose the discrepancy between Romanist schemes and those necessary to support forms of economic development in line with the evolution of liberal theories at the end of the 19th century. In fact, even the latter showed a growing impatience with individualist principles, which were considered as a basis for rules unsuitable to promote capitalist modernisation (II.1.7). In order to restore harmony between law and society, it was necessary to combine liberating and ordering instances, the latter being incompatible with the traditional use of Roman law.

3 NEXT: SUPPORTING AND FIGHTING FASCISM

In France and Italy too, references to Roman law played a certain role in the movement to reinterpret civil law in the light of economic trends. The latter inspired criticism of the rules that had 'found their legal formulation in classical Roman law' and neglected supra-individual consequences of individual behaviour: in particular its 'social function' (II.1.2).[26] It was now widely believed that Roman law was unsuitable for 'cementing the agreement of individual interest with the general and social interest'.[27]

To cope with the consequences of World War I, a chaotic legislative production was needed, which at least reflected irreversible tendencies towards the overcoming of individualistic patterns.[28] This is exemplified in Italy by Nicolò Gallo, minister of justice at the beginning of the 20th century, in the report accompanying the measure establishing a commission for the reform of private law. There he stigmatised in particular the law of property:

> The doctrine of property, almost abstractly considered, without or with minimal regard to its social function, was an error of the old legal conception, as it was an error of life. . . . Therefore the pure Roman definitions, legitimately acquired to modern law by secular observance with appropriate modifications, now need new integrations more in keeping with the present reality.[29]

25 O. Gierke, *Der Entwurf eines Bürgerlichen Gesetzbuchs und das deutsche Recht*, Leipzig, 1889, p. 2 f.
26 L. Duguit, *Les transformations générales du droit privé depuis le Code Napoléon*, 2nd ed., Paris, 1920, pp. 16 and 147 ff.
27 B. Brugi, *Introduzione enciclopedica alle scienze giuridiche e sociali*, 4th ed., Milano, 1907, p. 227.
28 See A. Somma, *Verso la grande trasformazione. Il primo conflitto mondiale e la disciplina dell'ordine economico nell'esperienza italiana*, in *Historia et ius*, 2019, p. 1 ff.
29 E. Bruni, *Socialismo e diritto privato*, Milano, 1910, p. 301.

In short, World War I had definitively demolished individualism (II.1.4). It had highlighted all the implications of the transition from bourgeois society to industrial society, first of all those connected to class division (II.2.4). This fuelled attempts to overcome the capitalist order following the example of the October Revolution, but also and above all the search for an alternative to classical liberalism as well as socialism.

Both Italy and Germany experienced a particular alternative. This was fascism, defined at the time as the third way beyond traditional liberalism and socialism (II.1.3), which was, in essence, a reform of economic liberalism achieved through the abolition of political liberalism.[30] In both Germany and Italy, the new course was accompanied by references to Roman law, adjusted to reflect the different construction of national identity in the two dictatorships. Those differences related to the use of Roman law as an instrument through which to identify the foundation of traditional forms of power, as fascist power was in many respects.

In Germany, the Nazis even addressed Roman law in their party's first programme, drafted at the beginning of 1920. The rhetoric there is similar to the one found in the Germanist literature (IV.3.2), such as in particular the idea that this law 'serves the materialistic world order', which is why they demanded it to be 'replaced by a general German law'.[31]

The bridge between the Germanist literature and the emerging Nazi legal thought, i.e. the deformation of Otto Gierke's thought including its association with racial issues, was built by a second-rate scholar: Arnold Wagemann. He described Roman law as a system that was perhaps an example to be imitated as far as forms were concerned, but which had to be rejected in terms of its contents, in particular those pertaining to the modes of exercising political power. For Wagemann, they were based on 'constraint' and therefore clashed with the Germanic idea of *Führertum*, which was instead centred on the concept of 'authoritativeness'.[32]

Wagemann then went on to discuss the characteristics of Germanic law as opposed to Roman law: the latter places the emphasis on individual's discretion, the former on the individual's obligations towards the community. This community was identified, like the concept of *Führertum*, on the basis of the ethnic origin of its members. More precisely:

> Since Roman law recognised only legitimations, the subject of law was the individual person, the single man, and he was the sole lord whose interests inspired the only directives for the formation of legal norms. In this way, rights were created that were not limited by duties and were conferred on their holder without consideration for the type of assets involved or the purpose of their acquisition. The Germanic conception never started from the non-binding character of human will. It has always sought to examine the consequences attributable to the type of acquisition of individual goods and how much leeway could be allowed to anyone without harming the interests of permanent institutions.[33]

Nazi literature made it clear that the attack was directed at Roman law following its transposition into Germany. It was seen as the victim of oriental and therefore non-Aryan interpolations, and for this reason as an instrument of the state to be wielded against the people, with the complicity of a science devoted to the apolitical and non-evaluative study of law. Quite different praise was reserved for Roman law 'of the first three hundred years', considered a monument of the past to be honoured as a 'racist' order of a 'Nordic people'.[34] That

30 See A. Somma, *I giuristi e l'Asse culturale Roma-Berlino. Economia e politica nel diritto fascista e nazionalsocialista*, Frankfurt M., 2005, p. 81 ff.
31 Point 19 of the Programme of the *Nationalsozialistische Deutsche Arbeiterpartei* of 24 February 1920.
32 A. Wagemann, *Geist des deutschen Rechts*, Jena, 1913, pp. 1 and 48.
33 *Ivi*, p. 28.
34 H. Frank, *Die Zeit des Rechts*, in *Deutsches Recht*, 1936, p. 1 ff.

Roman law was a legal order not yet undermined by conceptualism and was thus capable of providing the foundation for multiple constructions:

> For us jurists, the Roman creativity in producing law can be an example. This moved from the individual case and not from a system of rigid rules, issued decision after decision wisely, deviated, discarded, retraced its steps, opened up new avenues, and doing so notwithstanding the great decisional directives. It thus obtained, by means of a comprehensive direction, a legal science that did not float in the sky of concepts but kept both feet on the ground of the practice of law. . . . A systematising dogmatics drowned this ductility in the Byzantine era, considered obscure and contradictory the different possibilities of issuing decisions with which to break the rigidity of principles and to envisage multiple decisional models.[35]

Obviously, Italian fascism's references to Roman law were of a different tenor, particularly suited to evoking a tradition considered to be an essential part of the entire national history. Moreover, the Italian dictatorship, unlike the German one, was able to invoke a continuity with the immediately preceding period and its references to Roman law. The pre-fascist state was the expression of an authoritarian culture, the opposite of what the Weimar experience had intended to embody. In short, it was easy and rhetorically powerful for fascist Italy to repeat that the law 'came from Rome',[36] and that the revolution made by Mussolini represented 'the return to Roman greatness'.[37]

It is no wonder, then, that the fascists emphasised the Roman origin of the Civil Code of 1942. Despite the numerous crises proclaimed by those who considered it unsuitable for the construction of a non-individualist type of legal system, Roman law was in fact celebrated as the foundation of the Civil Code. In Putzolu's words:

> It relates directly to the tradition of Italic Roman law, our law, which all nations have plundered and often smuggled in as their own, and which we, in the age of guilty acquiescence, have at times re-imported under a foreign label, with the relative contaminations and deformations. . . . In order to understand this truth – which every fascist feels instinctively palpitating in the depths of his heart – it is not enough to say that this is the fundamental Code of a Nation of imperial stature and destiny, but it is above all necessary to remember that it lays down the tables regulating a new life, inspired by the principles of the revolution that is already triumphing in the spirits and arms of Europe and is soon destined to spread and assert itself throughout the world.[38]

Hence, the effort of fascist literature to legitimise the regime by exalting, in propagandistic terms, any identification between Roman tradition and the fascist order, thus documenting 'the intimate relations between Roman civilisation and culture and the civilisation and culture established by fascism in Italy'.[39] These relations were also capable of being the basis for autarchic and racist policies. For Grandi:

> Italic Roman law is the living law of the authoritarian, hierarchical, expansionist Roman state: the law of human common sense, and therefore universal. For the same reasons, we fascists have opposed the concept of latinity, which under an artificial universalist pretext tended towards the political pre-eminence of others, with the idea of romanity, which bears the fatal and unmistakable mark of our first-born race in the face of the races civilised by Rome.[40]

35 H. Lange, *Deutsche Romanistik?*, in *Deutsche Juristen-Zeitung*, 1934, c. 1499 f.
36 So Mussolini at the first 'Congresso giuridico italiano', in *Rivista penale*, 1932, p. 1299 ff.
37 P. De Francisci, *Ai giuristi italiani (Discorso inaugurale del I Congresso giuridico italiano)*, in *Lo Stato*, 1932, p. 674.
38 A. Putzolu, *Panorama del Codice civile fascista*, in *Rivista di diritto civile*, 1941, p. 396.
39 F. Casetti, *Leggi romane e leggi fasciste*, Roma, 1937, p. 3.
40 D. Grandi, *Tradizione e rivoluzione dei Codici mussoliniani*, Roma, 1940, p. 10.

It is curious at this point that, at the end of the Second World War, it was precisely a new emphasis on its connection with liberal culture that determined the fate of references to Roman law in Italy. In literature, the Roman roots of civil codification were again emphasised, capable of promoting a new individualism that could be reborn from the ashes of the totalitarian state. In other words, it was said that the 1942 Code did not have a 'fascist imprint' because it had been modelled on previous texts and doctrines. For this reason, it would have been easy to 'defascistise' it, that is, to recover the liberal tradition of the old plant by simply eliminating the 'new sprouts'.[41]

Statements of the same tenor were sometimes mediated by references to natural law, which, according to an approach inspired by the Enlightenment, was considered to have revealed itself in Roman law. The discourses of the jurists were thus returned to the function of validating the exercise of power by exalting the ahistorical and rational character of the acts of that power.

All this, while the authors sympathetic to fascism had emphasised what they considered the main characteristic of the 'current Roman law': the fact that it constituted a 'systematic method' based on principles that 'resist any new codification' and 'adapt themselves wonderfully to the new social demands', making it possible to express the contents contained even in the 'new social legislation'.[42] In this sense it was concluded that 'everything has changed from the point of view of content and value', but 'nothing has changed from the point of view of technique'.[43]

In this way, even the liberal code became compatible with fascist values and documented the merger of tradition and revolution, that is, 'the constant harmony of the new with the old order'. As Francesco Santoro Passarelli pointed out during the fascist era:

> In order for the civil code to continue proving for the future that our present social and political order also had to and could build up its own private law, it is not necessary to subvert the institutions of the family, property, contracts and inheritance. Indeed, such a civil code would have no mould of its own today. It is necessary and sufficient for the new civil legislator, in dictating his rules, to be attentive to those connections that bind all the various aspects of the law, which is one, to our current social and political reality, to the tendencies of legal scholars and more so of courts, which lives in daily contact with life, following its transformations and possibly adapting to these.[44]

From this point of view, the so-called mere rhetorical concessions to the political power made by scholars that wanted to present themselves, if not as anti-fascist, then at least as non-fascist, are particularly important. For the advocates of a reading of the fascist era as a mere parenthesis in national history, they were no more than a frill to be attached to speeches with an intimate liberal attitude. However, it was precisely this frill that contributed to the 'renewal of the law' that was 'inadvertently achieved through interpretation'[45] by reading the code 'in the context of all the often far more important norms in life that are outside it'.[46]

4 NEXT: PROMOTING SOCIALISM

Additional proofs of the versatility of Roman law are provided by its use in connection with a Marxist theory of law. Before considering this aspect, we must mention the traditional

41 B. Biondi, *Il diritto romano cristiano*, vol. 1, Milano, 1952, p. 55.
42 F.S. Azzariti, G. Martinez and G. Azzariti, *Diritto civile italiano*, 2nd ed., vol. 1, Padova, 1943, p. v.
43 G. Perticone, *Sui principî generali dell'ordinamento giuridico*, in Facoltà di giurisprudenza etc. (Eds.), *Studi sui principî generali dell'ordinamento giuridico*, Pisa, 1943, p. 56.
44 F. Santoro Passarelli, *Il diritto civile nell'ora presente*, in *Rivista italiana per le scienze giuridiche*, 1933, p. 62 f.
45 F. Ferrara, *Rinnovamento del diritto civile secondo i postulati fascisti*, in *Archivio di studi corporativi*, 1940, p. 44.
46 F. Vassalli, *Motivi e caratteri della codificazione civile* (1942), in *Rivista italiana per le scienze giuridiche*, 1947, p. 96.

aversion of its proponents to Roman law, which is regarded as the very basis of the 'bourgeois' and 'imperialist' West.[47]

More precisely, Roman law is seen as a superstructure that has established and reproduced social systems in which 'the inequalities of men had a much greater weight than any equality'[48]: its role was to supervise power relations between free men and slaves, and later those consistent with a society ruled by a merchant class.[49] References to Roman law have then accompanied class conflicts whether they be those typical of the feudal age, with the clash between landowners and workers on other people's land, or those resulting from the abolition of feudalism with the French Revolution.

Karl Marx himself, who had had the opportunity to follow Savigny's lectures in Berlin, points to Roman law as the moment of validation of normative systems centred on 'pure private property, which has cast off all semblance of a communal institution and has shut out the state from any influence on the development of property'. Precisely:

> Civil law develops simultaneously with private property out of the disintegration of the natural community. With the Romans the development of private property and civil law had no further industrial and commercial consequences, because their whole mode of production did not alter. . . . As soon as industry and trade developed private property further, first in Italy and later in other countries, the highly developed Roman civil law was immediately adopted again and raised, to authority. When later the bourgeoisie had acquired so much power that the princes took up its interests in order to overthrow the feudal nobility by means of the bourgeoisie, there began in all countries – in France in the sixteenth century – the real development of law, which in all countries except England proceeded on the basis of the Roman Codex. In England, too, Roman legal principles had to be introduced to further the development of civil law (especially in the case of movable property).[50]

When Roman law became the law of the bourgeoisie, and thus the instrument for overthrowing feudal society, it helped to create the conditions for the emergence of a classless society: it is therefore necessary to be 'grateful to Roman law, which favoured the historical function of the bourgeoisie'.[51] Moreover, the advent of the classless society presupposes that the function of law as a superstructure of bourgeois societies is finally revealed (II.3.8). In particular, it presupposes the recognition of how references to Roman law feed 'the illusion that law is the primary foundation of society' and not, on the contrary, the translation into normative terms of power structures functional to the promotion and maintenance of a given system of production. As Tumanov states:

> The legal forms of simple commodity production, as we encounter them historically in Roman private law, proved to be not only useful, but also necessary for capitalist production relations. . . . Roman law is an accomplished law of simple commodity production, i.e. of pre-capitalist commodity production, which, however, is also adapted to capitalist commodity production. . . . The bourgeois codification of private law in the 19th century certainly included non-Roman elements. Nevertheless, it developed from the reception of Roman law.[52]

On closer inspection, not all Marxist scholars agree with such statements. Some consider the idea that slavery is 'the main factor in the Roman legal experience' to be anti-historical,

47 For instance, J. Göring et al., *Grundfragen des sozialistischen Zivilrechts*, Berlin, 1979, p. 50.
48 F. Engels, *Antidühring* (1877), Roma, 1968, p. 109 ff.
49 For instance, M. Bartosek, *La periodizzazione del diritto romano*, in A. Guarino and L. Labruna (Eds.), *Synteleia Vincenzo Arangio-Ruiz*, Napoli, 1964, p. 1149 ff.
50 K. Marx, *The German Ideology* (1845), New York NY, 1970, p. 80 f.
51 G. Solari, *Socialismo e diritto privato*, cit., p. 18 nt. 32.
52 W.A. Tumanow, *Kritik der bürgerlichen Rechtsideologie* (1971), Berlin, 1975, p. 213.

and attribute the equation 'Roman law-capitalism' to the 'persistence of the Pandectist ideal'. Such an equation would thus apply not to historical Roman law, rather to the Romanist tradition.[53] Others conclude that, from this point of view, Roman law does not constitute an order based on individualist values, or at least that they are balanced by other characteristics. These characteristics are not of the collectivist character evoked by fascist literature (IV.3.3), but those in which the supremacy of the legal order over the individual act is a means of strengthening the point of view of the weak.

This view is confirmed to a certain extent by the research which seeks to document the existence of a Romanist substratum in the civil law of the socialist countries (II.3.8). It is supported, in particular, by Francesco De Martino, according to whom in Roman law 'the individual will has a very modest place':

> The claimed Roman individualistic tendencies are summed up in the vigour of the *pater*'s family powers and in the independence of property: both, however, are characteristics of an organism that had arisen as a political organism and as such had asserted itself free and autonomous from others. . . . The whole historical movement of private law developed, however, in the sense of receiving ideas and social forces into the positive legal system: Roman *aequitas* and Roman *bona fides*.[54]

Such defences do not aim at recovering Roman law as an instrument for implementing present policies, as it is the case for Neopandectism: they are mainly driven by the intention to promote historicising approaches. However, this is not the case for a journal published between 1999 and 2011 with the highly charged title 'Diritto romano attuale' (Current Roman Law), which contains also references to a Marxian, if not Marxist, vision of society.

The will to promote Roman law for present policies is evident: it is seen as a point of reference to build a 'conceptual system' different from that of Pandectism, but 'of equal scientific rigour', insofar as it aims to create a technique that is 'precise and stable in fundamental evaluations and flexible and mobile in case-by-case evaluations'. Instead, the assertions that legal science 'describes the evolution of the power relations between the interests present in society' – specifying that these are 'class relations' – are Marxian. The same applies to the remark, rather Marxist than Marxian, that the study of Roman law according to this model allows 'the transformation of legal solutions from one balance of class relations to another' – that is, from a situation of 'class domination' to one of 'pluralism of interests'.[55]

5 NEXT: RECONSTRUCTING EUROPEAN LAW

The use of Roman law to promote fascism or socialism may seem particularly far-fetched, but other uses are no less so, including the one we have already mentioned several times. That is its use in the construction of European private law by scholars on the basis of the common foundation of national laws (II.1.1). This has implications not only for the content of European law, but also for the role that scholars seek to play in contemporary societies (I.1.5). Indeed, they would have a considerable advantage in the competition with political and economic power: 'ancient Roman law may not be resurrected as a *norma iuris*, but may once again be

53 L. Raggi, *Materialismo storico e studio del diritto romano*, in *Rivista italiana per le scienze giuridiche*, 1955–1956, p. 596 f.
54 F. De Martino, *Individualismo e diritto romano privato*, in *Annuario di diritto comparato e studi legislativi*, 1943, p. 51.
55 *Il programma della rivista*, in *Diritto romano attuale*, 1999, p. 3 ff.

revived in the form of the literature of the case, the dominance of science over legislation, and the participation of jurists in jurisdiction'.[56]

Roman law, in short, should allow scholarship to return to being a formal source of law, or at least guarantee them a privileged place in the process of constructing the foundations of the law of the new millennium (II.1.5). We know that the term Neopandectism derives from this, and recalls the controversy surrounding the drafting of the German Civil Code, which the founder of the Historical School combated as he saw it as an obstacle to the constant renewal of the law through the popular spirit. We also know that first the Historical School and then the Pandectists were concerned above all at halting the loss of the power to create law, which had passed from scholars to legislators: This is the key link to the present phase of the making of European private law (I.1.1).

Links between the past and the present can also be found in the ideological inspiration of the rules drafted by Neopandectists. They are presented as neutral, in other words applicable regardless of the context in which they are applied, but are obviously designed for a bourgeois society. Indeed, the individualistic character of Roman contract law is presented as the point of reference for establishing the core of the common European tradition. In Zimmermann's words:

> That contracts based on nothing more than formless consent are, as a rule, actionable, is recognized today in all Western European legal systems. This is one of those latent underlying principles of European contract law. And this principle, like many others, is in characteristic fashion Roman and non-Roman at the same time: it is Roman law in modern clothing, no longer in a toga or in a medieval coat of mail.[57]

We know, however, that academics, as a professional class capable of expressing an autonomous idea of society, have had no influence whatsoever on the construction of European private law. They have merely been called upon to translate the political will to comply with neoliberal orthodoxy into technical formulae (II.1.5). And if this is true of academics in general, the verdict seems even more definitive for Neopandectism since the European institutions themselves consider the individualism of Roman law constructions unsuitable for an economic order centred on mass production and consumption. This can be seen in European Union documents that make this very point:

> Again, many of the national laws hark back to a time when manufacturing and marketing conditions were very different from what they are today. Traditional civil law rules governing the contract of sale were based on the paradigm of two equal citizens concluding a contract for the transfer of title from one to the other. Hence they are ill adapted to current manufacturing and marketing realities.[58]

In fact, neoliberalism is the ideology of industrial society rather than of bourgeois society: it does not condemn public authorities to inaction, but gives them the task of actively enforcing the functioning of the market. In this sense, neoliberalism overcomes individualism and promotes the dissolution of the individual. His behaviour must be functional to the development of the economic order and his social integration must be reduced to integration into the market (II.2.9).

56 F. Casavola, *Diritto romano e diritto europeo*, in *Labeo*, 1994, p. 168.
57 R. Zimmermann, *Roman Law and European Legal Unity*, in A. Hartkamp et al. (Eds.), *Towards a European Civil Code*, Nijmegen etc., 1994, p. 72.
58 *Proposal for a European Parliament and Council Directive on the sale of consumer goods and associated guarantees* of 18 June 1996, Com/1995/520 fin., p. 5.

If this is the case, the use of Roman law to promote capitalism as a cornerstone of the Western legal tradition seems destined to disappoint those who proposed it. Their aspiration to become 'a participant, albeit in a subordinate position, in the legal regulation of life' is destined to be frustrated.[59] Evidently, neither can one think of Roman law as the foundation of another cornerstone of the Western legal tradition: democracy. Although attempts to do so seem to surface in the statement that 'talking about European citizenship' makes 'sense if it means rediscovering the Roman *civis* and his dignity' and that ancient Rome promoted 'the recognition of human rights'.[60]

Instead, Roman law recurs in the reflections on Christianity as the third cornerstone of the Western legal tradition. That is to say, it is emphasised in its essence as the glue of the Christian West, in a rhetoric that may be derived from the conservative romanticism which was also invoked by Pandectism (II.2.3). Similar arguments are somewhat revived in the celebration of the historical common law, a reference model for today's constructions, as an order formed through the 'synergy of Christianity and Roman law', representing the 'constituent backbone of the history of Europe'.[61] All this is done to emphasise a contrast with the Islamicised East, just as was once done with the Sovietised East.[62] Broggini captures this mood:

> The new political identity, the *renovatio imperii romani*, arose from the fierce and violent struggle against Islam. . . . The Mediterranean Empire disappeared definitively and a new unity emerged in Charlemagne's *regna Francorum et Longobardorum*, who enlarged them and imposed on them the sceptre of Christian civilisation: *Imperium christianum*. The history of Roman law thus becomes, from Charlemagne onwards, the history of European law. . . . Neither the Byzantine tradition nor that of Islam participate in the evolution of the institutions of Roman law. The current influence of Roman law thus reflects the history of Europe and the borders of its civilisation, especially in relation to Islam. . . . Contrary to what one might think, it also encompasses the history of English law, which, developing independently, assimilates the essential values of classical Roman law.[63]

But even this use of Roman law seems unlikely, or at least destined to support a traditional power that does not need Roman law to brandish Christianity as an ideological glue. In terms of all three cornerstones of the Western legal tradition, then, this use appears to be a blunt weapon, limited to efforts to preserve or extend the power of the jurist in a society that has now turned to other fields of knowledge to find the tools for the technocratic governance of social life (I.1.5). Here too, however, these efforts are unable to halt the decline of the jurist as technocrat par excellence, which not coincidentally accompanies the decline of Roman law as a point of reference for his activity.

6 THE STRUCTURE OF CONTRACTUAL CONSENT: THE TRANSFER MODEL

After having assessed the dissociation between techniques and values in references to a system as a whole – which can be assimilated to situations in which references are made to

59 M. Brutti, *La solitudine del presente*, in I. Birocchi and M. Brutti (Eds.), *Storia del diritto e identità disciplinari: tradizioni e prospettive*, Torino, 2016, p. 297 f.
60 G. Crifò, *Dignità del cittadino ovvero "le stesse cose ritornano"*, in *Diritto romano attuale*, 2000, p. 9 f.
61 F. Casavola, *Diritto romano e diritto europeo*, cit., p. 163.
62 For instance. R. David, *Traité élémentaire de droit civil comparé*, Paris, 1950, p. 224.
63 G. Broggini, *Le droit romain et son influence actuelle*, B. Schmidlin (Ed.), *Vers un droit privé européen commun?*, Basel, 1994, p. 116.

particularly broad concepts – we can consider the same dissociation in relation to specific concepts. We will give examples from concepts related to the development of a general theory of contract.

This theory was born at the time of the Enlightenment's belief in the rational character of human nature,[64] which is why it coincides with the description of the procedure by which the contract is formed. The voluntarist approach to contract, while allowing for conceptual abstractions, emphasises that the legal relevance of the agreement derives from the matching intentions of the parties, i.e. it relies on their self-determination.[65]

This approach has long characterised the thinking of legal scholars and is still widespread today. For some time now, however, it has also been criticised for being incompatible with many approaches which, even if they do not start from a radical critique of the internal point of view on law, nonetheless emphasise the utility of distinguishing between the contract in its constitutive phase and the obligation which results from it. The former, it is said, is dominated by the contracting parties, while the latter is shaped by the legal system.

Comparative lawyers have undoubtedly contributed to this outcome in their role as profaners of the orthodoxy often cultivated by domestic law scholars, i.e. in homage to the subversive function of comparative law (I.1.1).

Particularly significant are the analyses of four different 'manifestations' of what is usually presented as the 'single inspiring notion' of contract. The 'contract as an instrument of unlimited autonomy' is the first one, conceived to express the full self-determination of the contracting parties, both in the formation of the contract and in the determination of its content: this notion of contract coincides with the German notion of bilateral legal act. A second manifestation is the 'contract as agreement', which equates the contract with consent, but then requires additional constitutive elements for contract formation: we find it in the French and in the Italian Civil Code. A third manifestation is the 'contract as exchange', i.e. an agreement which is legally relevant only if it contemplates a detriment for the creditor in consideration of the counter-performance: it is typical for common law. The fourth manifestation is the 'contract as reliance', whereby the agreement becomes binding – or is constructed starting from non-transactional conduct – insofar as it generates an expectation considered reasonable. This manifestation is now considered to be prevalent.[66]

Other comparative lawyers have noted that the model most consistent with the voluntarist approach – the scheme whereby the contract is simply a bilateral legal act – does not stand up to scrutiny that takes into account the functions of contract. We know that the scheme developed in the wake of Savigny's teachings was designed to develop a systematics whereby the contract, intended as a mere meeting of wills, is found as an autonomous concept in the various branches of the private law system: in the law of obligations, in property law, in family law and in inheritance law (IV.2.1). Only the contract of the law of obligations, however, constitutes a veritable expression of private autonomy, in the sense that it is accompanied by the recognition of a freedom to shape the many aspects of the contractual relationship. Not so, however, the contracts of the other branches of civil law, which do not contemplate such a freedom and are therefore not proper contracts. They are instead 'the gateway to a new status'; for example, of owner, or of spouse or of heir.[67]

On closer inspection, the analyses mentioned do not really challenge the traditional unifying accounts of the law of contract. Indeed, they pay little attention to the context in which

64 F. Galasso, *Il negozio giuridico. Lezioni di storia del diritto italiano*, 2nd ed., Milano, 1967, pp. 334 and 338.
65 P.S. Atiyah, *The Rise and Fall of Freedom of Contract*, Oxford, 1979, p. 256 ff.
66 R. Sacco and G. De Nova, *Il contratto*, t. 1, in *Trattato di diritto civile*, dir. R. Sacco, Torino, 2004, p. 51 ff.
67 K. Zweigert and H. Kötz, *An Introduction to Comparative Law* (1984), 2nd ed., Oxford, 1992, p. 352.

the technical-legal constructions are placed, which, on the contrary, is taken into consideration by dissociating the conceptual constructions from the values they are intended to implement. Doing so, one is able to highlighting the implications of a specific construction in terms of the values it is linked with: in particular, in the moments in which the construction asserts itself, as well as when it capitulates to other constructions and other values they aim to implement.

Three models for describing the structure of consent have been identified, which can be traced back to three different stages in the elaboration of a general theory of the contract, and to three different ways of distinguishing legal from merely social obligations. These are the transfer model elaborated by the adherents of rational natural law, the Pandectist model elaborated in the second half of the 19th century, and the current model.[68]

The transfer model describes the contract as the transfer of a promise, or rather of the right to demand the performance of the promise, or again as a cross-transfer of that right. This is the model that recurs above all in the literature presenting the contract as a species of the 'covenant', and the latter as a concept reconstructed around a promise, or rather two promises. In Pothier's terms:

> A convention or a covenant (they are synonyms) is the consent of two or more persons to form between them some commitment or to terminate a previous one or to modify it. . . . The species of convention which has for its object the formation of some commitment is that convention which is called a contract. The principles of Roman law on the different species of covenant and on the distinction between contracts and mere covenants are not admitted in our law, since they are not founded on natural law and are distant from its simplicity. . . .
>
> It follows that in our law one should not define contract as the interpreters of Roman law define it, namely as *conventio nomen habens a jure civili, vel causam*. A contract is to be defined as a convention by which one or both parties mutually promise and undertake to give, to do or not to do something. I said promise and commit themselves because only promises that we make with the intention of committing ourselves and granting the promisee the right to demand their fulfilment form a contract and a convention.[69]

There are two aspects of the formula describing the transfer model that highlight points of contact with two different approaches to the matter, or, rather two different conflicting values: the reference to the promise and the idea of the transfer of a right.

The reference to the promise refers back to constructions rooted in the Second Scholasticism, that is, the 16th-century Spanish school of natural law. It is thus an expression of a creed that emphasises, in holistic terms, the bonds of the individual in relation to the community, or rather that does not know the individual insofar as it conceives of him as dissolved within the community. This is precisely what is expressed by the references, typical among the authors of the Second Scholasticism, to the Aristotelian theme of commutative justice and thus to the idea that exchange must tend to be equal. All of this is derived from the Roman law discipline of 'abnormal harm'[70]: 'if you or your father sold property worth more for a lesser price, the humane course is that either you restore the farm to the buyers and recover the price under the authority of a *iudex*; or, if the buyer prefers, you recover the difference from the just price' (C. 4, 44, 2).

68 See B. Schmidlin, *La causa del contratto nel codice civile francese*, in L. Vacca (Ed.), *Causa e contratto nella prospettiva storico-comparatistica*, Torino, 1997, p. 287 f.
69 R.-J. Pothier, *Traité des obligations*, in Id. (Ed.), *Oeuvres*, vol. 1, Bruxelles and Amsterdam, 1829, p. 2 f. (n. 3).
70 Among others, J. Gordley, *The Philosophical Origins of Modern Contract Doctrine*, Oxford, 1991, p. 94 ff.

7 NEXT: FROM THE PANDECTIST MODEL TO THE CURRENT MODEL

The values to which the reference to the promise refers are obviously at odds with what a voluntarist approach to the contract envisages. This is because it contradicts the demand for a limitation of private autonomy beyond what is necessary and sufficient to recognise the intention of the contracting parties as the source of the legal obligation. It is the voluntarist approach, however, that promotes the image of the promisor, who is a promisor insofar as he or she has transferred to the promisee the right to demand what has been promised. This image is obviously based on a fiction that is useful for promoting, rhetorically, the individual will as the trigger of the legal effects of the act and can be retraced to Grotius:

> To understand the matter fully, we must carefully observe that there are three different ways of speaking, respecting things which are, or which, it is supposed, will be in our power. . . . The third way is, where such a determination is confirmed by evident signs of an intention to convey a peculiar right to another, which constitutes the perfect obligation of a promise, and is attended with consequences similar to an alienation of property.[71]

And it is precisely voluntarism that is celebrated by first modern codifications of civil law, in particular the French Civil Code of 1804. And yet the concepts used are in part still those typical of the era in which contract law was reconstructed starting from the promise. This was inspired more by the intention to identify a fair balance between performances than to underline individual self-determination. We can deduce this, for example, from the mention, among the essential elements of the contract, of the party's consent to be bound instead of the agreement of the parties (art. 1108). It can also be deduced from the way in which abnormal harm is conceptualised, following Roman law, still as a mere mathematical inequality between performance and counter-performance: 'if the vendor has suffered a loss of more than seven-twelfths of the price of an immoveable, he has a right to demand annulment of the sale, even though he should have expressly renounced in the contract the power of demanding such annulment' (art. 1674).

The Pandectist model's emphasis on the bilateral legal act as the contractual paradigm is fully consistent with the voluntarist approach (IV.2.1). Here, references to promises are definitively omitted and the wills of the parties are merged and protected by the legal system from the sole point of view of their free formation. Von Savigny explains:

> Legal facts may consist in: A) voluntary acts of the person concerned, i.e. of the person to whom the acquisition or loss in question relates. B) Casual circumstances, to which belong acts of persons other than the person concerned, as well as omissions. Furthermore, in voluntary acts the agent's will may operate in two ways: a) As aimed immediately at the creation or dissolution of the legal relationship, although these may perhaps be means to achieve other, even non-legal ends. These facts are called declarations of will or legal transactions. b) Or as immediately aimed at other non-legal ends, so that the legal effect recedes into a subordinate position in consciousness or is definitely not intended. Declarations finally manifest themselves in two ways: 1) As a unilateral will of the person concerned, the most important case of which is the last will, which, however, has its true seat only in the special part of the system, i.e. in inheritance law. 2) As a concordance of the will of the person concerned with the will of one or more other persons, i.e. as a contract.[72]

71 H. Grotius, *The Rights of War and Peace* (1625), vol. 2, London, 1814, p. 9 f. (Lib. 2, Cap. 11, n. 4)
72 F.C. von Savigny, *System des heutigen Römischen Rechts*, vol. 3, Berlin, 1840, p. 6 f.

This way of describing the structure of contractual consent derives from Kant's philosophy, at the basis of a conception which emphasises the perspective of individual action, to which the only limitation is respect for the sphere of others. Curiously, in the pages that Kant dedicates to the contract, all this still coexists with formulas that can be traced back to the transfer model.[73] Not so, however, in the aforementioned equation between contract and bilateral legal transaction, elaborated precisely in order to emphasise how it is now regarded as an instrument of unlimited autonomy (IV.2.1). From this perspective, the regulation of abnormal harm continues to be admitted; however, it is based on different motives. The institution is now an expedient through which to prevent abuse of the freedom of others, so much so that at the end of the 19th century it was even considered extraneous to the foundations of civil law.[74]

However, this is not exactly the notion of contract referred to in the German *Bürgeliches Gesetzbuch* of 1896, which, however, is largely based on the theory of the legal transaction (*Rechtsgeschäft*). It reformulates in the mentioned sense the regulation of the abnormal harm: 'a legal transaction is void by which a person, by exploiting the predicament, inexperience, lack of sound judgment or considerable weakness of will of another, causes a promise to be made to them or causes a promise of pecuniary advantages to be made to a third party, in exchange for an act of performance that are clearly disproportionate to the performance' (para. 138).

The articles do, however, contain references to good faith as a point of reference for interpreting the contract (para. 157), as well as for evaluating the performance owed by the debtor (para. 242). It is precisely on the basis of good faith, a concept which restricts individual self-determination in favour of heteronomous control over acts of private autonomy, that the current way of conceiving the contract as a 'sum of promises producing reliance' has developed.[75] Or possibly, if one intends to use a lexicon sensitive to voluntarist instances, as 'an agreement of concordant and reciprocal manifestations of will evaluated according to the principle of trust'.[76]

The notion of reliance refers in many respects to what was expressed in the past by the reference to the promise, which also appears in the current model. In this sense, reliance reinforces the intention not to reserve the assessment of the contractual relationship to the parties alone, whose intent cannot therefore be the sole trigger of its legal relevance. This explains the reason that, at a time when it erodes space for voluntarist conceptions of the contract, the new approach ends up shifting the focus from the formation of the contract to the performance of the obligation. That is, from the act to the relationship.

If in fact the focus on the formation of contact is functional to emphasising the principle of self-determination, the focus on the performance of the obligation underlines instead its exceptions.[77] All this is to do away with the vision of the 'contract as a means of unlimited autonomy' and the 'contract as agreement', and to promote the 'contract as exchange' and the 'contract as reliance'.

However, this is not the end of the story. European contract law is pushing a change in the values to be implemented through the restrictions on the principle of self-determination. It is no longer commutative justice that motivates these restrictions, but rather the will to make the behaviour of market actors conform to an economic order based on the principle

73 I. Kant, *The Metapphysics of Morals* (1797), Cambridge MA, 1991, p. 91 f.
74 See W. Flume, *Allgemeiner Teil des Bürgerlichen Gesetzbuches* (*Das Rechtsgeschäft*), 4th ed., vol. 2, Berlin etc., 1992, p. 381.
75 A. Gambaro, *Sintesi conclusiva in tema di causa e contratto*, in L. Vacca (Ed.), *Causa e contratto*, cit., p. 562 f.
76 B. Schmidlin, *La causa del contratto nel codice civile francese*, cit., p. 288.
77 Already L. Raiser, *Vertragsfunktion und Vetragsfreiheit*, in E. von Caemmerer et al. (Eds.), *Hundert Jahre deutsches Rechtsleben*, vol. 1, Karlsruhe, 1960, p. 120 ff.

of competition[78]: the will to comply with neoliberal orthodoxy in the shaping of European private law (II.1.5).

All this can certainly be shown by means of various methodological approaches, provided that the relations between technical-legal concepts and their implications observable from an external point of view on law are emphasised. However, the dissociation between techniques and values makes it possible to highlight the unstable nature of these relations, and this is why it should be taken into consideration by comparative law scholars.

SUMMARY

1. Law orients individual behaviour and shapes social life, and its sources are all those who actually have a power of conditioning. However, there is no one-to one correspondence between technical-legal constructions and concrete modes of exercising this power, at the very least because the interpretation of rules is an essentially political practice, constitutive of their meaning. This leads to an important methodological point, both for those who wish to promote a unifying comparison and for those who wish instead to compare in order to bring out identities: it is necessary to proceed to a dissociation between legal techniques and the values they aim at implementing. The link between society and law at the discursive level can thus be seen as an essentially unstable relationship between the techniques used by power and the values that power seeks to promote through controlling the legal discourse.
2. The dissociation between techniques and values can be seen in relation to a system as a whole: for example, to Roman law as a law capable of constituting the foundation of both traditional power and rational power. This law was invoked to legitimise the distinction between the political and the economic spheres at the basis of the bourgeois society born of the French Revolution; the same law then legitimised the Romantic reaction to that Revolution, and thus the constructions first of the Historical School and then of the Pandectism. Towards the end of the 19th century, however, the link between individualism and Roman law, which was used to establish a traditional and rational power at the same time, proved unsuitable for capitalist modernisation.
3. At the latest with the First World War, it became urgent to find a third way between classical individualist liberalism and socialism, which was committed to the overthrow of the capitalist order. In all this, the link between Roman law and individualism led to an only partial discrediting of Roman law. The fascist dictatorships that imposed their third way, which consisted of compressing political freedoms in order to reform economic freedoms, exalted Roman law in a traditional key: the Italians as the law of an authoritarian, hierarchical, expansionist Roman state, and the Germans as the racist order of a Nordic people. After the fall of fascism, the restoration of the link between individualism and Roman law allowed the latter to be re-credited as a barrier against the recurrence of dictatorship. It also allowed many jurists who had been involved with the regime to simulate their substantive distance from the dictatorship.

78 See A. Somma, *Introduzione critica al diritto europeo dei contratti*, Milano, 2007, p. 9 ff.

4. The socialist cause has been promoted by identifying Roman law as the reference point for the construction of bourgeois society. However, this is seen as an intermediate step towards overcoming capitalism, and from this point of view Roman law is also celebrated in literature with a Marxist sensibility. There are, however, authors who find in the history of Roman law other reasons for paying attention to this law and its evolution, ultimately linked to the denial of its individualistic character or at least to the underlining of its solidaristic elements.
5. Roman law has traditionally been used to promote the construction of European private law by those who emphasize its individualist character. Yet individualism is not suited to the regulation of a capitalist economic order, which as such is based on functionalised rights. Attempts to use Roman law to support the other cornerstones of the Western legal tradition are also unsuccessful: obviously this law is not suited to support democracy, while as the foundation of Christianity it can be used in an anti-Islamic key, but in a subordinate position to other, more incisive rhetoric. What remains is the reference to Roman law as a means for the jurist to play a leading role in the construction of European law. However, this is a role that the jurist has not held for some time, with no sign of a reversal of the trend.
6. The dissociation between techniques and values can also be studied in relation to specific concepts that recur in different legal systems: for example, the concepts that describe the structure of contractual consent. These correspond to three different models. The first, the transfer model developed by the adherents of rational natural law, describes the contract as a reciprocal exchange of the right to demand the fulfilment of a promise. The reference to the latter indicates the persistence of a sensitivity to the Aristotelian theme of commutative justice, as developed by the Second Scholastic analysing the legal doctrine of abnormal harm.
7. In the transfer model, the idea that one can transfer the right to enforce the promise, instead, anticipates the affirmation of a voluntaristic conception of contract, fully developed in the Pandectist model. In this latter model, the structure of contractual consent is that of the bilateral legal transaction. The current model is different, in which the contract is seen as a set of promises that engender reliance. Moreover, it focuses on the distinction between agreement and contractual obligation, thus recognising the role of the legislature and the courts in defining the latter. However, also because of the tendencies coming from the European level, this role is less and less about promoting commutative justice and more and more about pandering to neoliberal orthodoxy.

INDEX

For Product Safety Concerns and Information please contact our EU representative GPSR@taylorandfrancis.com Taylor & Francis Verlag GmbH, Kaufingerstraße 24, 80331 München, Germany